Fact File

Not a Pet

Bobcat
(Felis rufus)

Bobcats look like house cats, except that they stand nearly two feet tall and weigh as much as 30 pounds. They have a fierce snarl and hunt alone at night. Bobcats sometimes hunt large animals, such as deer.

A single male bobcat may occupy a territory as large as 25 square miles.

HOUGHTON MIFFLIN

California Science

HOUGHTON MIFFLIN

BOSTON

Program Authors

William Badders
Director of the Cleveland Mathematics and
Science Partnership
Cleveland Municipal School District, Cleveland, Ohio

Douglas Carnine, Ph.D.
Professor of Education
University of Oregon, Eugene, Oregon

James Feliciani
Supervisor of Instructional Media and Technology
Land O' Lakes, Florida

Bobby Jeanpierre, Ph.D.
Assistant Professor, Science Education
University of Central Florida, Orlando, Florida

Carolyn Sumners, Ph.D.
Director of Astronomy and Physical Sciences
Houston Museum of Natural Science, Houston, Texas

Catherine Valentino
Author-in-Residence
Houghton Mifflin, West Kingston, Rhode Island

Primary Grade Consultant

Kathleen B. Horstmeyer
Past President SEPA
Carefree, Arizona

Content Consultants
See Teacher's Edition for a complete list

California Teacher Reviewers

Robert Aikman
Cunningham Elementary
Turlock, California

Christine Anderson
Rock Creek Elementary
Rocklin, California

Dan M. Anthony
Berry Elementary
San Diego, California

Patricia Babb
Cypress Elementary
Tulare, California

Ann Balfour
Lang Ranch Elementary
Thousand Oaks, California

Colleen Briner-Schmidt
Conejo Elementary
Thousand Oaks, California

Mary Brouse
Panama Buena Vista Union
School District
Bakersfield, California

Monica Carabay
Four Creeks Elementary
Visalia, California

Printed in the U.S.A.

ISBN-13: 978-0-618-68620-9
ISBN-10: 0-618-68620-7

1 2 3 4 5 6 7 8 9-CS-15 14 13 12 11 10 09 08 07 06

California Teacher Reviewers (cont'd.)

Sheri Chu
Vineyard Elementary
Ontario, California

Teena Collins
Frank D. Parent Elementary
Inglewood, California

Gary Comstock
Cole Elementary
Clovis, California

Jenny Dickinson
Bijou Community School
South Lake Tahoe, California

Cheryl Dultz
Kingswood Elementary
Citrus Heights, California

Tom East
Mountain View Elementary
Fresno, California

Sharon Ferguson
Fort Washington Elementary
Fresno, California

Robbin Ferrell
Hawthorne Elementary
Ontario, California

Mike Freedman
Alta-Dutch Flat Elementary
Alta, California

Linda Gadis-Honaker
Banyan Elementary
Alta Loma, California

Lisa Gomez
Marshall James Elementary
Modesto, California

Lisa Green
Jordan Elementary
Orange, California

Tina Hubbard
Brentwood Elementary
Victorville, California

Carey Iannuzzo
Fitzgerald Elementary
Rialto, California

Teresa Lorentz
Banta Elementary
Tracy, California

Christine Luellig
Henderson Elementary
Barstow, California

Peggy MacArthur
Montevideo Elementary
San Ramon, California

Jeffrey McPherson
Parkview Elementary
Garden Grove, California

Susan Moore
Lang Ranch Elementary
Thousand Oaks, California

William Neddersen
Tustin Unified School District
Tustin, California

Josette Perrie
Plaza Vista School
Irvine, California

Lisa Pulliam
Alcott Elementary
Pomona, California

Jennifer Ramirez
Skyline North Elementary
Barstow, California

Lynda Rogers
Santa Cruz County Office of
Education
Capitola, California

Nancy Scali
Arroyo Elementary
Ontario, California

Janet Sugimoto
Sunset Lane School
Fullerton, California

Laura Valencia
Kingsley Elementary
Montclair, California

Sally Van Wagner
Antelope Creek Elementary
Rocklin, California

Jenny Wade
Stockton Unified School District
Stockton, California

Judy Williams
Price Elementary
Anaheim, California

Karen Yamamoto
Westmore Oaks Elementary
West Sacramento, California

Contents

UNIT A
Planet Earth

Big Idea Topography is reshaped by the weathering of rock and soil and by the transportation and deposition of sediment.

Chapter 1   **Earth's Structure** 2
          Vocabulary Preview 4
Lesson 1   What Makes Earth a Special Planet? 6
Lesson 2   What Is Earth's Structure? 16
          Focus On: Literature: A Journey to the Center of the Earth 24
Lesson 3   What Makes Up Earth's Surface? .26
          Extreme Science: Down in Death Valley 36

          Links for Home and School 38
          Careers in Science 39
          Review and Test Practice 40

Chapter 2   **Shaping Earth's Surface** 42
          Vocabulary Preview 44
Lesson 1   How Is Earth's Surface Worn Down? 46
          Focus On: Primary Source: Caves of the West 54
Lesson 2   How Do Rivers Shape the Landscape? 56
          Extreme Science: Masterpiece of Erosion 64
Lesson 3   How Do Beaches Change? 66

          Links for Home and School 74
          People in Science 75
          Review and Test Practice 76

          Unit Review and Test Practice 78
          Unit Wrap-Up 80

Mendocino Coast, California

UNIT B

The Dynamic Earth

Big Idea Plate tectonics accounts for important features of Earth's surface and major geological events.

Chapter 3

Evidence of Plate Tectonics 82

Vocabulary Preview 84

Lesson 1   What Do Rocks and Fossils Reveal? 86

      Focus On: Readers' Theater: Alfred Wegener and Pangaea 94

Lesson 2   What Are Tectonic Plates? 98

Lesson 3   How Do Tectonic Plates Move? 106

Lesson 4   What Happens at Plate Boundaries? 114

      Extreme Science: It's Alive! 122

      Links for Home and School 124

      Careers in Science 125

      Review and Test Practice 126

Chapter 4

Mountains, Earthquakes, and Volcanoes 128

Vocabulary Preview 130

Lesson 1   How Do Mountains Form? 132

Lesson 2   What Happens During an Earthquake? 140

Lesson 3   How Are Earthquakes Located and Measured? 148

      Focus On: Technology: Predicting Earthquakes 156

Lesson 4   How Do Volcanoes Form? 158

      Extreme Science: Sleeping Giant 168

      Links for Home and School 170

      People in Science 171

      Review and Test Practice 172

      Unit Review and Test Practice 174

Unit Wrap-Up 176

San Andreas fault

Contents

UNIT C
Earth's Energy Supply

Big Ideas Many phenomena on Earth's surface are affected by the transfer of energy through radiation and convection currents. Heat moves in a predictable flow from warmer objects to cooler objects until all the objects are at the same temperature.

Chapter 5

Heating Earth 178

Vocabulary Preview 180

Lesson 1 How Does Energy Travel from the Sun to the Earth? 182

Focus On: History of Science:
Great Moments for the Electromagnetic Spectrum 190

Lesson 2 How Is Earth Heated? 192

Lesson 3 What Are Convection Currents? 202

Extreme Science: Diablo Wind 210

Links for Home and School 212

Careers in Science 213

Review and Test Practice 214

Chapter 6

Energy and Weather 216

Vocabulary Preview 218

Lesson 1 What Causes Weather? 220

Focus On: Technology: Predicting Hurricanes 230

Lesson 2 What Are Global Weather Patterns? 232

Lesson 3 What Are California's Climates? 240

Extreme Science: Super Waves! 248

Links for Home and School 250

People in Science 251

Review and Test Practice 252

Unit Review and Test Practice 254

Unit Wrap-Up 256

Pigeon Point Lighthouse

UNIT D
Ecology

Big Idea Organisms in ecosystems exchange energy and nutrients among themselves and with the environment.

Chapter 7

The Biosphere 258
Vocabulary Preview 260

Lesson 1 What Are Ecosystems? 262
Lesson 2 What Are Earth's Biomes? 268
Focus On: Primary Source: Rain Forests 276
Lesson 3 What Cycles Through the Biosphere? 278
Extreme Science: A World in Your Hands 288

Links for Home and School 290
People in Science 291
Review and Test Practice 292

Chapter 8

Roles of Living Things 294
Vocabulary Preview 296

Lesson 1 What Is a Food Web? 298
Focus On: Technology: Food Web of the Farm 306
Lesson 2 What Roles Do Organisms Play? 308
Lesson 3 What Is Symbiosis? 316
Extreme Science: Dentists of the Deep 324

Links for Home and School 326
People in Science 327
Review and Test Practice 328

Bighorn sheep

Contents

Chapter 9 **Populations** 330

Vocabulary Preview 332

Lesson 1 What Limits Population Growth? 334

Extreme Science: Crab Crossing 342

Lesson 2 What Is Ecological Succession? 344

Lesson 3 How Do Humans Change Ecosystems? 350

Focus On: History of Science: Protecting the Environment 360

Links for Home and School 362

Careers in Science 363

Review and Test Practice 364

Unit Review and Test Practice 366

Unit Wrap-Up 368

Mohave Desert

UNIT E
Earth's Natural Resources

Big Idea Sources of energy and materials differ in amounts, distribution, usefulness, and the time required for their formation.

Chapter 10   **Energy Resources** 370

Vocabulary Preview 372

Lesson 1   How Do People Use Energy? 374

Lesson 2   Why Are Fossil Fuels Limited? 382

Focus On: Reader's Theater: Once There Were Fossil Fuels 390

Lesson 3   What Are Alternatives to Fossil Fuels? 394

Extreme Science: Power Tower 406

Links for Home and School 408

Careers in Science 409

Review and Test Practice 410

Chapter 11   **Material Resources** 412

Vocabulary Preview 414

Lesson 1   What Material Resources Are Nonrenewable? 416

Focus On: Technology: Landfills 426

Lesson 2   What Material Resources Are Renewable? 428

Extreme Science: Tired! 440

Links for Home and School 442

People in Science 443

Review and Test Practice 444

Unit Review and Test Practice 446

Unit Wrap-Up 448

Shasta Dam

Features

UNIT A

California Field Trip: Point Reyes National Seashore . . . . .Tab A

Directed Inquiry
Make a Sundial 7
A Model Earth 17
Model a Map 27
Rock Weathering 47
Set Up a Stream Slope 57
A World in a Grain of Sand 67

Express Lab
See How a Sundial Works 9
Make an Earth Model 21
Draw a Map 31
Model Chemical Weathering 51
Show How Sediments Build Up 62
Make Sand .71

UNIT B

California Field Trip: Channel Islands . . . . .Tab B

Directed Inquiry
Be a Time Traveler! 87
Model Pangaea! 99
Mantle Motion 107
Picking a Pattern 115
Make a Mountain 133
Make Waves! 141
Locating an Earthquake 149
Volcano Model 159

Express Lab
Model a Fossil 91
Solve a Puzzle 102
Make a Convection Current 109
Model Plate Motion 119
Make a Mountain 137
Model Waves 145
Find an Epicenter 152
Show Why Magma Rises 161

UNIT C

California Field Trip: Mount Shasta . . . . .Tab C

Directed Inquiry
Light and Dark 183
Lighten Up! 193
Circling Around! 203
Discovering Dew Point 221
Spin It! 233
Graph Your Climate! 241

Express Lab
Observe Solar Energy 185
Angles of Sunlight and Temperature .197
Transfer Thermal Energy 205
See Condensation 224
Create a Coriolis Effect 235
Graph Temperature 245

UNIT D

California Field Trip: Big Sur Ornithology Lab . . . . Tab D

Directed Inquiry

A Look at Life 263
Where Do They Live? 269
Bag It! 279
Identify Your Food 299
Role Playing 309
Hide and Seek! 317
Game of Numbers 335
Disaster Recovery 345
Tracking Water Pollution 351

Express Lab

Sample Soil 266
Classify What You See 274
See Water in the Air 285
Identify a Lunchbox Food Web 302
Make Food Connections 314
Test Camouflage 319
Act Out Competition 338
Clean Up an "Oil Spill" 347
Determine Habitat Loss 353

UNIT E

California Field Trip: Muir Woods . . . . Tab E

Directed Inquiry

Swing Time 375
3...2...1... Oil Game Over? 383
Heating a Home 395
Recycling! 417
What Is It Made From? 429

Express Lab

Observe Energy 379
Model Oil Reserves 387
Monitor Energy 403
See Recyclables 423
Find the Renewable Resource 437

California Science

Using Your Textbook

The Nature of Science

In the front of your book, you will be introduced to scientists and to ways of investigating science.

Every unit in your book has two or more chapters.

Science is an adventure. People all over the world do science. You can do science, too. You probably already do.

Independent Books are books you can read on your own.

Big Idea! tells you the part of your **California Science Standards** that connects the Main Ideas of each lesson.

EARTH UNIT A SCIENCE

Planet Earth

Chapter 1
Earth's Structure 2

Independent Books
- Earth's Structure
- Climbing High
- To the Center of the Earth!

Chapter 2
Shaping Earth's Surface 42

Independent Books
- Shaping Earth's Surface
- Along the Nile
- Acid Rain

Big Idea!
Standard Set 2
Shaping Earth's Surface
Topography is reshaped by the weathering of rock and soil and by the transportation and deposition of sediment.

McWay Cove, California

1

Lesson Preview gives information and asks questions about each lesson.

Writing Journal tells you to write or draw answers to the questions.

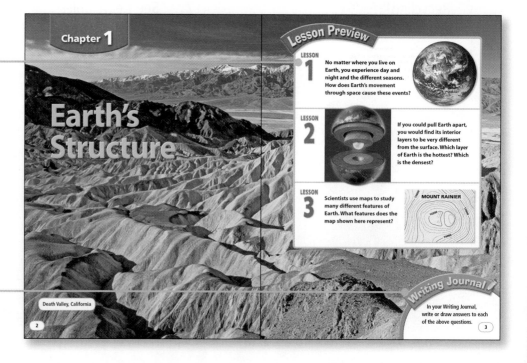

Chapter 1

Earth's Structure

Death Valley, California

2

Lesson Preview

LESSON 1
No matter where you live on Earth, you experience day and night and the different seasons. How does Earth's movement through space cause these events?

LESSON 2
If you could pull Earth apart, you would find its interior layers to be very different from the surface. Which layer of Earth is the hottest? Which is the densest?

LESSON 3
Scientists use maps to study many different features of Earth. What features does the map shown here represent?

MOUNT RAINIER

Writing Journal

In your Writing Journal, write or draw answers to each of the above questions.

3

xii

Vocabulary Preview

introduces important science terms, with pictures, and vocabulary skills.

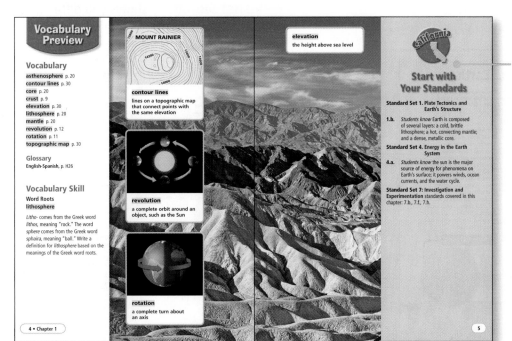

California Science Standards are identified for each chapter.

Every lesson in your book has two parts.
Lesson Part 1: Directed Inquiry

Building Background gives you science facts and information.

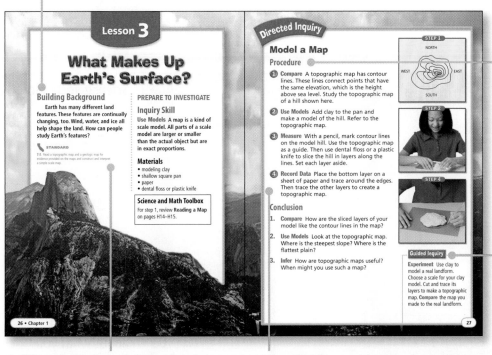

Procedure lists the steps you will follow to conduct your Investigation.

Guided Inquiry lets you take your investigation further.

California Science Standards appear in blue throughout each lesson.

Conclusion guides you in thinking about your investigation.

Lesson Part 2: Learn by Reading

Vocabulary lists the new science words that you will learn.

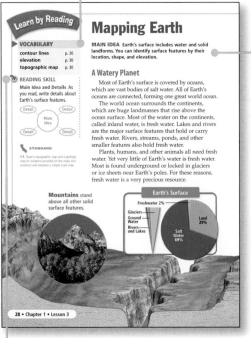

Main Idea tells you what is important.

Reading Skill helps you understand and organize information as you read.

Lesson Wrap-Up

Visual Summary shows you different ways to summarize what you've read.

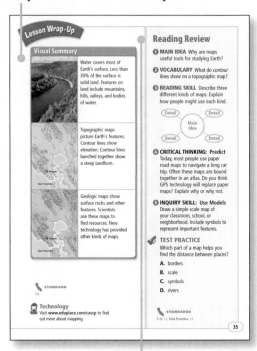

Reading Review lets you check your understanding after you read.

Focus On

Focus On lets you learn more about a key concept in a chapter.

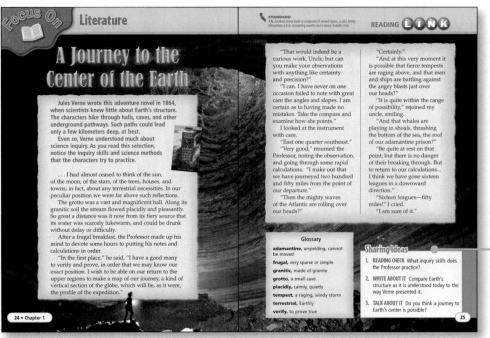

Focus On types include: History of Science, Technology, Primary Source, Literature, and Readers' Theater.

Sharing Ideas has you check your understanding and write and talk about what you have learned.

Extreme Science

Compares and contrasts interesting science information.

Writing Journal provides writing guidance for the Extreme Science lesson.

Links and Careers/People in Science

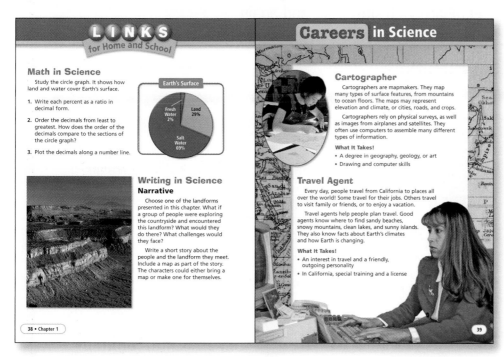

Links connects science to other subject areas.

Careers/People in Science tells you about the work of real scientists.

Chapter and Unit Review and Test Practice

Helps you to know you are on track with learning California science standards.

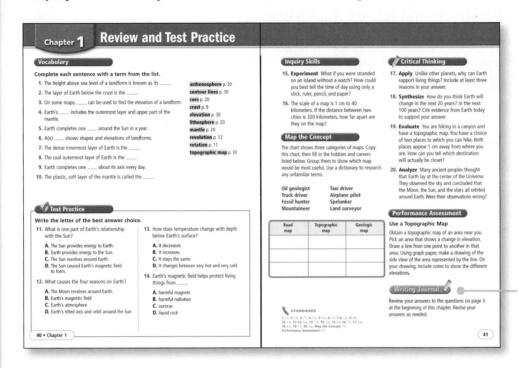

Chapter 1 — Review and Test Practice

Vocabulary

Complete each sentence with a term from the list.

1. The height above sea level of a landform is known as its ____.
2. The layer of Earth below the crust is the ____.
3. On some maps, ____ can be used to find the elevation of a landform.
4. Earth's ____ includes the outermost layer and upper part of the mantle.
5. Earth completes one ____ around the Sun in a year.
6. A(n) ____ shows shapes and elevations of landforms.
7. The dense innermost layer of Earth is the ____.
8. The cool outermost layer of Earth is the ____.
9. Earth completes one ____ about its axis every day.
10. The plastic, soft layer of the mantle is called the ____.

asthenosphere p. 20
contour lines p. 30
core p. 20
crust p. 9
elevation p. 30
lithosphere p. 20
mantle p. 20
revolution p. 12
rotation p. 11
topographic map p. 30

Test Practice

Write the letter of the best answer choice.

11. What is one part of Earth's relationship with the Sun?

A. The Sun provides energy to Earth.
B. Earth provides energy to the Sun.
C. The Sun revolves around Earth.
D. The Sun caused Earth's magnetic field to form.

12. What causes the four seasons on Earth?

A. The Moon revolves around Earth.
B. Earth's magnetic field
C. Earth's atmosphere
D. Earth's tilted axis and orbit around the Sun

13. How does temperature change with depth below Earth's surface?

A. It decreases.
B. It increases.
C. It stays the same.
D. It changes between very hot and very cold.

14. Earth's magnetic field helps protect living things from

A. harmful magnets
B. harmful radiation
C. auroras
D. liquid rock

Inquiry Skills

15. **Experiment** What if you were stranded on an island without a watch? How could you best tell the time of day using only a stick, ruler, pencil, and paper?

16. The scale of a map is 1 cm to 40 kilometers. If the distance between two cities is 320 kilometers, how far apart are they on the map?

Map the Concept

The chart shows three categories of maps. Copy this chart, then fill in the hobbies and careers listed below. Group them to show which map would be most useful. Use a dictionary to research any unfamiliar terms.

Oil geologist   Taxi driver
Truck driver   Airplane pilot
Fossil hunter   Spelunker
Mountaineer   Land surveyor

Road map	Topographic map	Geologic map

Critical Thinking

17. **Apply** Unlike other planets, why can Earth support living things? Include at least three reasons in your answer.

18. **Synthesize** How do you think Earth will change in the next 20 years? In the next 100 years? Cite evidence from Earth today to support your answer.

19. **Evaluate** You are hiking in a canyon and have a topographic map. You have a choice of two places to which you can hike. Both places appear 1 cm away from where you are. How can you tell which destination will actually be closer?

20. **Analyze** Many ancient peoples thought that Earth lay at the center of the Universe. They observed the sky and concluded that the Moon, the Sun, and the stars all orbited around Earth. Were their observations wrong?

Performance Assessment

Use a Topographic Map

Obtain a topographic map of an area near you. Pick an area that shows a change in elevation. Draw a line from one point to another in that area. Using graph paper, make a drawing of the side view of the area represented by the line. On your drawing, include notes to show the different elevations.

Writing Journal

Review your answers to the questions on page 3 at the beginning of this chapter. Revise your answers as needed.

STANDARDS
1: ??, 2: ??, 3: ??, 4: ??, 5: ??, 6: ??, 7–8: ??, 9: ??,
10: ??, 11–12: ??, 13: ??, 14: ??, 15: ??, 16: ??, 17: ??,
18: ??, 19: ??, 20: ??, Map the Concept: ??,
Performance Assessment: ??

40 • Chapter 1   41

Writing Journal instructs you to review the questions you answered at the start of the chapter.

Unit Wrap-Up

Learn more about science using the **Discover More** question. Also find a link to a simulation on the EduPlace web site.

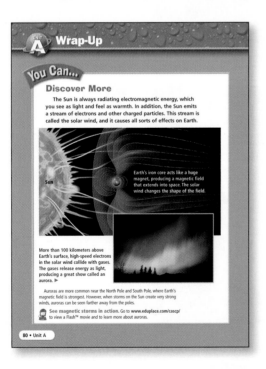

UNIT A — Wrap-Up

You Can...

Discover More

The Sun is always radiating electromagnetic energy, which you see as light and feel as warmth. In addition, the Sun emits a stream of electrons and other charged particles. This stream is called the solar wind, and it causes all sorts of effects on Earth.

Earth's iron core acts like a huge magnet, producing a magnetic field that extends into space. The solar wind changes the shape of the field.

Sun

More than 100 kilometers above Earth's surface, high-speed electrons in the solar wind collide with gases. The gases release energy as light, producing a great show called an aurora. ▶

Auroras are more common near the North Pole and South Pole, where Earth's magnetic field is strongest. However, when storms on the Sun create very strong winds, auroras can be seen farther away from the poles.

See magnetic storms in action. Go to www.eduplace.com/cascp/ to view a Flash™ movie and to learn more about auroras.

80 • Unit A

References

The back of your book includes sections you will refer to again and again.

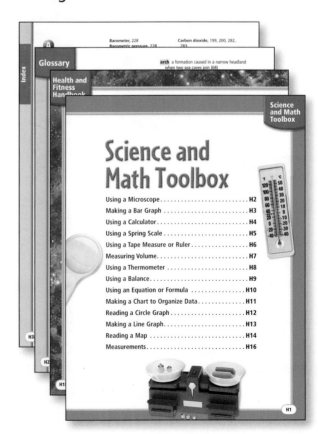

Barometer, 228
Barometric pressure, 228

Carbon dioxide, 199, 200, 282, 283

arch a formation caused in a narrow headland when two sea caves join (68)

Index

Glossary

Health and Fitness Handbook

Science and Math Toolbox

Science and Math Toolbox

Using a Microscope H2
Making a Bar Graph H3
Using a Calculator H4
Using a Spring Scale H5
Using a Tape Measure or Ruler H6
Measuring Volume H7
Using a Thermometer H8
Using a Balance H9
Using an Equation or Formula H10
Making a Chart to Organize Data H11
Reading a Circle Graph H12
Making a Line Graph H13
Reading a Map H14
Measurements H16

Start with Your Standards

Your California Science Standards

How Families Can Help S1

Set 1 Plate Tectonics and Earth's Structure S2

Set 2 Shaping Earth's Surface S3

Set 3 Heat (Thermal Energy) (Physical Science) S4

Set 4 Energy in the Earth System S4

Set 5 Ecology (Life Sciences) S5

Set 6 Resources S6

Set 7 Investigation and Experimentation S6

Your California
Science Standards

Welcome to the adventure of science!

Many famous scientists and inventors have lived and worked in California. Someday, you could be one, too!

Your science standards tell you what you should know by the end of Grade 6. They also tell what you should be able to do when you investigate and experiment. When you use your science book, you will find the standards printed next to each section of the lesson and chapter.

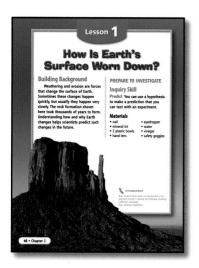

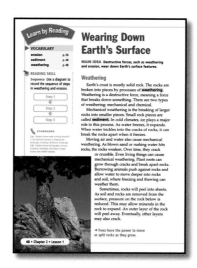

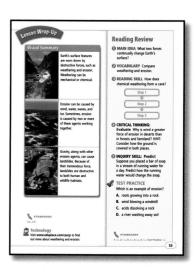

Houghton Mifflin Science will lead you to mastering your standards. Along the way, you will ask questions, do hands-on investigations, think critically, and read what scientists have discovered about how the world works. You will also get to know real people who do science every day.

How Families Can Help

- Get to know the California Science Content Standards on the pages that follow. If you want to learn more about science education, you can find the Science Framework for California Public Schools online at **www.cde.ca.gov/ci/**

- Relate the science of the standards to activities at home such as cooking, gardening, and playing sports.

- Get to know your child's science textbook, encouraging him or her to use the table of contents, index, and glossary. Point out the importance of titles and headings as a means to finding the information needed.

- Help your child choose library books to read about science, nature, inventors, and scientists. You can use the Recommended Literature for Math & Science online database at **www.cde.ca.gov/ci/sc/ll/**

- Find opportunities for your child to use numbers and mathematics skills and to measure and to estimate measurements, such as when planning a trip.

- Encourage your child to do experiments and enter science fairs.

Yosemite National Park

Science Content Standards

These Science Content Standards are learning goals that you will achieve by the end of sixth grade. Below each standard is the unit or chapter in this book where that standard is taught. In that unit and chapter, there are many opportunities to master the standard—by doing investigations, reading, writing, speaking, and drawing concept maps.

Set 1 Plate Tectonics and Earth's Structure

Plate tectonics accounts for important features of Earth's surface and major geologic events. As a basis for understanding this concept:
Unit B: The Dynamic Earth

Mount Shasta

1.a. *Students know* evidence of plate tectonics is derived from the fit of the continents; the location of earthquakes, volcanoes, and midocean ridges; and the distribution of fossils, rock types, and ancient climatic zones.
Chapter 3: Evidence of Plate Tectonics

1.b. *Students know* Earth is composed of several layers: a cold, brittle lithosphere; a hot, convecting mantle; and a dense, metallic core.
Chapter 1: Earth's Structure
Chapter 3: Evidence of Plate Tectonics
Chapter 4: Effects of Plate Movement

1.c. *Students know* lithospheric plates the size of continents and oceans move at rates of centimeters per year in response to movements in the mantle.
Chapter 3: Evidence of Plate Tectonics

1.d. *Students know* that earthquakes are sudden motions along breaks in the crust called faults and that volcanoes and fissures are locations where magma reaches the surface.
Chapter 4: Effects of Plate Movement

1.e. *Students know* majors geologic events, such as earthquakes, volcanic eruptions, and mountain building, result from plate motions.
Chapter 3: Evidence of Plate Tectonics
Chapter 4: Effects of Plate Movement

1.f. *Students know* how to explain major features of California geology (including mountains, faults, volcanoes) in terms of plate tectonics.
Chapter 3: Evidence of Plate Tectonics
Chapter 4: Effects of Plate Movement

1.g. *Students know* how to determine the epicenter of an earthquake and know that the effects of an earthquake on any region vary, depending on the size of the earthquake, the distance of the region from the epicenter, the local geology, and the type of construction in the region.
Chapter 4: Effects of Plate Movement

Set 2 — Shaping Earth's Surface

Topography is reshaped by the weathering of rock and soil and by the transportation and deposition of sediment. As a basis for understanding this concept:
Unit A: Planet Earth

2.a. *Students know* water running downhill is the dominant process in shaping the landscape, including California's landscape.
Chapter 2: Shaping Earth's Surface

2.b. *Students know* rivers and streams are dynamic systems that erode, transport sediment, change course, and flood their banks in natural and recurring patterns.
Chapter 2: Shaping Earth's Surface

2.c. *Students know* beaches are dynamic systems in which the sand is supplied by rivers and moved along the coast by the action of waves.
Chapter 2: Shaping Earth's Surface

2.d. *Students know* earthquakes, volcanic eruptions, landslides, and floods change human and wildlife habitats.
Chapter 2: Shaping Earth's Surface
Chapter 4: Effects of Plate Movement
Chapter 9: Populations

Laguna Beach

Set 3 Heat (Thermal Energy) (Physical Science)

Heat moves in a predictable flow from warmer objects to cooler objects until all the objects are at the same temperature. As a basis for understanding this concept:

Unit C: Earth's Energy Supply

3.a. *Students know* energy can be carried from one place to another by heat flow or by waves, including water, light and sound waves, or by moving objects.
Chapter 4: Effects of Plate Movements
Chapter 5: Heating Earth

3.b. *Students know* that when fuel is consumed, most of the energy released becomes heat energy.
Chapter 10: Energy Resources

3.c. *Students know* heat flows in solids by conduction (which involves no flow of matter) and in fluids by conduction and convection (which involves flow of matter).
Chapter 5: Heating Earth

3.d. *Students know* heat energy is also transferred between objects by radiation (radiation can travel through space).
Chapter 5: Heating Earth

Set 4 Energy in the Earth System

Many phenomena on Earth's surface are affected by the transfer of energy through radiation and convection currents. As a basis for understanding this concept:

Unit C: Earth's Energy Supply

4.a. *Students know* the sun is the major source of energy for phenomena on Earth's surface; it powers winds, ocean currents, and the water cycle.
Chapter 1: Earth's Structure
Chapter 5: Heating Earth
Chapter 6: Energy and Weather

4.b. *Students know* solar energy reaches Earth through radiation, mostly in the form of visible light.
Chapter 5: Heating Earth

4.c. *Students know* heat from Earth's interior reaches the surface primarily through convection.
Chapter 3: Evidence of Plate Tectonics

4.d. *Students know* convection currents distribute heat in the atmosphere and oceans.
Chapter 5: Heating Earth
Chapter 6: Energy and Weather

4.e. *Students know* differences in pressure, heat, air movement, and humidity result in changes of weather.
Chapter 6: Energy and Weather

 Set 5

Ecology (Life Sciences)

Organisms in ecosystems exchange energy and nutrients among themselves and with the environment. As a basis for understanding this concept:

Unit D: Ecology

Sicklefin lemon shark ▼

5.a. *Students know* energy entering ecosystems as sunlight is transferred by producers into chemical energy through photosynthesis and then from organism to organism through food webs.
Chapter 7: The Biosphere
Chapter 8: Roles of Living Things

5.b. *Students know* matter is transferred over time from one organism to others in the food web and between organisms and the physical environment.
Chapter 7: The Biosphere
Chapter 8: Roles of Living Things

5.c. *Students know* populations of organisms can be categorized by the functions they serve in an ecosystem.
Chapter 8: Roles of Living Things

5.d. *Students know* different kinds of organisms may play similar ecological roles in similar biomes.
Chapter 8: Roles of Living Things

5.e. *Students know* the number and types of organisms an ecosystem can support depends on the resources available and on abiotic factors, such as quantities of light and water, a range of temperatures, and soil composition.
Chapter. 7: The Biosphere
Chapter 9: Populations

Set 6 Resources

Sources of energy and materials differ in amounts, distribution, usefulness, and the time required for their formation. As a basis for understanding this concept: Unit E: Earth's Natural Resources

6.a. *Students know* the utility of energy sources is determined by factors that are involved in converting these sources to useful forms and the consequences of the conversion process.
Chapter 10: Energy Resources

6.b. *Students know* different natural energy and material resources, including air, soil, rocks, minerals, petroleum, fresh water, wildlife, and forests, and know how to classify them as renewable or nonrenewable.
Chapter 10: Energy Resources   Chapter 11: Material Resources

6.c. *Students know* the natural origin of the materials used to make common objects.   Chapter 11: Material Resources

Set 7 Investigation and Experimentation

Scientific progress is made by asking meaningful questions and conducting careful investigations. As a basis for understanding this concept and addressing the content in the other three strands, students should develop their own questions and perform investigations. Students will:
Directed Inquiry and Guided Inquiry investigations in every lesson

7.a. Develop a hypothesis.

7.b. Select and use appropriate tools and technology (including calculators, computers, balances, spring scales, microscopes, and binoculars) to perform tests, collect data, and display data.

7.c. Construct appropriate graphs from data and develop qualitative statement about the relationships between variables.

7.d. Communicate the steps and results from an investigation in written reports and oral presentations.

7.e. Recognize whether evidence is consistent with a proposed explanation.

7.f. Read a topographic map and a geologic map for evidence provided on the maps and construct and interpret a simple scale map.

7.g. Interpret events by sequence and time from natural phenomena (e.g., the relative ages of rocks and intrusions).

7.h. Identify changes in natural phenomena over time without manipulating the phenomena (e.g., a tree limb, a grove of trees, a stream, a hillslope).

The Nature of Science

Science is an adventure. People all over the world do science. You can do science, too. You probably already do.

Big Idea

Scientific progress is made by asking meaningful questions and conducting careful investigations.

Start with Your Standards

STANDARD SET 7. Investigation and Experimentation

7. Scientific progress is made by asking meaningful questions and conducting careful investigations. As a basis for understanding this concept and addressing the content in the other three strands, students should develop their own questions and perform investigations.

7.a. Develop a hypothesis.

7.b. Select and use appropriate tools and technology (including calculators, computers, balances, spring scales, microscopes, and binoculars) to perform tests, collect data, and display data.

7.c. Construct appropriate graphs from data and develop qualitative statements about the relationships between variables.

7.d. Communicate the steps and results from an investigation in written reports and oral presentations.

7.e. Recognize whether evidence is consistent with a proposed explanation.

7.f. Read a topographic map and a geologic map for evidence provided on the maps and construct and interpret a simple scale map.

7.g. Interpret events by sequence and time from natural phenomena (e.g., the relative ages of rocks and intrusions).

7.h. Identify changes in natural phenomena over time without manipulating the phenomena (e.g., a tree limb, a grove of trees, a stream, a hillslope).

The Nature of Science

You Can Do What Scientists Do . . . S10

You Can Think Like a Scientist S12

You Can Be an Inventor S18

You Can Make Decisions S22

Science Safety S24

You Can...

Do What Scientists Do

Meet Dr. Jorge Vazquez. He is a physical oceanographer at the Jet Propulsion Laboratory (JPL) in Pasadena, California. JPL is part of the National Aeronautics and Space Administration (NASA). A physical oceanographer is an Earth scientist who studies the properties of Earth's ocean and the changes that can be observed in ocean water. At JPL, Dr. Vazquez studies data about the ocean that has been collected by Earth-orbiting NASA science satellites.

Satellites are an important tool of oceanographers. They are used to collect huge quantities of data about water temperature, wave height, and changes in ocean currents.

Scientists formulate explanations about the natural world. They then test their explanations with different kinds of investigations. Some, including those of Dr. Vazquez, involve making and analyzing observations. Other investigations involve collecting specimens, experimenting, or building models.

Dr. Vazquez is interested in ocean temperature data. He looks for patterns of change with the seasons and from year to year. He tries to understand why these patterns occur and then formulates better explanations of how ocean temperature variations affect ocean currents and climate.

In addition to working to answer his own questions, Dr. Vazquez helps other scientists by distributing the ocean data they need for their investigations.

Scientific progress comes from challenges to current theories.

Dr. Vazquez shares his knowledge of oceanography with future scientists in the classroom. The science of oceanography includes concepts related to biology, Earth science, space science, and physics. The students he teaches may eventually challenge current scientific theories as they make observations and carry out experiments.

Think Like a Scientist

The ways scientists ask and answer questions about the world around them is called **scientific inquiry.** Scientific inquiry requires certain attitudes, or approaches to thinking about a problem. To think like a scientist you have to be:

- curious and ask a lot of questions.

- willing to answer them by planning careful experiments.

- able to keep an open mind. That means you listen to the ideas of others.

- willing to use mathematics at every step of scientific inquiry.

- open to changing what you think when your investigation results surprise you.

- skeptical of what other people tell you, and willing to question ideas.

How does a prism change white light into all the different colors? Are the colors part of the white light?

Use Critical Thinking

When you think critically you evaluate what you hear and read. You can decide if what you hear on TV or read on a website is fact or opinion. A *fact* can be checked to make sure it is true. An *opinion* is what you think about the facts.

Did you ever hear a claim that was hard to believe? When you think, "What evidence is there to support that claim?" you are thinking critically. Critical thinkers evaluate sources of information and the strengths and weaknesses in statements.

Observations can be interpreted in many ways. Scientists decide whether a conclusion is supported by the data collected.

It looks like this prism [sep]arates the beam of white [light] into all the different colors. [Cou]ld the white light contain [li]ght of different colors?

I read that white light is made of a rang[e] of wavelengths of light, e[ach] different color. A prism ben[ds] [each] wavelength differently a[nd] separates the colors.

Science Inquiry

Applying scientific inquiry helps you understand the world around you. Suppose you have decided to investigate two different ways that tennis balls reach the ground.

Observe You notice a tennis player drop a ball straight down to the ground. You notice the same player hit or throw the ball horizontally.

Ask a Question When you think about what you saw, heard, or read you may have questions. Choose a question that can be answered by making observations or experimenting.

Hypothesis Think about facts you already know. Do you have an idea about the answer? Write it down. That is your hypothesis.

Experiment Design a test that will tell if the hypothesis is true or not. Choose the tools and materials you will need. Write the steps you will follow. Make sure that you keep all conditions the same except the one you are testing. That condition is called the *independent variable*.

Conclusion Think about your results. What do they tell you? Did your results support your hypothesis or show it to be false?

Describe your experiment to others. Communicate your results and conclusion.

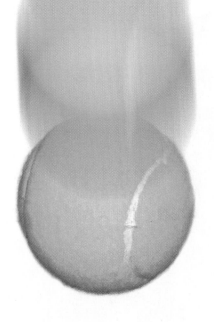

STANDARDS

7.a. Develop a hypothesis.
7.e. Recognize whether evidence is consistent with a proposed explanation.

My Tennis Ball Experiment

Observe A ball that is dropped falls straight down and hits the ground. Balls that are hit or tossed move sideways before they hit the ground.

Ask a Question I wonder, does the ball that moves sideways take the same amount of time to hit the ground as the one that is dropped?

Hypothesis A ball thrown horizontally takes the same amount of time to hit the ground as the ball that drops.

Experiment I'm going to have two students release tennis balls at the same time. One student will roll the ball along a table to start the sideways motion. When that ball moves off the table the other student will drop his ball from the same height. I will watch to see whether one ball hits the ground first.

Conclusion The results of my experiment support my hypothesis. A ball thrown horizontally takes the same amount of time to reach the ground as a ball that is dropped from the same height.

Inquiry Process

The processes scientists use to conduct investigations vary with the kinds of questions they ask. Here is a process that some scientists follow when it is possible to do an experiment.

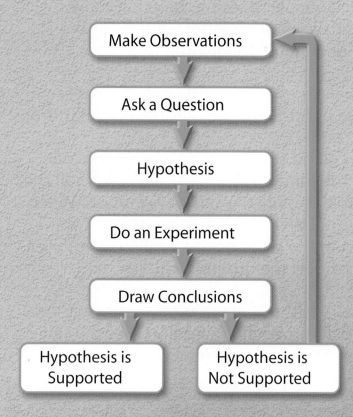

Science Inquiry Skills

You'll use many of these skills of inquiry when you investigate and experiment.

- Ask Questions
- Observe
- Compare
- Classify
- Predict
- Measure
- Hypothesize
- Use Variables
- Experiment
- Use Models
- Communicate
- Use Numbers
- Record Data
- Analyze Data
- Infer
- Collaborate
- Research

Try It Yourself!

Experiment with Mystery Sand

When you gently sprinkle a spoonful of Mystery Sand onto the surface of water in a clear cup, the sand does not sink. However, if you pour a heaping spoonful of Mystery Sand into the water, the sand makes unusual formations on the bottom of the cup.

1. What questions do you have about the Mystery Sand?

2. How would you find out the answers?

3. How could you use the Mystery Sand to test a hypothesis?

4. Write your plan for an experiment with one independent variable using Mystery Sand. Predict what the results will be.

Be an Inventor

Dean Kamen made his first important invention in the 1970s when he was in college. His brother, a medical student, told Dean that there was no good way to give steady doses of needed medicines to people with serious illnesses. After Kamen thought about the problem, he invented a small pump that could deliver a steady dose of medicine to a person at exactly the right time.

Since then, Kamen has become one of the world's great inventors. He is famous for inventing a robotic wheelchair that can climb stairs and move over rocky ground. Kamen invents more than just medical devices. He also invented an electric scooter called the Segway human transporter. A person can stand and move on this upright scooter without falling because the Segway uses a gyroscope to keep its balance.

"To me, life is a blur of activities. I mean, it's only a job if you'd rather be doing something else."

What Is Technology?

The tools people make and use, the things they build with tools, and the methods used to accomplish a practical purpose are all **technology.** A paper airplane is an example of technology. So is a jumbo jet that carries passengers or cargo from one city to another.

Scientists use technology to make their observations more accurate. For example, Earth-orbiting satellites make it possible for scientists to take photographs of Earth's surface. Remote-sensing instruments can also measure small changes in ocean temperatures, making scientists' observations more exact. Possibly the most useful technology for scientists is the computer. Computers make it possible to store, organize, and analyze huge amounts of data.

Many technologies make the world a better place to live. Sometimes, though, a technology that solves one problem can cause other problems. For example, air conditioners make living and working in places with warm climates easier and more comfortable. However, a chemical used for decades in air conditioners destroyed other chemicals high in the atmosphere that protected living things from the harmful rays of the Sun.

A Better Idea

"I wish I had a better way to _____." How would you fill in the blank? Everyone wishes he or she could do his or her job more easily or have more fun. Inventors try to make those wishes come true. Inventing or improving an invention requires time and patience. You can be an inventor, too.

Portable Digital Audio Player

LCD screen

control button

A portable digital audio player is a computer built into a listening device. People can listen to music from a player that easily fits into a pocket.

How to Be an Inventor

1 Identify a problem. It may be a problem at school, at home, or in your community.

2 List ways to solve the problem. Sometimes the solution is a new tool. Other times it may be a new way of doing an old job or activity.

3 Choose the best solution. Decide which idea will work best. Think about which one you can carry out.

4 Make a sample. A sample, called a *prototype,* is the first try. Your idea may need many materials or none at all. Choose measuring tools that will help your design work better.

5 Try out your invention. Use your prototype, or ask some else to try it. Keep a record of how it works and what problems you find. The more times you try it, the more information you will have.

6 Improve your invention. Use what you learned to make your design work better. Draw or write about the changes you made and why you made them.

7 Share your invention. Show your invention to others. Communicate how you made it and how it works. Tell how it makes an activity easier or more fun. If it did not work as well as you wanted, tell why.

Make Decisions

Danger in the Sun

Think back to your early years in elementary school. Possibly your favorite time of day was just before or after lunch when everyone went outdoors to play. Outdoor play is great exercise and reduces stress. Yet playing outdoors when the Sun is highest in the sky creates health risks.

There are different types of skin cancer, and most can be easily cured if caught early. One type, called melanoma, can be deadly. If left untreated, melanoma spreads to other parts of the body. Severe sunburns on people under the age of 18 can cause melanoma later in their lives.

Deciding What to Do

How can young children get the benefits of outdoor play at school and still avoid the risk of skin cancer?

Here's how to make your decision. You can use the same steps to help solve problems in your home, in your school, and in your community.

1 Learn Learn about the problem. Take the time needed to get the facts and understand what scientists know about it. You could talk to an expert, read reference books, or explore websites.

2 List Make a list of actions you could take. Add actions other people could take.

3 Decide Think about each action on your list and identify related risks and benefits. Decide which choice is the best one for you, your school, or your community.

4 Share Communicate your decision to others.

Always use a Sunscreen when you work or play outdoors.

Science Safety

☑ Know the safety rules of your school and classroom and follow them.

☑ Read and follow the safety tips in each Investigate activity.

☑ When you plan your own investigations, predict possible hazards and write down how to avoid them.

☑ Know how to dispose of hazardous materials and chemicals and put away science materials. Keep your work area clean, and tell your teacher about spills right away.

☑ Know how to safely use equipment, including electrical devices.

☑ Wear safety goggles and use other safety equipment when your teacher tells you.

☑ Unless your teacher tells you to, never put any science materials in or near your ears, eyes, or mouth.

☑ Wear gloves when handling live animals.

☑ Wash your hands when your investigation is completed.

Caring for Living Things

☑ Learn how to care for the plants and animals in your classroom so that they stay healthy and safe. Learn how to hold animals carefully.

EARTH UNIT A SCIENCE

Planet Earth

Let's Go!

Point Reyes National Seashore

Point Reyes Lighthouse is one of the best places along the California coast for seeing California Gray Whales on their annual migration from Alaska to Mexico.

Banana slugs can have up to 27,000 teeth on their long tongues.

Gray whales can live to be 70 years old.

Planet Earth

Chapter 1
Earth's Structure 2

Independent Books

- Earth's Structure
- Climbing High
- To the Center of the Earth!

Chapter 2
Shaping Earth's Surface 42

Independent Books

- Shaping Earth's Surface
- Along the Nile
- Acid Rain

McWay Cove, California

Topography is reshaped by the weathering of rock and soil and by the transportation and deposition of sediment.

Earth's Structure

Death Valley, California

LESSON 1

No matter where you live on Earth, you experience day and night and the different seasons. How does Earth's movement through space cause these events?

LESSON 2

If you could pull Earth apart, you would find its interior layers to be very different from the surface. Which layer of Earth is the hottest? Which is the densest?

LESSON 3

Scientists use maps to study many different features of Earth. What features does the map shown here represent?

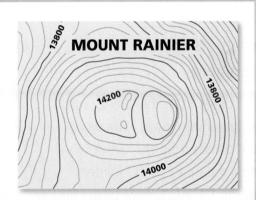

MOUNT RAINIER
13800
13800
14200
14000

Writing Journal

In your Writing Journal, write or draw answers to each of the above questions.

Vocabulary Preview

Vocabulary

asthenosphere p. 20
contour lines p. 30
core p. 20
crust p. 9
elevation p. 30
lithosphere p. 20
mantle p. 20
revolution p. 12
rotation p. 11
topographic map p. 30

Glossary

English-Spanish, p. H26

Vocabulary Skill

Word Roots
lithosphere

Litho- comes from the Greek word *lithos*, meaning "rock." The word *sphere* comes from the Greek word *sphaira*, meaning "ball." Write a definition for *lithosphere* based on the meanings of the Greek word roots.

contour lines

lines on a topographic map that connect points with the same elevation

revolution

a complete orbit around an object, such as the Sun

rotation

a complete turn about an axis

elevation
the height above sea level

Start with Your Standards

Standard Set 1. Plate Tectonics and Earth's Structure

1.b. *Students know* Earth is composed of several layers: a cold, brittle lithosphere; a hot, convecting mantle; and a dense, metallic core.

Standard Set 4. Energy in the Earth System

4.a. *Students know* the sun is the major source of energy for phenomena on Earth's surface; it powers winds, ocean currents, and the water cycle.

Standard Set 7: Investigation and Experimentation standards covered in this chapter: 7.b., 7.f., 7.h.

What Makes Earth a Special Planet?

Building Background

When will the Sun rise tomorrow, and when will it set? What causes seasons, and why do some places have longer summers and winters than others? The movement of Earth through space is the key to answering these questions. Earth rotates about its tilted axis and revolves around the Sun.

The Sun affects every aspect of life on Earth. It provides light and heat, and powers the weather.

STANDARDS

4.a. *Students know* the Sun is the major source of energy for phenomena on Earth's surface; it powers winds, ocean currents, and the water cycle.

7.h. Identify changes in natural phenomena over time without manipulating the phenomena (e.g., a tree limb, a grove of trees, a stream, a hillslope).

PREPARE TO INVESTIGATE

Inquiry Skill

Observe When you observe, you use your senses and tools to identify properties, including changes over time.

Materials

- atlas or Internet access
- orienteering compass
- protractor
- 8-cm × 8-cm piece of card stock
- paper plate
- scissors
- tape

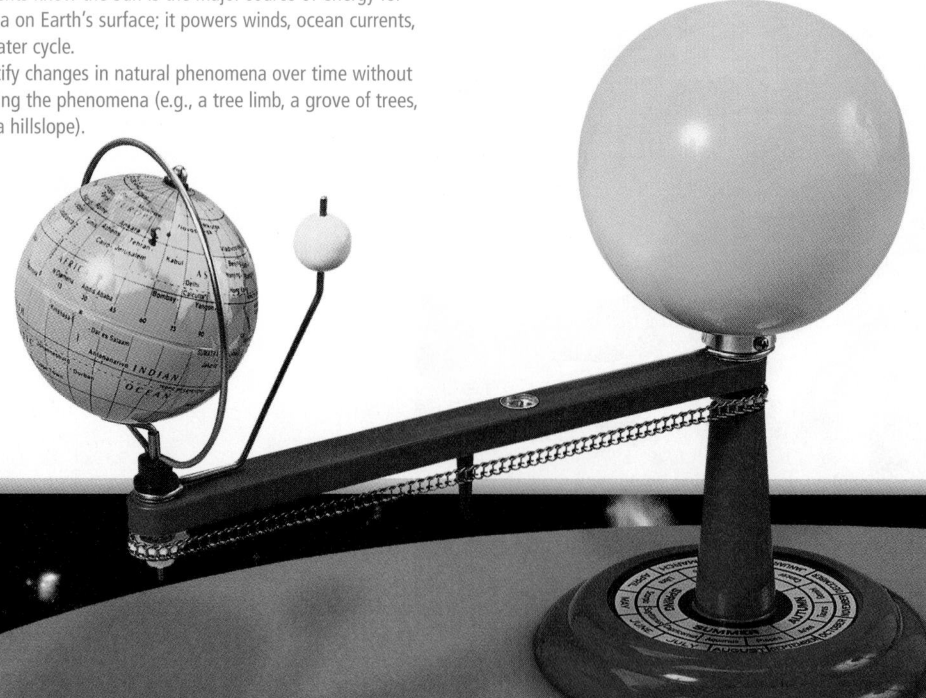

Make a Sundial

Procedure

Safety: Exercise caution when using scissors. Never look directly at the Sun.

STEP 1

1. **Measure** Work with a partner. Use an atlas to find the latitude of your community. On card stock, use the protractor to draw and label an angle equal to that latitude. Make the rays of the angle 6 cm long.

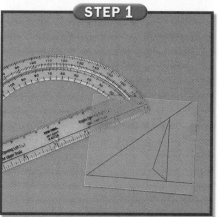

STEP 1

2. **Collaborate** Cut along the angle line to form a triangle. This will be your gnomon (NOH mahn), or sundial stick. Fold the gnomon to make it stand up straight. Cut out a wedge from the vertical side.

3. Cut a slit in the paper plate and slide in the gnomon. Tape it to the back of the plate.

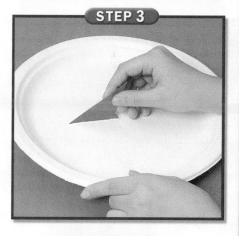

STEP 3

4. **Observe** Place the sundial outdoors in a sunny spot. Use the compass to align the gnomon so it points north. Tape down the sundial. Mark where the straight side of the gnomon's shadow crosses the circle. Record the time next to the mark.

5. **Record Data** Each hour on the hour, mark and label the gnomon's shadow. Continue throughout the school day.

Conclusion

1. **Analyze Data** What patterns do you see in the day's time markings ?

2. **Use Numbers** Take your sundial outside at a time other than on the hour. Point the gnomon north. Read the sundial to estimate the time. Compare its time to the actual time. How accurate is your sundial?

Guided Inquiry

Experiment Record the date on your sundial. Repeat the activity at different times during the year, using a different color pen to record the data. Look for changes in your data. **Infer** what might cause these changes.

VOCABULARY

crust	p. 9
revolution	p. 12
rotation	p. 11

READING SKILL

Cause and Effect As you read, list effects on Earth that are caused by the Sun.

Cause → Effect

STANDARD

4.a. *Students know* the sun is the major source of energy for phenomena on Earth's surface; it powers winds, ocean currents, and the water cycle.

Earth

MAIN IDEA The Sun is the major source of energy for Earth. Different locations on Earth receive different amounts of solar energy.

A Special Planet

Earth is the third planet from the Sun in the solar system. Like the other planets, Earth receives nearly all its energy from the Sun. However, it's the only planet known to support life.

There are several reasons why Earth is so special. The range of temperatures on Earth allows water to exist in liquid form, a necessary condition for life. In fact, liquid water covers about 70 percent of Earth's surface! If Earth were closer to the Sun and did not have an atmosphere to protect it, the water would boil or evaporate. If Earth were farther away, all the water would freeze.

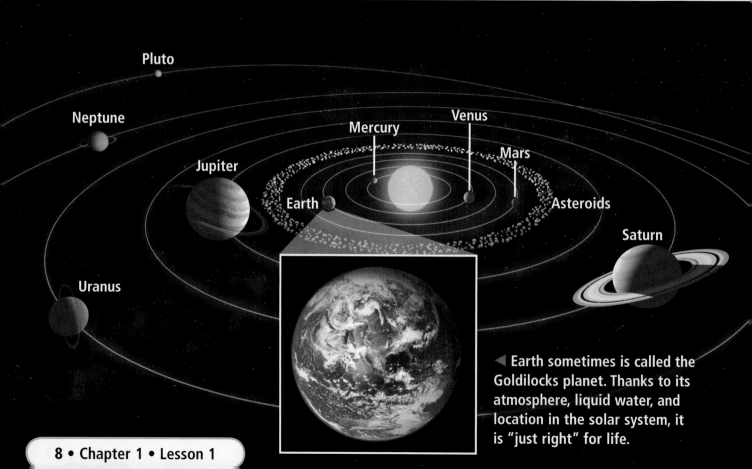

◄ Earth sometimes is called the Goldilocks planet. Thanks to its atmosphere, liquid water, and location in the solar system, it is "just right" for life.

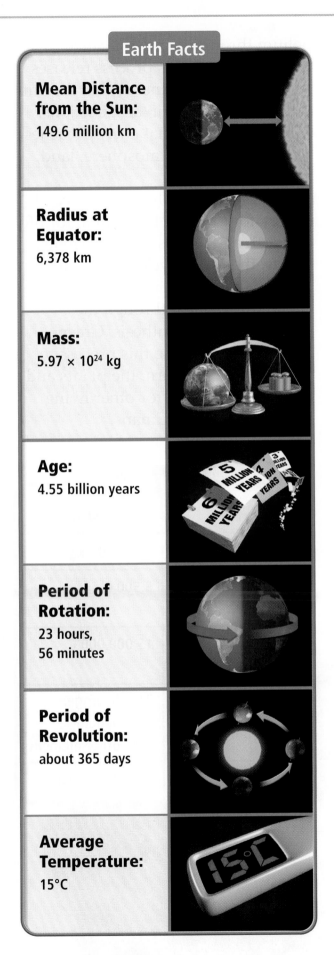

Earth Facts

Mean Distance from the Sun:
149.6 million km

Radius at Equator:
6,378 km

Mass:
5.97×10^{24} kg

Age:
4.55 billion years

Period of Rotation:
23 hours, 56 minutes

Period of Revolution:
about 365 days

Average Temperature:
15°C

Look at the photo of Earth taken from space. The planet looks like a giant blue-and-white swirled marble. The blue color comes from Earth's oceans. The white swirls are clouds.

Earth's gravity is strong enough to retain an atmosphere—the blanket of air that surrounds the planet. Currents in the atmosphere and the oceans help redistribute the energy Earth receives from the Sun, moderating the surface temperatures.

The atmosphere is made up mostly of nitrogen and oxygen, with small amounts of other gases mixed in. Earth's atmosphere and magnetic field protect the planet from harmful radiation. The atmosphere also helps protect Earth from meteoroids.

Earth's thin rocky outer layer is called the **crust.** This is where all living things live. The crust is made up mostly of minerals called silicates. Silicates are combinations of oxygen and silicon. On average, oxygen makes up 46 percent and silicon, 28 percent of Earth's crust. Aluminum, iron, and other elements make up the rest.

You can find more Earth facts in the table on the left.

 **READING CHECK** Why is Earth able to support life?

Activity Card 1
See How a Sundial Works

The Sun

The Sun is a huge sphere of hot glowing gas, called *plasma*. At a mean distance of nearly 150 million km (93 million mi), it is the closest star to Earth. Of the billions of stars in the Universe, the Sun is average in most ways. It is a medium-sized yellow star that is about 4.6 billion years old. The Sun is so large that more than 1 million Earths could fit inside it!

The Sun's mass makes up about 99.8 percent of all the mass in the solar system. Its gravitational pull is strong enough to keep Earth and all the other objects in the solar system in orbit around it.

As you can see in the table, the Sun is extremely hot. At the Sun's core, hydrogen is converted into helium through a process called nuclear fusion. This process releases a huge amount of energy that the Sun radiates into space in all directions. A tiny fraction of that energy reaches Earth, heating its atmosphere, land, and oceans.

The Sun is the ultimate source of energy for Earth. It is essential for life on Earth and drives ocean currents, winds, the water cycle, and weather.

Earth's living things use the energy of sunlight through the process of photosynthesis. Green plants and algae use this process to produce food. In turn, the plants and algae provide food for other living things, including humans.

The Sun continuously generates both light and heat. ▼

Sun Facts	
Diameter	1,390,000 km
Mass	2.0×10^{30} kg
Surface Temperature	5,500°C
Core Temperature	15,000,000°C
Composition	74% hydrogen 24% helium 2% other elements
Age	4.6 billion years

Day and Night

Seen from Earth, the Sun appears to move across the sky every day. It rises in the east, climbs to its highest point at midday, then lowers to the west until it sets. This apparent motion is due to Earth rotating like a spinning top about its axis. Earth rotates from west to east.

Earth's axis is an imaginary straight line that passes through the geographic North and South poles. Each full **rotation,** or complete turn about its axis, takes one day. As Earth rotates, the half facing the Sun has daytime, while the other half has night. This gives rise to the endless cycle of night and day.

To help you understand, try this simple activity. First, select an object, such as a clock or a lamp shade, to represent the Sun. Think of yourself as Earth. Stand so that you can just

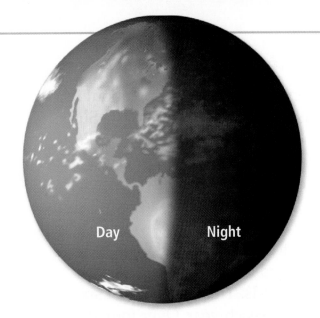

▲ At any moment, it is day on half of Earth's surface and night on the other.

see the model Sun out of the left corner of your eye. Then slowly rotate in a counterclockwise circle.

As you move, the model Sun comes into full view, then is visible only in the far right corner of your eye, and later is out of sight completely. It remained in place while you—the model Earth—rotated.

🎯 **CAUSE AND EFFECT** What keeps Earth in orbit around the Sun?

▲ Earth's rotation changes how the shadow falls on a sundial. What time does this sundial show?

11

The Year and the Seasons

In addition to rotating about its axis, Earth travels around the Sun in a nearly circular orbit. It takes Earth one year to complete one **revolution,** or orbit around the Sun. Ordinary calendars show that one year lasts a total of 365 days. However, the actual time for a revolution is longer by exactly 5 hours, 48 minutes, and 46 seconds. This adds almost six hours to each year. Over four years, that adds almost 24 hours, or one day.

To keep calendars in line with Earth's movement around the Sun, one day is added to the calendar every four years. That day is February 29. The extra-long years are called leap years.

Why does Earth have seasons? As you learned, Earth rotates about its axis. The axis is not vertical but is tilted about 23.5° with respect to the vertical. Because of the tilt, each pole is oriented either toward or away from the Sun, depending on Earth's position in its orbit. This is why Earth has seasons.

In the middle of the calendar year, the Northern Hemisphere tilts toward the Sun. As a result, the Sun climbs higher in the sky and the days are longer. The Sun's rays strike the ground more directly, resulting in the warmer days of spring and summer.

During the rest of the year, the Northern Hemisphere tilts away from the Sun. The Sun is lower in the sky and stays above the horizon for fewer hours. The Sun's rays are angled as they strike the ground, which spreads out the sunlight. The Northern Hemisphere experiences cooler days of fall and winter.

Earth's Seasons in the Northern Hemisphere

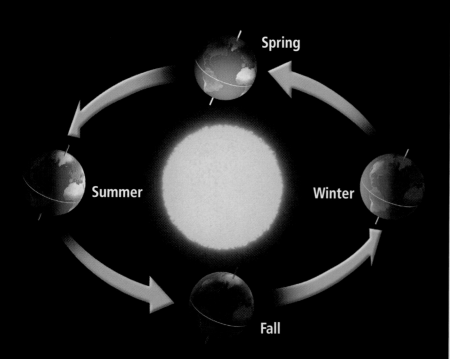

Spring

Summer

Winter

Fall

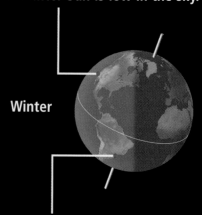

On a December day, Los Angeles has less than 10 hours of daylight. The winter Sun is low in the sky.

Winter

South of the equator, Buenos Aires has more than 14 hours of daylight. The summer Sun is high in the sky.

▲ Earth enjoys relatively stable, mostly moderate climates. This makes Earth a wonderful place to live for a huge variety of living things—including you.

Earth's Climates

The shape of Earth's orbit around the Sun, the wobble and angle of Earth's axis, and Earth's rotational speed vary very slowly with time.

As a result, the amount of solar energy Earth receives varies slowly. Therefore Earth's climates do not change much over hundreds of years. This means that weather patterns and temperature ranges can be predicted fairly accurately.

For example, people living in Chicago, Illinois, can rely on average temperatures of about ⁻6°C (22°F) every January. People living east or west of Chicago can expect similar low temperatures.

Yet the weather changes when you head south from Chicago. As you move through St. Louis, Memphis, and Houston, the temperatures increase. Houston's average January temperature is a warm 11°C (52°F). This trend is present during other seasons, too.

What causes this trend? As you move south through the United States, you move closer to the equator. Places closer to the equator receive more solar radiation, and thus are warmer.

As you will learn, many factors affect temperature and climate. For example, oceans tend to moderate the temperature of coastal areas. This is why California cities have warmer winter weather than places farther inland.

CAUSE AND EFFECT **What causes the climates on Earth to stay about the same year after year?**

13

Earth's Future

Earth is a wonderful planet for living things, just as it has been for a very long time. Yet humans are changing Earth in many ways. Over the last 50 years, scientists have begun to understand these changes and their effects. In many cases, people have changed their behavior to help protect the planet.

For example, in the 1970s, scientists discovered the side effects of certain chemicals used in refrigerators, air conditioners, and spray cans. These chemicals are called chlorofluorocarbons, or CFCs.

▲ You can help Earth's resources last longer by recycling plastics, metals, and paper.

They were destroying the ozone layer, a layer in the upper atmosphere that protects Earth from the Sun's harmful ultraviolet rays. To stop this damage, governments all over the world banned the use of CFCs.

Today, scientists are studying the effects of many types of human activities. Burning fossil fuels, cutting down forests, overfishing— these activities and many more could have long-lasting effects. You will learn more about these issues as you read on.

Every day, you make choices that affect Earth's future. You can choose wisely by learning as much about Earth as you can! You also can do many simple things to help make your community a better place to live.

 **CAUSE AND EFFECT** How did CFCs harm the atmosphere?

◀ Earth is the only home that people have. Taking care of it is a job for everyone.

Visual Summary

Earth is sometimes called the "Goldilocks planet." Its position in the solar system, its atmosphere, abundant water, and moderate temperatures make it "just right" for life to exist.

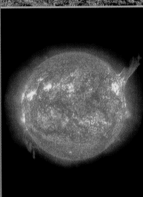

The Sun is the ultimate source of energy for Earth. It powers winds, ocean currents, and the water cycle. Living things also gain their energy from sunlight.

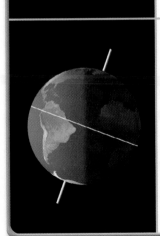

Earth rotates on its axis, causing day and night. Earth also revolves around the Sun. Earth's axis is tilted, causing the seasons of the year.

STANDARD

4.a.

 Technology
Visit **www.eduplace.com/cascp** to learn more about the Earth-Sun relationship.

Reading Review

① MAIN IDEA Explain how the Sun is important to all life on Earth.

② VOCABULARY Define *rotation* and *revolution*, using Earth as the example.

③ READING SKILL Why are Earth's average temperatures highest near the equator and lowest near the North and South poles?

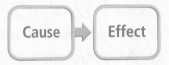

④ CRITICAL THINKING: Predict Earth's axis tilt is the reason Earth has seasons. Predict how Earth's seasons might change if the angle of its axis tilt changed.

⑤ INQUIRY SKILL: Observe How could you observe and measure the way the Sun appears to move across the sky? Remember that you should never look directly at the Sun!

 **TEST PRACTICE**
What does the Sun provide Earth with every day?

A. CFCs

B. atmosphere

C. water

D. energy

STANDARD

1–5: 4.a., **Test Practice:** 4.a.

15

What Is Earth's Structure?

Building Background

Earth has a layered structure. At the surface is a layer of solid rock called the crust. Below is the mantle, made of softened rock. Below the mantle is Earth's core, a very dense layer made mainly of iron. By studying Earth's structure, scientists can predict how the surface will change.

 STANDARDS

1.b. *Students know* Earth is composed of several layers: a cold, brittle lithosphere; a hot, convecting mantle; and a dense, metallic core.
7.b. Select and use appropriate tools and technology (including calculators, computers, balances, spring scales, microscopes, and binoculars) to perform tests, collect data, and display data.

PREPARE TO INVESTIGATE

Inquiry Skill

Use Models When you make a model, you are using a representation of an object to better understand how it works.

Materials

- modeling clay, 2 colors
- a small marble
- metric measuring tape
- scissors
- aluminum foil
- plastic knife

Science and Math Toolbox

For step 4, review **Using a Tape Measure or Ruler** on page H6.

A Model Earth

Procedure

STEP 1

1 **Collaborate** Working with a partner, roll modeling clay into two balls of different colors. Make one the size of a golf ball and the other the size of a baseball.

2 **Use Models** The smaller clay ball represents Earth's outer core. The marble represents its inner core. Push the marble into the center of the smaller clay ball and reshape the clay around it. You now have a model of Earth's two-part core.

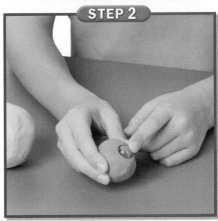
STEP 2

3 **Observe** The larger clay ball represents Earth's mantle. Using the plastic knife, cut this clay ball in half. Reshape the clay so that this ball can be wrapped around the two-part core. You now have a model of Earth's core and mantle.

4 **Measure** Use a measuring tape to find the distance around your model at its "equator." Cut a rectangle of foil equal to that distance in length and one-half that distance in width. Wrap the foil around the mantle and smooth it out. This thin layer of foil represents Earth's crust.

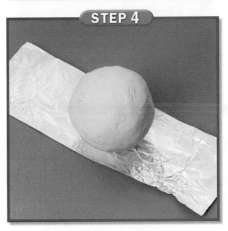
STEP 4

Conclusion

1. **Use Models** In your *Science Notebook*, draw what your model of Earth would look like if you could slice it in half. Label the layers.

2. **Communicate** Write a report in your *Science Notebook* explaining the steps and results of your investigation.

Guided Inquiry

Ask Questions What questions do you have about the temperatures of Earth's layers? Make a plan to **research** your questions, including choosing tools to collect and display data.

Earth's Structure

MAIN IDEA Earth is made up of different layers. Each layer has its own unique characteristics.

VOCABULARY

asthenosphere	p. 20
core	p. 20
lithosphere	p. 20
mantle	p. 20

READING SKILL

Compare and Contrast As you read, note how Earth's layers are similar to and different from one another.

Compare	Contrast

STANDARD

1.b. *Students know* Earth is composed of several layers: a cold, brittle lithosphere; a hot, convecting mantle; and a dense, metallic core.

Hot Inside

In many parts of the world, columns of steaming hot water can be found shooting up through Earth's surface. These boiling fountains are known as *geysers* (GUY zuhrs). Geysers form where water drains down a deep channel in Earth's surface. At the bottom of the channel, hot rocks heat the water, forming steam that pushes water to the surface. Finally, the built-up pressure forces the remaining water to erupt in a sudden explosion. The existence of geysers suggests that Earth is hot inside.

Yellowstone National Park in Wyoming is well known for its numerous geysers and hot springs. Long before this region became a tourist attraction, Jim Bridger explored its wonders. Bridger was a fur trader, scout, and mountain man. He told everyone he met about the many geysers and amazing sights of the region.

Visit Yellowstone today, and you, too, can see evidence of Earth's hot interior. But just how hot is it inside Earth?

66 Geysers spout up 70 feet, with a terrible hissing noise, at regular intervals. In this section are the great springs, so hot that meat is readily cooked in them.... **99**

Jim Bridger (1804–1881)
Geyser Gazer

▲ Yellowstone National Park's hot springs, geysers, and mudpots are evidence of Earth's hot interior.

Earth's temperature increases about 25°C per km in the crust, then more slowly from the upper mantle to its center. ▶

Temperature of Earth's Interior

Earth's Center

Temperature (°C) — vertical axis: 1,000 2,000 3,000 4,000 5,000 6,000

Depth (km) — horizontal axis: 0 1,000 2,000 3,000 4,000 5,000 6,000 7,000

By studying mines and holes drilled in the crust, scientists know that the temperature increases about 2 to 3°C for every 100 m (300 ft) below Earth's surface. However, the deepest drill holes reach less than 15 km (9 mi) below the surface. So scientists depend on indirect evidence, such as geysers and volcanic activity, to learn what Earth is like inside. They also conduct experiments on surface rocks and minerals under conditions of high pressure and temperature.

Scientists have found that much of Earth's internal heat comes from energy released when radioactive elements such as potassium, uranium, and thorium break down. Some heat is left over from Earth's formation.

More information about Earth's interior can be gained by observing seismic waves. These waves are vibrations that travel through the solid Earth during earthquakes. Seismic waves change as they move through different kinds of materials at different temperatures.

COMPARE AND CONTRAST How does Earth's temperature change with depth below the surface?

19

Earth's Layers

Earth has a layered structure. Most of these layers are made up of solid rock. The innermost layers are mostly a mixture of metals.

Earth's layers vary in thickness. The crust, the uppermost layer, is much thinner than the other layers. The crust is nearly all solid rock. Under the continents, the crust is mostly granite and other low-density rocks. Below the oceans, the crust is mostly made of basalt—a dark, dense rock.

The crust is by far the thinnest of Earth's layers. Under the continents, the average thickness of the crust is about 40 km (24 mi), but it may be as much as 70 km (42 mi) in mountainous regions. The crust is even thinner under the oceans. The ocean-floor crust has a thickness of about 7 km (4 mi).

The solid layer just below Earth's crust is the **mantle.** The mantle is denser than the crust and contains more iron and less silica. The mantle is about 2,900 km (1,800 mi) thick. It makes up more than two-thirds of Earth's mass. This rigid upper mantle and crust combine to form a rigid shell called the **lithosphere** (LITH oh sfir).

Below the lithosphere, the rock material in the upper mantle is much softer. This material can flow very slowly, like plastic that has been heated almost to its melting point. The solid lithosphere can be thought of as "floating" on this upper mantle. The plastic part of the mantle beneath the lithosphere is called the **asthenosphere** (as THEN uh sfir).

The innermost of Earth's layers is the **core,** which extends to the center of Earth. The core is divided into two regions, or layers—the outer core and the inner core. The outer core is about 2,200 km (1,400 mi) thick and is the only layer that is in a liquid state. It is made up of molten iron, with some nickel, sulfur, and oxygen also present.

The solid inner core, about 1,200 km (720 mi) thick, is even hotter than the outer core. Made up of nearly pure iron, the inner core is about the size of the Moon. Its temperature is about 5,000°C, about as hot as the surface of the Sun! The extremely high pressure from above keeps the iron from melting.

A hard-boiled egg is often used to model Earth's structure. Others compare Earth to a peach or similar fruit with a thin skin and a pit in the center.

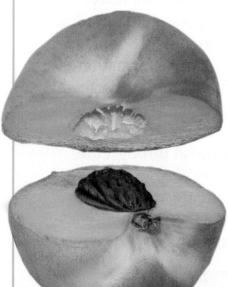

◄ When a peach is used as a model of Earth, what does the peach pit represent?

COMPARE AND CONTRAST How is Earth like a peach? How is it different?

Layers of Earth

Crust

Earth's thin outermost layer is solid rock. It is about five times thicker under the continents than it is under the oceans.

Mantle

This thick layer lies between the crust and the outer core. The rigid upper mantle together with the crust forms the lithosphere.

Outer Core

Consisting mostly of molten iron, this is Earth's only liquid layer.

Inner Core

Pressure keeps this super-hot metallic region in a solid state.

Express Lab

Activity Card 2
Make an Earth Model

Earth's Magnetic Field

If you have ever used an orienteering compass, you have detected Earth's magnetic field. Earth's magnetic field is similar to the magnetic field surrounding a bar magnet. Like the bar magnet, Earth has a north magnetic pole and a south magnetic pole. The magnetic field lines fan out from the north magnetic pole, loop around, and come together at the south magnetic pole.

Scientists attribute Earth's magnetic field to the presence of molten iron in Earth's outer core. Circulating electric currents are produced as the liquid iron core rotates. These electric currents create Earth's magnetic field.

Like a bar magnet, Earth is surrounded by a magnetic field. ▼

▲ Auroras are common near Earth's North and South poles. Sometimes, during extra strong bursts of solar wind, auroras may be seen as far south as California and Texas!

Earth's magnetic poles are tilted about 11° with respect to the geographic poles. Moreover, Earth's magnetic north pole is near the geographic South Pole, and vice versa. Earth's magnetic field has reversed direction many times in the course of millions of years. As you will learn later, scientists have used this fact to help explain how continents move.

Earth's magnetic field protects humans and other living things from the solar wind, a stream of fast, electrically charged particles from the Sun. The particles are guided by Earth's magnetic field into Earth's upper atmosphere near the poles. There, the particles collide with atoms and molecules of oxygen and nitrogen. The collisions produce beautiful ribbons and curtains of light known as auroras, or northern lights.

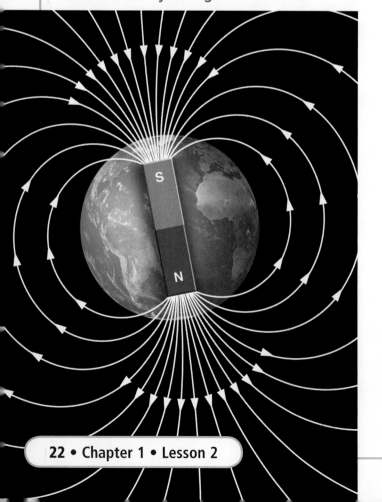

COMPARE AND CONTRAST How is Earth like a compass?

Visual Summary

Hot springs and geysers are one sign that Earth has a very hot interior. Scientists have inferred that Earth's temperatures increase with depth, rising to nearly 5,000°C at its center.

Earth has a layered structure consisting of a cold, brittle lithosphere; a hot mantle; and a dense, metallic core.

Earth's magnetic field is created by its rotating outer core of liquid iron. The magnetic field protects living things on Earth from harmful radiation.

STANDARD
1.b.

Technology
Visit www.eduplace.com/cascp to find out more about Earth's structure.

Reading Review

❶ MAIN IDEA Name the four layers that make up Earth's structure.

❷ VOCABULARY What makes up the *lithosphere*? How is the lithosphere different from the layer beneath it?

❸ READING SKILL How is Earth's crust different from the layers beneath? Why are these differences important?

Compare	Contrast

❹ CRITICAL THINKING: Evaluate One of your classmates says that Earth's interior is not important because it does not affect life on the surface. Do you agree or disagree? Cite evidence to support your answer.

❺ INQUIRY SKILL: Use Models How would you build a model of Earth's layers? Compare your model with Earth's actual layers.

TEST PRACTICE

Which is the thinnest layer of Earth?

A. the crust

B. the lithosphere

C. the inner core

D. the mantle

STANDARDS
1–5: 1.b., **Test Practice:** 1.b.

A Journey to the Center of the Earth

Jules Verne wrote this adventure novel in 1864, when scientists knew little about Earth's structure. The characters hike through halls, caves, and other underground pathways. Such paths could lead only a few kilometers deep, at best.

Even so, Verne understood much about science inquiry. As you read this selection, notice the inquiry skills and science methods that the characters try to practice.

. . . I had almost ceased to think of the sun, of the moon, of the stars, of the trees, houses, and towns; in fact, about any terrestrial necessities. In our peculiar position we were far above such reflections.

The grotto was a vast and magnificent hall. Along its granitic soil the stream flowed placidly and pleasantly. So great a distance was it now from its fiery source that its water was scarcely lukewarm, and could be drunk without delay or difficulty.

After a frugal breakfast, the Professor made up his mind to devote some hours to putting his notes and calculations in order.

"In the first place," he said, "I have a good many to verify and prove, in order that we may know our exact position. I wish to be able on our return to the upper regions to make a map of our journey, a kind of vertical section of the globe, which will be, as it were, the profile of the expedition."

STANDARD
1.b. *Students know* Earth is composed of several layers: a cold, brittle lithosphere; a hot, convecting mantle; and a dense, metallic core.

READING LINK

"That would indeed be a curious work, Uncle; but can you make your observations with anything like certainty and precision?"

"I can. I have never on one occasion failed to note with great care the angles and slopes. I am certain as to having made no mistakes. Take the compass and examine how she points."

I looked at the instrument with care.

"East one quarter southeast."

"Very good," resumed the Professor, noting the observation, and going through some rapid calculations. "I make out that we have journeyed two hundred and fifty miles from the point of our departure."

"Then the mighty waves of the Atlantic are rolling over our heads?"

"Certainly."

"And at this very moment it is possible that fierce tempests are raging above, and that men and ships are battling against the angry blasts just over our heads?"

"It is quite within the range of possibility," rejoined my uncle, smiling.

"And that whales are playing in shoals, thrashing the bottom of the sea, the roof of our adamantine prison?"

"Be quite at rest on that point; but there is no danger of their breaking through. But to return to our calculations... I think we have gone sixteen leagues in a downward direction."

"Sixteen leagues—fifty miles!" I cried.

"I am sure of it."

Glossary

adamantine, unyielding, cannot be moved

frugal, very sparse or simple

granitic, made of granite

grotto, a small cave

placidly, calmly, quietly

tempest, a raging, windy storm

terrestrial, Earthly

verify, to prove true

Sharing Ideas

1. **READING CHECK** What inquiry skills doe the Professor practice?

2. **WRITE ABOUT IT** Compare Earth's structure as it is understood today to t way Verne presented it.

3. **TALK ABOUT IT** Do you think a journey Earth's center is possible?

What Makes Up Earth's Surface?

Building Background

Earth has many different land features. These features are continually changing, too. Wind, water, and ice all help shape the land. How can people study Earth's features?

STANDARD

7.f. Read a topographic map and a geologic map for evidence provided on the maps and construct and interpret a simple scale map.

PREPARE TO INVESTIGATE

Inquiry Skill

Use Models A map is a kind of scale model. All parts of a scale model are larger or smaller than the actual object but are in exact proportions.

Materials

- modeling clay
- shallow square pan
- paper
- dental floss or plastic knife

Science and Math Toolbox

For step 1, review **Reading a Map** on pages H14–H15.

Model a Map

Procedure

1 **Compare** A topographic map has contour lines. These lines connect points that have the same elevation, which is the height above sea level. Study the topographic map of a hill shown here.

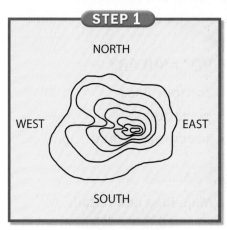

STEP 1

NORTH

WEST   EAST

SOUTH

2 **Use Models** Add clay to the pan and make a model of the hill. Refer to the topographic map.

3 **Measure** With a pencil, mark contour lines on the model hill. Use the topographic map as a guide. Then use dental floss or a plastic knife to slice the hill in layers along the lines. Set each layer aside.

STEP 2

4 **Record Data** Place the bottom layer on a sheet of paper and trace around the edges. Then trace the other layers to create a topographic map.

Conclusion

1. **Compare** How are the sliced layers of your model like the contour lines in the map?

2. **Use Models** Look at the topographic map. Where is the steepest slope? Where is the flattest plain?

3. **Infer** How are topographic maps useful? When might you use such a map?

STEP 4

Guided Inquiry

Experiment Use clay to model a real landform. Choose a scale for your clay model. Cut and trace its layers to make a topographic map. **Compare** the map you made to the real landform.

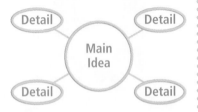

Mapping Earth

MAIN IDEA Earth's surface includes water and solid landforms. You can identify surface features by their location, shape, and elevation.

A Watery Planet

Most of Earth's surface is covered by oceans, which are vast bodies of salt water. All of Earth's oceans are connected, forming one great world ocean.

The world ocean surrounds the continents, which are huge landmasses that rise above the ocean surface. Most of the water on the continents, called inland water, is fresh water. Lakes and rivers are the major surface features that hold or carry fresh water. Rivers, streams, ponds, and other smaller features also hold fresh water.

Plants, humans, and other animals all need fresh water. Yet very little of Earth's water is fresh water. Most is found underground or locked in glaciers or ice sheets near Earth's poles. For these reasons, fresh water is a very precious resource.

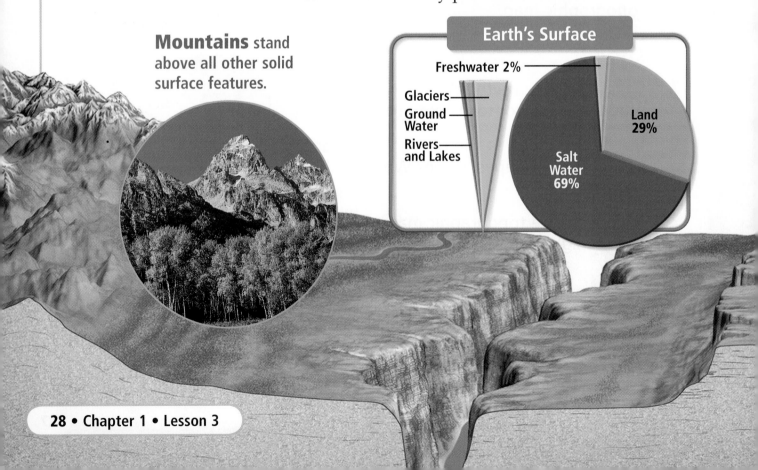

Mountains stand above all other solid surface features.

Earth's Surface

Freshwater 2%
Glaciers
Ground Water
Rivers and Lakes
Salt Water 69%
Land 29%

Land Features

Mountains are the tallest of Earth's landforms. Their steep slopes rise to tall peaks. Mountains can be found as single peaks or in chains, ranges, and mountain systems. Six major mountain ranges form the Rocky Mountain system.

Hills are smaller than mountains. Although hills do not rise as high as mountains, their rounded crests still stand above the land around them.

Mountain valleys are long, narrow regions of low land between ranges of mountains or hills. Canyons are deep valleys with steep sides that are carved out by rivers or streams. In fact, running water is responsible for shaping much of the landscape.

Plateaus (plah TOES) are high landforms with fairly flat surfaces. Plateaus are often found along the tops of canyons and can extend for many miles on either side of a canyon.

Like plateaus, plains are broad and flat. However, plains are lower than their surroundings. Plains make up most of the Midwest region of the United States.

A flood plain is the floor of a river valley on either side of the river. Water covers a flood plain when a river overflows its banks. The flood plains of some river valleys are hundreds of kilometers wide.

In North America, the Atlantic Coastal Plain extends from Canada all the way to Florida. This coastal plain slopes gently from the Appalachian Mountains to the shores of the Atlantic Ocean.

There is no coastal plain along the shores of the Pacific Ocean. In many places, the coastline is rocky. Steep cliffs and mountains extend to the water's edge.

Beaches are flat landforms along an ocean or a large lake. You will learn more about beaches in the next chapter.

MAIN IDEA AND DETAILS What are the tallest landforms? What are the flattest?

River Valleys occur between mountains and hills and on plains.

Coastal Plains are low-lying areas that slope gently from the mainland toward the shore.

Mapping Surface Features

When did you last use a map? Maybe you used a road map for a city or state, or maybe you studied a trail map for a nature hike. There are many kinds of maps. A map is a representation of Earth or a region of Earth.

One special type of map is a topographic map. A **topographic map** is a map that shows the shape of surface features and their **elevations,** or heights above sea level. **Contour lines** connect points on the map that have the same elevation. The distance between neighboring contour lines represents the same change in elevation.

By studying contour lines, you can learn about the shape and steepness of the land. Contour lines make it possible to measure the height of a mountain, the depths of the ocean floor, or the steepness of a slope.

Notice that contour lines never cross. When contour lines are very close together, the slope of the land is steep. If contour lines are farther apart, the ground is more gently sloped or even relatively level.

Topographic maps usually also show rivers, lakes, and different types of vegetation. They also show features of a coastline in great detail. For example, special symbols may show whether a beach is sandy or rocky. Symbols might also show a coral reef off the coast, or even a sunken ship!

MAIN IDEA AND DETAILS Name some features a topographic map may show.

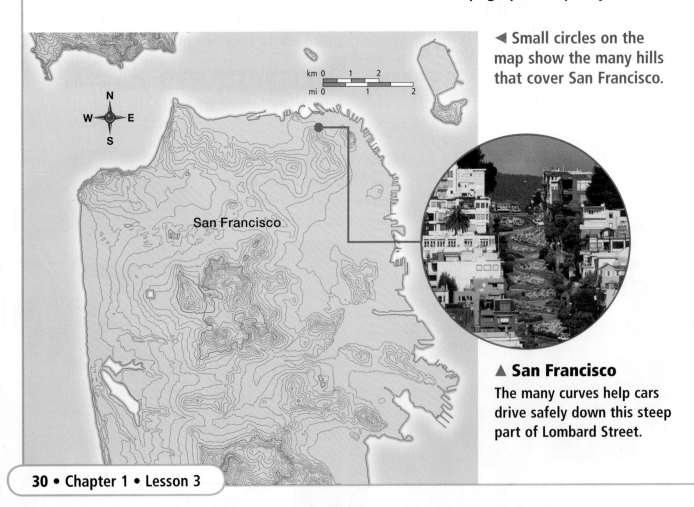

◄ Small circles on the map show the many hills that cover San Francisco.

▲ **San Francisco**
The many curves help cars drive safely down this steep part of Lombard Street.

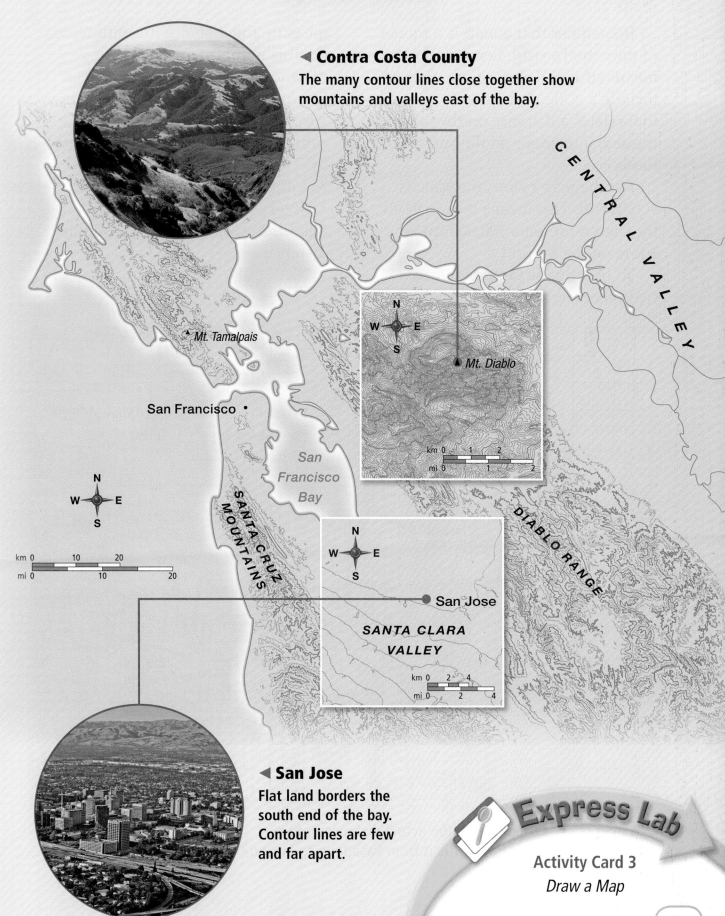

Topographic Map

◀ Contra Costa County
The many contour lines close together show mountains and valleys east of the bay.

CENTRAL VALLEY

Mt. Diablo

N
W E
S

km 0   1   2
mi 0   1   2

Mt. Tamalpais

San Francisco •

San Francisco Bay

SANTA CRUZ MOUNTAINS

DIABLO RANGE

N
W E
S

km 0   10   20
mi 0   10   20

N
W E
S

San Jose

SANTA CLARA VALLEY

km 0   2   4
mi 0   2   4

◀ San Jose
Flat land borders the south end of the bay. Contour lines are few and far apart.

Express Lab

Activity Card 3
Draw a Map

Map Scale

Remember that a map is a model of the actual world. For a map to be meaningful and easy to use, it must include a scale. A map scale is a ratio that relates a distance on the map to the actual distance on the surface of Earth.

For the map below, the scale is 1 : 300,000. This means that 1 cm on the map represents 300,000 cm, or 3 km, on the ground.

To find the distance between two places on a map, use a ruler to measure the distance in centimeters. On this map, for example, the distance between the Los Angeles International Airport and Van Nuys Airport is about 12 cm. To find the actual distance, multiply this value by 3 km. So the actual distance is 36 km (22 mi).

Every map has a unique scale. Read the scale carefully to estimate distance.

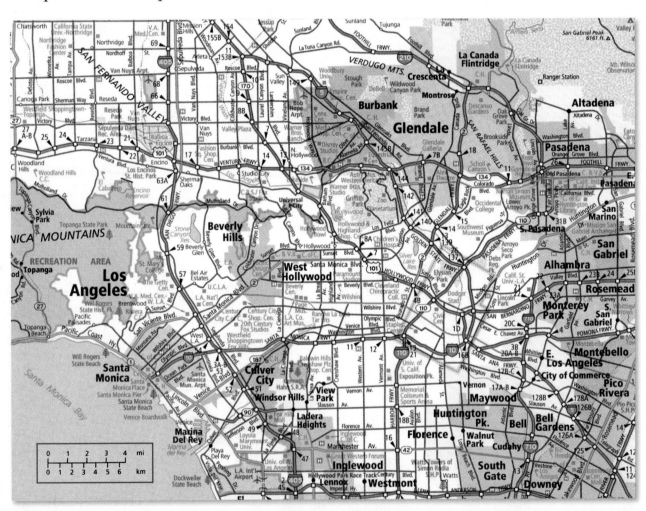

▲ A map scale is used to find the actual distance between places. Approximately how far is it from Pasadena to Encino?

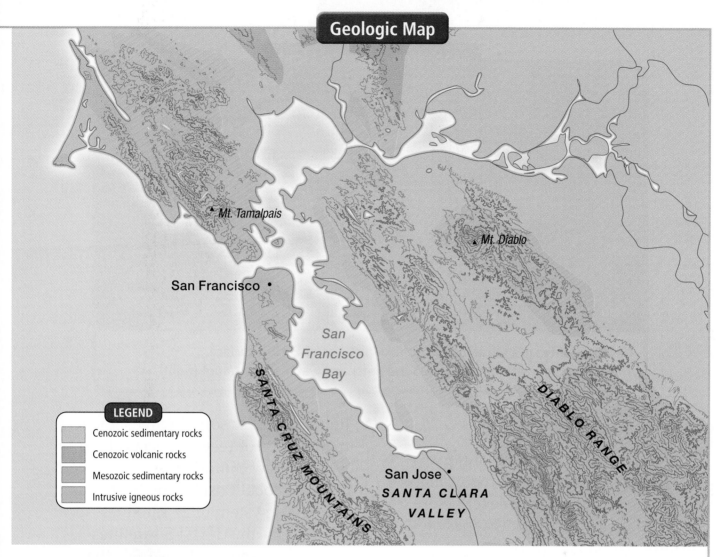

LEGEND
- Cenozoic sedimentary rocks
- Cenozoic volcanic rocks
- Mesozoic sedimentary rocks
- Intrusive igneous rocks

▲ On this geologic map of the San Francisco Bay area, colors show the different types of surface rocks. Notice that contour lines are included to show the topography.

Geologic Maps

Some maps show very specific kinds of information. One such map is a geologic map. A geologic map usually shows types and distributions of surface rocks. It may also show other surface features, such as rivers and lakes.

Scientists often study geologic maps to learn about the different types of rock in an area. This can help them find resources such as minerals, ores, groundwater, coal, or petroleum. They also use geologic maps to identify areas where dangerous events such as landslides, sinkholes, earthquakes, or volcanic eruptions may happen.

Engineers and builders also use geologic maps. By studying the composition of the ground, they can design and safely construct buildings, roads, and bridges.

 **MAIN IDEA AND DETAILS** Why is a map's scale important?

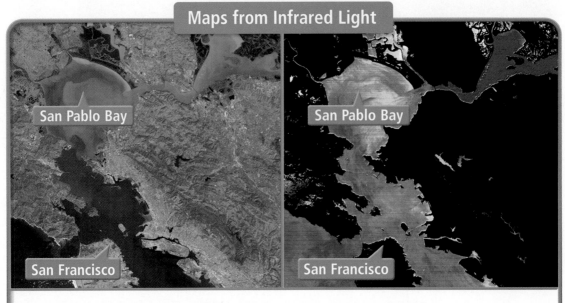

Maps from Infrared Light

San Pablo Bay

San Francisco

San Pablo Bay

San Francisco

NASA satellites use infrared light to take pictures of Earth's surface.
The colors show differences in land use (left) and water temperature (right).

New Types of Maps

People have been making maps for thousands of years. Today, maps are more accurate than ever before, and they also show new types of information.

For example, NASA has developed maps using images from satellites. These images show land and water surfaces all over the world and can be updated as often as needed. Satellites are also used to observe large-scale weather systems, helping meteorologists make weather maps and forecasts.

Scientists have been able to map the ocean floor by using sonar. In this technology, sound waves are sent down from a ship, then "bounce up" from the ocean floor below. A similar technique called lidar is used to map coral reefs. Lidar stands for "light detection and ranging." It uses laser light instead of sound waves. Lidar-made maps of reefs are accurate to within a few centimeters!

The Global Positioning System (GPS) is a system of 27 satellites orbiting Earth. The GPS satellites continually send radio signals that can be picked up by anyone with the proper receiver. Airplanes are equipped with GPS receivers, as are many cars. By measuring the distance to at least four of the satellites, the receiver pinpoints location very accurately.

As technology continues to change and improve, so will the maps that people use to understand Earth. Maybe people will still get lost, but that shouldn't happen because of their maps.

MAIN IDEA Identify some types of maps made possible using modern technology.

Visual Summary

Water covers most of Earth's surface. Less than 30% of the surface is solid land. Features on land include mountains, hills, valleys, and bodies of water.

Topographic maps picture Earth's features. Contour lines show elevation. Contour lines bunched together show a steep landform.

Mt. Tamalpais

San Francisco •

Geologic maps show surface rocks and other features. Scientists use these maps to find resources. New technology has provided other kinds of maps.

Mt. Tamalpais

San Francisco •

 STANDARD

7.f.

 Technology
Visit **www.eduplace.com/cascp** to find out more about mapping.

Reading Review

1 **MAIN IDEA** Why are maps useful tools for studying Earth?

2 **VOCABULARY** What do *contour lines* show on a topographic map?

3 **READING SKILL** Describe three different kinds of maps. Explain how people might use each kind.

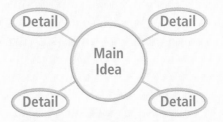

4 **CRITICAL THINKING: Predict**
Today, most people use paper road maps to navigate a long car trip. Often these maps are bound together in an atlas. Do you think GPS technology will replace paper maps? Explain why or why not.

5 **INQUIRY SKILL: Use Models**
Draw a simple scale map of your classroom, school, or neighborhood. Include symbols to represent important features.

 TEST PRACTICE
Which part of a map helps you find the distance between places?

A. borders

B. scale

C. symbols

D. rivers

 STANDARDS

1–5: 7.f., **Test Practice:** 7.f.

EXTREME Science

STANDARDS 7.f. Read a topographic map and a geologic map for evidence provided on the maps and construct and interpret a simple scale map.

Down in Death Valley

Pop Quiz: Which state holds the lowest spot in the continental U.S.? How about the highest? Hint: same answer!

California has them both. In fact, Death Valley contains the lowest spot in the entire Western Hemisphere—a salt flat called Badwater, which is 86 meters, or 282 feet below sea level.

Less than 160 km away towers Mt. Whitney, the highest mountain peak in the adjacent United States. Rising from the western rim of the Great Basin Desert, Mt. Whitney stands tall at an impressive 4,418 meters, or 14,495 feet. When it comes to topography, California is a land of extremes.

Mount Whitney Peak

California's Highs and Lows

Sea Level
0 m

Mount Whitney
4,418 m

Death Valley
−86 m

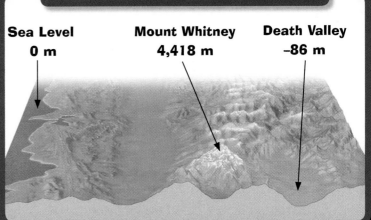

Death Valley is also one of the hottest, driest places on the entire planet. The temperature there once reached 56° C, or 134° F!

Writing Journal

The mean, or average, elevation of the state of California is 884 meters. How much higher is Mt. Whitney than the mean elevation?

Math in Science

Study the circle graph. It shows how land and water cover Earth's surface.

1. Write each percent as a ratio in decimal form.

2. Order the decimals from least to greatest. How does the order of the decimals compare to the sections of the circle graph?

3. Plot the decimals along a number line.

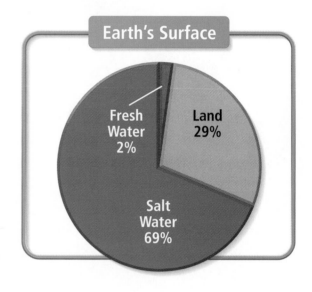

Earth's Surface

Fresh Water 2%

Land 29%

Salt Water 69%

Writing in Science
Narrative

Choose one of the landforms presented in this chapter. What if a group of people were exploring the countryside and encountered this landform? What would they do there? What challenges would they face?

Write a short story about the people and the landform they meet. Include a map as part of the story. The characters could either bring a map or make one for themselves.

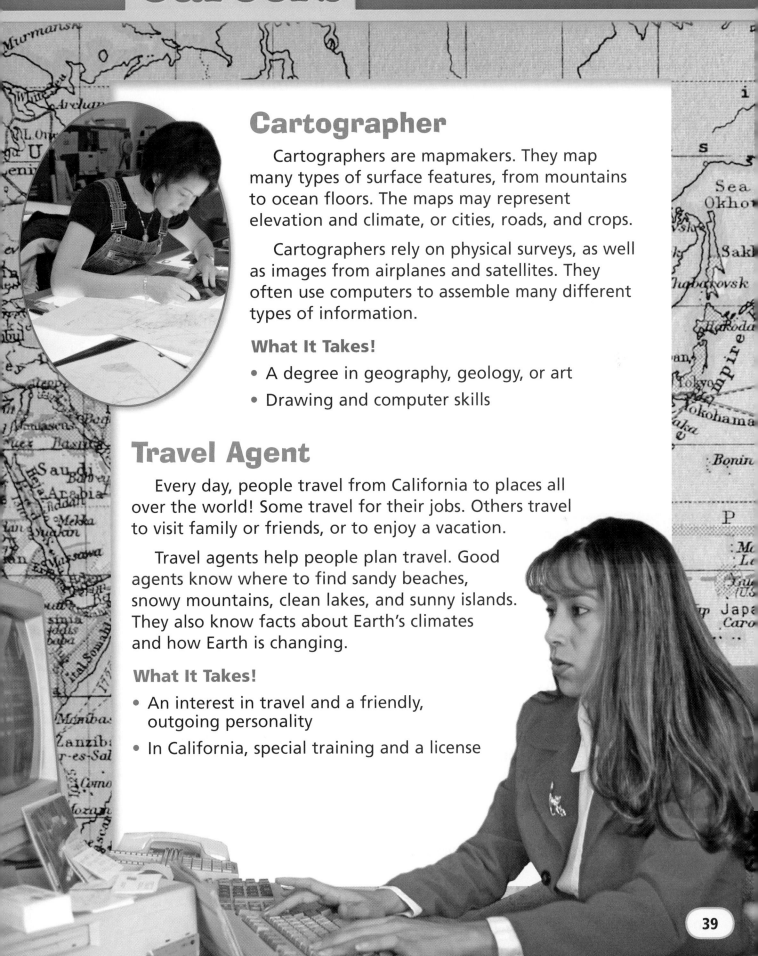

Cartographer

Cartographers are mapmakers. They map many types of surface features, from mountains to ocean floors. The maps may represent elevation and climate, or cities, roads, and crops.

Cartographers rely on physical surveys, as well as images from airplanes and satellites. They often use computers to assemble many different types of information.

What It Takes!

• A degree in geography, geology, or art

• Drawing and computer skills

Travel Agent

Every day, people travel from California to places all over the world! Some travel for their jobs. Others travel to visit family or friends, or to enjoy a vacation.

Travel agents help people plan travel. Good agents know where to find sandy beaches, snowy mountains, clean lakes, and sunny islands. They also know facts about Earth's climates and how Earth is changing.

What It Takes!

• An interest in travel and a friendly, outgoing personality

• In California, special training and a license

Vocabulary

Complete each sentence with a term from the list.

1. The height above sea level of a landform is known as its ____.

2. The layer of Earth below the crust is the ____.

3. On some maps, ____ can be used to find the elevation of a landform.

4. Earth's ____ includes the outermost layer and upper part of the mantle.

5. Earth completes one ____ around the Sun in a year.

6. A(n) ____ shows shapes and elevations of landforms.

7. The dense innermost layer of Earth is the ____.

8. The cool outermost layer of Earth is the ____.

9. Earth completes one ____ about its axis every day.

10. The plastic, soft layer of the mantle is called the ____.

asthenosphere p. 20
contour lines p. 30
core p. 20
crust p. 9
elevation p. 30
lithosphere p. 20
mantle p. 20
revolution p. 12
rotation p. 11
topographic map p. 30

Test Practice

Write the letter of the best answer choice.

11. What is one part of Earth's relationship with the Sun?

    A. The Sun provides energy to Earth.
    B. Earth provides energy to the Sun.
    C. The Sun revolves around Earth.
    D. The Sun caused Earth's magnetic field to form.

12. What causes the four seasons on Earth?

    A. The Moon revolves around Earth.
    B. Earth's magnetic field
    C. Earth's atmosphere
    D. Earth's tilted axis and orbit around the Sun

13. How does temperature change with depth below Earth's surface?

    A. It decreases.
    B. It increases.
    C. It stays the same.
    D. It changes between very hot and very cold.

14. Earth's magnetic field helps protect living things from ____.

    A. harmful magnets
    B. harmful radiation
    C. auroras
    D. liquid rock

Inquiry Skills

15. Experiment What if you were stranded on an island without a watch? How could you best tell the time of day using only a stick, ruler, pencil, and paper?

16. The scale of a map is 1 cm to 40 kilometers. If the distance between two cities is 320 kilometers, how far apart are they on the map?

Map the Concept

The chart shows three categories of maps. Copy this chart, then fill in the hobbies and careers listed below. Group them to show which map would be most useful. Use a dictionary to research any unfamiliar terms.

Oil geologist   Taxi driver
Truck driver   Airplane pilot
Fossil hunter   Spelunker
Mountaineer   Land surveyor

Road map	Topographic map	Geologic map

Critical Thinking

17. Apply Unlike other planets, why can Earth support living things? Include at least three reasons in your answer.

18. Synthesize How do you think Earth will change in the next 20 years? In the next 100 years? Cite evidence from Earth today to support your answer.

19. Evaluate You are hiking in a canyon and have a topographic map. You have a choice of two places to which you can hike. Both places appear 1 cm away from where you are. How can you tell which destination will actually be closer?

20. Analyze Many ancient peoples thought that Earth lay at the center of the Universe. They observed the sky and concluded that the Moon, the Sun, and the stars all orbited around Earth. Were their observations wrong?

Performance Assessment

Use a Topographic Map

Obtain a topographic map of an area near you. Pick an area that shows a change in elevation. Draw a line from one point to another in that area. Using graph paper, make a drawing of the side view of the area represented by the line. On your drawing, include notes to show the different elevations.

Writing Journal

Review your answers to the questions on page 3 at the beginning of this chapter. Revise your answers as needed.

STANDARDS

1: 7.f., **2:** 1.b., **3:** 7.f., **4:** 1.b., **5:** 4.a., **6:** 7.f., **7–8:** 1.b., **9:** 4.b., **10:** 1.b., **11–12:** 4.a., **13:** 1.b., **14:** 3.d., **15:** 4.b., **16:** 7.f., **17:** 5.e., **18:** 4.a., **19:** 7.f., **20:** 4.a., **Map the Concept:** 7.f., **Performance Assessment:** 7.f.

Shaping Earth's Surface

Big Sur, California

LESSON 1

Weathering and erosion wear down the surface of Earth. How do you think this stone arch was formed?

LESSON 2

A stream can begin as a trickle, then flow into rivers that carry huge amounts of water. How do rivers shape Earth's surface?

LESSON 3

Ocean waves pound coastlines day after day. What kinds of structures form at beaches?

Writing Journal

In your Writing Journal, write or draw answers to each question.

43

Vocabulary Preview

sea stack
an offshore column of rock created by wave erosion

Vocabulary

alluvial fan p. 61

arch p. 68

barrier island p. 69

beach p. 69

cliff p. 68

delta p. 61

deposition p. 60

erosion p. 50

headland p. 68

meander p. 60

sandbar p. 69

sea cave p. 68

sea stack p. 68

sediment p. 48

spit p. 69

tributary p. 58

weathering p. 48

Glossary
English-Spanish, p. H26

Vocabulary Skill
Root Words and Suffixes
deposition

The verb *deposit* means to lay down or leave behind by a natural process. When the suffix *-ion* is added to deposit, the word becomes a noun. It means the act of laying down sediment.

alluvial fan

a fan-shaped deposit of sediment that forms when water flows from a steep slope onto a flat plain

spit

a sandbar that has one end attached to land

tributary

a river or a stream feeding into a major river

Start with Your Standards

Standard Set 2. Shaping Earth's Surface

2.a. *Students know* water running downhill is the dominant process in shaping the landscape, including California's landscape.

2.b. *Students know* rivers and streams are dynamic systems that erode, transport sediment, change course, and flood their banks in natural and recurring patterns.

2.c. *Students know* beaches are dynamic systems in which the sand is supplied by rivers and moved along the coast by the action of waves.

2.d. *Students know* earthquakes, volcanic eruptions, landslides, and floods change human and wildlife habitats.

Standard Set 7: Investigation and Experimentation standards covered in this chapter: 7.a., 7.b., 7.d., 7.h.

How Is Earth's Surface Worn Down?

Building Background

Weathering and erosion are forces that change the surface of Earth. Sometimes these changes happen quickly, but usually they happen very slowly. The rock formation shown here took thousands of years to form. Understanding how and why Earth changes helps scientists predict such changes in the future.

PREPARE TO INVESTIGATE

Inquiry Skill

Predict You can use a hypothesis to make a prediction that you can test with an experiment.

Materials

- nail
- mineral kit
- 2 plastic bowls
- hand lens
- eyedropper
- water
- vinegar
- safety goggles

 STANDARDS

2.a. *Students know* water running downhill is the dominant process in shaping the landscape, including California's landscape.
7.a. Develop a hypothesis.

Rock Weathering

Procedure

Safety: Wear goggles during this activity.

STEP 1

1 **Experiment** Using a nail, scratch the calcite over a plastic bowl to make a small pile of dust. Tilt the bowl to spread the dust as evenly as possible across the bottom and up the sides.

2 **Observe** Use the eyedropper to drip several drops of water along one side of the bowl. Observe what happens to the dust that the water meets. Use a hand lens to observe more closely. Record your observations.

STEP 2

3 **Predict** What do you think will happen to calcite when it comes in contact with vinegar? Write your predictions in your *Science Notebook*.

4 **Observe** Using another bowl, repeat Step 1. Then repeat Step 2, but use vinegar instead of water. Observe and record what happens.

STEP 4

Conclusion

1. **Compare** Describe how the calcite dust changed when it came in contact with water and with vinegar. Compare the two changes.

2. **Hypothesize** In nature, how could pieces of rock change when exposed to rushing water? How could rock change when exposed to acids? Use your results to support your hypothesis.

3. **Infer** Why are most caves and caverns formed in limestone, a kind of rock made from calcite?

Guided Inquiry

Experiment Can water break apart rocks when it freezes into ice? Design an experiment using chalk, water, a plastic bag, and a freezer. Write a report to **communicate** the steps you followed, your results, and your conclusion.

VOCABULARY

erosion	p. 50
sediment	p. 48
weathering	p. 48

READING SKILL

Sequence Use a diagram to record the sequence of steps in weathering and erosion.

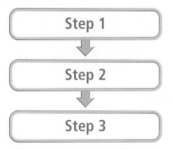

Step 1

↓

Step 2

↓

Step 3

STANDARDS

2.a. *Students know* water running downhill is the dominant process in shaping the landscape, including California's landscape.
2.d. *Students know* earthquakes, volcanic eruptions, landslides, and floods change human and wildlife habitats.

Wearing Down Earth's Surface

MAIN IDEA Destructive forces, such as weathering and erosion, wear down Earth's surface features.

Weathering

Earth's crust is mostly solid rock. The rocks are broken into pieces by processes of **weathering.** Weathering is a destructive force, meaning a force that breaks down something. There are two types of weathering: mechanical and chemical.

Mechanical weathering is the breaking of larger rocks into smaller pieces. Small rock pieces are called **sediment.** In cold climates, ice plays a major role in this process. As water freezes, it expands. When water trickles into the cracks of rocks, it can break the rocks apart when it freezes.

Moving air and water also cause mechanical weathering. As blown sand or rushing water hits rocks, the rocks weaken. Over time, they crack or crumble. Even living things can cause mechanical weathering. Plant roots can grow through cracks and break apart rocks. Burrowing animals push against rocks and allow water to move deeper into rocks and soil, where freezing and thawing can weather them.

Sometimes, rocks will peel into sheets. As soil and rocks are removed from the surface, pressure on the rock below is reduced. This may allow minerals in the rock to expand. An outer layer of the rock will peel away. Eventually, other layers may also crack.

◄ Trees have the power to move or split rocks as they grow.

Cave Formation

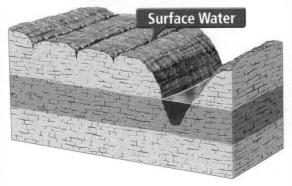

Surface Water

Weak acids formed in rainwater seep into the ground, where they weather rock.

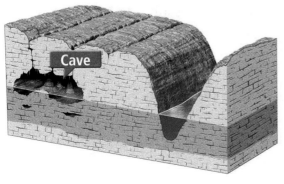

Cave

Over time, holes are produced. Eventually, the holes grow into caves.

▲ Caves are a result of weathering.

Although mechanical weathering breaks rocks, it does not change the type of rock. In chemical weathering, the compositions of rocks change.

Water is the main factor that causes chemical weathering. Water can dissolve some minerals that make up rocks. Water can also dissolve compounds in the air and soil to form weak acids. This acidic water can dissolve certain minerals. For example, weak acids dissolve minerals in limestone and marble easily.

Generally, a combination of different types of weathering is at work in a region. Most weathering takes place at or near Earth's surface. However, water trickling through the ground can affect rocks far beneath the surface. Caves are underground hollow areas created by weathering. Large caves are often called caverns.

Most caverns are made from limestone. Weak acids seep into the ground until they reach a zone soaked with water. As the ground water becomes more acidic, it dissolves calcite and other minerals in the rock.

Over time, the action of the acidic water produces holes in the rock. The holes grow, creating passages, chambers, and pits, and eventually become caves. At first, the caves are full of water. Later, the water drains away.

SEQUENCE How can water from Earth's surface create a cave?

49

Erosion

Weathering is the process that breaks down rock into smaller pieces called sediments. The carrying away of sediments is called **erosion** (e ROH zhuhn). Agents of erosion include moving water, such as streams and rivers, which you will learn more about in the next lesson. Wind, ice, and gravity are also erosion agents.

Wind erosion is especially powerful in deserts and other dry areas. Strong winds readily pick up and carry small grains of sediment. They may blow the loose sediment onto larger rocks, which in turn weathers them. Exposed rock is open to even further weathering.

Have you ever seen sand dunes on a beach or in a desert? Dunes are also caused by wind erosion. When the wind picks up large pieces of sediment, it usually drops them less than a meter away. The falling

▲ Wind sweeps sand into sand dunes. Sand dunes—like the ones shown above—form on the inland part of beaches.

sediment hits other pieces, moving them along in a creeping motion. This bunches the sediment into dunes.

Frozen water also wears down and shapes Earth's surface features. Thousands of years ago, glaciers covered large areas of Asia, Europe,

In Bryce Canyon, Utah, water and wind erosion helped create a spectacular landscape.

▲ In high mountains, glaciers can carve out bowl-shaped hollows called cirques.

▲ Melting glaciers left many lakes behind.

and North America. The ice in some of these glaciers was a kilometer thick. The weight of the ice was so great that it pushed and dented the ground beneath it. Glaciers helped shape the rolling plains in the northern United States. They also carved out the Great Lakes.

In arctic regions and in high mountains, glaciers continue to shape Earth today. Gravity moves rivers of ice downhill toward the sea. Although glaciers move very slowly, their weight and size make them very powerful. Mountain glaciers can transform V-shaped river valleys into U-shaped valleys.

Glaciers can also move huge amounts of soil and rock. These sediments are carried along the bottoms and sides of the ice. As the ice inches forward, sediments in

the ice grind against the surface below.

Glaciers often carve out hollows in the land they erode. When the glaciers melt, these hollows fill with water to form lakes. Glaciers created more than 10,000 such lakes in Minnesota.

Ocean waves and currents also erode Earth's surface. In another lesson, you will learn how ocean water shapes coastlines.

SEQUENCE Describe how erosion wears down Earth's surface.

Activity Card 4
Model Chemical Weathering

Landslides and Sinkholes

The ongoing process of erosion keeps the landscape changing. In general, such destructive forces act very slowly. However, sometimes changes happen much faster.

Landslides are one example. Landslides are large masses of rocks and sediments that tumble down a steep slope. Mudflows, rock falls, and avalanches are examples of landslides. Landslides happen suddenly, sometimes in minutes.

Although gravity is the main cause of a landslide, other destructive forces are involved. Erosion from rivers, rain, glaciers, or ocean water may steepen a slope and loosen sediments. If the sediments become soaked with water, they may slide

When sediments slide down a steep slope, buildings on them slide, too. This landslide took place in southern California. ▼

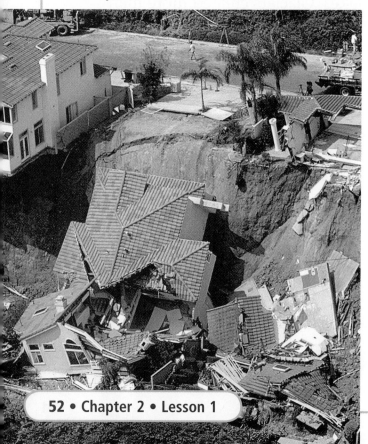

▲ *Sinkhole* is a very descriptive term: Land above weathered rock sinks into a hole. This sinkhole occurred in Florida.

more easily. Any disturbance, such as a minor earthquake, can create cracks or shake rocks loose. This action can start landslides.

Volcanoes can also cause landslides. Volcanic eruptions can deposit ash and other materials on steep slopes. Heavy rains added to this material can cause a landslide.

The tremendous force of tons of falling matter in a landslide can quickly destroy homes and businesses, and bury highways. Landslides can also destroy vegetation and habitats, harming ecosystems.

You have read that chemical weathering creates caves in certain types of rock. This process can take thousands of years. However, after a cave has formed, the rock above the cave often has little support. At some point, this rock may collapse, forming a sinkhole.

 **SEQUENCE** How does a landslide occur?

Visual Summary

Earth's surface features are worn down by destructive forces, such as weathering and erosion. Weathering can be mechanical or chemical.

Erosion can be caused by wind, water, waves, and ice. Sometimes, erosion is caused by two or more of these agents working together.

Gravity, along with other erosion agents, can cause landslides. Because of their tremendous force, landslides are destructive to both human and wildlife habitats.

STANDARDS

2.a., 2.d.

 Technology
Visit **www.eduplace.com/cascp** to find out more about weathering and erosion.

Reading Review

1 MAIN IDEA What two forces continually change Earth's surface?

2 VOCABULARY Compare *weathering* and *erosion*.

3 READING SKILL How does chemical weathering form a cave?

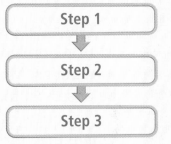

| Step 1 |
| Step 2 |
| Step 3 |

4 CRITICAL THINKING:
Evaluate Why is wind a greater force of erosion in deserts than in forests and farmland? HINT: Consider how the ground is covered in both places.

5 INQUIRY SKILL: Predict
Suppose you placed a bar of soap in a stream of running water for a day. Predict how the running water would change the soap.

 TEST PRACTICE
Which is an example of erosion?

A. roots growing into a rock

B. wind blowing a windmill

C. acids dissolving a rock

D. a river washing away soil

 STANDARDS

1: 1.a., **2:** 1.a., **3:** 2.a., **4:** 2.a., **5:** 1.a., **Test Practice:** 1.a.

53

Caves of the West

Over 100 years ago, American naturalist John Muir marveled at the beauty of caves in the Sierra mountains. Most of the sights he described can still be observed today.

Scientists classify caves according to how and where they form. A cave may form in many ways depending on rock type, climate, landscape, and the effects of wind or water.

If you like caves, you are lucky to live in California. The west coast is home to a wide variety of caves, including the three types shown here.

> **66** … so much splendor in darkness, so many mansions in the depths of the mountains, buildings ever in process of construction, yet ever finished, developing from perfection to perfection. **99**
>
> John Muir, from
> *The Mountains of California*,
> published in 1894

Limestone Cave, Mitchell Caverns, California
This cave formed when groundwater dissolved and washed away limestone. Columns form from seeping water that leaves minerals behind.

STANDARDS
2.a. *Students know* water running downhill is the dominant process in shaping the landscape, including California's landscape.

SOCIAL STUDIES **LINK**

Lava Tube,
Mt. Saint Helens, Washington

After a volcano erupts, some lava may flow away while the lava around it hardens. The result is a cave called a lava tube.

Sea Cave,
Santa Cruz Islands

Pounding wind and ocean waves shape caves along the coast. In California, sea caves provide shelter for seals and sea lions.

Sharing Ideas

1. **READING CHECK** What factors affect how and where caves form?

2. **WRITE ABOUT IT** Describe three different kinds of caves and the way they formed.

3. **TALK ABOUT IT** Read the quote from John Muir. Do you agree with his opinions of caves?

How Do Rivers Shape the Landscape?

Building Background

High up in the mountains, water collects in small brooks and streams. The streams combine and gather more water as they travel downhill, eventually becoming a river that flows to the ocean.

As rivers flow across the landscape, they shape and change it. Over the course of hundreds, even thousands of years, rivers have shaped some of Earth's most interesting landforms.

STANDARDS

2.a. *Students know* water running downhill is the dominant process in shaping the landscape, including California's landscape.
7.h. Identify changes in natural phenomena over time without manipulating the phenomena (e.g., a tree limb, a grove of trees, a stream, a hillslope).

PREPARE TO INVESTIGATE

Inquiry Skill

Infer When you infer, you use known facts and logical reasoning to make interpretations.

Materials

- soil
- aluminum pan
- metric ruler
- pencil
- paper cup
- bottle of water

Science and Math Toolbox

For step 2, review **Using a Tape Measure or Ruler** on page H6.

Set Up a Stream Slope

Procedure

STEP 1

1. **Use Models** With a partner, build a soil slope on one end of an aluminum pan. The slope can be steep or gentle. Draw and label a picture of the soil slope in your *Science Notebook.* Use a metric ruler to measure the height and length of the slope.

2. **Predict** You will drip water from a paper cup onto the soil at the top of the slope. Predict what you think will happen. Record your prediction.

STEP 3

3. **Experiment** Use a pencil to poke a small hole in the bottom of a paper cup. Cover the hole with your finger. Have your partner fill the cup with water. Hold the cup above the soil at the top of the slope. Remove your finger and let the water flow over the soil slope.

4. **Observe** What happened to the soil? Measure the height and length of the slope now. Draw a picture and describe the changes in your *Science Notebook.*

5. **Hypothesize** How do you think your results would change if you vary the steepness of the slope, or the speed or amount of water? Develop a hypothesis. Then experiment to test your hypothesis.

Conclusion

1. **Compare** Look at the pictures you drew of your soil slopes. Do the pictures support your prediction?

2. **Infer** What can you infer about the way water and gravity shape Earth's surface?

Guided Inquiry

Ask Questions Observe a nearby creek or stream. What questions do you have about how it changes? Plan an investigation to answer your questions. Select the tools you will need to **record data**.

Rivers

MAIN IDEA Water running downhill is a powerful force in changing Earth's landscape. Rivers erode, move sediment, change course, and flood their banks in a continuous pattern.

VOCABULARY

alluvial fan	p. 61
delta	p. 61
deposition	p. 60
meander	p. 60
tributary	p. 58

 READING SKILL

Main Idea and Details As you read, think about the most important facts and the details that support those facts.

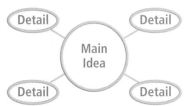

STANDARDS

2.a. *Students know* water running downhill is the dominant process in shaping the landscape, including California's landscape.
2.b. *Students know* rivers and streams are dynamic systems that erode, transport sediment, change course, and flood their banks in natural and recurring patterns.

How Rivers Form

Rivers typically begin high in the mountains. Water collects as runoff, which is rain water or melting snow that flows over the ground. Because of gravity, the runoff flows downhill, gathering first into tiny trickles, then into brooks and streams.

Further downhill, streams join other streams, eventually forming a large body of flowing fresh water—a river. Most large rivers are joined by many **tributaries,** which are streams and small rivers.

Rivers will take the shortest and steepest path downhill. Sometimes, stretches of white water or waterfalls form part of a river's course. Sometimes, its course changes direction because huge boulders or other obstacles block the most direct path. All rivers ultimately empty into large bodies of water, such as lakes or the ocean.

Tributaries

Flood plain

With a length of 615 km (382 mi), the Sacramento River is the longest in California. From its source near Mount Shasta, it flows through the northern part of the Central Valley before it empties into San Francisco Bay.

As a stream or river moves downhill, its rushing water weathers and erodes the ground over which it flows. Bedrock is broken down and minerals dissolved. Soil, pebbles, and other sediment are picked up and transported by the river. Over time, the river carves out a wider and deeper channel.

As the flow of water increases, the moving water and rocks carried by it further erode the riverbed. Sediment is carried away from the riverbank. A river valley forms. Sometimes, rapid cutting of the valley floor in the upper part of a river creates a canyon.

The amount of sediment carried by a river is called the sediment load. The larger and faster a river, the greater its sediment load. A faster river has more energy than a slow river, so it can carry more sediment and bigger pieces of sediment.

 **MAIN IDEA** What path does a river usually follow?

▲ A mountain stream in California weathers rocks as it rushes over them. It carries sediment downstream.

▲ Over time, some rivers create the deep V-shaped valleys known as canyons.

Ocean

Mouth

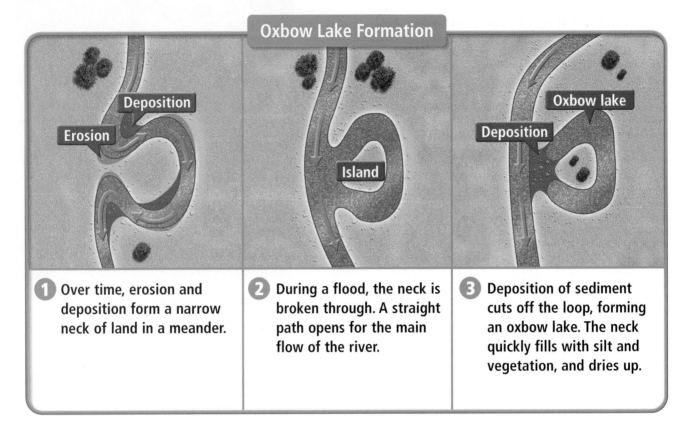

Oxbow Lake Formation

1. Over time, erosion and deposition form a narrow neck of land in a meander.

2. During a flood, the neck is broken through. A straight path opens for the main flow of the river.

3. Deposition of sediment cuts off the loop, forming an oxbow lake. The neck quickly fills with silt and vegetation, and dries up.

Deposition

Rivers usually drop sediment they carry somewhere along their course to the ocean. The process of dropping sediments is called **deposition** (dep uh ZISH uhn). While erosion is a destructive force, deposition is a constructive force. It builds up the land.

Deposition helps create a variety of surface features. Several of these features occur as part of river systems.

Recall that rivers usually begin at high elevations. The water flows swiftly downhill, picking up sediment. When the river gets closer to the ocean, the land gradually levels out. This leveling causes the water to lose energy and slow down. Sediment drops out of the slower water and is deposited.

Meanders and Oxbow Lakes When a river moves across wide, flat regions, it begins to wind in curves called **meanders** (me AN duhrs). Meanders increase in size as water erodes the outside of each curve and deposits

◄ As a river flows across a flat plain, its course begins to wind in curves called meanders.

sediment on the inside. Meanders occur because the flow of the river slows down on the inside and speeds up on the outside of each curve. Sediment is deposited by the slowing water and eroded by the fast current.

Sometimes, one curve in a meander will catch up with another curve that is farther downstream. A loop forms in the river. The loop is eventually cut off by the deposition of silt and clay, creating an oxbow lake.

Alluvial Fans and Deltas When the flow of water in a river decreases quickly, special kinds of deposits are formed. An **alluvial fan** is a fan-shaped landmass that forms after water rushes down a steep slope, then slows over a flat plain.

The heaviest, coarsest material is dropped first, so the head of the fan is its steepest part. The size of the sediment gets smaller and the steepness of the slope decreases as you move farther down the fan.

Alluvial fans are common in Death Valley, California. Mountain waters suddenly slow down as they drop from steep canyons onto the flat valley floor.

A **delta** is a low plain that forms where a river enters the ocean. Sediment that is still being carried by the river is dropped here. Deltas often take the shape of a triangle. If the river is large, the delta it creates will be large, too. The Mississippi River has a vast delta that extends into the Gulf of Mexico.

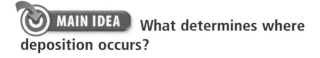 **MAIN IDEA** What determines where deposition occurs?

▲ Alluvial fans and deltas are formed when rushing waters slow suddenly and their sediments are deposited.

▲ The Mississippi River delta is called a "bird's foot" delta. Why do you think it got this name?

Floods

Flooding is a natural agent of change to Earth's surface. Most flooding occurs because of seasonal changes in rainfall or snowfall. In the United States, seasonal flooding usually occurs in spring.

After a very snowy winter or a sudden warm spell, a large amount of melt water may enter a river in a short period of time. When the water reaches flat lowlands, it spills over the riverbanks.

▲ The Mississippi flood of 1993 affected communities along the river, destroying homes and businesses.

During the winter of 1996 and 1997, parts of northern Minnesota and North Dakota received 250 cm (98 in.) of snow from eight blizzards, a much greater snowfall than normal. When the snow melted, the Red River reached 8 m (26 ft) above its banks. Water covered most of the towns of Grand Forks and East Grand Forks.

In 1993, heavy rains fell over much of the Midwest. The Mississippi River flooded. Near St. Louis, the river was above flood stage for 144 days.

Severe storms can also cause floods. When the soaked ground can hold no more water, all rain water becomes runoff. A sudden flood after a storm is called a flash flood.

Broken dams or levees also can cause floods or make flooding worse. Levees are mounds built to hold back reservoirs, rivers, or other bodies of water. When Hurricane Katrina struck in 2005, Lake Pontchartrain burst through part of its levee, sending floodwaters into New Orleans.

Receding floodwaters leave behind ruined homes, businesses, and crops. Flooding can be especially dangerous in cities, where overflowing sewers create health hazards.

MAIN IDEA What causes seasonal flooding?

Express Lab

Activity Card 5
Show How Sediments Build Up

Visual Summary

Rivers form from natural streams of fresh water. Rivers shape the landscape by weathering and erosion.

Flowing waters also shape the landscape by deposition. Water picks up and carries sediment from one place and deposit it in another.

Flooding affects people, animals, and plants by destroying habitats and altering the landscape.

STANDARDS

2.a., 2.b.

Technology
Visit **www.eduplace.com/cascp** to find out more about rivers.

Reading Review

1 **MAIN IDEA** Describe how rivers form.

2 **VOCABULARY** What factors affect the rate of *deposition*?

3 **READING SKILL** Describe ways that rivers change the landscape. Use specific examples to illustrate your answer.

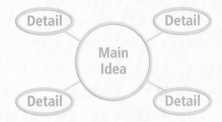

4 **CRITICAL THINKING:**
Synthesize Flooding is a natural process. Do you think engineers and scientists should do more to prevent flooding? If so, what should they do?

5 **INQUIRY SKILL: Infer** Study a map that shows the Mississippi River. Where does it have more meanders—in its northern half or southern half? Why do you think it has so many meanders?

TEST PRACTICE
The dropping of sediment by a river is called _____.

A. deposition

B. erosion

C. melting

D. flowing

STANDARDS

1: 2.a., 2.b., **2–5:** 2.b., **Test Practice:** 2.b.

Masterpiece of Erosion

What a drop! You're looking down into one of the biggest, deepest canyons in the world. In fact, this canyon system is so deep and vast it was named the Grand Canyon.

How did the Grand Canyon form? Erosion—mostly in the form of water running downhill. The Colorado River has been steadily wearing its way into the plateau underneath it for millions of years. Wind, rain, gravity, and other forces have helped shape the canyon walls. The result is a natural wonder. The Grand Canyon winds more than 434 km at an average depth of 1,219 m. In some places, if you could throw a rock far enough out, it would fall more than a mile before hitting bottom.

At the Grand Canyon's deepest point, it would take over four and a half stacked Empire State Buildings to reach the rim!

Writing Journal

The Empire State Building is 381 m tall. Calculate how many, end to end, it would take to equal the Grand Canyon's length of 434 km.

How Do Beaches Change?

Building Background

Have you ever picked up grains of sand at the beach? Those grains may come from many different sources. Some sand comes from rock. Other sand comes from the remains of sea creatures.

Waves can carry sand and deposit it on the shore. Rivers can deposit sand on their way to the sea. Beaches are always changing due to the action of wind and water.

STANDARDS

2.c. *Students know* beaches are dynamic systems in which the sand is supplied by rivers and moved along the coast by the action of waves.
7.g. Interpret events by sequence and time from natural phenomena (e.g. the relative ages of rocks and intrusions).

PREPARE TO INVESTIGATE

Inquiry Skill

Analyze Data When you analyze data, you look for patterns or other evidence in order to make an inference, a prediction, a hypothesis, or draw a conclusion.

Materials

- sand samples
- black paper
- white paper
- hand lens
- microscope
- magnet
- plastic bags

Science and Math Toolbox

For step 2, review **Using a Microscope** on page H2.

A World in a Grain of Sand

Procedure

STEP 1

1. **Observe** Use a hand lens to examine each sand sample. To make viewing easier, place light-colored sand on dark paper, and place dark-colored sand on white paper. Record your observations in your *Science Notebook.*

2. **Compare** Feel the sand samples with your fingertips. Note how the samples are alike and different. Record your observations.

STEP 3

3. **Observe** Place a few grains of one sand sample on a slide. Look at the grains through the microscope. Repeat this process with the other sand samples. Record your observations in your *Science Notebook.*

4. **Experiment** Put each sand sample in a plastic bag and pass a magnet over it. Are any of the grains of sand attracted to the magnet? Record what you observe.

Conclusion

1. **Compare** How were the sand samples similar to one another? How were they different?

2. **Analyze Data** Where might the materials making up the sand in your samples have come from? Give reasons for your answers.

3. **Hypothesize** Form a hypothesis to explain how sand forms. How could you test this hypothesis?

Guided Inquiry

Experiment How does sand on a beach change from day to day, or month to month? Assume you can visit a beach every day. List the steps you would take to **observe** changes on the beach.

Beaches

VOCABULARY

arch	p. 68
barrier island	p. 69
beach	p. 69
cliff	p. 68
headland	p. 68
sandbar	p. 69
sea cave	p. 68
sea stack	p. 68
spit	p. 69

READING SKILL

Compare and Contrast As you read, note how different types of coast features are alike and different.

Group	Group

STANDARDS

2.c. *Students know* beaches are dynamic systems in which the sand is supplied by rivers and moved along the coast by the action of waves.

MAIN IDEA Beaches are formed through erosion and deposition. Sand is supplied by rivers and moved along the coast by waves.

Shaping Shorelines

Moving ocean water continually changes the shape of a shoreline, as do winds. Waves gradually wear down the rock. Water is forced into cracks in the rocks, wedging them apart over time. Salt helps dissolve or weaken the rock.

Land that sticks out into the ocean is eroded first. **Headlands** are narrow sections of land that jut out into the ocean. Waves first erode the bases of the headlands. Overhanging rock may collapse, forming steep rock features called **cliffs.**

Weaker rock is worn away more quickly than stronger rock. Holes called **sea caves** are left behind. If the headland is narrow, sea caves on both sides of it may join to form an **arch.**

As erosion continues, the top of the arch may collapse. The ocean side of the arch is left standing alone. This rock column is called a **sea stack.**

Sea Cave

▲ **Sea stacks** are offshore columns of rock created by wave erosion.

Beach

Waves move sand down a beach.

Sandbar

Barrier Island

Recall that rivers deposit sediment as they empty into the ocean. Ocean waves can pick up sediment from one spot and deposit it farther down the shoreline. Sand and larger sediment are deposited, while finer silt is washed out to sea.

When more sediment is deposited than eroded, a beach forms. A **beach** is made up of sand or other loose sediment that has been deposited along a shoreline. Beaches are dynamic systems, meaning they are continually changing.

Like waves, ocean currents also carry sediment. Longshore currents run parallel and very close to the shore. Such currents carry sediment from one place to another along a shoreline. The current may deposit a **sandbar,** a ridge of sand below the water's surface.

A **spit** is a sandbar that rises above the water level and has one end attached to the shore. The end of the spit that is not attached to land is often shaped like a hook.

A **barrier island** is a sandbar that runs parallel to the shore. Some barrier islands start out as spits and become detached from the shore by wave erosion or a rise in sea level. Others form after storm waves pick up sediment from the ocean floor and deposit it in one area. Still others were sand dunes that became flooded when the sea level rose thousands of years ago.

Barrier islands extend along the Atlantic coast of the United States. Some of these islands are 160 km (100 mi) long or more. Barrier islands protect the shoreline from storm damage. They also provide fragile habitats for wildlife and plants.

COMPARE AND CONTRAST How does a sandbar compare to a beach?

Spits are sandbars with one end attached to land. ▶

Cliff

Headland

▲ **Arches** form when erosion cuts a hole through a narrow headland.

Black sand is common on Hawaii and other volcanic islands.

On California beaches, shell fragments are mixed with finely-weathered rocks.

Rivers may deposit silt along their shores to form thin, narrow beaches.

Sand: Up Close

Sand forms from a variety of rocks and minerals. The type of sand found on a beach depends upon the rocks and minerals in that area. Rivers and wind carry sediment from inland areas to the oceans. As sediment pieces continue to rub against water and one another, they eventually form sand. A sand grain may be no bigger than a grain of salt.

Sand on California beaches is typically made from quartz, feldspar, shell fragments, and magnetite. The combination of these minerals and shells makes the sand a light tan color. Magnetite is an iron ore, so it is magnetic. Feldspar is a mineral that can be a number of colors. Quartz is the most common mineral found in deserts and coastal areas.

Not all sand is light tan. Many beaches in Hawaii are made from basalt, which colors them a dark gray. The beaches on the Pacific island of Tahiti are made of black sand. This sand comes from lava and ash from volcanoes. Along the coast of Belize, in Central America, some sand is made mostly from the remains of algae or larger plants. Sand may also contain weathered coral from coral reefs, as found on some Florida beaches.

When you look closely at grains of sand, you will see that they are different sizes, shapes, and colors.

COMPARE AND CONTRAST What are some different types of beach sand?

Low tide

High tide

▲ Because of tides, ocean water covers parts of the shoreline for only a part of each day. In these photos, notice where the trees are growing. Why don't trees grow on the lower ground?

Changes in Sea Level

Changes in sea level also shape shorelines. For example, tides are daily changes in sea level caused primarily by the Moon's gravitational pull on Earth's oceans. Most ocean shorelines experience two high tides and two low tides each day.

Tides create currents that can move sediment from one place to another, especially in bays and inlets. Outgoing tides can pick up sediment from the shore and deposit it farther out in the inlet, forming a tidal delta.

The difference between high tide and low tide varies greatly from place to place. Factors that affect tide height include the shapes of the shoreline and the ocean floor.

The highest tides on Earth are found in the Bay of Fundy, which is along the Atlantic coast of Canada. Here, sea levels can rise and fall as much as 16 meters (52 feet) in a single day!

Other changes in sea level are more dramatic than tides, and they last longer as well. Sea level has risen and fallen many times throughout Earth's history. Scientists have found evidence of such changes by studying old shoreline features and sediment cores. They also have discovered traces of human settlements in places now under the ocean!

What caused these changes? The biggest reason was Earth's changing temperature. When Earth was colder, more water was stored in huge glaciers and ice sheets, and ocean levels dropped. When temperatures rose and the ice sheets melted, ocean levels rose as well.

 **COMPARE AND CONTRAST** How do ocean levels change with Earth's temperature?

Activity Card 6
Make Sand

Beach Issues

Like many other places, beaches face many challenges. Beach pollution is a problem in every coastal state in the United States today.

Polluted water is one of the major causes. Rivers and streams may carry pollutants into the oceans, which in turn wash them onto beaches. After a heavy storm, overflowing sewers may dump untreated wastes into rivers. Runoff picking up pollution from the ground will also make its way to the ocean.

Petroleum can destroy a beach ecosystem quickly. Spills from offshore oil wells or oil tankers do not happen often, but when they do, the effects can be devastating. If the oil reaches the beach, then animals, plants, rocks, and sand all become coated in thick layers of oil that are hard to remove.

Many Californians dream of owning a home right next to the Pacific Ocean. However, construction along beaches can disrupt the natural shaping of that beach by the ocean. Construction can also damage or destroy salt marshes and other sensitive beach ecosystems.

To protect beaches, the state government sponsors the California Coastal Commission. The state has also established several beaches as parks and nature reserves.

Beaches are special places—the meeting of Earth's land, air, and oceans. Keeping beaches clean and healthy is an important goal.

COMPARE AND CONTRAST How does pollution on beaches compare to pollution in other places?

Oil can wash ashore far away from where it is spilled. Cleaning oil spills is a difficult but necessary task. ▼

Visual Summary

Erosion and deposition work together to constantly reshape shorelines. Waves cause both deposition and erosion.

Changes in sea level also shape shorelines. Tides rise and fall every day. Sea levels also change over thousands of years as Earth's climate becomes warmer or cooler.

Beach sand can be made up of different types of minerals, rocks, plant remains, and shells. Different kinds of beach sand are common in different places.

 **STANDARD**

2.c.

 Technology
Visit **www.eduplace.com/cascp** to find out more about beaches.

Reading Review

1 MAIN IDEA What changes the shape of beaches?

2 VOCABULARY What is the difference between *erosion* and *deposition*?

3 READING SKILL How are beach sands alike and different? Consider their physical features, such as size, shape, and color, as well as how the sands formed.

Group	Group

4 CRITICAL THINKING: Apply Laws protect people against building houses on many barrier islands. Why is a barrier island a poor location for a house?

5 INQUIRY SKILL: Analyze Data Scientists are constantly looking for ways to clean up oil spills. Research modern clean-up methods. Which methods seem to be the most effective?

 TEST PRACTICE
A shoreline is built up through the process of _____.

A. pollution

B. erosion

C. deposition

D. wave action

 STANDARDS
1–5: 2.c., **Test Practice:** 2.c.

Math in Science

Students are tracking the depth of a stream near their school. They measured the depth every school day for 2 weeks. They plotted their results in the bar graph shown at right. Their first measurement was on Monday, April 3rd.

1. From April 3rd to April 7th, by how many centimeters did the stream rise? What percent increase is this rise?

2. Calculate the range, mean, and mode of the students' data on stream depth.

3. When was the stream depth closest to 4 inches? (1 cm = 0.39 in.)

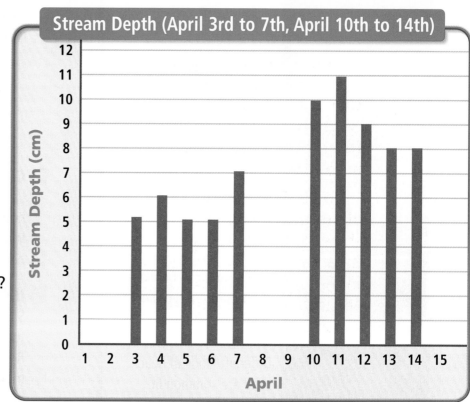

Stream Depth (April 3rd to 7th, April 10th to 14th)

Writing in Science
Research Report

What is acid rain? How does acid rain affect Earth's water, land, and people? Research acid rain and its effects, then write a report to present your findings. Be sure to correctly cite the sources of your information.

Alexandria Boehm

As a girl in Hawaii, Ali Boehm loved to play on beaches and in the ocean. When she noticed how pollution was ruining some of her favorite beaches, she made an important decision about her career.

Today, Dr. Boehm is a professor of environmental engineering at Stanford University and an expert on beach and water pollution. She studies pollution from chemicals and from bacteria and other microorganisms.

In 2005, Dr. Boehm published a surprising report about the beaches of Southern California. She showed that their water quality changes with the lunar cycle and the tides! The water typically holds more harmful bacteria under a full Moon or new Moon than during other moon phases.

Review and Test Practice

Vocabulary

Complete each sentence with a term from the list.

1. A smaller river that flows into a larger river is called a(n) ____.

2. A(n) ____ is a deposit of sediment along a shoreline.

3. When sediment is deposited very quickly from a river, a(n) ____ may form.

4. An area of land that forms parallel to a coastline is a(n) ____.

5. A smooth winding curve in a river is a(n) ____.

6. A(n) ____ is a sandy area that is connected to the coastline on one end.

7. The ____ of rock can be either mechanical or chemical.

8. A(n) ____ is formed after a sea arch collapses.

9. ____ is the process of moving sediment.

10. Sediment from rivers is deposited as it merges with the ocean in an area called a(n) ____.

alluvial fan p. 61
barrier island p. 69
beach p. 69
delta p. 61
deposition p. 60
erosion p. 50
headland p. 68
meander p. 60
sandbar p. 69
sea stack p. 68
sediment p. 48
spit p. 69
tributary p. 58
weathering p. 48

Test Practice

Write the letter of the best answer choice.

11. An area of land jutting out from a coastline is called a ____.

    A. tributary
    B. delta
    C. headland
    D. sea stack

12. Small pieces of rock called ____ may be carried by water.

    A. waves
    B. sea cave
    C. sandbar
    D. sediment

13. The act of building up land is ____.

    A. deposition
    B. erosion
    C. sediment
    D. weathering

14. Rivers shape the landscape through ____.

    A. erosion
    B. deposition
    C. erosion and deposition
    D. tributaries

Inquiry Skills

15. Infer The sand from beach *A* has sediment that is attracted to a magnet. The sand from beach *B* does not have any such sediment. What can you infer about the sand from each beach?

16. Juan precisely measures one cup of sand from two different beaches. Both sand samples are alike in color and texture. How can Juan compare the samples further?

Map the Concept

Landforms near a coastline are formed through erosion or deposition. Classify the landforms below according to how they were formed.

barrier island   sea arch
beach   sea cave
delta   sea stack
sandbar   spit

Erosion	Deposition

Critical Thinking

17. Apply Describe some of the challenges in keeping beaches clean and free of pollution.

18. Synthesize What solutions would you propose to a town that suffers extensive damage from seasonal flooding?

19. Evaluate You are attending a town meeting about a proposed housing development near the mouth of a river. What arguments would you give against such a development? How would you support your arguments?

20. Analyze What can you infer about a relatively flat area that features many large lakes and U-shaped valleys?

Performance Assessment

Make a River Model

Create a model of a river that forms in the mountains, travels down to the lowlands, and flows into the ocean. Use materials that are readily available. Include several tributaries in your model and note how the water movement changes as they join. On your model, note how the water behaves as it speeds up and slows down.

Writing Journal

Review your answers to the questions on page 43 at the beginning of this chapter. Change your answers as needed, based on what you have learned.

STANDARDS

1: 2.b., **2:** 2.c., **3:** 2.b., **4:** 2.b., **5:** 2.b., **6:** 2.c., **7:** 2.a., **8:** 2.c.,
9: 2.b., **10:** 2.c., **11:** 2.c., **12:** 2.b., **13:** 2.c., **14:** 2.c., **15:** 7.g.,
16: 7.b., **Map the Concept:** 2.c., **17:** 2.c., **18:** 2.d., **19:** 2.c.,
20: 2.c., **Performance Assessment:** 2.b.

Write the letter of the best answer choice.

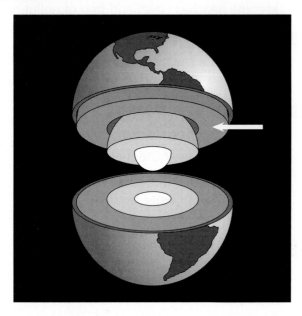

1. To which layer of Earth is the arrow pointing?
   A. outer core
   B. mantle
   C. crust
   D. lithosphere

2. What provides the energy that drives winds and the water cycle?
   A. Earth's rotation
   B. Earth's hot interior
   C. gravity
   D. the Sun

3. What makes up Earth's inner core?
   A. solid iron
   B. plasma
   C. partly-melted rock
   D. water vapor

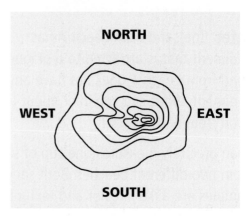

4. In this topographic map, what does each line represent?
   A. land at one elevation
   B. the bed of a river or stream
   C. a highway or other road
   D. a path for walking around the hill

5. Water carrying away sediment is an example of what process?
   A. weathering
   B. erosion
   C. deposition
   D. burrowing

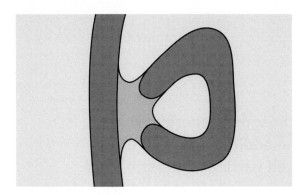

6. What best describes the way an oxbow lake forms?

   A. Heavy rains formed the lake.
   B. The river flooded to form the lake.
   C. A glacier carved out the lake.
   D. Deposition changed the river's course.

7. Which of these features is NOT formed by the actions of ocean waves?

   A. spit

   B. sea arch

   C. alluvial fan

   D. barrier island
   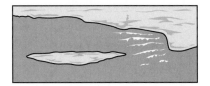

8. What best describes how a landslide changes a habitat?

   A. suddenly and with much destruction
   B. slowly and with little effect
   C. slowly and quietly
   D. suddenly, but with temporary effects

Answer the following in complete sentences.

9. What evidence shows that Earth has a hot interior? Include two examples.

10. How can water shape the land along a hillside? Discuss examples of weathering and erosion in your answer.

 STANDARDS

1. 1.b., 2. 4.a., 3. 1.b., 4. 7.f., 5. 2.a., 6. 2.b., 7. 2.c., 8. 2.d., 9. 1.b., 10. 2.a., 7.h.

You Can...

Discover More

The Sun is always radiating electromagnetic energy, which you see as light and feel as warmth. In addition, the Sun emits a stream of electrons and other charged particles. This stream is called the solar wind, and it causes all sorts of effects on Earth.

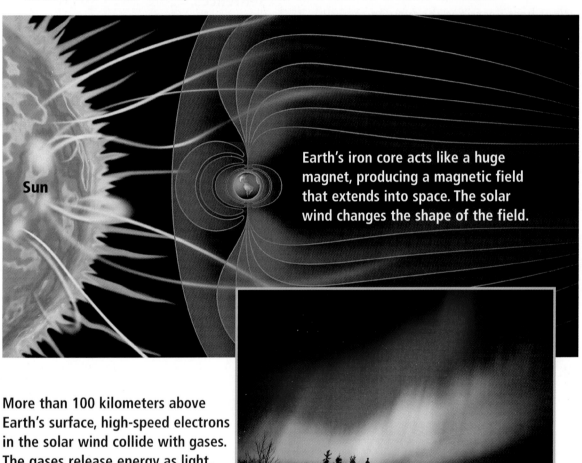

Sun

Earth's iron core acts like a huge magnet, producing a magnetic field that extends into space. The solar wind changes the shape of the field.

More than 100 kilometers above Earth's surface, high-speed electrons in the solar wind collide with gases. The gases release energy as light, producing a great show called an aurora. ▶

Auroras are more common near the North Pole and South Pole, where Earth's magnetic field is strongest. However, when storms on the Sun create very strong winds, auroras can be seen farther away from the poles.

 See magnetic storms in action. Go to www.eduplace.com/cascp/ to view a Flash™ movie and to learn more about auroras.

The Dynamic Earth

California Connection

Visit www.eduplace.com/cascp/ to learn more about Earth's tectonic activity.

Channel Islands

One hundred and forty five species of plants and animals are unique to the Channel Islands and found nowhere else in the world.

In the water, harbor seals paddle with their front flippers and steer with their back flippers.

Spanish shawls feed on sea anemone and store an anemone's stinging cells in order to protect themselves from predators.

The Dynamic Earth

Chapter 3

Evidence of Plate Tectonics 82

Independent Books

• Evidence of Plate Tectonics
• The Hawaiian Islands
• The Story of Sue: T. Rex

Chapter 4

Mountains, Earthquakes, and Volcanoes 128

Independent Books

• Mountains, Earthquakes, and Volcanoes
• Volcano: Pompeii
• Keiiti Aki and the Southern California Earthquake Center

Lava from a volcano

Plate tectonics accounts for important features of Earth's surface and major geologic events.

Chapter 3

Evidence of Plate Tectonics

Death Valley, California

LESSON 1

Scientists studying Earth's surface in the early 1900s faced some surprising discoveries. What was it about the continents that puzzled them?

LESSON 2

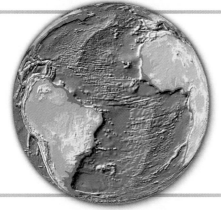

Beneath Earth's vast and powerful oceans, what changes take place that shift and reshape the surface?

LESSON 3

Continents collide, pull apart, and slide past one another. What causes these motions?

LESSON 4

Volcanoes and earthquakes are among the most powerful and destructive forces of nature. What causes a volcano to erupt or an earthquake to strike?

Writing Journal

In your Writing Journal, write or draw answers to each question.

Vocabulary Preview

Vocabulary

convection p. 110
convection current p. 110
fault p. 101
fossil p. 90
magma p. 102
plate boundary p. 104
sea-floor spreading p. 102
strata p. 89
subduction p. 117
tectonic plates p. 100

Glossary

English-Spanish, p. H26.

Vocabulary Skill

Root Words
subduction

This word comes from the Latin words *sub*, meaning "below," and *ducere*, meaning "to lead." Together, the word parts mean "to draw away from below."

strata
horizontal layers of rock

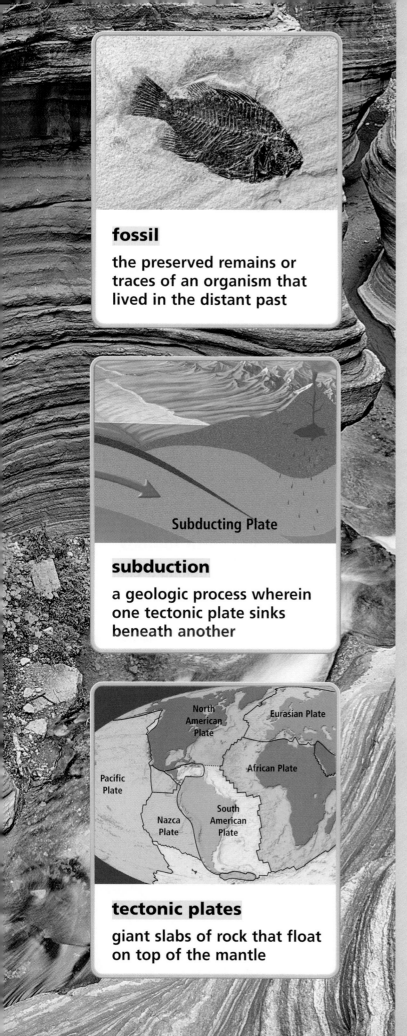

fossil

the preserved remains or traces of an organism that lived in the distant past

Subducting Plate

subduction

a geologic process wherein one tectonic plate sinks beneath another

North American Plate

Eurasian Plate

African Plate

Pacific Plate

Nazca Plate

South American Plate

tectonic plates

giant slabs of rock that float on top of the mantle

California

Start with Your Standards

Standard Set 1. Plate Tectonics and Earth's Structure

1.a. *Students know* evidence of plate tectonics is derived from the fit of the continents; the location of earthquakes, volcanoes, and midocean ridges; and the distribution of fossils, rock types, and ancient climatic zones.

1.c. *Students know* lithospheric plates the size of continents and oceans move at rates of centimeters per year in response to movements in the mantle.

1.e. *Students know* major geologic events, such as earthquakes, volcanic eruptions, and mountain building, result from plate motions.

1.f. *Students know* how to explain major features of California geology (including mountains, faults, volcanoes) in terms of plate tectonics.

Standard Set 4. Energy in the Earth System

4.c. *Students know* heat from Earth's interior reaches the surface primarily through convection.

Standard Set 7: Investigation and Experimentation standards covered in this chapter: 7.a., 7.d., 7.e., 7.g.

What Do Rocks and Fossils Reveal?

Building Background

Rocks and fossils reveal facts about more than just themselves. They are evidence of long-term changes in Earth's climate and of major changes to continents and oceans.

 STANDARDS

1.a. *Students know* evidence of plate tectonics is derived from the fit of the continents; the location of earthquakes, volcanoes, and midocean ridges; and the distribution of fossils, rock types, and ancient climatic zones.

7.g. Interpret events by sequence and time from natural phenomena (e.g., the relative ages of rocks and intrusions).

PREPARE TO INVESTIGATE

Inquiry Skill

Infer When you infer, you use known facts and logical reasoning to make interpretations.

Materials

- 3 fossil samples (labeled A, B, and C)
- hand lens

Science and Math Toolbox

For step 1, review **Making a Chart to Organize Data** on page H11.

Be a Time Traveler!

Procedure

1. **Collaborate** Work in a small group. Gather your fossil samples and a hand lens. In your *Science Notebook*, make a chart like the one shown.

2. **Observe** Look closely at Fossil A. Use the hand lens to see more detail.

3. **Record Data** Record your observations about Fossil A in your chart. Include its shape, size, and other visible details.

4. **Infer** Using your observations of Fossil A and what you already know about fossils, decide which modern organism the fossil most closely resembles. Write the name of that organism in your chart.

5. **Observe** Repeat steps 2 to 4 for Fossils B and C.

Conclusion

1. **Classify** Classify each fossil as a plant or an animal. Describe the evidence that supports your classification.

2. **Infer** Based on what you know about organisms that resemble the fossils, what additional information can you infer about the organism that left the fossil?

3. **Hypothesize** For each fossil, develop a hypothesis about the environment in which the plant or animal lived.

4. **Draw Conclusions** Can you tell how old the fossils are? Explain why or why not.

STEP 1

	Fossil A	Fossil B	Fossil C
Shape			
Size			
Other details			
Type of organism			

STEP 2

STEP 4

Guided Inquiry

Ask Questions What fossils are found in California? Where else are they found? Ask questions like these at a science museum or university, or visit Internet sites. **Research** what fossils reveal about changes on Earth.

Earth's History

READING SKILL

Draw Conclusions As you read, note conclusions about Earth based on rocks, fossils, and other evidence.

```
┌─────────────────┐
│      Data       │
└─────────────────┘
         ↓
┌─────────────────┐
│      Data       │
└─────────────────┘
         ↓
┌─────────────────┐
│   Conclusion    │
└─────────────────┘
```

MAIN IDEA Earth's rock layers and fossils contain evidence that can be used to explain Earth's history.

Evidence of Change

Rocks are always changing from one form to another. They do so through weathering, erosion, heating and cooling, and many other processes. These same processes shape Earth's surface.

Glaciers, which are thick sheets of ice, have been one important agent of change. As they advance and retreat, they slowly grind rock and sculpt the land. During the ice ages, glaciers once covered large land areas. The most recent ice age ended about 15,000 years ago.

Rocky objects from space also form features on Earth's surface. Most of these objects are small, so they burn up in the atmosphere. But larger objects can strike the surface, forming impact craters.

By studying rocks, scientists can infer events in Earth's history. The information in rocks is known as the rock record.

The Rocky Mountains are relatively young. Their sharp peaks reveal that not much erosion has occurred.

Compared to the Rocky Mountains, the Appalachian Mountains are old. Their rounded shapes show more evidence of erosion.

▲ Scientists ask questions and develop theories to make sense of their observations. How do you think long layers of rock can bend into curved shapes?

The Rock Record

In 1669, Danish scientist Nicolaus Steno observed that sediment is always deposited horizontally in layers, or **strata.** He concluded that if the strata were not disturbed or deformed, the layers at the bottom would always be the oldest. The location of any layer in the rock provided a clue to the age of the sediment that formed it.

By the early 1900s, scientists had gathered much information on sedimentary rock layers around the world. They had observed that each layer had specific properties, such as mineral and chemical composition, color, texture, and thickness.

Scientists also made maps of the rock layers with detailed descriptions of each layer. They noticed that similar rock layers often occurred in different parts of the world.

Certain types of strata were quite puzzling. For example, scientists knew that fish and animals with shells live in the ocean and settle to the bottom when they die. Yet strata containing the remains of fish and shells are found inside mountains, far from any body of water. How were they moved hundreds or even thousands of meters above sea level?

Furthermore, scientists observed strata in mountains that appeared curved and folded. They were not able to explain these observations until they learned more about the way mountains form.

DRAW CONCLUSIONS What puzzled scientists about Earth's rock strata?

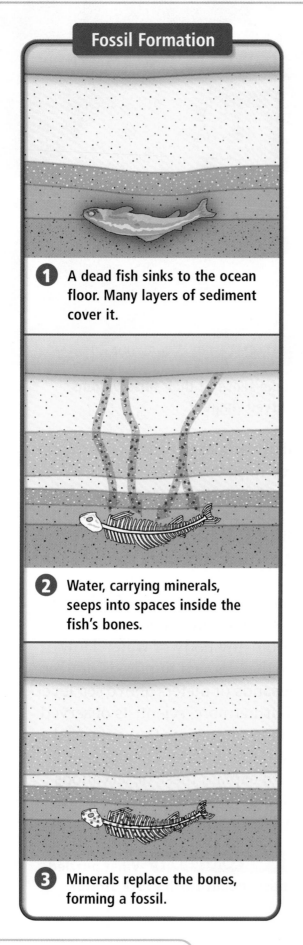

Fossil Formation

1. A dead fish sinks to the ocean floor. Many layers of sediment cover it.

2. Water, carrying minerals, seeps into spaces inside the fish's bones.

3. Minerals replace the bones, forming a fossil.

The Fossil Record

A **fossil** (FAHS uhl) is the preserved remains or traces of an organism that lived in the distant past. Fossils are often found in layers of sediment and are important to the rock record. Information they provide about Earth's history is called the fossil record.

Fossils are evidence of the plants, animals, and other organisms that lived long ago. By studying fossils, scientists get an idea of what now-extinct organisms looked like and how they lived.

How Fossils Form Typically, fossils come from an animal's bones, shells, or other hard parts. These parts are not easily decomposed or eaten. Hard parts also resist weathering by wind and rain.

To be preserved as a fossil, a dead organism usually must be buried quickly. Burial protects it from air, rain, and wind. It also hides it from scavengers and many decomposers. Eventually the soft parts decay, leaving the hard parts behind.

Over time, minerals dissolved in water collect in the pores of a shell or bone. The minerals preserve the shape and size of these parts, and the organism becomes a fossil.

Plants and animals without hard parts can also create fossils. These organisms make imprints, like leaving a footprint in mud or snow. Such imprints are called trace fossils. A trace fossil of a leaf, for example, may look like a very detailed drawing of a leaf. Trace fossils can be prints of body parts, such as feet or tails, or they can show the whole organism.

This fossil of a tropical fern was found in a polar climate. Thus, you can infer that this region once had a much warmer climate.

This fossil fish came from a mountain in Wyoming. This shows that the land was once underwater.

Fossils of this small freshwater reptile have been found both in South America and Africa.

Relative Dating How can scientists tell the age of a fossil? One way is to study the strata of sedimentary rock where the fossil was found. Recall that the oldest strata are on the bottom and the more recent are on top. Scientists infer that fossils are about the same age as the rock around them.

This is called relative dating. It does not tell a fossil's exact age, but does allow scientists to compare the ages of fossils from different rock strata.

Clues About the Past Some fossils provide clues to the climate and environment in which the organism lived. For example, a fossil of a tropical fern indicates that the land was once warm, humid, and marshy—the kind of environment in which tropical ferns thrive.

When scientists find fossils of fish far from water, they know that the climate of the area was once very different. The rock layer containing the fish fossil must have formed under water. In fact, in Earth's geologic past, shallow seas once covered parts of the United States.

Fossils of the same plant and animal species have been found on different continents. How could this be explained?

 **DRAW CONCLUSIONS** What evidence does a fossil provide?

 Express Lab

Activity Card 7
Model a Fossil

Continental Drift

As you've read, fossils of ferns can be found in places that now are cold all year long, places where no ferns grow. How are such finds possible?

Wegener's Hypothesis In 1915, German meteorologist Alfred Wegener proposed an explanation for findings such as this one. He hypothesized that Earth's continents slowly move about its surface. This idea was called continental drift.

Wegener's hypothesis was based on four pieces of evidence. First, the coastlines of South America and western Africa appear to fit together, like pieces of a puzzle. Second, fossils from the same plant and animal species were uncovered in both South America and western Africa. For example, the reptile shown on page 91 lived in freshwater! It could not have swum across the large, salty Atlantic Ocean and survived.

Third, deposits from glaciers were discovered in places that now have warm weather all year long. Fourth, mountain ranges across North America and western Europe seemed to link up, as if these landmasses were once connected.

Wegener hypothesized that all of this evidence could be explained if the continents had once been joined together. He called this landmass *Pangaea* (pan JEE uh), meaning "all land."

Although his evidence was strong, Wegener could not explain how continents could have moved. Yet 30 years after his death, scientists found evidence to support Wegener's ideas. They began to accept the idea of moving continents.

DRAW CONCLUSIONS What was Wegener's hypothesis of continental drift?

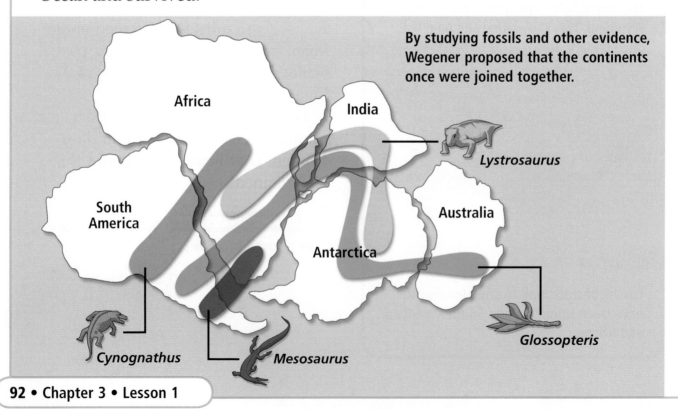

By studying fossils and other evidence, Wegener proposed that the continents once were joined together.

Africa

India

Lystrosaurus

South America

Australia

Antarctica

Cynognathus

Mesosaurus

Glossopteris

Visual Summary

The rock record provides clues about changes to Earth's surface. At first, scientists could not explain tilted rock layers and other observations.

Fossils preserved in sedimentary rock are the remains of once-living plants and animals. Fossils from the same species have been found on different continents.

Evidence from the rock record, the fossil record, and ancient climatic zones led scientists to conclude that the continents have moved.

STANDARD
1.a.

Technology
Visit **www.eduplace.com/cascp** to find out more about Earth's history.

Reading Review

❶ MAIN IDEA What do fossils show about Earth's climate?

❷ VOCABULARY Write a paragraph describing how *fossils* are formed. Include an example.

❸ READING SKILL What evidence supports Wegener's hypothesis of continental drift?

❹ CRITICAL THINKING: Evaluate Sal watches a mountain and does not see it move. He concludes that continents do not move from place to place. Evaluate this conclusion.

❺ INQUIRY SKILL: Infer If you found a fossil of a shark in your back yard, what could you infer about the region in which you live?

TEST PRACTICE
A fish fossil lies in the top layer of a sample of sedimentary rock. What does this show?

A. Fish once lived on dry land.

B. The fish lived after the fossil animals from layers below.

C. The fish lived in a warm area.

D. The fish lacked hard parts.

STANDARDS
1–4: 1.a., **5:** 1.a., 7.g., **Test Practice:** 1.a.

93

Alfred Wegener and Pangaea

What is Pangaea? Scientist Alfred Wegener (1880–1930) believed that long ago the seven continents were joined together, forming a supercontinent he called Pangaea.

Characters

Alfred Wegener

The Seven Continents:
Africa, Antarctica, Asia, Australia, Europe, North America, South America

STANDARD
1.a. *Students know* evidence of plate tectonics is derived from the fit of the continents; the location of earthquakes, volcanoes, and midocean ridges; and the distribution of fossils, rock types, and ancient climatic zones.

READING

The setting is planet Earth, and Wegener is taking the stage.

Wegener *(to audience)*: Good afternoon, I am German scientist Alfred Wegener.

Europe *(aside)*: His name is pronounced "VAY-guh-ner."

Wegener: My friends and I are here to present my theory of continental drift, which I published in the year 1915.

North America *(shocked)*: Did you say "continental drift"? Are you suggesting that continents move?

Wegener: Don't act so surprised! Surely you know that continents move during earthquakes and volcanic eruptions.

North America: Yes, but—

Wegener *(holding up one hand at North America)*: Let me tell you my story. Then you will understand. It all started when I was a young man fascinated by maps. One day I noticed that the coasts of two continents appear to fit together, like pieces of a jigsaw puzzle. Africa and South America, will you demonstrate?

Africa *(moving toward South America)*: If I turn a little this way, and South America rotates that way ...

South America: Yes, we *could* fit together, couldn't we?

Wegener: Yes! That got me thinking. I found out that nearly identical fossils have been discovered on both sides of the Atlantic Ocean, as well as identical rock layers. There are similar pairs of mountain ranges, too, such as the Scottish Highlands in Europe and the Appalachians in North America.

Asia: What are you driving at? Are you saying that some of the continents were once joined together?

Wegener: Not *some* of the continents— *all* of the continents! That's my theory.

Antarctica: Incredible!

Wegener: Isn't it? I call this joined continent *Pangaea*. That's Greek for "all the Earth." Might the seven of you demonstrate what Pangaea looked like?

Wegener waves directions. The continents move together to form Pangaea.

Australia *(stumbling)*: This is terribly disorienting. Am I still Down Under?

South America: Hey, someone's stepping on my Galápagos Islands!

Antarctica: It's getting a bit too warm around here.

Wegener: Stop right there! Perfect! As you can see, the continents fit together into one supercontinent. According to my theory, this is how Earth looked about 200 million years ago.

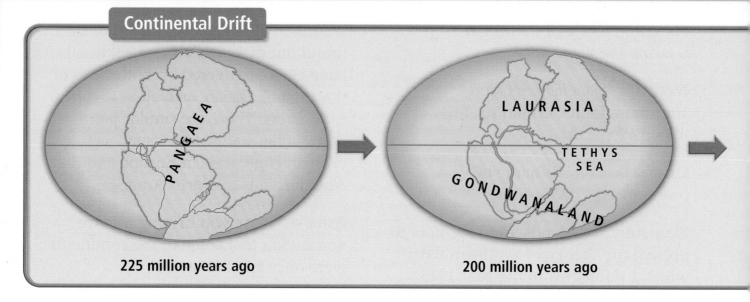

Continental Drift

225 million years ago

200 million years ago

LAURASIA

TETHYS SEA

GONDWANALAND

PANGAEA

Africa: So animals could wander from me to South America, is that right?

South America: Plant seeds could travel easily, too.

Wegener: Right and right. But over the years, slowly but surely, the continents drifted apart.

Wegener gestures at the continents. They drift apart, back to their modern-day positions.

Australia: Well, it was fun while it lasted!

Europe (*to the others*): Maybe I'll see you again in another 200 million years or so.

Wegener: Perhaps, perhaps. My theory about Pangaea explains a great deal about Earth's geography. For example, have you noticed that mountain ranges are found mostly near the edges of continents?

South America: Now that you mention it, I have a rugged mountain range running along my west coast.

North America: That's funny, so do I!

Asia: And I have the Himalayas, that tall mountain range just north of India.

Wegener: According to my theory, mountains arise when continents move into each other. For example, the Himalayas rose when India slammed into the rest of Asia.

Asia: Ouch!

North America: Well, Mr. Wegener, you seem to have solved all the mysteries of our planet. So tell us: Just how did continents move around the planet?

Wegener (*shaking his head*): Well, you've hit upon the weakness of my theory. I could only guess at how the continents moved. Many of my critics enjoyed pointing this out.

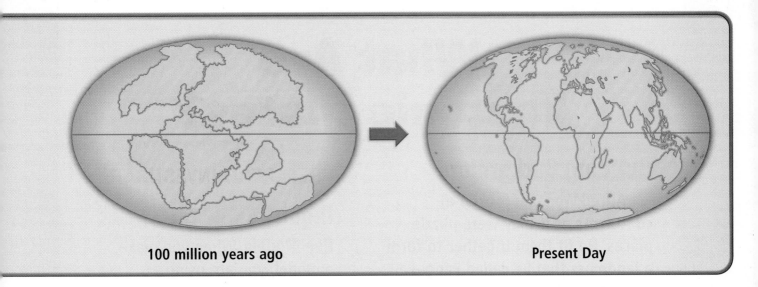

100 million years ago   **Present Day**

Continents gather around Wegener and pat him on the back in consolation.

Wegener: It's okay. After my time, people decided that I was correct. You see, scientists began studying the ocean floor.

Asia: What do oceans have to do with anything?

Wegener: A great deal! Scientists have discovered giant mountain chains, called mid-ocean ridges, in the ocean's depths. In these ridges, molten rocks rise from below Earth's surface and become part of the ocean floor.

Europe: So what does that mean?

Wegener: It means that the ocean floors are moving, too! Oceans and continents move in giant slabs that scientists call tectonic plates. If I'd lived long enough, I would have studied tectonic plates myself.

Australia: I'd like to thank Mr. Wegener for proposing new ideas that challenged old ones. That's very important in science!

Africa: Plus, he used evidence from many different branches of science.

North America: A keen observer and a logical thinker—that's our Mr. Wegener!

Wegener: Why thank you, my friends, I am truly—moved!

All laugh.

Sharing Ideas

1. **READING CHECK** What is Wegener's theory of continental drift?

2. **WRITE ABOUT IT** Describe facts about Earth's geography that Wegener's theory explains.

3. **TALK ABOUT IT** What lessons about science does Wegener's story illustrate?

What Are Tectonic Plates?

Building Background

Alfred Wegener looked at continents as if they were puzzle pieces. He fit them together to form a landmass that he called Pangaea.

Today, scientists accept the idea that continents move. However, the "pieces" are not quite as simple as Wegener had proposed.

STANDARDS

1.a. *Students know* evidence of plate tectonics is derived from the fit of the continents; the location of earthquakes, volcanoes, and midocean ridges; and then distribution of fossils, rock types, and ancient climatic zones.
7.g. Interpret events by sequence and time from natural phenomena (e.g., the relative ages of rocks and intrusions).

PREPARE TO INVESTIGATE

Inquiry Skill

Use Models When you make a model, you are using a representation of a process to better understand how it works.

Materials
- world map
- tracing paper
- construction paper
- glue
- scissors

Science and Math Toolbox

For step 1, review **Read a Map** on pages H14–H15.

Model Pangaea!

Procedure

1. **Observe** Look at the shapes of the continents on the world map. Based on their shapes, describe how they might have once fit together as the supercontinent called Pangaea.

STEP 2

2. **Use Models** Trace the shapes of all the continents onto tracing paper. Glue the tracing paper to the construction paper. Cut out the continents. **Safety:** Be careful when using scissors.

STEP 2

3. **Hypothesize** How might the continents fit together into a supercontinent? Try piecing the paper continents together. When you are done, check the map of Pangaea on page 96. How closely does your map match?

STEP 3

4. **Predict** Based on how the continents fit together in Pangaea, predict the locations where you would expect to find similar rock types and fossils.

Conclusion

1. **Use Models** Using your model, rearrange the continents in another way. How might the world be different today if the continents were in these positions?

2. **Infer** Based on its locations in Pangaea and in the modern world, explain how the climate of North America might have changed from 200 million years ago to the present.

Guided Inquiry

Experiment Globes are more accurate than flat maps. Use everyday materials to create a spherical model of continental drift. **Compare** the spherical model to the flat model.

Tectonic Plates

VOCABULARY

fault	p. 101
magma	p. 102
plate boundary	p. 104
sea-floor spreading	p. 102
tectonic plates	p. 100

READING SKILL

Main Idea As you read, fill in the main ideas and details to organize the information in the lesson.

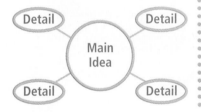

STANDARDS

1.a. *Students know* evidence of plate tectonics is derived from the fit of the continents; the location of earthquakes, volcanoes, and midocean ridges; and the distribution of fossils, rock types, and ancient climatic zones.

1.c. *Students know* lithospheric plates the size of continents and oceans move at rates of centimeters per year in response to movements in the mantle.

MAIN IDEA The solid, outermost layer of Earth is divided into large, moving plates. Evidence for these plates includes the locations of earthquakes, volcanoes, and mid-ocean ridges.

Continents and Tectonic Plates

In the 1960s, scientists proposed a new theory that expanded on Wegener's ideas. This theory is called plate tectonics. *Tectonics* (tek TAHN iks) is the term for large-scale processes that deform Earth's crust.

Recall that the continents are part of Earth's crust. The crust and the upper part of the mantle form the rigid rocky layer called the lithosphere. According to the theory of plate tectonics, the lithosphere is broken up into huge, irregular slabs called **tectonic plates.**

It is the tectonic plates that move, not the continents themselves. The continents merely ride along on top, like cargo on a container ship.

The Himalaya Mountains formed from the collision of the Indian Plate and the Eurasian Plate. ▼

Evidence of Moving Plates Evidence of moving plates is visible in places where plates come together, pull apart, or slide past one another. These places are found all over the world, including California.

The Himalaya Mountains in Central Asia formed from colliding plates. These mountains are among the highest on Earth. They began forming about 65 million years ago when India collided with mainland Asia. The pressure caused the plates to buckle and fold, creating the mountains. This collision is still in progress today.

In California, two plates are sliding past one another along the San Andreas Fault. A **fault** is a crack in Earth's crust along which movement takes place. As rocks in each plate grind past each other, pressure builds up. Eventually the rocks break and shift. The sudden movement along the fault is felt as an earthquake.

In places where plates pull apart, a rift valley, or long narrow valley, forms on Earth's surface. An example is the Great Rift Valley in East Africa. This 5,000-km (3,100-mi) long rift began forming 35 million years ago.

MAIN IDEA Describe evidence that supports the movement of plates.

▲ Sliding plates will break apart any structure built across them.

At the northern part of the Great Rift Valley, the rift valley is filled in by the Red Sea. ▶

Red Sea

Sea-Floor Spreading

In the years before and after World War II, scientists began mapping the ocean floor. They made a surprising discovery. Along the middle of the Atlantic Ocean was an underwater mountain chain. Scientists today call it a mid-ocean ridge. Further studies show that mid-ocean ridges are part of all of Earth's oceans.

Today, scientists know that these ridges mark the areas where two plates are moving apart. These ridges are connected, stretching tens of thousands of kilometers across the ocean floor.

The Mid-Atlantic Ridge is very distinct. It even has the same shape as the coastline of South America and western Africa. You can clearly see that the two continents broke apart along this line.

In the center of these ridges are deep valleys, called rift valleys. As the plates spread apart, magma flows up and fills the space in a process called **sea-floor spreading. Magma** is melted rock below Earth's surface.

The discovery of sea-floor spreading provided three pieces of evidence to support the plate tectonic theory. First, it explained how plates grow and shrink. If one plate is growing, another must be shrinking. After all, the planet is not changing size!

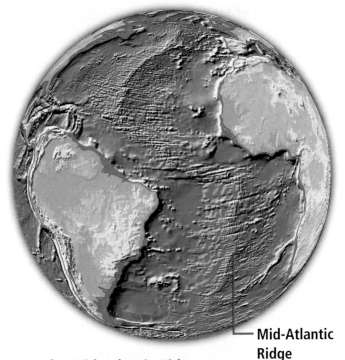

Mid-Atlantic Ridge

▲ The Mid-Atlantic Ridge runs down the center of the Atlantic Ocean floor.

A plate is destroyed where one plate moves beneath another, such as at a deep ocean trench. The sinking plate descends into the mantle, melts, and is recycled. Plates are enlarged when two plates move apart. Magma rises up through the crack between them. As the magma cools and hardens, the new rock becomes part of the plates.

Second, the oldest ocean floor is only about 200 million years old—far younger than Earth. The ocean floor is youngest, and the sediment thinnest, next to the rift valley. It becomes older farther away. At places where plates come together, the floor is being destroyed. Any ocean floor made more than 200 million years ago has been recycled.

Activity Card 8
Solve a Puzzle

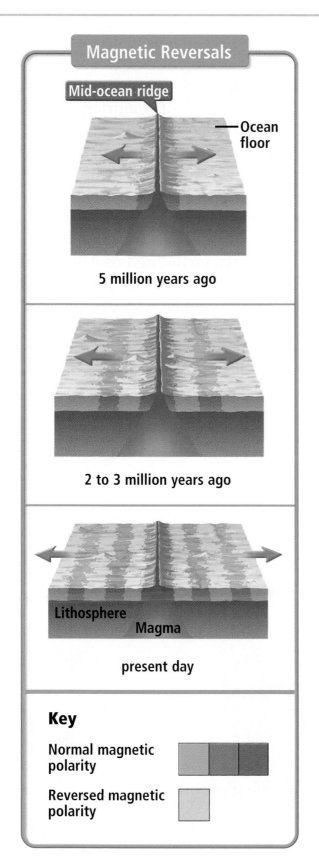

Magnetic Reversals

Mid-ocean ridge

Ocean floor

5 million years ago

2 to 3 million years ago

Lithosphere

Magma

present day

Key

Normal magnetic polarity

Reversed magnetic polarity

▲ Matching bands of iron minerals prove that the sea floor is spreading. Over millions of years, new rock has spread outward from the mid-ocean ridge.

Third, and perhaps most important, is evidence involving Earth's magnetic field. Recall that Earth is like a big magnet with a north pole and a south pole. The magma that flows out of the mid-ocean ridge is rich in iron.

Iron minerals act like compass needles. As magma cools and hardens, iron minerals in the rock line up in the direction of Earth's magnetic field. On either side of a mid-ocean ridge are bands of newly formed rock with a record of Earth's magnetic field.

Earth's magnetic field reverses polarity from time to time. The north magnetic pole and the south magnetic pole switch places. As scientists have discovered, this has happened hundreds of times over the past 150 million years.

Iron minerals in rock act as a record of Earth's magnetic field when the rock formed. On either side of the mid-ocean ridges are parallel bands of rock with matching records. This proves that the plates are moving apart from a common source.

One final piece of evidence comes from volcanic and earthquake activity. You will learn more about this in Lesson 4.

 **MAIN IDEA** How does sea-floor spreading support plate tectonics?

Earth's Tectonic Plates

Scientists have identified seven major plates and many smaller plates. As you can see from the map, the major plates can be all ocean crust or a combination of ocean and continental crust. A few small plates are continental crust only. The largest plate includes almost the entire Pacific Ocean!

The plates vary greatly in size and shape. Some span only a few hundred kilometers, while others are thousands of kilometers wide. Plates also change in size as they collide and pull apart. The huge Pacific Plate, for example, is slowly shrinking because the Eurasian Plate is pushing against it.

The edge of a tectonic plate is called a **plate boundary.** Note that plate boundaries don't line up with the boundaries of countries, states, or even continents!

For example, the North American Plate covers most of North America, but not all of it. Look closely at the western edge of the continent. The Pacific Plate covers a section of California, including Los Angeles and San Diego. As you will discover, this fact helps explain why earthquakes are so common in California.

MAIN IDEA What does the map reveal about tectonic plates?

Major Tectonic Plates

This map shows Earth's major tectonic plates. Plates interact along their boundaries.

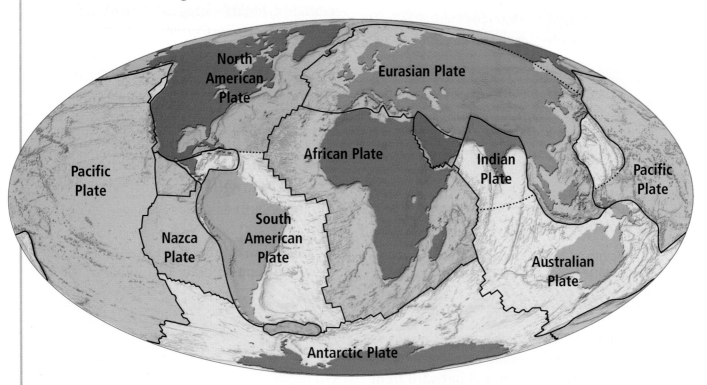

Visual Summary

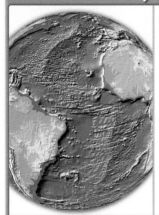

A mid-ocean ridge is an underwater mountain chain on the floor of the ocean. The Mid-Atlantic Ridge has the same shape as the coastlines of Africa and South America.

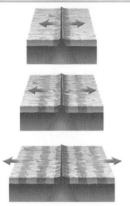

During sea-floor spreading, ocean floor is created at mid-ocean ridges. The record of magnetic reversals proves that tectonic plates are moving apart at mid-ocean ridges.

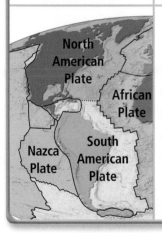

Earth's lithosphere is broken into seven large plates and numerous smaller ones. The plates slowly change shape as they collide and pull apart.

North American Plate

African Plate

Nazca Plate

South American Plate

STANDARDS

1.a., 1.c.

Technology
Visit **www.eduplace.com/cascp** to find out more about tectonic plates.

Reading Review

① MAIN IDEA What causes the continents to move over time?

② VOCABULARY Write a sentence using the term *tectonic plates* to explain how Earth changes.

③ READING SKILL In two or three sentences, summarize the main idea of the *Sea-Floor Spreading* section.

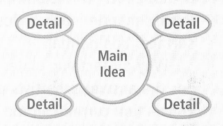

Detail   Detail

Main Idea

Detail   Detail

④ CRITICAL THINKING: Synthesize What role did sea-floor spreading play in arranging the continents as they are today?

⑤ INQUIRY SKILL: Use Models Describe how you would create a model of sea-floor spreading using everyday materials.

 TEST PRACTICE
How many major tectonic plates have scientists identified?

A. three

B. five

C. seven

D. nine

STANDARDS

1: 1.c., **2–3:** 1.a., 1.c., **4:** 1.a., **5:** 1.c., **Test Practice:** 1.a.

How Do Tectonic Plates Move?

Building Background

The Hawaiian Islands formed over a "hot spot." This is a region where Earth's mantle reaches closer to the surface than normal.

Why do tectonic plates move? For the answer, scientists point to convection currents in the mantle.

STANDARDS

4.c. *Students know* heat from Earth's interior reaches the surface primarily through convection.
7.d. Communicate the steps and results from an investigation in written reports and oral presentations.

PREPARE TO INVESTIGATE

Inquiry Skill

Communicate You can communicate the steps and results of investigations in the form of written reports and oral presentations.

Materials

- mantle-model fluid
- square glass container (bottle or dish)
- ring stand
- desk lamp with 75-W bulb

Mantle Motion

Procedure

STEP 1

1. **Collaborate** Work in a large group or as a class. Shake the bottle of mantle-model fluid until it is thoroughly mixed. Carefully fill the glass container with the fluid. Place the container on the ring stand. Place the desk lamp underneath, as shown.

2. **Predict** What do you think will happen in the fluid when you turn on the lamp? Write down your prediction in your *Science Notebook.*

STEP 3

3. **Observe** Turn on the lamp. For 5 minutes, look closely at the fluid both from the side and from above. Record your observations in words and a labeled diagram.

4. **Analyze Data** Do your observations support your prediction? Explain why or why not.

5. **Compare** How is the model similar to what happens in Earth's mantle? How is it different?

Conclusion

1. **Communicate** Write a report summarizing your investigation and results. Include drawings both of the apparatus and of the fluid motions you observed.

2. **Hypothesize** The pattern you observed is called a convection current. Form a hypothesis about how convection currents arise.

Guided Inquiry

Experiment Use small pieces of foam, mantle-model fluid, and a heat lamp to model how continents move. Estimate the speed of the model continents by using a stopwatch and ruler. **Compare** the speeds of your model continents and real ones.

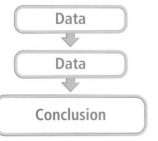
READING SKILL

Draw Conclusions As you read, draw conclusions about the relationship between plate movements and convection currents.

Data
↓
Data
↓
Conclusion

STANDARDS

1.c. *Students know* lithospheric plates the size of continents and oceans move at rates of centimeters per year in response to movements in the mantle.
4.c. *Students know* heat from Earth's interior reaches the surface primarily through convection.

Moving Plates

MAIN IDEA Heat from Earth's interior drives convection currents in the mantle. These currents move tectonic plates at rates of centimeters per year.

Oceans and Continents

When scientists began studying the ocean floor, they expected it to be much like the land they had left behind. Instead, they discovered some important differences.

Continental crust is composed of granitic rocks. Granitic rocks are made of lightweight minerals such as quartz and feldspar. Oceanic crust is composed of basaltic rocks, such as basalt and gabbro. These are igneous rocks, meaning they formed from hot, molten rocks as they cooled. Basaltic rocks are denser than granitic rocks.

The illustration on the next page shows how scientists understand Earth's crust today. Note that continental crust is much thicker than oceanic crust. On average, continental crust is about 40 km thick. Under oceans, the crust typically is about 7 km thick.

Earth's vast oceans cover a rocky floor. These rocks are denser than those that make up the continents. The photograph shows the coast of California and the Pacific Ocean.

Cross-Section of Earth's Crust

Lithosphere

Asthenosphere

◄ Continental crust is made of less dense, granitic rock.

◄ Oceanic crust is made of denser, basaltic rock.

Floating Plates

Earth's crust and the rigid upper part of the mantle together form the lithosphere. The lithosphere is broken into sections called tectonic plates. Underneath, the mantle is hot and plastic-like. This part of the mantle is called the asthenosphere (as THEN uh sfihr).

Why doesn't the lithosphere sink into the hot layer below it? The reason is that the rocks in the asthenosphere are denser than the rocks above them, both the granitic rocks on land and the basaltic rocks of the ocean. You can think of Earth's tectonic plates as giant slabs of continents and ocean, all afloat on a sea of soft rock!

Density also explains why continental crust is much thicker than ocean crust. Granitic rocks are less dense than basaltic rocks, so continental crust can grow thicker than oceanic crust and still float on the asthenosphere beneath.

Much like other things that float, Earth's tectonic plates are in constant motion. They slam into one other, slide over or under each other, and grow larger or smaller. Yet the total size of the planet is not changing. This means that if one plate is enlarging, another must be shrinking. You will learn more about these motions as you read on.

DRAW CONCLUSIONS Why don't continents sink into the mantle?

Activity Card 9
Make a Convection Current

Plate Motion

How do tectonic plates move across Earth? Recall that Earth's interior is much hotter than its surface. This temperature difference causes a convection current to form in the asthenosphere.

Convection is the transfer of thermal energy by the mass movement in a fluid, such as air, water, or molten rock. In a **convection current,** convection drives the fluid through a circular path.

Convection currents form in Earth's atmosphere and oceans, in an aquarium, and even in a pot of water heated on a stove. In a heated pot, the water near the bottom heats up first. The hot water is less dense than the cooler water above it and rises. Cooler, denser water moves in to take its place. When the hot water reaches the top of the pot, it cools, becomes denser, and sinks back down to be heated again.

A similar process takes place in Earth's interior. As rock material is heated deep in the asthenosphere, it expands and becomes less dense. Because it is less dense than surrounding rock, it rises. Eventually it cools, becomes denser, and sinks again, forming a convection current. The current transfers thermal energy from Earth's hot interior to its surface.

The asthenosphere contains many slow-moving convection currents. According to one theory, these currents move the tectonic plates above them. They drag plates along, much like a conveyor belt drags groceries at the supermarket.

According to one theory, convection currents in Earth's mantle drag along tectonic plates. Here the currents move two plates apart. ▼

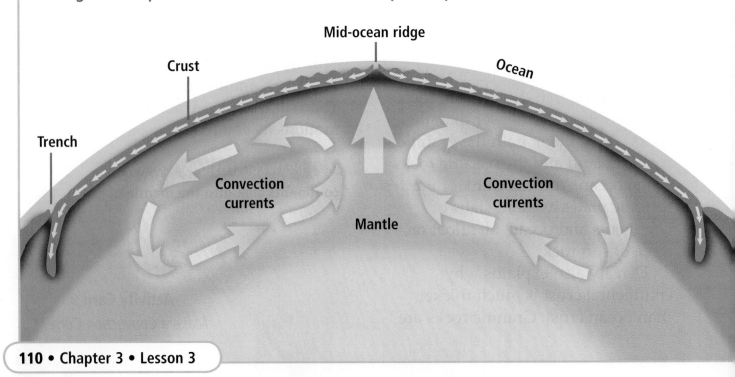

Slow Motion

As you might guess, tectonic plates move very slowly. Recall that Pangaea started to break up about 200 million years ago. It took millions of years for the supercontinent to break apart, and millions more for the modern continents to move to their present positions.

Scientists have measured tectonic plates moving at an average speed of about 10 cm (4 in.) per year. That is about the rate at which fingernails grow! However, this slow rate of movement adds up over time.

Suppose that a plate moves at a speed of 2 cm per year. Over the course of 100,000 years, the plate will have moved 2 km! Over 200 million years the plate would have traveled some 4,000 km.

What kinds of changes can slow-moving plates cause? The answer includes mountain building, earthquakes, and volcanoes! You will learn more about these changes in the next chapter.

You might think that Earth would be a better home without its tectonic activity. However, earth scientists would argue otherwise. Without mountain building, for example, the forces of weathering and erosion would gradually flatten all of Earth's landforms. How do you think flat continents would affect life on Earth?

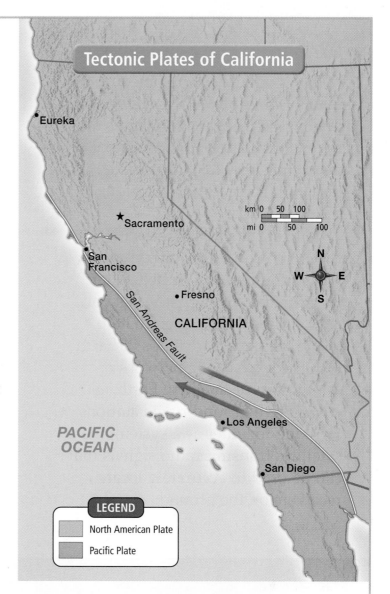

Tectonic Plates of California

•Eureka

★ Sacramento

•San Francisco

San Andreas Fault

•Fresno

CALIFORNIA

•Los Angeles

PACIFIC OCEAN

•San Diego

km 0 50 100
mi 0 50 100

N W E S

LEGEND
North American Plate
Pacific Plate

▲ The Pacific Plate slides past the North American Plate at about 5 cm per year. At this rate, when will Los Angeles meet San Francisco?

 **DRAW CONCLUSIONS** What would happen to tectonic plates if Earth's interior cooled?

Measuring Plate Movement

Deep oceans cover some tectonic plates. Other plates are made of large landmasses that are thousands of kilometers wide. How do scientists determine how fast these plates are moving? They observe Earth from the sky!

One of the most successful types of technology for accurately measuring location is the Global Positioning System (GPS). As you read earlier, GPS is used to help create very accurate maps of Earth.

GPS consists of a network of satellites in orbit above Earth, as well as five ground-based stations. Working together as a system, the satellites transmit radio signals that can be used to accurately locate receivers on the ground.

By measuring distances between specific points over time, scientists can measure how fast plates are moving. GPS data have recently confirmed that the African Plate is moving north at a rate of 1 cm per year.

In addition to satellites, scientists use ground-based radar and laser technology to directly measure plate movements. Using these technologies, the distance between two locations on different plates can be measured to within 1 cm, or even less. By repeating the measurements, the rate of movement of the plates can be calculated.

DRAW CONCLUSIONS **Why do scientists need advanced technology to measure plate movements?**

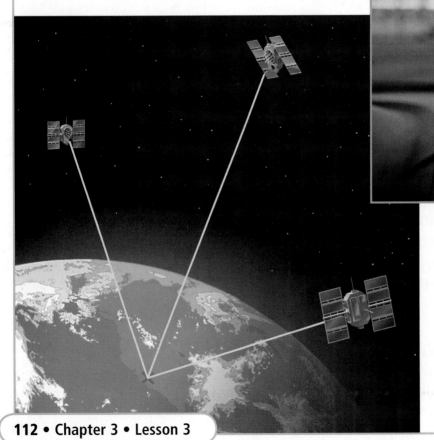

Scientists are using GPS signals to measure the motions of tectonic plates. How else is this technology being used?

Visual Summary

Continental crust is made of different kinds of rock than oceanic crust. As a result, continental crust is less dense and thicker than oceanic crust.

Convection currents in Earth's mantle drive tectonic plate motion. According to one model, plates are dragged along like groceries on a conveyor belt.

Tectonic plates move at an average rate of 10 cm per year. Scientists use satellites, radar, and lasers to measure plate movement.

 **STANDARDS**

1.c., 4.c.

 Technology
Visit **www.eduplace.com/cascp** to find out more about GPS.

Reading Review

❶ MAIN IDEA What causes plates to move?

❷ VOCABULARY Write a sentence to define the term *convection*. Give two examples of convection.

❸ READING SKILL Is oceanic crust denser than continental crust? What evidence supports your answer?

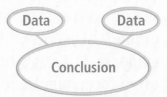

❹ CRITICAL THINKING: Apply What question would you ask if you were interviewing a scientist who measured rates of plate movement?

❺ INQUIRY SKILL: Communicate How would you describe Earth's moving tectonic plates to a fourth-grader? You may use words, pictures, or models to communicate.

 TEST PRACTICE
Tectonic plates are made of sections of ____.

A. outer core

B. lithosphere

C. mantle

D. asthenosphere

 STANDARDS

1–2: 1.b., 4.c., **3:** 1.b., **4–5:** 1.c., **Test Practice:** 1.b.

What Happens at Plate Boundaries?

Building Background

Visit the Old Faithful Geyser of Calistoga, California, and you will see hot water shooting up from the ground. Geysers and hot springs are evidence of Earth's hot interior. They often form near boundaries of tectonic plates.

As tectonic plates move, they cause all sorts of changes to Earth's surface. Those changes are clues to what is happening below.

PREPARE TO INVESTIGATE

Inquiry Skill

Analyze Data When you analyze data, you look for patterns or other evidence in order to make an inference, a prediction, a hypothesis, or draw a conclusion.

Materials

- world atlas
- blank world map
- red pencil
- green pencil

Science and Math Toolbox

For steps 2 and 3, review **Read a Map** on pages H14–H15.

 STANDARDS

1.e. *Students know* major geologic events, such as earthquakes, volcanic eruptions, and mountain building, result from plate motions.
7.e. Recognize whether evidence is consistent with a proposed explanation.

Picking a Pattern

Procedure

1. **Compare** Read and compare the lists of earthquake and volcano locations below. What similarities do you find?

Earthquakes	Year		Volcanoes	Year
Banda Sea, East Indonesia	1938		Arenal, Costa Rica	1968
Concepción, Chile	1751		Krakatau, Indonesia	1883
Esmeraldas (offshore), Ecuador	1906		Momotombo, Nicaragua	1609
Kamchatka Peninsula, Russia	1952		Mt. Fuji, Japan	1707
Kobe, Japan	1995		Mt. Hood, Oregon	1865
Prince William Sound, Alaska	1964		Mt. Pinatubo, Phillippines	1991
San Francisco, California	1906		Mt. St. Helens, Washington	1980
Tangshan, China	1976		Tiatia (Kurile Islands), Russia	1973

STEP 2

2. Use an atlas to find the locations of the earthquakes and volcanoes.

3. **Record Data** Mark each location on the blank world map. Draw a red triangle for a volcano. Draw a green circle for an earthquake. Check your work.

STEP 3

Conclusion

1. **Analyze Data** In your *Science Notebook*, draw conclusions about the pattern you see.

2. **Infer** Using what you know about Earth's structure, infer the relationship between the planet's plates and the places where most volcanoes and earthquakes occur.

Guided Inquiry

Ask Questions How has plate tectonics shaped California? Use the Internet, almanacs, or other reference resources to find volcano and earthquake data. Then plot these data on a blank map of California. What can you **infer** from your data?

115

READING SKILL

Cause and Effect As you read, use a graphic organizer to show the effects of moving tectonic plates.

Cause → Effect

STANDARDS

1.e. *Students know* major geologic events, such as earthquakes, volcanic eruptions, and mountain building, result from plate motions.
1.f. *Students know* how to explain major features of California geology (including mountains, faults, volcanoes) in terms of plate tectonics.

Plate Boundaries

MAIN IDEA Movement along plate boundaries causes geologic events such as earthquakes, volcanic eruptions, and mountain building.

Plate Interactions

As you have learned, tectonic plates move very slowly. Typically, this motion can hardly be felt. But at times, it can cause sudden and unexpected changes to Earth's surface.

Why do some regions of the world experience violent volcanic eruptions and devastating earthquakes while other regions do not? The answer lies at the edges, or boundaries, of Earth's tectonic plates. Where tectonic plates meet edge-to-edge, movement and interactions produce earthquakes, volcanoes, and other geologic events and structures.

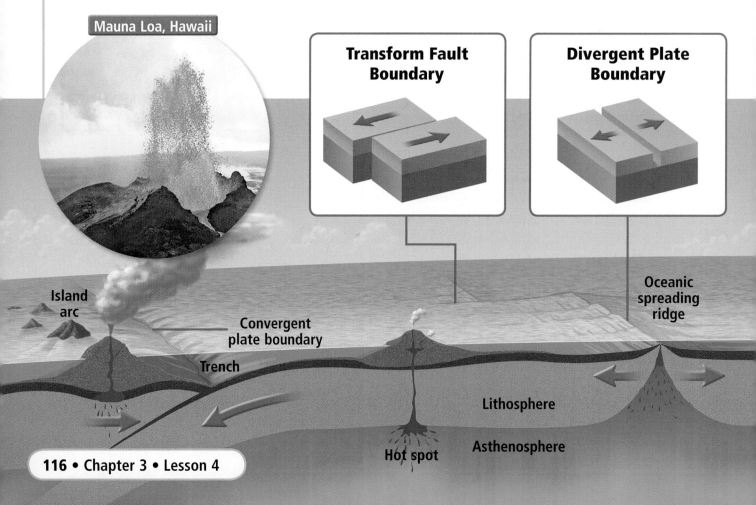

Mauna Loa, Hawaii

Transform Fault Boundary

Divergent Plate Boundary

Island arc

Convergent plate boundary

Trench

Oceanic spreading ridge

Lithosphere

Hot spot

Asthenosphere

Types of Plate Boundaries

There are three types of plate boundaries: convergent, divergent, and transform fault. Each has characteristic features and causes different events and landforms.

At converging boundaries, two plates converge, or move toward each other. Eventually, they collide. When plates collide, one may ride up over the other. The upper plate forces the edge of the lower plate under the surface. This process is called **subduction.** (suhb DUCK shuhn)

At diverging boundaries, two plates move away, or diverge, from each other. Molten rock rises up the gap between the plates, forming new crust. This usually happens along mid-ocean ridges. As you have learned, the process is called sea-floor spreading.

At transform fault boundaries, plates slide horizontally past each other. Crust is not created or destroyed. Instead, it is buckled and deformed.

Whether they are converging, diverging, or sliding past one another, Earth's plates never stop moving and changing. New rock is added to Earth's crust in some places, while old rock is "lost" to the mantle in other places.

CAUSE AND EFFECT Why do only some areas experience volcanic eruptions?

Yellowstone National Park

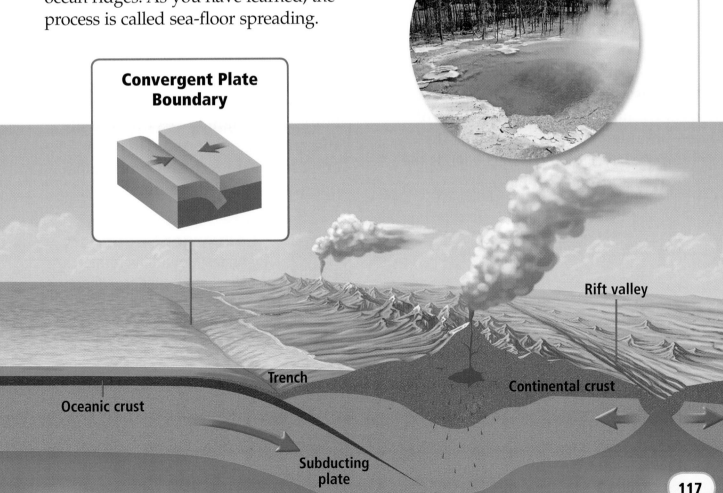

Convergent Plate Boundary

Oceanic crust

Trench

Subducting plate

Rift valley

Continental crust

Convergent Boundaries These boundaries form where two plates push together. There are three types of convergent boundaries.

At *continental-continental boundaries*, two plates both made of continental crust collide. Because continental crust is relatively light, neither plate is subducted. Instead, the land crumples into high mountains. The Himalaya Mountains and Tibetan Plateau formed this way 50 million years ago.

At *oceanic-continental boundaries*, an oceanic plate collides with a continental plate. Because the oceanic plate is denser, it will be subducted below the continental plate. A deep narrow valley on the ocean floor, called a trench, forms where the oceanic plate dives down.

Two oceanic plates converge at *oceanic-oceanic boundaries*. A subduction zone forms as the cooler, denser plate sinks below the other. A trench is formed at this type of boundary, too. The Mariana Trench, at nearly 11,000 m (36,000 ft), is the deepest trench on Earth.

Subduction zones are usually accompanied by volcanic and earthquake activity. As the sinking plate melts, some of the resulting magma reaches the surface, forming volcanic island arcs such as the Aleutian Islands of Alaska.

Divergent Boundaries Divergent boundaries form where plates move apart. This usually occurs along the mid-ocean ridges between two oceanic plates. At the Mid-Atlantic Ridge, plates move apart at a rate of 2.5 cm per year, on average.

Some divergent boundaries are on land. The Great Rift Valley in Africa is one example. Over time, a new ocean basin may form in the gap between the diverging plates.

Iceland sits over two plates and the Mid-Atlantic Ridge. As a result, Iceland is slowly being pulled apart. Volcanic activity and hot springs are common in Iceland.

Along an oceanic divergent boundary, magma rises through the rift, creating new crust. This new crust forms underwater mountains often as tall as the mountains on

◄ **Convergent Boundary**
The Andes Mountains formed at a convergent boundary, where the Nazca Plate sinks beneath the South American Plate.

▲ Divergent Boundary
Iceland sits on top of the divergent boundary in the Atlantic Ocean.

▼ Transform Fault Boundary
The San Andreas Fault zone is a transform fault boundary. Here, the Pacific Plate moves past the North American Plate.

land. Volcanoes and earthquakes are common along underwater ridges.

Transform Fault Boundaries Transform fault boundaries form where two plates are sliding horizontally past each other. A fault is a crack in Earth's crust caused by sliding plates.

Most transform fault boundaries form along mid-ocean ridges between oceanic plates. However, a well-known example, the San Andreas Fault, runs along the west coast of California.

As you have read, the San Andreas Fault zone is at the boundary of the North American Plate and the Pacific Plate. Part of the California coast—from San Francisco south to San Diego—is on the Pacific Plate and is moving north.

The rest of California is part of the North American Plate. This plate is moving north, too, but at a slower rate than the Pacific Plate. Earthquakes are common as pressure builds up along the fault, then is suddenly released.

You will learn much more about earthquakes, volcanoes, and mountain building when you read the next chapter.

 **CAUSE AND EFFECT** What causes faults in Earth's crust?

Activity Card 10
Model Plate Motion

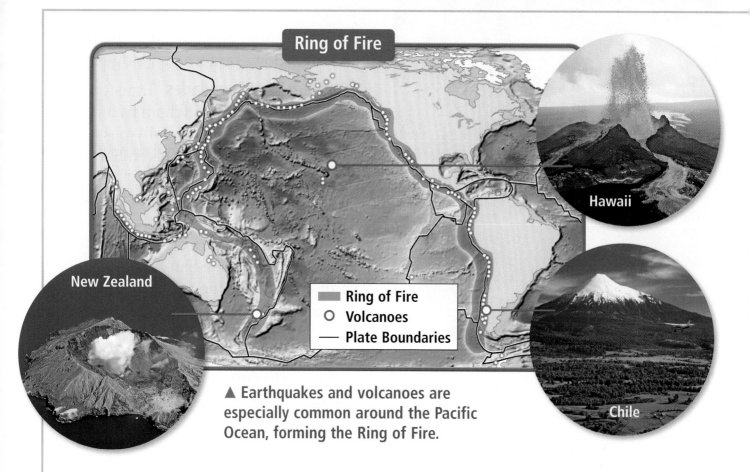

Ring of Fire

Legend:
- ▬ Ring of Fire
- ○ Volcanoes
- — Plate Boundaries

New Zealand

Hawaii

Chile

▲ Earthquakes and volcanoes are especially common around the Pacific Ocean, forming the Ring of Fire.

The Ring of Fire

Many earthquakes and volcanoes occur in a zone that borders the Pacific Ocean. For that reason, this zone has been named the Ring of Fire. It extends from the eastern coast of Asia, across the northern Pacific, and down the west coasts of North and South America.

The Ring of Fire outlines Earth's subduction zones. As the map shows, the Pacific Plate converges with several continental plates along the Ring of Fire.

Faulting during subduction causes earthquakes and can also lead to volcanic activity. As you have learned, subduction zones are associated with deep-ocean trenches. As the subducting plate sinks into the mantle, it melts to form magma. The magma may later rise to the surface, forming a line of volcanoes that often parallels the trench.

Not all earthquakes and volcanoes occur along the Ring of Fire. Remember, diverging plates also cause earthquakes and volcanoes. Diverging boundaries are usually located near the middle of ocean basins. At these boundaries, magma rises to the surface between separating plates, creating volcanic mountain ridges. Faulting at the ridges leads to earthquakes.

This pattern of earthquakes and volcanoes along plate boundaries is further evidence in support of plate tectonics.

 **CAUSE AND EFFECT** What creates volcanoes in the Ring of Fire?

Visual Summary

The movement of tectonic plates causes changes on Earth's surface. These changes include earthquakes, volcanoes, and mountain building. All occur in California.

Plate boundaries can be convergent, divergent, or transform fault. Earthquakes and volcanic eruptions are common along many plate boundaries.

Many earthquakes and volcanoes occur in subduction zones around the Pacific Ocean. This set of zones is called the Ring of Fire.

STANDARDS
1.e., 1.f.

Technology
Visit **www.eduplace.com/cascp** to find out more about plate boundaries.

Reading Review

1 MAIN IDEA What geologic events are likely to be found at convergent plate boundaries?

2 VOCABULARY Write a sentence using the term *subduction*.

3 READING SKILL Why do so many earthquakes and volcanoes occur around the Pacific Ocean?

Cause → Effect

4 CRITICAL THINKING: Analyze How would Earth be different if tectonic plates did not move?

5 INQUIRY SKILL: Analyze Data Research at least five recent earthquakes or volcanic eruptions. Add them to the list on page 115. Do the additional data support the conclusions that this lesson presents about plate interactions?

 TEST PRACTICE

Which type of plate boundary is associated with the San Andreas Fault?

A. convergent boundary

B. subduction zone

C. divergent boundary

D. transform fault boundary

STANDARDS
1–5: 1.e., **Test Practice:** 1.f.

121

EXTREME Science

STANDARDS **1.e.** *Students know* major geologic events, such as earthquakes, volcanic eruptions, and mountain building, result from plate motions.

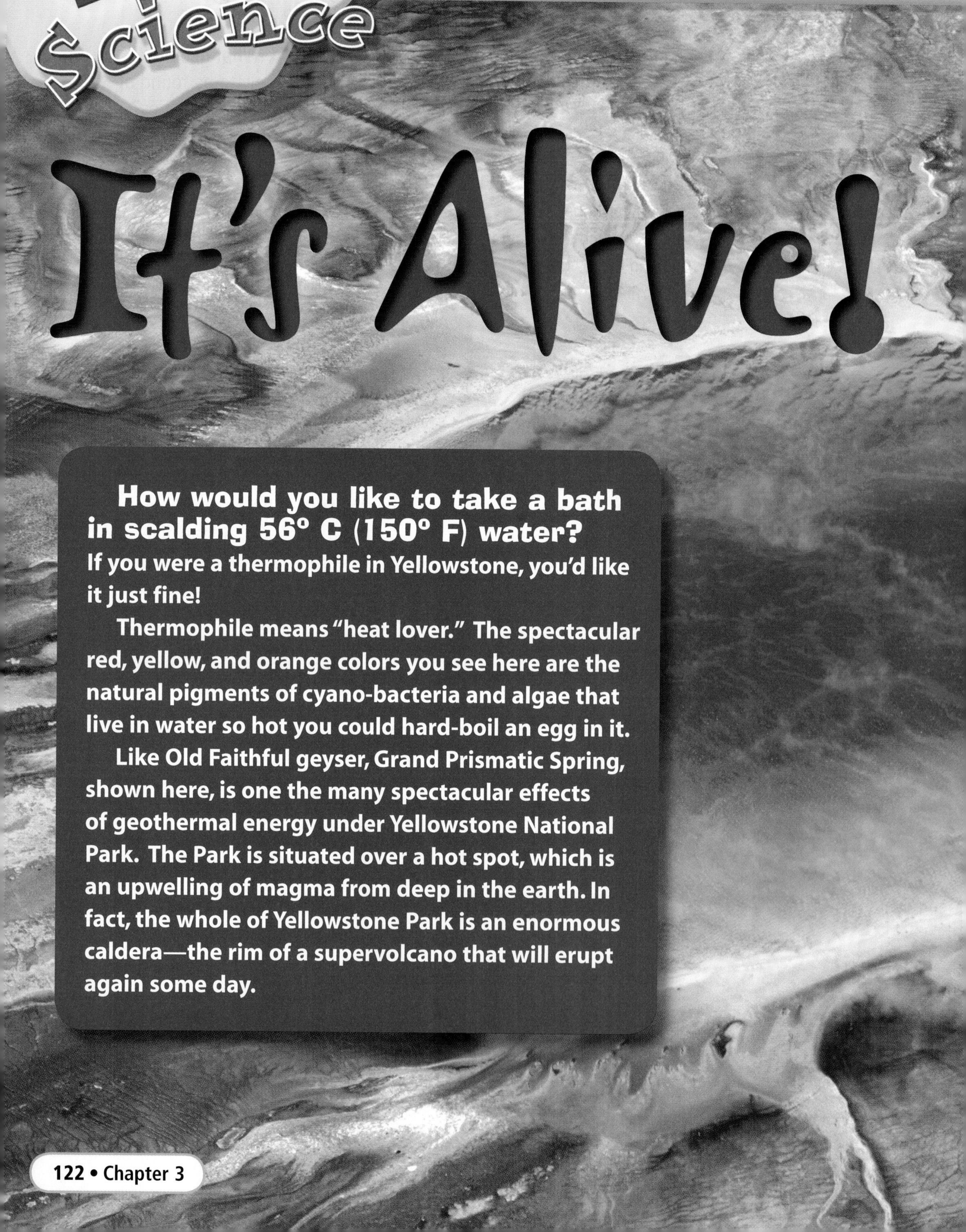

It's Alive!

How would you like to take a bath in scalding 56° C (150° F) water?
If you were a thermophile in Yellowstone, you'd like it just fine!

Thermophile means "heat lover." The spectacular red, yellow, and orange colors you see here are the natural pigments of cyano-bacteria and algae that live in water so hot you could hard-boil an egg in it.

Like Old Faithful geyser, Grand Prismatic Spring, shown here, is one the many spectacular effects of geothermal energy under Yellowstone National Park. The Park is situated over a hot spot, which is an upwelling of magma from deep in the earth. In fact, the whole of Yellowstone Park is an enormous caldera—the rim of a supervolcano that will erupt again some day.

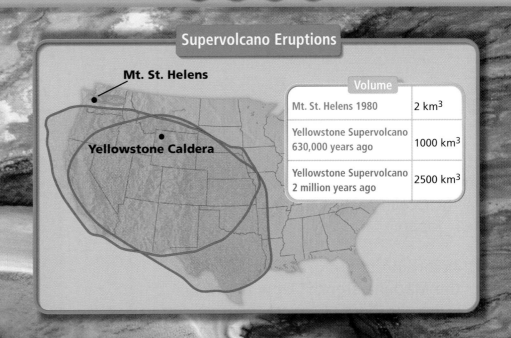

Supervolcano Eruptions

Mt. St. Helens

Yellowstone Caldera

Volume	
Mt. St. Helens 1980	2 km^3
Yellowstone Supervolcano 630,000 years ago	1000 km^3
Yellowstone Supervolcano 2 million years ago	2500 km^3

The center of the Grand Prismatic Spring is 87° C (188° F)—too hot for anything to live. The blue color there is refracted light from the sky.

Writing Journal

Is it possible that extremophiles might be found on other planets? Do some library and Internet research and write in your journal about what you find.

Math in Science

The Mariana Trench is the deepest part of Earth's oceans, and is far deeper than any canyon on land. It is located in the Pacific Ocean east of the Mariana Islands, near Japan.

1. According to the graph, how deep is the Mariana Trench? How far away is it from shore? Convert these values to miles. (1 km = 0.62 mi)

2. The top of Mt. Everest is the highest point on Earth, about 9 km above sea level. What is the difference in elevation between Mt. Everest and the Mariana Trench?

3. If you walked down the ocean floor from the shoreline into the trench, how far would you descend, on average, for every 1 km you moved away from shore?

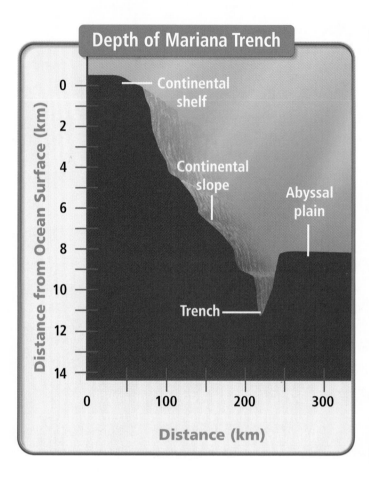

Depth of Mariana Trench

Continental shelf

Continental slope

Abyssal plain

Trench

Distance from Ocean Surface (km)

Distance (km)

Writing in Science
Research Report

Research the San Andreas Fault and the effect it has had on California. Search the Internet or at the library. You may also interview classmates or adults about their experiences with earthquakes.

Building Contractor

Building contractors plan and manage the construction of homes, schools, and other buildings. They must consult with architects, purchase building materials, and hire the construction team. In California, they also must meet strict building codes to prepare houses for earthquakes.

What It Takes!

- A broad understanding of construction
- The ability to plan, to coordinate tasks, and to manage a budget
- Management and communication skills

Paleontologist

Have you admired the exhibits of dinosaurs at a museum of natural history? Those exhibits are the work of paleontologists, scientists who study ancient life.

Paleontologists travel the world to dig fossils out of the ground. They study the fossils carefully and compare them to living animals. Their work shows the history of living things. It also provides clues to how Earth's land and climate have changed.

What It Takes!

- Master's degree or doctorate
- Skills in the laboratory and in the field
- Enthusiasm for science and teaching

Vocabulary

Complete each sentence with a term from the list.

1. Earth's lithosphere is broken up into ____.

2. The preserved remains of an organism is called a ____.

3. Sedimentary rock is deposited in layers called ____.

4. Molten rock beneath Earth's surface is called ____.

5. At mid-ocean ridges, magma flows up and fills the space in a process known as ____.

6. The transfer of thermal energy by mass movement in a fluid is called ____.

7. The sinking of one tectonic plate beneath another is called ____.

8. The edge of a tectonic plate is known as a ____.

9. The rising and sinking motion of a heated fluid forms a cyclic pattern called a ____.

10. A crack in Earth's crust along which movement takes place is called a ____.

convection p. 110
convection current p. 110
fault p. 101
fossil p. 90
magma p. 102
plate boundary p. 104
sea-floor spreading p. 102
strata p. 89
subduction p. 117
tectonic plates p. 100

Test Practice

Write the letter of the best answer choice.

11. The Himalaya Mountains, Andes Mountains, and other tall mountains formed at ____.

    A. divergent boundaries
    B. transform fault boundaries
    C. sea-floor spreading
    D. convergent boundaries

12. Tectonic plates float upon the ____.

    A. crust
    B. core
    C. asthenosphere
    D. ocean

13. Because new crust is constantly being created in rift valleys, the ____ on Earth are relatively young.

    A. continents
    B. volcanoes
    C. ocean floors
    D. mountain chains

14. Beneath Earth's crust lies the layer known as the ____.

    A. outer core
    B. mantle
    C. sea floor
    D. inner core

15. **Use Models** How would you design a model that shows different types of plate boundaries?

16. A region has just experienced a series of major earthquakes. What can you infer about that region's position on its underlying tectonic plate?

Map the Concept

The chart shows three types of plate boundaries. Copy the chart. Write each word or term in the list in the correct column. Some terms will appear in more than one column.

earthquakes   rift valleys
faults   sea-floor spreading
mid-ocean ridges   trenches
mountains   volcanoes

Divergent	Convergent	Transform

Critical Thinking

17. **Synthesize** What could you conclude about an area where new sea floor was forming from cooling magma?

18. **Evaluate** Consider the fossil evidence that Wegener used to support his hypothesis of continental drift. What facts related to the fossils did he use? What conclusions did he draw from those facts?

19. **Apply** Los Angeles is located on the Pacific Plate, which is moving northwest at a rate of about 50 mm (2 in.) per year. About how far from its present location will Los Angeles have moved in 1,000 years?

20. **Synthesize** Pangaea extended north and south across the equator. Present-day North America was positioned over the equator. How might the climate of the United States have been different from today? What was the climate like in Antarctica?

Performance Assessment

Boundary Models

Make a three-dimensional model that shows the different types of plate boundaries. Include typical geological features found at each type of boundary. You may use modeling clay, cardboard, and other everyday materials. Include labels on your model, and write captions.

Writing Journal

Review your answers to the questions on page 83 at the beginning of this chapter. Change your answers as needed, based on what you have learned.

STANDARDS

1: 1.c., **2–3:** 1.a., **4:** 1.b., **5:** 1.a., **6:** 4.c., **7:** 1.c., **8:** 1.c., 1.e.,
9: 1.e., 4.c., **10:** 1.f., **11:** 1.a., **12:** 1.b., **13:** 1.a., **14:** 1.b.,
15: 1.e., **16:** 7.e., **17:** 1.e., **18:** 1.a., **19:** 1.c., 1.f., **20:** 1.a.,
Performance Assessment: 1.e., **Map the Concept:** 1.e.

Chapter 4

Mountains, Earthquakes, and Volcanoes

The San Andreas Fault

LESSON 1

Some mountains are tall and jagged. Others are rounded and covered by trees. How do mountains form?

LESSON 2

Earthquakes can crack roads and shake down buildings. What makes earthquakes so powerful?

LESSON 3

Scientists use special tools to determine the location and strength of earthquakes. What do these tools show?

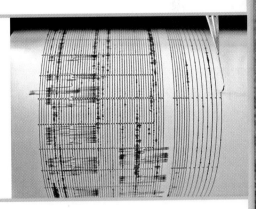

LESSON 4

Most volcanoes form at or near plate boundaries. What causes volcanoes to form in these locations?

Writing Journal

In your Writing Journal, write or draw answers to each question.

Vocabulary Preview

Vocabulary

cinder cone volcano p. 162
composite volcano p. 162
dome mountain p. 136
epicenter p. 150
fault-block mountain p. 134
focus p. 150
fold mountain p. 134
hot spot p. 136
intensity p. 151
island arc p. 161
lava p. 160
magnitude p. 146
seismic wave p. 144
seismograph p. 146
shield volcano p. 162
tsunami p. 154
volcano p. 136

Glossary
English-Spanish, p. H26

Vocabulary Skill
Word Parts
epicenter

Learning common prefixes can help you understand new words. The prefix *epi-* means *on, over,* or *above.* An earthquake's epicenter is a point on the surface, directly over the spot where the earthquake began.

cinder cone volcano

a volcano with slopes made mostly of rock and ash

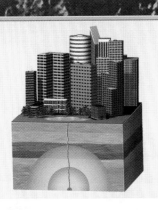

focus

the point underground where an earthquake begins

fold mountain

a mountain formed where plates collide, causing Earth's crust to fold and crumple

lava

molten rock, or magma, that reaches Earth's surface

Standard Set 1. Plate Tectonics and Earth's Structure

1.d. *Students know* that earthquakes are sudden motions along breaks in the crust called faults and that volcanoes and fissures are locations where magma reaches the surface.

1.e. *Students know* major geologic events, such as earthquakes, volcanic eruptions, and mountain building, result from plate motions.

1.f. *Students know* how to explain major features of California's geology (including mountains, faults, volcanoes) in terms of plate tectonics.

1.g. *Students know* how to determine the epicenter of an earthquake and how the effects of an earthquake on any region vary, depending on the size of the earthquake, the distance of the region from the epicenter, the local geology, and the type of construction in the region.

Standard Set 2. Shaping Earth's Surface

2.d. *Students know* earthquakes, volcanic eruptions, landslides, and floods change human and wildlife habitats.

Standard Set 3. Heat (Thermal Energy) (Physical Science)

3.a. *Students know* energy can be carried from one place to another by heat flow or by waves, including water, light and sound waves, or by moving objects.

Standard Set 7: Investigation and Experimentation standards covered in this chapter: 7.a., 7.b., 7.d.

How Do Mountains Form?

Building Background

Have you ever wondered why mountains form in some places, but not in others? Why are some mountains jagged and pointy, while others look like rounded, wrinkled pieces of clay? For the answers, study the movement of Earth's tectonic plates. They tell the story of Earth's mountains.

 **STANDARDS**

1.e. *Students know* major geologic events, such as earthquakes, volcanic eruptions, and mountain building, result from plate motions.
7.b. Select and use appropriate tools and technology (including calculators, computers, balances, spring scales, microscopes, and binoculars) to perform tests, collect data, and display data.

PREPARE TO INVESTIGATE

Inquiry Skill

Compare When you compare, you describe how two or more events are alike and how they are different.

Materials

- shoebox lid
- scissors
- slightly moist sand
- wax paper
- goggles
- ruler

Make a Mountain!

Procedure

Safety: Be careful when using scissors. Wear goggles for this investigation.

1. **Collaborate** Work with a partner. Place a shoebox lid upside down on a flat surface. Then cut a narrow slit along one end of the lid where it bends up.

2. **Use Models** Line the top of the lid with wax paper. The wax paper should be the width of the slit and about 2.5 cm (1 in.) longer than the lid.

3. Place the wax paper in the lid. Pull one end of the paper about 2.5 cm (1 in.) through the slit. Spread half of the sand at the end of the lid near the slit.

4. **Record Data** Spread the other half near the center of the lid. Each pile of sand represents the crust on one of Earth's plates. Draw the model setup in your *Science Notebook.*

5. **Use Models** Slowly pull the wax paper through the slit to model the movement of one of Earth's plates.

STEP 1

STEP 5

Conclusion

1. **Communicate** In your *Science Notebook,* draw what happened to the sand as accurately as you can.

2. **Compare** How does what happened to the sand compare with what happens to rocks in Earth's crust when two tectonic plates collide?

Guided Inquiry

Experiment Select materials to model what happens along a divergent plate boundary. Design the model, and then try it out. In a brief oral presentation, **communicate** how it models plate movement.

Mountain Building

MAIN IDEA Mountains form from plate motions.

VOCABULARY

dome mountain   p. 136

fault-block
 mountain   p. 135

fold mountain   p. 134

hot spot   p. 136

volcano   p. 136

READING SKILL

Classify Use a chart to list the types of mountains and the processes that form them.

Group	Group	Group

STANDARDS

1.e. *Students know* major geologic events, such as earthquakes, volcanic eruptions, and mountain building, result from plate tectonics.
1.f. *Students know* how to explain major features of California geology (including mountains, faults, volcanoes) in terms of plate tectonics.

Folding and Faulting Forces

Mountains are Earth's tallest landforms. Some reach several kilometers above Earth's surface! Ranges such as Asia's Himalayas and California's Sierra Nevada form huge barriers hundreds of miles long. Even with modern roads and bridges, mountains can be difficult to cross.

Because mountains are so huge, you might think they are permanent. But that is not so. Just like Earth's other surface features, mountains are continually being created and destroyed. The actions of tectonic plates build up mountains, while weathering and erosion wear them down.

Scientists classify mountains into five basic types: folded, fault-block, volcanic, dome, and erosion mountains. You will learn about each type in this lesson.

Most mountains form at or near plate boundaries, especially those where two plates push together. In these zones, fold mountains are common. A **fold mountain** forms where continental plates collide, causing the crust to fold and crumple.

Folding
Folding occurs when continental tectonic plates collide, creating some of Earth's tallest mountain ranges.

Faulting

Faulting can produce dramatic cliffs when a large section of rock is forced upward or downward, as in this formation in the Rocky Mountains.

Over time, erosion wears down and softens the folds. That is why some of the oldest fold mountains, such as Arkansas' Ouachita Mountains, have rounded peaks.

In other cases, stress on the crust causes it to crack instead of fold. This creates *faults,* or fractures, in the crust. Fault-block mountains may form wherever faulting occurs. A **fault-block mountain** is a mountain that forms from a block of crust that is pushed upward or downward along a fault.

In most cases, fault-block mountains form when stress splits the crust. Land on one side of the fault is raised, while the other side drops downward. The Grand Teton range in Wyoming is one example of fault-block mountains.

As with fold mountains, erosion helps shape fault-block mountains. Older mountains have softer edges. Many of the valleys near the mountains are partly filled by material that has eroded from the nearby mountainsides.

In eastern and southeastern California, lines of parallel mountain ridges and valleys dominate the landscape. These ridges are blocks of land raised or lowered along fault lines. California's Death Valley is a block of land that has been dropped between parallel faults. It dropped so far that Death Valley is the lowest point in the United States.

 **CLASSIFY** How do fold mountains form?

Volcanic Forces

Volcanoes make the news when they erupt—sometimes in huge, fiery explosions. But not all volcanoes erupt. **Volcanoes** are mountains formed by magma that escaped from Earth's interior, then cooled.

Volcanic activity often happens at convergent boundaries, when the edge of one plate sinks beneath another. The edge of the sinking plate melts into magma deep underground. The magma rises. If it bursts through the crust, it can build up over time to form a volcanic mountain. Many of the peaks of South America's Andes Mountains are volcanoes that formed in this way.

At divergent boundaries, magma rises up in the gap between the two plates that are pulling apart. It then cools on either side as ridges of new crust. Recall that mid-ocean ridges form in this way at divergent boundaries on the ocean floor. The buildup of cooled magma under the sea has created the world's longest mountain chain.

Volcanic mountains can form away from plate boundaries as well. Magma plumes rising from the mantle create **hot spots** under some areas of the crust. As a plate moves over a hot spot, volcanic material can erupt through the plate, creating volcanic mountains.

Sometimes, magma rises toward the surface but doesn't break through the crust. It may push up underneath, creating a dome mountain. A **dome mountain** is a dome-shaped mound that forms in Earth's crust. Examples include the Black Hills in South Dakota and the Adirondack Mountains in New York.

Hardened magma

Dome
Dome mountains form when volcanic material bulges upward under the crust, hardening as it cools. A number of dome mountains lie to the east of the Rocky Mountains.

Erosion Mountains

Weathering and erosion continually shape Earth's landforms. Although all mountains are affected by these forces, a few mountains were formed entirely by them. These are called erosion mountains.

The Catskills in New York State are one example. The Catskills were once a plateau, or raised area of flat land. Mountains began forming during the last ice age, when glaciers carved the plateau into peaks and valleys. Later, rushing streams further sculpted the land. Today, the Catskills include 98 peaks that are more than 900 m (3,000 feet) high.

Erosion has shaped other kinds of mountains after they formed originally. The results often are irregular peaks and valleys. The Black Hills dome mountain, for example, has been eroded into the shape you see today.

The forces of glaciers, rivers, and gravity all helped shape the gentle, rolling hills of the Catskills. ▼

▲ At the Delaware Water Gap, erosion has exposed the tilted rock layers of Mount Minsi, Pennsylvania.

California's largest mountain range, the Sierra Nevada, was also shaped by erosion. Glaciers shaped some of the peaks and carved out bowls, now filled with small lakes. Glaciers also widened V-shaped mountain valleys into the U-shaped valleys now seen in parts of the Sierras.

CLASSIFY How are dome mountains different from most other mountains?

Express Lab

Activity Card 11
Make a Mountain Type

California Mountains

Most of California is on the North American Plate. Some of western California is on the Pacific Plate. The movements of these plates has helped shape the mountains of California.

The Sierra Nevada chain is a huge range of fault-block mountains. The mountains are a block of granite tilted westward from a fault that runs along their eastern edge.

Other mountain ranges in California are the result of squeezing forces that crumple and fold Earth's crust. Fold mountains have formed as a result.

About 30 million years ago, the interaction between the Pacific and North American Plates pushed up the Coast Ranges. These include the King and Santa Cruz Mountains. As the plates slipped past each other, the ocean floor folded and crumpled to form the mountains.

Mount Shasta and Lassen Peak are volcanic mountains that are part of the Cascades. The Cascade Range is a chain of volcanoes, formed where several smaller tectonic plates are subducted beneath the North American Plate.

CLASSIFY What is an example of fault-block mountains in California?

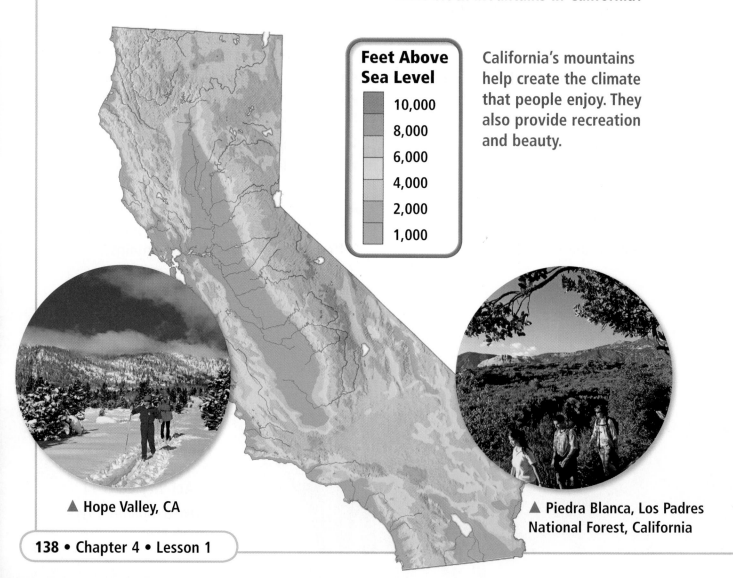

Feet Above Sea Level

10,000
8,000
6,000
4,000
2,000
1,000

California's mountains help create the climate that people enjoy. They also provide recreation and beauty.

▲ Hope Valley, CA

▲ Piedra Blanca, Los Padres National Forest, California

Visual Summary

Mountains often form at plate boundaries. Fold mountains form where continental plates collide. The moving plates fold and crumple the crust.

A fault is a fracture in Earth's crust. Fault-block mountains form when a block of crust is lifted up along a fault. Other types of mountains include volcanic, dome, and erosion mountains.

California's mountains include the Sierra Nevadas, Mount Shasta, and Lassen Peak. These mountains affect the state's climate and provide natural beauty.

STANDARDS

1.e., 1.f.

Technology
Visit **www.eduplace.com/cascp** to find out more about mountain building.

Reading Review

1 MAIN IDEA List the five types of mountains.

2 VOCABULARY Where do *fold mountains* form? Why don't they form at divergent boundaries?

3 READING SKILL Which two types of mountains are formed by volcanic activity?

Group	Group

4 CRITICAL THINKING: Synthesize You observe warped and wrinkled rock layers on the side of a tall California mountain with jagged peaks. What can you conclude about the mountain? What do you predict about its future?

5 INQUIRY SKILL: Observe Can mountain building be observed directly? Can the forces that wear down mountains be observed? Explain your answers.

 TEST PRACTICE

What best describes the Sierra Nevada mountains?

A. folded crust

B. a string of volcanoes

C. erosion mountains

D. a block of crust lifted along a fault

STANDARDS

1–3: 1.e., **4:** 1.f., **5:** 1.e., **Test Practice:** 1.f.

What Happens During an Earthquake?

Building Background

Have you felt the ground shake under your feet? Minor earthquakes strike California quite often. More serious earthquakes happen here, too.

Earthquakes begin with movements of Earth's tectonic plates. Sudden plate movements along a fault release stored energy in the rocks. Seismic waves travel outward in all directions.

STANDARDS

3.a. *Students know* energy can be carried from one place to another by heat flow or by waves, including water, light and sound waves, or by moving objects.
7.a. Develop a hypothesis.

PREPARE TO INVESTIGATE

Inquiry Skill

Record Data When you record data, you write observations and measurements in an organized way, including constructing graphs.

Materials

- short pieces of colored yarn
- meter stick
- coiled spring toy
- masking tape

Science and Math Toolbox

For step 1, review **Making a Chart to Organize Data** on page H11.

Make Waves!

Procedure

1 **Collaborate** Waves released during an earthquake are called seismic waves. Work in a group. In your *Science Notebook,* make a chart like the one shown.

2 **Experiment** Use a spring to model seismic waves. Tie a piece of yarn every 25 cm along the spring. Stretch the spring across the floor. Use tape to mark the position of one piece of yarn.

3 **Observe** As your partner holds steady the far end of the spring, shake the other end sideways over a few centimeters. This models a type of seismic wave called *S*-waves. Mark how far the yarn moved. Measure and record the distance.

4 **Record Data** Repeat step 3, shaking a bit harder or softer. Record your observations.

5 **Experiment** Place the meter stick on the floor under the spring, as shown. Align the 50-cm mark with one of the pieces of yarn. Tape the meter stick in place.

6 **Observe** Squeeze some coils together, then release them. This models a type of seismic wave called *P*-waves. Measure and record how far the yarn travels. Repeat.

Conclusion

1. **Compare** How are the two types of waves similar? How are they different? Refer to your observations of the yarn in your answer.

2. **Infer** How do you think waves transfer energy?

STEP 1

Wave Type	Trial	Distance (cm)
Transverse (S-wave)		
Longitudinal (P-wave)		

STEP 3

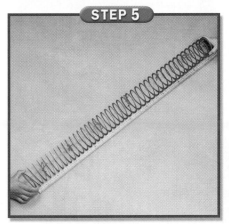
STEP 5

Guided Inquiry

Design an Experiment
Stretch two identical springs between you and a partner. Model *S*-waves in one spring and *P*-waves in the other spring. **Compare** the speeds of the two waves. What equipment or tools would let you measure the speeds?

Earthquakes

MAIN IDEA Earthquakes are caused by sudden motions along breaks in the crust called faults.

VOCABULARY

| seismic wave | p. 144 |
| seismograph | p. 146 |

READING SKILL

Cause and Effect Use the graphic organizer to identify the causes and effects of rock movement along faults.

| Cause | → | Effect |

STANDARDS

1.d. *Students know* that earthquakes are sudden motions along breaks in the crust called faults and that volcanoes and fissures are locations where magma reaches the surface.

3.a. *Students know* energy can be carried from one place to another by heat flow or by waves, including water, light and sound waves, or by moving objects.

At the Faults

Movements in Earth's crust are usually so small and slow you can't even feel them. But at times, these movements can be quick and violent, causing sudden and unexpected changes to Earth's surface. Such movements typically happen at faults. Remember that faults are cracks in the crust, typically along plate boundaries.

Earthquakes are one of these sudden changes. Why do earthquakes happen? The answer lies with the stress that builds up in rocks along faults. As you study the types of motions along faults, think about how rocks deep underground are affected.

On October 17, 1989, a powerful earthquake struck Northern California. It shook apart this freeway near downtown Oakland. ▼

Types of Faults

Faults can be classified into three main groups. The groups are based on the type of force that forms the faults and the way they move. Look at the drawings at right.

Normal faults occur at or near divergent boundaries, places where the Earth's crust is being stretched apart. Eventually, the rock breaks. A fault forms when one block moves down the edge of a sloping crack.

Most normal faults are small, with blocks of rock moving down by just a meter or so. Some faults, however, extend across many kilometers! In western United States, normal faults run along the edges of several mountains ranges, such as the Tetons and the Sierra Nevadas. Mid-ocean ridges are also typical locations for this type of fault.

Reverse faults usually occur at convergent plate boundaries, where rock is being squeezed. As the rock breaks, one block is pushed up along a sloping crack. This type of fault often occurs in regions where one plate subducts below the other.

Strike-slip faults occur where tectonic plates slide past each other at transform-fault boundaries. In contrast to the other two types of fault, the movement is horizontal, as one block grinds past the other. California's San Andreas Fault is a strike-slip fault.

CAUSE AND EFFECT What happens when stresses build up along a fault?

Normal
As sections of the crust move apart, rocks are stretched until they snap, causing one block to move down along a sloping crack.

Reverse
Rocks are compressed as they come together, causing one block to move up along a sloping crack as the other moves down.

Strike-slip
Rocks grind against each other as they move horizontally past each other in opposite directions. Pressure builds up along the fault until the rocks break.

Seismic Waves

Remember that tectonic plates move very slowly. Sometimes rocks move along easily with the plates, but they also can jam up against a plate or between two plates. Over time, stress builds up within the rock as the plates strain against each other.

Eventually, the stress becomes so great that rocks break. The plates shudder and jolt into a new position. This causes an earthquake.

The released energy travels in waves in all directions, including up to the surface. These waves are called **seismic waves.** They cause the motion that is felt as an earthquake.

Body Waves Seismic waves that travel through Earth's interior are called body waves. There are two kinds of body waves: *P*-waves and *S*-waves.

P-waves, or primary waves, are an example of longitudinal waves. Rocks move back and forth in the same direction the wave travels. *P*-waves are the fastest kind of seismic wave, traveling at about 6 km/s (3.7 mi/s) through rock.

During an earthquake, the first jolt or thud you feel is the arrival of the *P*-waves. The *P*-waves push and pull on rock along their path. As *P*-waves reach the surface, the ground cracks and crumples.

The second type of body wave is the *S*-wave, or secondary wave. *S*-waves are transverse waves. Rocks move up and down or side-to-side, at right angles to the direction the wave travels. *S*-waves are slower than *P*-waves. They are called secondary waves because they arrive after the *P*-waves in an earthquake.

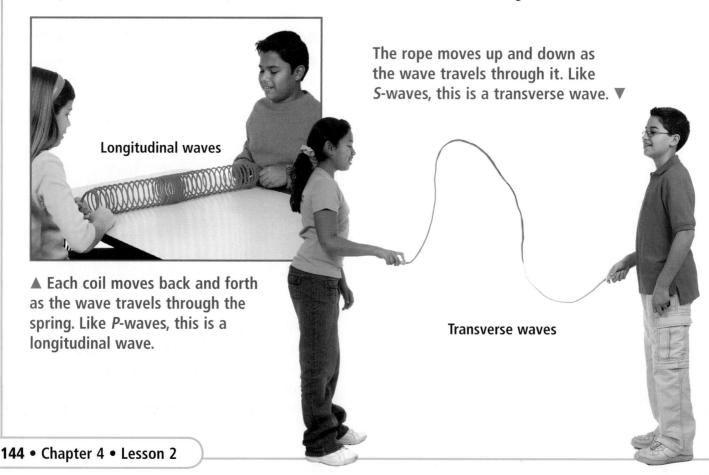

Longitudinal waves

▲ Each coil moves back and forth as the wave travels through the spring. Like *P*-waves, this is a longitudinal wave.

The rope moves up and down as the wave travels through it. Like *S*-waves, this is a transverse wave. ▼

Transverse waves

Seismic Waves

P-Waves
P-waves are the first to arrive at the surface. They are longitudinal waves.

S-Waves
S-waves come next. They are transverse waves.

L-Waves
L-waves are a type of surface wave. These are typically very destructive.

When *S*-waves hit, you might feel a strong side-to-side motion. *P*-waves can travel through solids and liquids, including Earth's liquid outer core. *S*-waves, however, can only travel through solid rock.

Surface Waves Other waves, called surface waves, travel only across Earth's surface. One type of surface wave is the *L*-wave, or Love wave. It is named for the British scientist who discovered it.

L-waves travel the slowest. They arrive just after both *P*-waves and *S*-waves. Surface waves do not travel as far from an earthquake's origin as body waves. They cause a rolling motion on the surface that can cause great damage to structures. *L*-waves often are the most destructive.

Although each type of wave differs in velocity, all seismic waves travel very fast—several kilometers per second. As Californians know, they can cause huge damage.

Scientists and engineers have learned all sorts of ways to prepare for earthquakes. But there is no way to stop them altogether.

CAUSE AND EFFECT Compare the surface movements caused by *P*-waves and *S*-waves.

Express Lab

Activity Card 12
Model Waves

Recording Seismic Waves

When an earthquake strikes, scientists can quickly locate its origin and measure its strength. This is possible because of a huge network of instruments that monitor movement in Earth's crust. The network covers California especially well.

Seismographs are the main tool for measuring the strength and duration of an earthquake. A **seismograph** detects and measures the amount of ground motion during a quake. Scientists interpret these data to measure the strength of an earthquake, also called its magnitude.

A seismograph produces a written trace of seismic waves called a seismogram. Data are recorded as lines on a drum or by a computer.

One type of seismograph measures horizontal motion. It consists of a rotating drum attached firmly to the bedrock underground. A weighted pen is suspended over the drum like a pendulum. The pen marks the paper wrapped around the rotating drum.

When a quake strikes, the drum attached to the bedrock moves with Earth's motion. The suspended pen does not move. So it traces the movement of the drum beneath it.

Seismographs also record aftershocks, which are smaller earthquakes that follow the first one. Aftershocks can occur for several days after an earthquake. Some aftershocks are destructive.

CAUSE AND EFFECT In what order do waves appear on a seismogram?

Typically on a seismogram, *P*–waves appear first, followed by larger *S*–waves. Surface waves come last. They often are the most powerful and destructive waves.

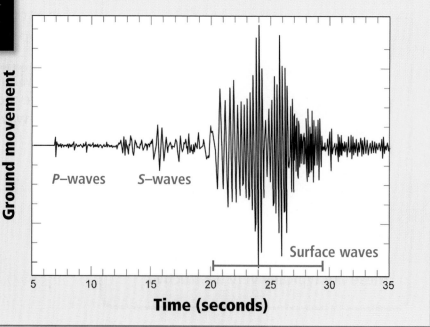

P–waves   *S*–waves   Surface waves

Ground movement

Time (seconds)

5   10   15   20   25   30   35

Visual Summary

Sudden movements along faults cause earthquakes. Rocks build up stress along moving plate boundaries, then suddenly release energy as they break. Seismic waves travel to the surface.

Examples of seismic waves include *P*-waves, *S*-waves, and surface waves. Each travels in a different way. Surface waves often carry the most energy and cause the most damage.

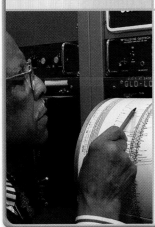

Scientists measure the strength of earthquakes by using a tool called a seismograph. The seismic waves appear as wavy lines that show how the ground is moving.

 STANDARDS

1.d., 3.a.

Technology
Visit **www.eduplace.com/cascp** to find out more about faults and earthquakes.

Reading Review

1 MAIN IDEA Where do most earthquakes begin?

2 VOCABULARY Compare how different types of *seismic waves* move through rock.

3 READING SKILL Tectonic plates move very slowly. Why do their motions cause sudden, violent events such as earthquakes?

Cause ➡ Effect

4 CRITICAL THINKING: Apply You are sitting at home and you feel a small jolt. A few seconds later, the ground starts to shake more violently. Explain the events you just experienced.

5 INQUIRY SKILL: Record Data What if you were asked to design a new tool to measure the strength of seismic waves? Is it important that the invention work automatically, at all times of the day? Explain.

 TEST PRACTICE

Which of these is NOT a type of seismic wave?

A. surface wave

B. secondary wave

C. interior wave

D. primary wave

 STANDARDS

1: 1.d., **2:** 3.a., **3:** 1.d., **4–5:** 3.a., **Test Practice:** 3.a.

147

How Are Earthquakes Located and Measured?

Building Background

When an earthquake strikes California, scientists very quickly know its epicenter and strength. The epicenter is the point on the surface just above the center of the earthquake underground.

By studying earthquakes, scientists have learned how people can prepare for them—and survive them. In the future, they may be able to predict earthquakes, too.

 STANDARDS

1.g. *Students know* how to determine the epicenter of an earthquake and know that the effects of an earthquake on any region vary, depending on the size of the earthquake, the distance of the region from the epicenter, the local geology, and the type of construction in the region.
7.b. Select and use appropriate tools and technology (including calculators, computers, balances, spring scales, microscopes, and binoculars) to perform tests, collect data, and display data.

PREPARE TO INVESTIGATE

Inquiry Skill

Measure When you measure, you select and use appropriate tools and units to make numerical observations.

Materials

- calculator
- drawing compass
- ruler
- outline map of the United States

Locating an Earthquake

Arrival Time of Seismic Waves for 3 Cities (hr: min: sec)			
City	Tucson, AZ	Billings, MT	Houston, TX
P-wave	5:06:35	5:07:10	5:09:10
S-wave	5:08:50	5:10:00	5:13:35
Difference	_____	_____	_____
Distance (km)	_____	_____	_____
Scaled Distance	_____	_____	_____

Procedure

1. **Collaborate** Work with a partner. Copy the table into your *Science Notebook.*

2. **Analyze Data** For each city, calculate and record the difference in seconds between the arrival times of *P*-waves and *S*-waves. Remember that 1 minute equals 60 seconds.

3. **Use Numbers** To find the distance from each city to the epicenter, multiply the time differences from step 2 by 8.6 km/s.

4. **Use Numbers** For each distance you calculated, use the scale of the outline map to calculate the corresponding distance on the map.

5. **Measure** Locate each city on the map. Use the ruler and drawing compass to draw a circle around each city. The radius should be the distance you calculated in step 4.

STEP 5

Conclusion

1. **Analyze Data** Where did the three circles intersect? What does this indicate? Explain.

2. **Draw Conclusions** What are the fewest number of locations needed to locate an epicenter? Explain your answer.

Guided Inquiry

Ask Questions Only a few earthquakes are serious events. Most are too weak for people to feel. How often do earthquakes strike in California and elsewhere? **Research** this question. Show the data in a graph.

Locating Quakes

MAIN IDEA Scientists can locate earthquakes and measure their strength. Earthquakes damage human and wildlife habitats.

Focus and Epicenter

When an earthquake strikes, scientists are able to locate its center very quickly. The **focus** of an earthquake is the point underground where the earthquake begins. The point on the surface directly above the focus is called the **epicenter.** The epicenter is often where the quake is most strongly felt and the damage is greatest.

To find the epicenter, scientists analyze data from seismographs. Recall that *P*-waves and *S*-waves travel at different speeds through the ground. The difference in their arrival times corresponds to the distance to the epicenter. By calculating distances from three or more seismograph stations, the epicenter can be pinpointed precisely.

To find the epicenter of an earthquake, scientists draw a circle around each seismograph station. Each radius is the distance to the epicenter, where the circles meet. ▼

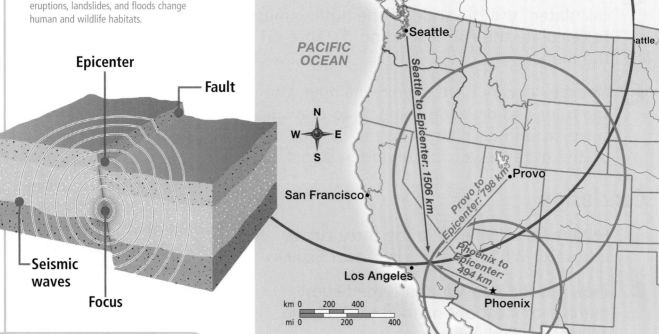

Measuring Earthquakes

Earthquakes can release a huge amount of energy, or very little. It depends on how much rock breaks at a fault and how far rocks shift.

Scientists usually measure earthquakes in one of two ways. The first is **intensity**—a measure of the amount of damage the quake produces.

Intensity scales depend on observations of earthquake effects. The most widely used intensity scale is the Modified Mercalli scale. The scale has intensity numbers that run from I (no damage) to XII (almost total destruction). See the table on page 152.

In 1935, Charles Richter devised the Richter scale to measure earthquake magnitude. **Magnitude** is the amount of energy that an earthquake releases. It is a more precise measure of the strength of an earthquake than observed damage.

The Richter scale is based on seismograph readings. Each increase in whole numbers on the Richter scale represents a 10-fold increase in ground shaking. So during a magnitude 6 quake, the ground shakes 10 times as much as during a magnitude 5 quake.

The table and map show major earthquakes that have struck California. Minor, low-magnitude earthquakes strike much more frequently.

MAIN IDEA What determines the amount of energy an earthquake releases?

In California, major earthquakes can and do strike anywhere along the San Andreas Fault. ▼

Richter Scale	Place and Date of Earthquake
Major Earthquakes in California	
8.25	San Francisco; April 18, 1906
7.4	Yucca Valley; June 28, 1992
7.1	Loma Prieta; Oct. 17–18, 1989
6.7	Northridge; Jan. 17, 1994
6.6	Superstition Hills; Nov. 24, 1987

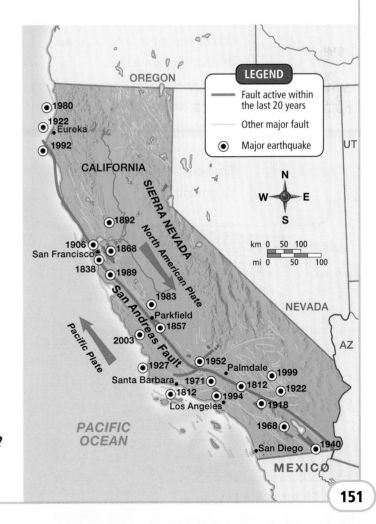

Modified Mercalli Scale

Scale	Observations
I to III	Minimally felt
IV	Felt indoors, like a heavy truck passing by
V	Felt by all, trees and poles shake
VI	Moves furniture, loosens plaster
VII	Damages poorly built houses and buildings
VIII	Damages most buildings, walls collapse
IX	Cracks appear in ground, mass destruction, landslides
X	Ground badly cracked, buildings and foundations destroyed
XI to XII	Total destruction, waves seen on ground

Effects of Earthquakes

Thousands of earthquakes happen each year. The most serious cause landslides and destroy plants, animals, and their habitats. In cities, they damage buildings, crack open gas and water mains, start fires, and fell trees and power lines.

Several factors determine the effects of earthquakes. Recall that shaking is strongest at the epicenter. In general, shaking decreases with distance from this point. The strength of the earthquake and how long it lasts also help determine its effects.

The makeup of Earth's surface in the quake zone is also important. Shaking tends to be more intense on ground with loose or soft soils, or over landfills. In fact, an area of hard stable bedrock close to the epicenter might suffer less damage than an area with loose soils farther away.

In 1989, the Loma Prieta earthquake helped prove this point. Years before, engineers had dumped rock and soil to fill in part of San Francisco Bay. This part of San Francisco, called the Marina District, suffered much more shaking and damage than other parts of the city.

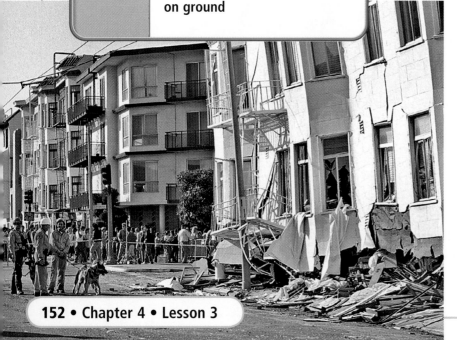

◄ The loosely-packed ground under San Francisco's Marina District led to great damage from the Loma Prieta earthquake.

Preparing for Earthquakes

In 1906, a powerful earthquake toppled or damaged nearly every building in San Francisco. About 80 years later, the Loma Prieta earthquake left the city damaged, but not nearly as ruined as before.

What caused the difference? The city was much better prepared! Today, buildings in California are constructed to withstand earthquakes. Laws require earthquake-resistant construction in many new structures, especially schools, hospitals, and dams.

Small structures are anchored strongly to their foundations. Concrete-covered steel rods strengthen walls. In some larger buildings, special foundations absorb much of the ground motion and cushion buildings against shocks. Buildings are made of flexible materials such as wood, rather than bricks that break and crumble.

Laws also require older buildings to be made safer. In many cases, braces are added to bind walls more securely to foundations and roofs.

To keep safe during an earthquake, remember to follow some simple rules. If you're inside, duck under a table or stand under a door frame. Stay away from windows and walls. If you're outside, move away from buildings, power lines, and tall trees.

Always keep a battery-operated radio in your home. During an earthquake or other emergency, listen for news and instructions.

MAIN IDEA **What affects the damage done by an earthquake?**

A triangle-shaped framework is very stable. It helps this building stand during an earthquake. So does the hinge-like reinforcement shown in the inset. ▼

Tsunamis

Earthquakes can also strike under the ocean. They can cause a **tsunami,** a huge sea wave produced by an earthquake, a landslide, or volcanic eruption on the ocean floor.

A tsunami isn't noticeable in deep water in the middle of the ocean. But the waves rise as they approach the shallow coast. Sea level can rise 30 meters (90 feet) above normal, sweeping away people and structures on shore.

The most deadly tsunami ever recorded occurred in the Indian Ocean on December 26, 2004. A huge undersea earthquake struck near the coast of Indonesia's island of Sumatra. It sent waves as high as 9 m (30 feet) crashing into the shores of eastern India, Thailand, and other areas of Southeast Asia and East

▲ The Indian Ocean tsunami of 2004 was one of the worst natural disasters in history. Why are tsunamis so difficult to predict?

Africa. More than 200,000 people were killed.

Not all undersea earthquakes cause tsunamis, so they are often hard to predict. Today, scientists use instruments called tsunameters.

The instruments are anchored to the ocean floor and can detect changes in water pressure. When that happens, they beam a signal to a satellite, which signals tsunami warning centers.

A detection system is now in place in the Pacific Ocean. But no system existed in the Indian Ocean in 2004. World leaders hope to establish one.

MAIN IDEA What causes a tsunami?

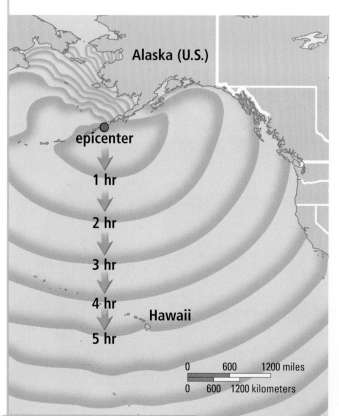

Alaska (U.S.)

epicenter

1 hr

2 hr

3 hr

4 hr

Hawaii

5 hr

0   600   1200 miles
0   600 1200 kilometers

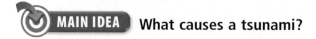

◄ In 1946, an earthquake in Alaska caused a deadly tsunami in Hawaii, nearly 5,000 kilometers away. Tsunamis may travel as fast as 950 km/h (600 mi/h).

Visual Summary

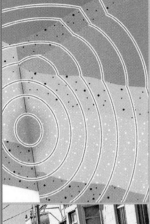

The epicenter of an earthquake is the point on the surface directly above the focus. Scientists analyze seismograms to determine the epicenter.

The effects of earthquakes depend on several factors, including strength of the earthquake, distance from the epicenter, rocks and soil in the ground, and building construction.

Earthquakes and tsunamis can destroy land and human habitats. Earthquakes can strike any time, so people should be prepared.

 STANDARDS

1.g., 2.d.

 Technology
Visit **www.eduplace.com/cascp** to find out more about earthquakes.

Reading Review

❶ MAIN IDEA What do magnitude and intensity measure about an earthquake?

❷ VOCABULARY Compare an earthquake's *focus* and its *epicenter*.

❸ READING SKILL Why is magnitude a better measure of the strength of earthquakes than intensity?

❹ CRITICAL THINKING: Evaluate A California family is building a new house. They want to make the house more earthquake resistant. What factors should the family evaluate?

❺ INQUIRY SKILL: Measure How do scientists pinpoint the epicenter of an earthquake?

 TEST PRACTICE
A tsunami typically forms after _____.

A. an earthquake strikes the ocean floor

B. a large fault opens on land

C. a mountain builds up

D. an earthquake strikes anywhere

STANDARDS

1: 2.d., **2:** 1.g., **3–4:** 2.d., **5:** 1.g., **Test Practice:** 2.d.

Predicting Earthquakes

When and where will the next major earthquake strike? Finding the answer could save lives and property.

Scientists are working hard to learn more about faults and to develop ways to predict earthquakes. As shown on these two pages, new technology is helping them.

Global Positioning System (GPS)

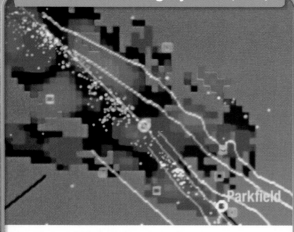

Parkfield

GPS allows scientists to accurately locate positions on Earth, including those near faults. By measuring and comparing positions of ground stations over time, scientists can track fault movements.

Lasers

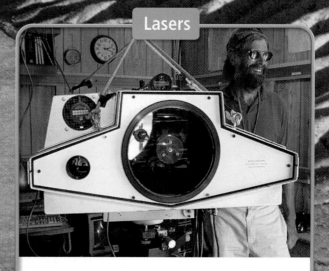

A technique using laser beams can measure a 12-km distance to within a millimeter! Scientists are using lasers to measure movements along the fault.

STANDARDS
1.d. *Students know* that earthquakes are sudden motions along breaks in the crust called faults and that volcanoes and fissures are locations where magma reaches the surface.
1.e. *Students know* major geologic events, such as earthquakes, volcanic eruptions, and mountain building, result from plate motions.

MATH

The San Andreas Fault Observatory at Depth (SAFOD)

The San Andreas Fault

This fault lies along the plate boundary that cuts across California. Movement along the fault causes California's earthquakes.

This is a deep borehole being drilled into the San Andreas Fault! It will house instruments and let scientists collect samples. Scientists will use these data to improve their earthquake models.

Sharing Ideas

1. **READING CHECK** How are scientists using technology to study earthquakes?

2. **WRITE ABOUT IT** Do you think scientists will be able to predict earthquakes in the future? Explain why or why not.

3. **TALK ABOUT IT** How else are people using GPS and laser technology?

How Do Volcanoes Form?

Building Background

More than 500 active volcanoes are spread around Earth. About 15 of them erupt each week. They can spew fiery hot lava and gases, and blast rock and ash high into the air.

PREPARE TO INVESTIGATE

Inquiry Skill

Infer When you infer, you use known facts and logical reasoning to make interpretations.

Materials

- pencil
- modeling clay
- cardboard
- white glue

 STANDARDS

1.d. *Students know* that earthquakes are sudden motions along breaks in the crust called faults and that volcanoes and fissures are locations where magma reaches the surface.
7.d. Communicate the steps and results from an investigation in written reports and oral presentations.

Volcano Model

Procedure

Safety: Wear goggles for this activity.

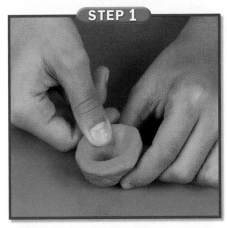
STEP 1

1. **Collaborate** Work with a partner. Shape modeling clay into a small hollow cone, about the size of a thimble. Give the cone thick walls without holes. This is your model volcano.

2. **Use Models** Hold the volcano upside down and carefully fill it with glue. Then press the cardboard against the glue and the bottom rim of the volcano. Press more clay around the rim to seal the glue tightly inside.

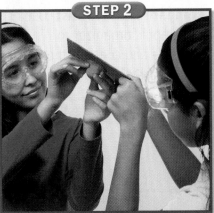
STEP 2

3. **Use Models** Carefully turn over the cardboard and volcano, as shown in the photo. Use the pencil to make a hole in the top of the volcano.

4. **Observe** Quickly squeeze the sides of the volcano. Step back and observe the results.

STEP 3

5. **Record Data** In your *Science Notebook*, draw and label a diagram of your model volcano. Continue watching the volcano every 5 minutes for 20 minutes. Record what you observe.

Conclusion

1. **Compare** How does your model compare to a real volcano? Describe the similarities and differences.

2. **Infer** When a volcano erupts, how can it change the land around it?

Guided Inquiry

Ask Questions Volcanoes can be very destructive. Do they provide any benefits to Earth's land and people? **Research** answers to this question. Discuss what you learn with the class.

Volcanoes

cinder cone volcano	p. 162
composite volcano	p. 162
island arc	p. 161
lava	p. 160
shield volcano	p. 163

READING SKILL

Compare and Contrast Use the graphic organizer to compare and contrast the three types of volcanoes.

Compare	Contrast

STANDARDS

1.d. *Students know* that earthquakes are sudden motions along breaks in the crust called faults and that volcanoes and fissures are locations where magma reaches the surface.
2.d. *Students know* earthquakes, volcanic eruptions, landslides, and floods change human and wildlife habitats.

MAIN IDEA Volcanoes form where magma reaches Earth's surface.

Inside a Volcano

A **volcano** is an opening in Earth's crust through which melted rock, hot gases, rock fragments, and ash reach the surface. The melted rock beneath Earth's crust is magma. Gas-filled magma rises toward the surface because it is less dense than the solid rock around it.

Near the surface, magma can burst through an opening or a weak area in the crust as lava. **Lava** is magma that reaches Earth's surface. Over time, the cooling lava can build up around the opening, forming a volcanic mountain. Such a mountain is also called a volcano.

Different types of material may be ejected from a volcano, and all of them are very hot. Lava may be hotter than 1,100°C (2,000°F). Rock fragments, dust, ash, steam, and a variety of gases can also burst from a volcano and scald anything in their paths.

Inside an Erupting Volcano
A volcano may erupt through one or more side vents as well as its central vent. The mountain forms from layers of lava, ash, and other debris.

Volcanoes and Plate Tectonics

If you look at a map, you will notice that volcanoes seem to cluster in some areas. They are especially common around the rim of the Pacific Ocean.

Because so many volcanoes and earthquakes occur around the Pacific Ocean, it is often called the Ring of Fire. The Ring exists because of the many plate boundaries there.

Volcanoes often form at convergent plate boundaries. In places where an ocean plate and a continental plate meet, the ocean plate is pushed under the land plate. As the edge of the ocean plate dives into the mantle, its leading edge melts into magma. The magma rises and bursts through cracks in the crust. The volcanoes of California's Cascade Range formed in this way.

Volcanoes also form where two oceanic plates meet. In this case, one plate is pushed under the other. A trench forms at the boundary. Just as when land-sea plates meet, magma rises through cracks in Earth's surface. Eventually, volcanoes build up from the ocean floor.

These volcanoes may form a string of islands called an **island arc.** The Aleutian Islands of Alaska are an example.

COMPARE AND CONTRAST Compare different ways that a chain of volcanoes may form.

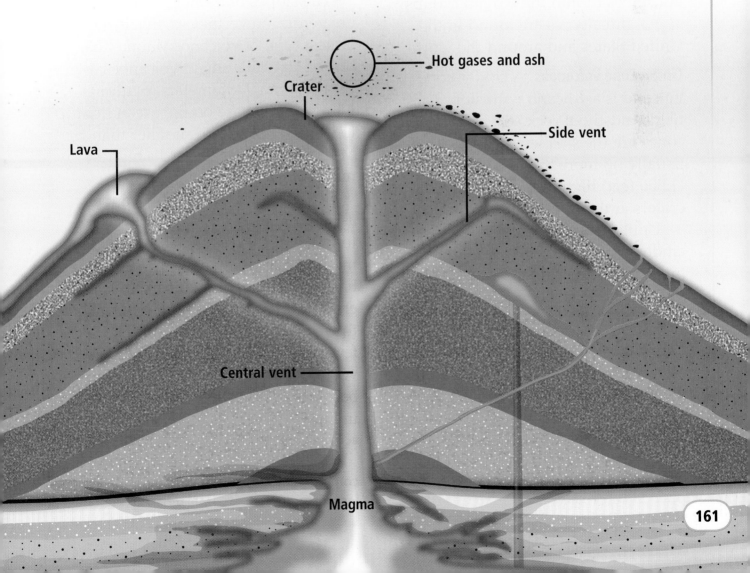

Hot gases and ash

Crater

Side vent

Lava

Central vent

Magma

Classifying Volcanoes

Not all volcanoes are alike. One reason is that they erupt in different ways. The lava's thickness and the amount of dissolved gases can affect the eruption.

As magma rises in a volcano, pressure decreases and gases can escape. Thick lava traps water vapor and other gases in huge pockets. As the magma rises, pressure builds until the gases are released, carrying magma and rock in a huge eruption. When magma is thinner, gases bubble out easily, and the eruption is gentler.

Scientists use characteristics such as type of eruption, shape, and structure to classify volcanoes. Most volcanoes fit into three main groups. All three types are found in the United States and around the world.

Cinder Cone Volcanoes A **cinder cone volcano** is a volcano with slopes made mostly of rock and ash. Cinder cones are the smallest volcanoes— usually no more than 500 meters (1,500 feet) high. Most have deep craters at their summits.

Unlike other types of volcanoes, cinder cones are usually produced by just one eruption. Sunset Crater in Arizona is a cinder cone volcano.

Composite Volcanoes A **composite volcano** is composed of alternating layers of lava and ash. Composite volcanoes are cone-shaped and have steep slopes. They are often called stratovolcanoes. Each eruption of a composite volcano adds a layer of volcanic material to its slope.

Composite volcanoes often explode violently because their thick lava traps gas underneath. Washington's Mount Rainier and Japan's Mount Fuji are both composite volcanoes. Another example is Mount Saint Helens, in Washington, which erupted explosively in 1980. It also spewed steam and ash in 2004.

Shield Volcanoes A **shield volcano** has a gentle slope and is made almost entirely of layer upon layer of lava. Shield volcanoes often have several vents, or openings. The thin, smooth lava of a shield volcano flows quickly and without the explosiveness of composite volcanoes.

The slopes of a shield volcano are gentle. Nevertheless, this is the largest type of volcano. Mauna Loa, one of Hawaii's shield volcanoes, is more than 9 kilometers (6 miles) high from its base on the ocean floor to its top. That makes it taller than Mount Everest, the world's highest mountain on land.

Scientists also classify volcanoes as active, dormant, or extinct. These terms refer to when and if a volcano might erupt again. An active volcano has erupted recently or is likely to erupt soon. (For volcanoes, however, the recent past could have been a few hundred years ago!) A dormant volcano is not active, but could become so. An extinct volcano is unlikely to erupt again.

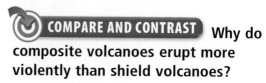 **COMPARE AND CONTRAST** Why do composite volcanoes erupt more violently than shield volcanoes?

Cinder Cone Volcano

A single eruption piled these ashes into a cone shape.

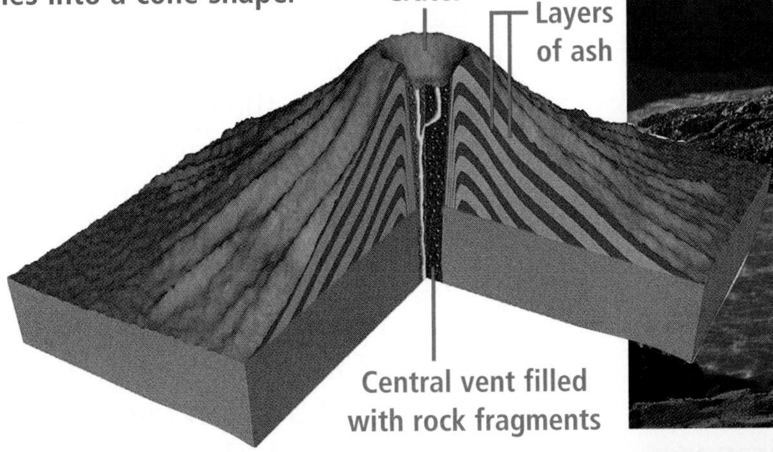

Crater

Layers of ash

Central vent filled with rock fragments

Mount Rinjani, Indonesia

Composite Volcano

Each eruption adds a new layer along the slope. Mount Fuji in Japan last erupted in 1707.

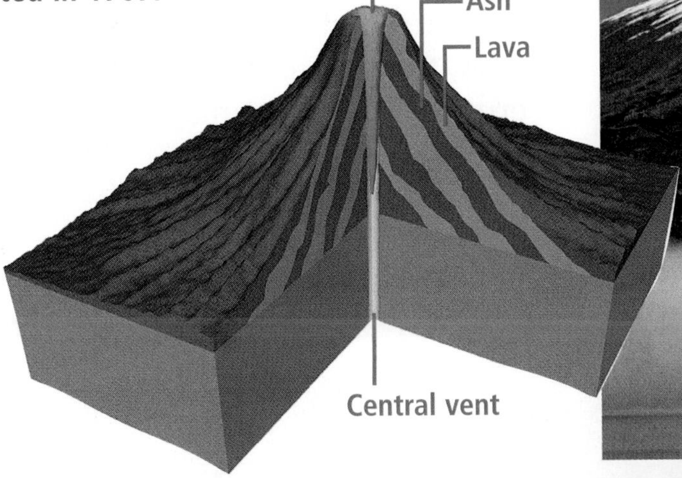

Crater

Ash

Lava

Central vent

Mount Fuji, Japan

Shield Volcano

Most shield volcanoes have bases on the ocean floor. The islands of Hawaii are all shield volcanoes.

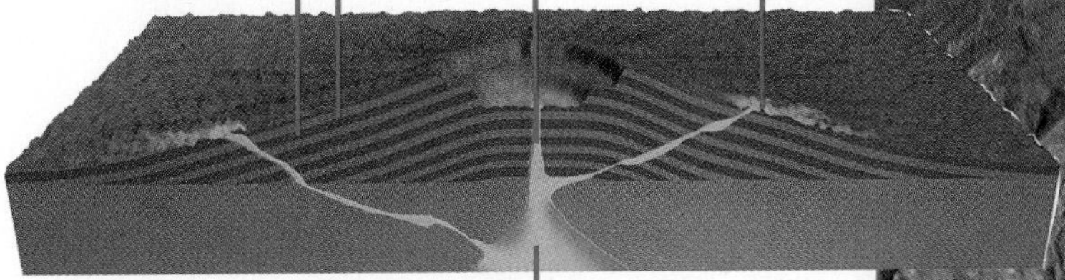

Layers of lava

Central vent

Lava flow

Magma

Mauna Loa, Hawaii

163

Effects of Volcanoes

Like earthquakes, volcanic eruptions can quickly change Earth's surface. Volcanic eruptions do have some helpful results. Weathered lava produces very fertile soil near volcanoes. But most often, volcanoes are hazards for people who live near them. Volcanic eruptions can set fires to forests, expel hot and poisonous gases, kill wildlife and bury their habitats — even destroy whole cities.

Records of destructive volcanoes go back thousands of years. In A.D. 79, Vesuvius in modern-day Italy erupted suddenly. For hours, the volcano showered the nearby town of Pompeii with ash and rock. Then a deadly cloud of hot gases swept down from the volcano. About 2,000 people died.

In 1883, the volcanic island Krakatau blew itself apart. The eruption produced a huge tsunami that killed more than 30,000 people.

More recently, the explosive eruption of Mount Saint Helens in 1980 greatly changed the landscape in the northwestern United States. It also killed dozens of people.

The eruption blew the top off the mountain. Hot gases rushed outward, leaving burned trees on the ground like matchsticks. A plume of ash blanketed towns more than 100 kilometers (62 miles) away.

Scientists monitor many active volcanoes around the world. By studying seismographs and measuring physical changes to the land, they can predict when an eruption is upcoming.

Hot ash from Mount Saint Helens killed trees and destroyed habitats. Fortunately, scientists had warned people to leave the area. ▼

California's Volcanoes

California's largest volcanoes are two mountains of the Cascade Range—Mount Shasta and Lassen Peak. They are at the southern end of a chain that runs to British Columbia in Canada. Mount Saint Helens is one of the volcanoes in this chain.

The Cascades volcanoes formed in a zone where two small oceanic plates—the Gorda Plate and the Juan de Fuca Plate—are diving under the North American Plate. Recall that in such areas, the plate's edge melts as it dives into the mantle. The newly formed magma rises through the crust to form a chain of volcanic mountains.

Mount Shasta, California's largest volcano, has not erupted for more than 200 years. But Lassen Peak released steam, ash, and lava in a series of eruptions between 1914 and 1921.

The eruption of Lassen Peak was the last major volcanic eruption in California. Lava swept away some buildings, and a hot cloud of gas burned nearby trees. But there was little other damage because few towns or people were in the area.

COMPARE AND CONTRAST What is the difference between a dormant volcano and an extinct one?

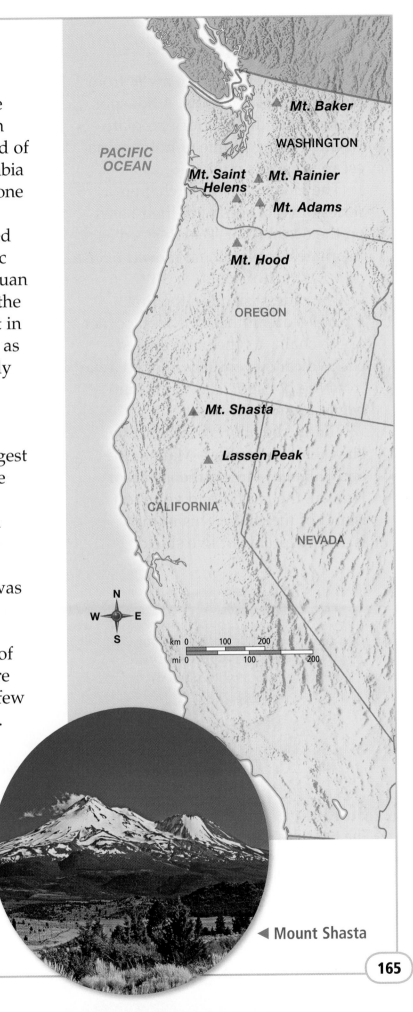

The map shows several volcanic mountains of the Cascade Range. California's Mount Shasta is in Siskiyou County, close to the Oregon border.

◀ Mount Shasta

Hawaiian Islands

Some volcanoes form away from plate edges at hot spots. A hot spot is an area in the interior of a plate where a rising plume of hot magma escapes Earth's crust.

The Hawaiian island chain is a series of volcanoes with their bases on the ocean floor. They formed as the plate carrying them moved over a mid-Pacific hot spot.

The oldest islands—the first formed—are in the northwest corner of the chain. As the plate moved, each volcano eventually moved away from the hot spot. A new volcano began to grow east of it.

Today, the only recently active Hawaiian volcanoes—Mauna Loa and Kilauea—are on the island of Hawaii, the largest and youngest island of the chain. This island is actually made of five shield volcanoes that have grown together. The island is still over the hot spot, but is moving away.

Fed by magma from the hot spot, a new volcano is emerging southeast of Hawaii. It is named Loihi. In time, Loihi will break through the ocean's surface and become the newest island in the Hawaiian chain.

COMPARE AND CONTRAST How do the islands of Hawaii compare to volcanoes on land?

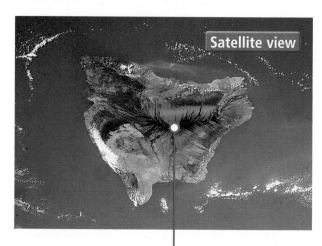

Satellite view

Mauna Loa

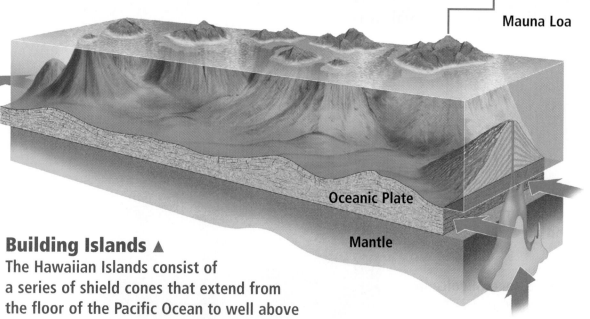

Oceanic Plate

Mantle

Building Islands ▲

The Hawaiian Islands consist of a series of shield cones that extend from the floor of the Pacific Ocean to well above its surface. As the crust continues to move over the magma plume, new mountains form.

The oceanic plate moves across the hot spot.

Visual Summary

Most volcanoes form at plate boundaries. Volcanoes are especially common along the edges of the Pacific Ocean, a region called the Ring of Fire.

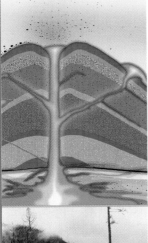

Volcanoes are locations where magma reaches Earth's surface. Three common types of volcanoes are cinder cone, composite, and shield volcanoes.

A volcanic eruption can change the natural environment and human habitats. Hot lava and ashes can scorch anything they contact. Over time, they enrich the soil for new life.

STANDARDS

1.d., 2.d.

Technology
Visit **www.eduplace.com/cascp** to find out more about volcanoes.

Reading Review

❶ MAIN IDEA At which types of plate boundary do most volcanoes form?

❷ VOCABULARY What is the difference between *magma* and *lava*?

❸ READING SKILL Compare and contrast the eruption of a shield volcano with that of a composite volcano. Explain the difference.

Compare	Contrast

❹ CRITICAL THINKING: Analyze There are no volcanoes along California's San Andreas Fault. Why do you think this so?

❺ INQUIRY SKILL: Infer Study the photo on page 164. What can you infer about the land before the volcanic eruption?

 TEST PRACTICE
Which of these is NOT a type of volcano?

A. cinder cone

B. shield

C. composite

D. tsunami

 **STANDARDS**
1–4: 1.d., **5:** 2.d., **Test Practice:** 1.d.

STANDARDS 1.d. *Students know* that earthquakes are sudden motions along breaks in the crust called faults and that volcanoes and fissures are locations where magma reaches the surface.

SLEEPING GIANT ERUPTS!

Talk about waking up on the wrong side of the bed!

Snowcapped Mount St. Helens slept for a hundred years. Then on May 18, 1980, the volcano blew its top in one of the greatest explosions in recorded history. The sideways blast blew down enough trees to build 300,000 homes. Debris over 182 meters deep even blocked nearby rivers!

Before the eruption, the mountain was 2,949 meters tall. Afterward it was 400 meters shorter! Recently, the volcano has shown new signs of activity. Scientists are monitoring underground magma closely to determine if another major eruption will occur.

In 1980, plumes of ash reached ▶ a height of 24 km.

The View from Inside
This picture is taken from inside the blown-out top of Mount St. Helens. Here you can see the inner walls of the volcano's cone.

steam plume

Danger Mounting
This rising, steaming lump is called a lava dome. As magma pushes up from underneath, it rises higher and higher—until the next big eruption. When will it be?

Writing Journal
Mount St. Helens' blast reached a speed of 1,078 km/hr. Calculate how soon the blast would reach a point 10 km away.

LINKS
for Home and School

Math in Science

The map shows the state of Hawaii. Each island is the top portion of one or more volcanoes. The volcanoes extend down to the ocean floor.

1. Using the map key and a ruler, calculate the distance in kilometers from Honolulu to Hilo.

2. If an airplane flies at a speed of 250 km/h, how long will it take to fly from Honolulu to Hilo?

3. Topography is a description of the surface features of the land. Predict the topography of any of the Hawaiian Islands. Where is the land flat, and where is it mountainous? Explain your answer.

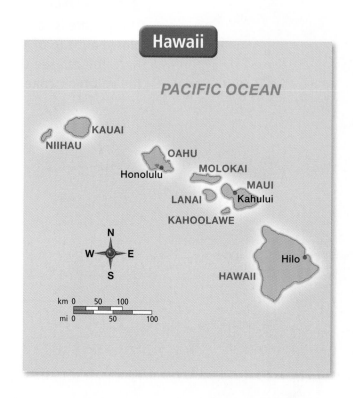

Hawaii

PACIFIC OCEAN

KAUAI
NIIHAU
OAHU
Honolulu
MOLOKAI
MAUI
LANAI   Kahului
KAHOOLAWE

N
W   E
S

Hilo

HAWAII

km 0   50   100
mi 0   50   100

Writing in Science
Expository

Prepare an information card that gives a step-by-step procedure to follow for Earthquake Safety. The card should explain the dangers of earthquakes and why safety is important.

Peter Malin

If you were studying earthquakes, how would you want to measure them? Scientist Peter Malin wants to place seismographs and other tools as close to an earthquake's focus as possible—several kilometers below the surface!

Professor Malin and other scientists are working on a project called SAFOD, which stands for San Andreas Fault Observatory at Depth. The project involves drilling down 3.2 kilometers into the fault. By installing tools to measure pressure, temperature, rock strain, and other data, Malin and his colleagues hope to discover just what happens when an earthquake strikes.

Part of Malin's challenge is to build instruments that can work deep underground. At a depth of 2 kilometers, temperatures are high enough to boil water. The air pressure is three times greater than on the surface.

◄ The task of building the observatory is much like drilling for oil.

Vocabulary

Complete each sentence with a term from the list.

1. A(n) ____ is used to record seismic waves.

2. Magma that reaches Earth's surface is called ____.

3. A volcano made entirely of layers of lava is a(n) ____.

4. Mountains that form when plates collide and cause Earth's crust to crumple and fold are ____.

5. A volcano with slopes made mostly of rock and ash is a(n) ____.

6. A huge wave produced by an earthquake, landslide, or volcanic eruption on the ocean floor is a(n) ____.

7. Mountains that form from a block of crust that is pushed up along a fault are ____.

8. Waves set in motion by earthquakes are called ____.

9. A dome-shaped mound that forms in Earth's crust is a(n) ____.

10. A volcano made of alternating layers of lava and ash is a(n) ____.

cinder cone volcano p. 162
composite volcano p. 162
dome mountain p. 136
epicenter p. 150
fault-block mountain
　　　 p. 135
focus p. 150
fold mountain p. 134
hot spot p. 136
intensity p. 151
island arc p. 161
lava p. 160
magnitude p. 146
seismic wave p. 144
seismograph p. 146
shield volcano p. 162
tsunami p. 154
volcano p. 136

 Test Practice

Write the letter of the best answer choice.

11. How are longitudinal and transverse waves different?

　　A. Only one is produced by earthquakes.
　　B. One causes damage, and the other does not.
　　C. They cause different motions in rock and on the ground.
　　D. Earthquakes produce one, and volcanoes produce the other.

12. Where do hot spots form?

　　A. the interior part of tectonic plates
　　B. at convergent plate boundaries
　　C. at divergent plate boundaries
　　D. where faults break Earth's surface

13. The San Andreas Fault is an example of a ____.

　　A. strike-slip fault
　　B. reverse fault
　　C. normal fault
　　D. mid-ocean ridge

14. Where is an earthquake's epicenter?

　　A. underneath the focus
　　B. on the surface, directly above the focus
　　C. at the point of greatest damage
　　D. at the point underground where an earthquake begins

Inquiry Skills

15. **Observe** A convergent plate boundary runs through an area. It is a place where a continental plate collides with an oceanic plate. What would you observe on land in the area of the plate boundary?

16. Two earthquakes occur in different places within days of each other. The first quake causes much more damage than the second quake. Some people conclude that the first quake was much stronger than the second. Is there enough evidence to support that conclusion? Explain.

Map the Concept

Fill in the concept map to identify characteristics of the major types of volcanoes.

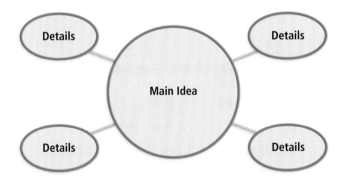

Details

Details

Main Idea

Details

Details

STANDARDS

1: 1.e., **2:** 1.d., **3:** 1.d., **4:** 1.e., **5:** 1.e., **6:** 1.e., **7:** 1.e., **8:** 1.d., **9:** 1.d., **10:** 1.d., **11:** 1.d., **12:** 1.e., **13:** 1.e., **14:** 1.f., **15:** 1.e., **16:** 1.e., **Map the Concept:** 1.d., **17:** 2.d., **18:** 1.d., **19:** 1.e., **20:** 2.d., **Performance Assessment:** 1.e.

Critical Thinking

17. **Apply** After a major volcanic eruption, scientists study the population of deer in forests near the volcano. What do you think they will find? Explain your answer.

18. **Synthesize** The Great Plains is a huge region that covers much of the interior of North America. There are no active volcanoes on the Great Plains. Offer a possible explanation.

19. **Analyze** In the seconds after an earthquake occurs, people in homes a few miles from the epicenter feel the ground move with a rolling motion. What is causing the motion?

20. **Evaluate** The state of California has passed laws that make it illegal for people to build homes near fault lines. Why do you think such laws were enacted?

Performance Assessment

Draw a Map

Draw a map of California that includes the San Andreas Fault. Include symbols for major volcanoes and major earthquakes that have occurred in the last 50 years. Write a short description that explains the relationship between earthquakes, volcanoes, plate boundaries, and faults.

Writing Journal

Review your answers to the Lesson Preview questions.

Write the letter of the best answer choice.

1. The tectonic plates are pieces of Earth's _____.

   A. inner core
   B. outer core
   C. asthenosphere
   D. lithosphere

2. The continents were once all together, as shown below, as a supercontinent called _____.

   A. Gondwanaland
   B. Pangaea
   C. Utopia
   D. Wegener

3. Partly melted rock that is heated moves upward in a process called convection. This happens because the partly melted rock is _____ than rock around it.

   A. heavier
   B. more fluid
   C. smoother
   D. less dense

4. Which picture best demonstrates the activity of the plate boundary at the San Andreas Fault?

   A.

   B.

   C.

   D.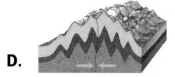

5. Which of the following LEAST affects the amount of damage to a city caused by an earthquake?

   A. the strength of the earthquake
   B. the distance from the city to the epicenter
   C. the season the earthquake occurs
   D. the type of construction in the region

6. The mountain shown below is a(n) _____.

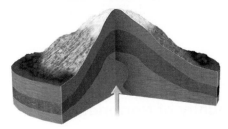

    A. dome mountain
    B. erosion mountain
    C. fold mountain
    D. volcanic mountain

7. The first shaking that you feel when an earthquake hits is the energy that travels through _____.

    A. *L*-waves
    B. *P*-waves
    C. *R*-waves
    D. *S*-waves

8. The fault shown below is a _____ fault.

    A. normal
    B. reverse
    C. strike-slip
    D. transform

Answer the following in complete sentences.

9. Describe how earthquakes are measured using the Modified Mercalli scale and the Richter scale. What type of information does each scale present?

10. Explain why rocks on the ocean floor are almost always much younger than rocks found on land.

STANDARDS

1–2: 1.c., **3:** 1.e., **4:** 1.f., **5:** 1.g., **6:** 1.e.,
7: 1.g., **8:** 1.e., **9:** 1.g., **10:** 1.a.

You Can...

Discover More

On January 17, 1994, a strong earthquake struck southern California. The epicenter was near the community of Northridge, and the magnitude was 6.7 on the Richter scale. The map shows how strongly the shaking was felt in different places.

Richter Scale

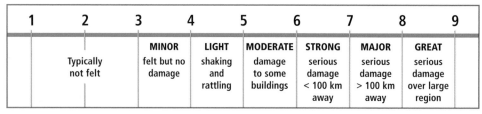

1	2	3	4	5	6	7	8	9
	Typically not felt	MINOR felt but no damage	LIGHT shaking and rattling	MODERATE damage to some buildings	STRONG serious damage < 100 km away	MAJOR serious damage > 100 km away	GREAT serious damage over large region	

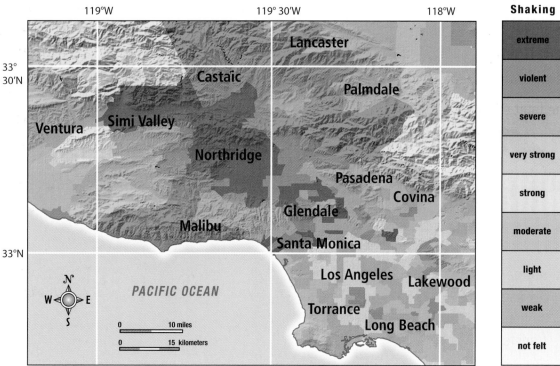

In a severe earthquake, the shock waves can topple buildings and collapse bridges. Earthquakes are common along the edge of the Pacific Ocean, where tectonic plates are slowly sliding against one another.

See an earthquake in action. Go to www.eduplace.com/cascp/ to view a Flash™ movie and to learn more about earthquakes.

PHYSICAL UNIT C SCIENCE

Earth's Energy Supply

Mount Shasta

Mount Shasta is a volcano that was formed over the last 100,000 years.

Skiing, snow-boarding, and sledding are popular winter sports at Mount Shasta.

Fishing is a popular summer sport at Shasta Lake.

PHYSICAL UNIT **C** SCIENCE

Earth's Energy Supply

Chapter 5
Heating Earth...178

Independent Books

- Heating Earth
- The Solar-Powered Home
- Waves and Rays

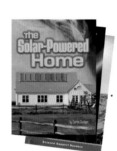

Chapter 6
Energy and Weather...216

Independent Books

- Energy and Weather
- In the Eye of a Hurricane
- Is Earth Getting Warmer or Colder?

Death Valley, California

California Big Ideas!

Standard Sets 3, 4.
Physical Sciences

Heat moves in a predictable flow
from warmer objects to cooler objects until
all objects are at the same temperature.

Many phenomena on Earth's surface
are affected by the transfer
of energy through radiation and
convection currents.

Chapter 5

Heating Earth

California poppies

LESSON

1

Earth is about 150 million kilometers away from the Sun. How does solar energy reach Earth through space?

LESSON

2

The North Pole is very cold, while places near the equator are very hot. Why do different regions of Earth receive different amounts of solar energy?

LESSON

3

Inside this balloon, hot air rises and cold air sinks. How do motions like this distribute thermal energy throughout Earth's atmosphere and oceans?

Writing Journal

In your Writing Journal, write or draw answers to each question.

Vocabulary Preview

convection

the transfer of thermal energy by the motion of a liquid or gas

Vocabulary

atmosphere p. 187
conduction p. 205
convection p. 205
convection current p. 205
density p. 205
electromagnetic radiation p. 186
electromagnetic spectrum p. 186
greenhouse effect p. 198
heat p. 204
land breeze p. 207
sea breeze p. 207
temperature p. 204
thermal energy p. 204
wave p. 184

Glossary

English-Spanish, p. H26

Vocabulary Skill

Word Origins
convection

This word comes from the Latin word *convehere,* which means "to bring together." The Latin word *vehere* means "to carry."

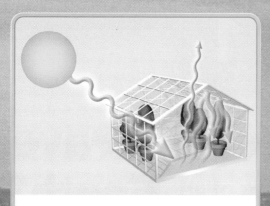

greenhouse effect

the trapping of heat by certain gases in Earth's atmosphere

heat

an amount of thermal energy transferred between objects or regions

wave

a disturbance that transfers energy from one location to another

Start with Your Standards

Standard Set 3. Heat

3.a. *Students know* energy can be carried from one place to another by heat flow or by waves, including water, light and sound waves, or by moving objects.

3.c. *Students know* heat flows in solids by conduction (which involves no flow of matter) and in fluids by conduction and by convection (which involves flow of matter).

3.d. *Students know* heat energy is also transferred between objects by radiation (radiation can travel through space).

Standard Set 4. Energy in the Earth System

4.a. *Students know* the sun is the major source of energy for phenomena on Earth's surface; it powers winds, ocean currents, and the water cycle.

4.b. *Students know* solar energy reaches Earth through radiation, mostly in the form of visible light.

4.d. *Students know* convection currents distribute heat in the atmosphere and oceans.

Standard Set 7: Investigation and Experimentation standards covered in this chapter: 7.b., 7.c., 7.e.

How Does Energy Travel From the Sun to Earth?

Building Background

Energy from the Sun travels through space to reach Earth. The energy is carried not by matter, but by electromagnetic waves. Solar energy provides Earth with light and heat.

 STANDARDS

4.b. *Students know* solar energy reaches Earth through radiation, mostly in the form of visible light.
7.c. Construct appropriate graphs from data and develop qualitative statements about the relationships between variables.

PREPARE TO INVESTIGATE

Inquiry Skill

Ask Questions When you ask questions that are based on facts and observations, you should be able to answer them with an experimental test.

Materials

- 2 identical metal cans
- 2 thermometers
- water
- clock or timer
- 2 sheets of newspaper

Science and Math Toolbox

For step 5, review **Making a Line Graph** on page H13.

Light and Dark

Procedure

1. **Collaborate** Work in a small group. In your *Science Notebook*, make a chart like the one shown.

2. **Record Data** Half-fill each of two cans with water at room temperature. Place a thermometer in each can. Measure and record the water temperature.

3. **Use Variables** Move one can into direct sunlight. Move the other can into a dark place. Put a folded sheet of newspaper under each can.

4. **Predict** What do you think will happen to the water temperature in each can? Record your prediction.

5. **Record Data** Measure and record both water temperatures every 5 minutes for 30 minutes. Plot the temperatures in a double line graph to show how temperature changes with time. Use a different color to show the data for each can.

Conclusion

1. **Analyze Data** What happened to the water temperature in the two cans? Was your prediction correct?

2. **Infer** Where did the energy that warmed the water come from? Explain.

3. **Ask Questions** What questions do you have about the way water changes temperature? Do you think the color of the can affects the water temperature? Describe a test that would help answer your questions.

STEP 1

Time	Can in Sunlight	Can in the Dark
Start		
After 5 min.		
After 10 min.		

STEP 2

STEP 3

Guided Inquiry

Experiment Will water or soil warm to a higher temperature in sunlight? **Predict** the answer. Then design and run an experiment to test your prediction.

183

Energy from the Sun

VOCABULARY

atmosphere   p. 187

electromagnetic
    radiation   p. 186

electromagnetic
    spectrum   p. 186

wave   p. 184

READING SKILL

Sequence Order and describe the parts of the electromagnetic spectrum.

1	
2	
3	
4	

STANDARDS

3.a. *Students know* energy can be carried from one place to another by heat flow or by waves, including water, light and sound waves, or by moving objects.
4.b. *Students know* solar energy reaches Earth through radiation, mostly in the form of visible light.

MAIN IDEA Waves carry energy but not matter from one place to another. Energy from the Sun travels through space as electromagnetic waves.

Waves and Energy

Have you ever watched ripples spread across a pond, or watched crests of water roll across the surface of the ocean? If so, you have seen waves. A **wave** is a disturbance that transfers energy from one location to another.

Energy is the ability to cause change or to do work. Waves carry energy but not matter. For example, when a wave travels through the ocean, the water molecules move briefly from their rest positions. The disturbance that caused the wave is passed from one molecule to the next. As a result, energy is transported through the water. The water itself is not transported across the ocean.

Sound waves form when objects vibrate. To observe this, place your hand against your neck and make a noise. Can you feel your vocal cords

Wave Energy
Water waves, sound waves, and light waves all carry energy. Which waves do you think travel the fastest?

Water

Sound

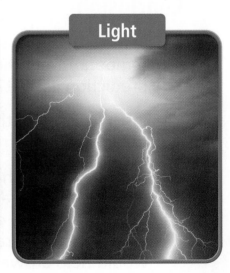
Light

The Sun is Earth's ultimate source of energy.

vibrating? Musical instruments, barking dogs, and alarm clocks all produce sound because they all vibrate.

Like sound, light also travels in waves. Yet light waves do not need a medium, or substance to travel through. They can travel through a vacuum, which is empty space.

Have you ever watched and listened to a thunderstorm? If so, you may have heard a clap of thunder several seconds after seeing the lightning flash, especially if the storm was far away. This happens because of the different speeds of sound waves and light waves.

The speed of light through a vacuum is 300,000 km/s (186,000 mi/s). This is the highest possible speed in the Universe! Light travels almost as fast in air. By contrast, the speed of sound in air is much slower, only about 340 m/s (1,110 ft/s).

Light allows you to see, and plants use the energy of light to make food and to grow. As you know, Earth's source of light comes from far away. This source is the Sun.

The Sun produces light because it is very hot. All hot objects give off light. You can see this every time you switch on a lamp. The light bulb glows because it is hot. A hot stove glowing red is another example.

While the Sun is very interesting to study, you should never look at it directly. Staring directly at such bright light can damage your eyes.

SEQUENCE Explain what happens when you toss a pebble into a quiet pond.

Express Lab

Activity Card 15
Observe Solar Energy

Electromagnetic Waves

Just what is light? Scientists took hundreds of years to discover the answer to this question.

Light is not matter, but rather a type of electromagnetic radiation. **Electromagnetic radiation** is energy transferred by waves that can travel through empty space. Along with visible light, familiar types of electromagnetic radiation include radio waves, microwaves, and x-rays.

Each type has different properties that depend on wavelength. In the diagram below, wavelength is modeled by the distance between two peaks of the wave.

Radio waves have the longest wavelengths and carry the least energy. In contrast, gamma rays have the shortest wavelengths and carry the most energy. In fact, gamma rays are so powerful they can penetrate most materials. To contain gamma rays, scientists use thick walls of lead or concrete.

The Sun emits waves across the entire **electromagnetic spectrum,** which is a continuous band that includes all types of electromagnetic radiation. The illustration models the electromagnetic spectrum.

Scientists have developed technologies for both generating and using different types of electromagnetic waves. Radio and television stations transmit information by using radio waves. Microwave ovens use microwaves to heat food, and toasters use infrared waves to toast bread.

Medical doctors use x-rays to look inside the human body. They may also use gamma rays to treat cancer and other diseases.

The Electromagnetic Spectrum

A radio receiver picks up and "decodes" radio waves to produce sound. ▶

Microwave ovens work because food absorbs microwaves. Very little heat is wasted. ▼

Radio waves

Microwaves

Lower Energy

Visible Light

Visible light makes up a very small part of the electromagnetic spectrum. Visible light, also called white light, is a mixture of colors. In order from lower to higher energy, the colors are red, orange, yellow, green, blue, indigo, and violet. The colors form a continuous band called the visible spectrum.

You can use a glass prism to separate white light into its component colors. Sunlight entering tiny water droplets in the air is also separated into colors. That is how a rainbow forms! Rainbows are common after a rainstorm or near a waterfall, but you can see rainbows even in mist from a garden hose.

Most of the radiation from the Sun that reaches Earth's surface is in the form of visible light. In addition, a small fraction reaches the surface as ultraviolet light and infrared light.

What happens to the other types of electromagnetic radiation? Most are blocked by Earth's **atmosphere,** the blanket of air that surrounds Earth. As you will discover, the atmosphere interacts with solar radiation in a number of very important ways.

SEQUENCE How does radiation change across the electromagnetic spectrum?

Inside a toaster, electrical energy is changed into thermal energy. Infrared waves toast the bread. ▼

White light can be separated into its individual colors by a glass prism or by raindrops. ▼

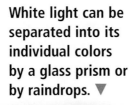

X-rays mostly pass through soft tissues, but are absorbed by bones. Doctors use them to take pictures of the body. ▼

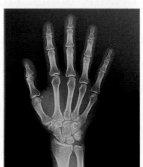

| Infrared light | Visible light | Ultraviolet light | X-rays | Gamma rays |

Higher Energy

Sun Safety Tips

 Wear a broad-spectrum sunscreen with a Sun protection factor (SPF) of at least 15.

 Use sunscreen if your skin will be exposed to sunlight for more than 20 minutes.

 Reapply sunscreen every two hours, or after swimming or strenuous activity.

 Wear sunglasses that offer protection from UV radiation.

Ultraviolet and Infrared Light

Ultraviolet (UV) light carries more energy than visible light and can harm humans and other organisms. Fortunately, certain gases in Earth's atmosphere block much of the Sun's UV light from reaching the surface. These gases include ozone, a form of oxygen found in a layer high in Earth's atmosphere.

Some UV light still reaches the surface. Some exposure to UV light is necessary. It helps your body manufacture vitamin D, which is needed for healthy bones. However, too much exposure can cause sunburn and eye damage. It can also cause early aging of the skin, which may lead to skin cancer.

To enjoy the Sun safely, follow the Sun Safety Tips shown above. Being outdoors is important for your health. But remember to protect yourself, too.

Earth's atmosphere also absorbs most of the infrared light it receives from the Sun. Infrared (IR) light carries less energy than visible light. When your skin absorbs IR radiation, you will feel warm.

The Sun is not the only source of infrared radiation. Other sources include electric heaters, toasters, coals from a barbeque grill, and heat lamps. Infrared radiation is generally not harmful to humans.

 **SEQUENCE** **How do UV and IR radiation compare to visible light?**

The campfire emits infrared waves, which radiate in all directions and warm the campers. ▼

Visual Summary

Energy can be carried from one place to another by waves, including water waves, light waves, and sound waves.

The Sun is Earth's ultimate source of energy. Solar energy travels to Earth as electromagnetic radiation, providing light and heat.

Most of the solar radiation that reaches Earth is in the form of visible light. The atmosphere absorbs other types.

 STANDARDS

3.a., 3.d., 4.b.

Technology

Visit **www.eduplace.com/cascp** to find out more about the electromagnetic spectrum.

Reading Review

1 MAIN IDEA How does energy travel from the Sun to Earth?

2 VOCABULARY How does Earth's *atmosphere* help to protect people from the Sun?

3 READING SKILL Arrange the different regions of the electromagnetic spectrum in order from least to most energy.

1	
2	
3	
4	

4 CRITICAL THINKING: Synthesize You are listening to a baseball game over the radio. Would you hear the announcers sooner if you were near the stadium or in a city far away? Explain.

5 INQUIRY SKILL: Ask Questions Imagine using a spring toy to learn about energy waves. What questions could you ask that you could test with an investigation?

 TEST PRACTICE

Which type of radiation carries the most energy?

A. radio waves

B. visible light

C. x-rays

D. gamma rays

 STANDARDS

1: 4.b., **2:** 3.d., **3:** 4.b., **4–5:** 3.a., **Test Practice:** 4.b.

Great Moments for the Electromagnetic Spectrum

The electromagnetic spectrum has been part of many great events! Can you spot the different forms of radiation in this timeline?

Prisms Isaac Newton shined white light through two prisms. The first prism separated it into colors; the second prism combined the colors into white light again.

Sunscreen French chemist Eugene Schueller invented the first sunscreen. Like products today, it blocked the Sun's dangerous ultraviolet (UV) radiation.

| 1660s | 1895 | 1930s | 1940s |

Medicine German scientist William Roentgen discovered X-rays. Passing X-rays through the body produces shadows of bones and other tissues.

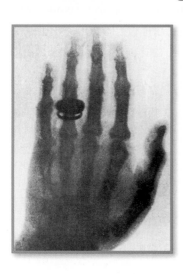

Broadcasting Los Angeles, already home to movie studios, became a center for radio and television.

STANDARD
3.a. *Students know* energy can be carried from one place to another by heat flow or by waves, including water, light and sound waves, or by moving objects.

SOCIAL STUDIES **LINK**

Computer artwork of Sedna ▼

Cooking The first microwave oven was nearly 2 meters tall! As technology improved, ovens became smaller, sleeker, and more popular.

Astronomy At California's Mt. Palomar Observatory, scientists discovered Sedna, a planet-like body beyond Pluto.

1940s   **1971**   **2003**

Medicine In the 1970s, doctors began scanning for bone disease with a technique that used gamma rays. This scan shows a normal skeleton.

Sharing Ideas

1. **READING CHECK** What types of electromagnetic radiation are presented on the timeline?

2. **WRITE ABOUT IT** How do you use electromagnetic radiation?

3. **TALK ABOUT IT** What other events or discoveries could be included in this timeline?

How Is Earth Heated?

Building Background

Earth's surface absorbs radiation from the Sun and is heated as a result. However, not all places on Earth receive the same amount of solar energy. One reason is the angle of the incoming sunlight on Earth's surface. As a result, Earth's surface is heated unevenly.

STANDARDS

4.a. *Students know* the sun is the major source of energy for phenomena on Earth's surface; it powers winds, ocean currents, and the water cycle.

7.c. Construct appropriate graphs from data and develop qualitative statements about the relationships between variables.

PREPARE TO INVESTIGATE

Inquiry Skill

Compare When you compare, you describe how two or more events are alike and how they are different.

Materials

- graph paper, 2 sheets
- meterstick
- protractor
- large flashlight

Science and Math Toolbox

For step 2, review **Using a Tape Measure or Ruler** on page H6.

Lighten Up!

Procedure

Safety: Do not shine the light into anyone's eyes, including your own.

STEP 2

① **Collaborate** Work with a partner. Place a sheet of graph paper on the floor in your work area.

② **Measure** Hold the flashlight 25 cm above the graph paper and pointed directly at it. When the room has been darkened, shine the flashlight directly onto the center of the graph paper at an angle of 90 degrees.

③ **Record Data** While you hold the light steady, have your partner carefully trace the lighted area of the graph paper. Label the drawing and put it aside. Replace it with a new sheet of graph paper.

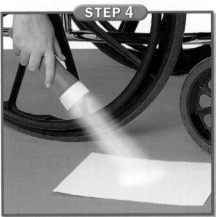

STEP 4

④ **Measure** Hold the flashlight 25 cm above the graph paper but tilt it at an angle of about 45 degrees to the graph paper. Use a protractor to help you determine the angle.

⑤ **Record Data** Repeat step 3.

⑥ **Use Numbers** Count the squares inside each shape traced on the sheets of graph paper to find each area. Record the areas in your *Science Notebook*.

Conclusion

1. **Compare** What differences do you notice between the two lighted areas? How does the area illuminated depend on angle?

2. **Infer** How might the differences in the lighted areas explain why Earth's surface is not evenly heated by the Sun?

Guided Inquiry

Experiment How can striking a curved surface, such as a large ball, affect the angle of the Sun's rays? **Predict** what will happen, and test your prediction. Write a report in which you graph and interpret your data.

Heating Earth

VOCABULARY

greenhouse effect p. 198

READING SKILL

Compare and Contrast
Note how different areas of Earth are heated differently.

Compare	Contrast

STANDARDS

3.d. *Students know* heat energy is also transferred between objects by radiation (radiation can travel through space).
4.a. *Students know* the Sun is the major source of energy for phenomena on Earth's surface; it powers winds, ocean currents, and the water cycle.

MAIN IDEA For many reasons, energy from the Sun does not heat Earth evenly.

Uneven Heating

From moment to moment, the Sun emits about the same amount of energy. When sunlight strikes Earth, some of the energy is absorbed by land, water, and the atmosphere. The absorbed energy is changed to thermal energy, heating Earth.

So why does Earth have such a variety of weather? How can the same day be warm and pleasant in California, icy cold in the far north, and steaming hot near the equator? The reason is that Earth is not heated evenly.

At the equator, sunlight strikes the surface at a 90-degree angle. As you move north toward higher latitudes, Earth's surface curves away from the equator. So sunlight strikes at an increasingly smaller angle. As a result, the same amount of solar energy is spread out over a larger area.

To state this another way, the amount of solar energy per square meter of Earth's surface is greatest at the equator. It decreases as you move away from

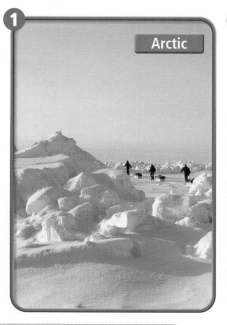

1 Arctic

2 Temperate

3 Equatorial

the equator. A square meter of land near the North Pole or South Pole receives little solar energy.

Another angle effect occurs because of Earth's rotation about its axis. The air is cooler in the morning and evening, when the Sun is low in the sky. The hottest time is often around noon, when the Sun is most directly overhead.

In any given place, the Sun changes position in the sky because Earth curves toward or away from the Sun as it rotates. When the Sun is high in the sky, its rays strike Earth most directly. During the morning and evening, however, the rays strike at a smaller angle. This spreads solar energy over a greater area.

When sunlight travels through the atmosphere at an angle, the light has to take a longer path through the atmosphere. A longer path means that the light has a greater chance to be absorbed, reflected, or scattered. Less light reaches Earth's surface.

A third reason why Earth is unevenly heated is because its axis is tilted. As Earth moves through its orbit, it is tilted either toward or away from the Sun. As you learned in Chapter 1, this causes the seasons.

For example, when it is summer in North America, the Northern Hemisphere is tilted toward the Sun. The days are longer and the Sun is higher in the sky, resulting in more sunlight per square meter.

COMPARE AND CONTRAST Why do different places on Earth receive different amounts of solar energy?

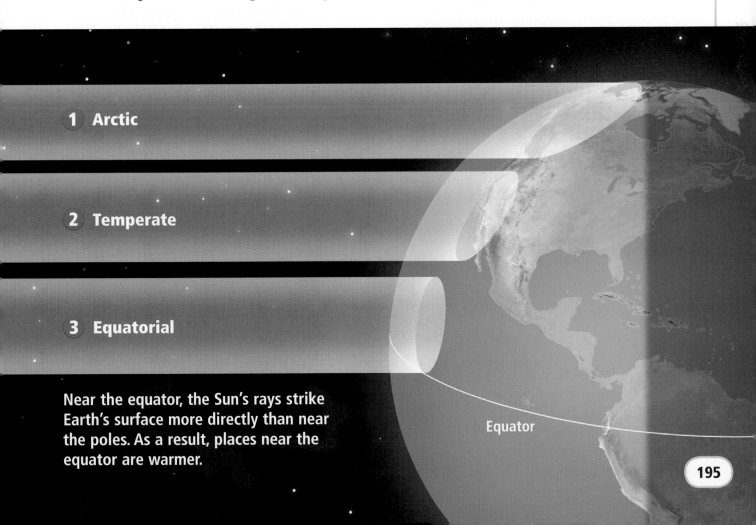

1 **Arctic**

2 **Temperate**

3 **Equatorial**

Near the equator, the Sun's rays strike Earth's surface more directly than near the poles. As a result, places near the equator are warmer.

Equator

Earth's Energy Balance

As you have read, Earth receives only a tiny fraction of the total energy that the Sun gives off. However, this small amount is enough to power Earth's water cycle, create weather, and provide the energy that plants and other living things need to grow.

When sunlight strikes your skin, you'll notice that your skin feels warm. This happens because the sunlight absorbed by your skin is changed into thermal energy. Your skin is not the only thing that absorbs sunlight and becomes warm. This happens to Earth's surface, too.

As shown in the diagram below, only some of the Sun's radiation reaches Earth's surface. This fraction is eventually re-radiated as infrared radiation. On average, the amount of energy Earth receives from the Sun balances the amount it loses into space. That is why average global temperatures don't vary much.

The diagram presents an average energy budget for the entire Earth. For any given place, actual numbers may vary a lot over time. On cloudy days, for example, the clouds reflect incoming solar radiation back into space. That is why cloudy days are cooler than clear days.

Clouds at night have the opposite effect. At night, Earth's warm surface emits infrared radiation into the atmosphere. Clouds absorb that radiation and re-radiate some of it back toward the surface. That's why cloudy nights tend to be warmer than clear nights. On clear nights, radiation from the surface escapes into space.

As a general rule, light-colored surfaces, such as clouds, snow, and ice, tend to reflect more light than dark-colored surfaces, such as forests or the ocean surface. These differences also help explain why Earth's surface is heated unevenly.

Only about half of the incoming solar energy reaches Earth's surface. What happens to the rest? ▼

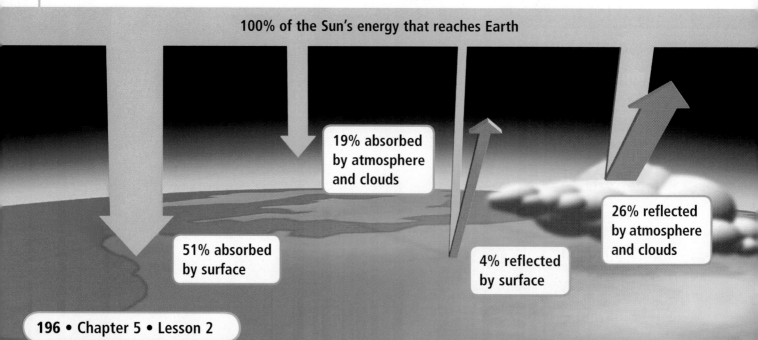

100% of the Sun's energy that reaches Earth

19% absorbed by atmosphere and clouds

26% reflected by atmosphere and clouds

51% absorbed by surface

4% reflected by surface

Earth

Moon

▲ Earth's atmosphere keeps surface temperatures in a moderate range, allowing water to stay liquid.

▲ Lacking an atmosphere, temperatures on the Moon vary greatly. Daytime temperature reaches 130°C (266°F). At night, the temperature plunges to −173°C (−279°F).

Comparing Earth and the Moon As you have seen, Earth's atmosphere helps moderate the warming effects of the Sun. What would Earth's temperatures be like without its atmosphere? For a useful comparison, consider the Moon.

The Moon is the same distance from the Sun as Earth, and it receives the same amount of solar energy per square meter. Yet with essentially no atmosphere, the Moon's surface temperatures vary dramatically.

During the day, the Moon's surface absorbs most of the incoming solar radiation. So the surface is extremely hot! At night, the Moon's warmed surface emits infrared radiation that escapes easily into space. The surface becomes very, very cold!

Another difference between Earth and the Moon is the way the daylight sky looks. Why is Earth's sky blue while the Moon's sky is black? Once again, the explanation is atmosphere.

Sunlight entering Earth's atmosphere scatters, or bounces, off molecules in the air. Light at the blue end of the spectrum is scattered more effectively than other colors. As a result, more blue light is scattered toward Earth's surface and the sky appears blue. Because the Moon has no atmosphere, no molecules scatter incoming sunlight. The sky takes on the blackness of space.

Study the two photos closely. What other differences do you observe between Earth and its Moon?

 **COMPARE AND CONTRAST** Why do temperatures on Earth and the Moon differ so greatly?

Express Lab

Activity Card 16
Angles of Sunlight and Temperature

The Greenhouse Effect

Have you ever been inside a greenhouse? You may have noticed that the air inside a greenhouse is warmer than the air outside. A greenhouse works because it traps some of the Sun's energy inside.

In a greenhouse, radiation from the Sun enters through clear glass panels and warms the surfaces inside. The warmed surfaces radiate energy back in the form of infrared radiation. However, the glass panels do not let much of the infrared radiation pass through. The energy is trapped inside.

On a much larger scale, certain gases in Earth's atmosphere act somewhat like the glass panels of a greenhouse. Like the glass, these gases allow radiation from the Sun to pass through and warm Earth's surface. Earth's warm surface radiates energy back into the atmosphere as infrared radiation. The gases absorb most of the infrared radiation, letting only a little of it pass through to space. The absorbed radiation is re-emitted in all directions, warming the surface and lower atmosphere.

This mechanism for warming the surface and lower atmosphere of a planet is known as the **greenhouse effect.** Without an atmosphere to create a greenhouse effect, life on Earth would be impossible. As you learned earlier, places with little or no atmosphere—such as the Moon—experience very large temperature changes from day to night.

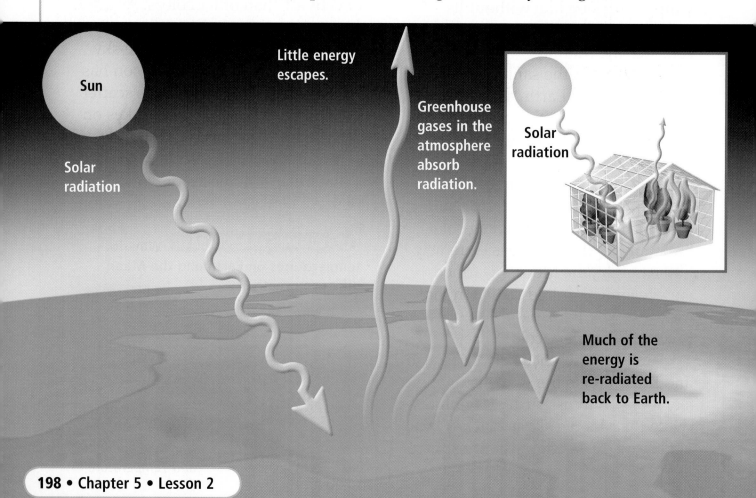

Sun

Solar radiation

Little energy escapes.

Greenhouse gases in the atmosphere absorb radiation.

Solar radiation

Much of the energy is re-radiated back to Earth.

The greenhouse effect depends on certain gases, called greenhouse gases, that occur naturally in the atmosphere. These gases include water vapor, methane, nitrous oxide, and, especially, carbon dioxide. The greater their amounts, the more solar energy is trapped and the warmer the atmosphere and surface become.

How important are greenhouse gases? To find the answer, compare Earth with its two neighbors in space: Venus and Mars. All three are rocky planets. But each has a very different atmosphere.

Venus has a very thick atmosphere. The atmospheric pressure at Venus's surface is about 90 times that of Earth's. And unlike Earth, the atmosphere of Venus consists mainly of carbon dioxide—almost a million times the amount in Earth's atmosphere. As a result, it traps most of the infrared radiation from Venus's surface.

The average temperature on Venus is about 480°C (900°F)! This is the highest surface temperature on any planet in the solar system. It is even higher than on Mercury, the planet closest to the Sun.

Like Venus, Mars also has an atmosphere that is mostly carbon dioxide. Yet Mars has a very thin atmosphere. The pressure is about $\frac{1}{100}$ that of Earth's. On Mars, infrared radiation can easily escape into space. As a result, the surface temperature on Mars averages −65°C (−85°F).

Venus and Mars illustrate a lesson for anyone who cares about life on Earth. The lesson is that the right

Comparing Atmospheres

Venus's atmosphere

Venus has a very thick atmosphere of carbon dioxide, creating a large greenhouse effect. The surface of Venus is extremely hot.

Mars's atmosphere

Mars has a very thin atmosphere, and the greenhouse effect is slight. Temperatures on Mars can be very low.

amount of gases in the atmosphere is important. Temperatures on Earth's surface depend on them.

COMPARE AND CONTRAST How does Earth's atmosphere compare to those of Mars and Venus?

Global Warming

Over the past 100 years, Earth's average surface temperature has increased by about 0.5°C (0.9°F). This trend of rising temperature is known as global warming. Over the same period, concentrations of carbon dioxide and other greenhouse gases in Earth's atmosphere have also risen gradually. The graph below shows the increase in carbon dioxide over the past 50 years.

Recall that greenhouse gases trap heat, warming Earth's surface and the lower parts of the atmosphere. Increased concentrations of greenhouse gases would work to enhance Earth's natural greenhouse effect, further warming the planet.

Where does the extra carbon dioxide come from? Most scientists agree that human activity is responsible for adding carbon dioxide to the atmosphere. Burning of fossil fuels produces carbon dioxide. Humans are also cutting down or burning forests. As you may know, plants take up carbon dioxide as they grow.

Rising average temperatures would eventually melt the ice sheets on Greenland and Antarctica, as well as mountain glaciers. Global ocean levels would rise as a result.

Most scientists agree that global warming is occurring and that human activity contributes to greenhouse gases. However, scientists disagree about the importance of the human contribution compared to natural variations in climate. Today, scientists and government leaders continue to discuss global warming and its possible consequences.

COMPARE AND CONTRAST How might the atmosphere change if people burned less fossil fuel?

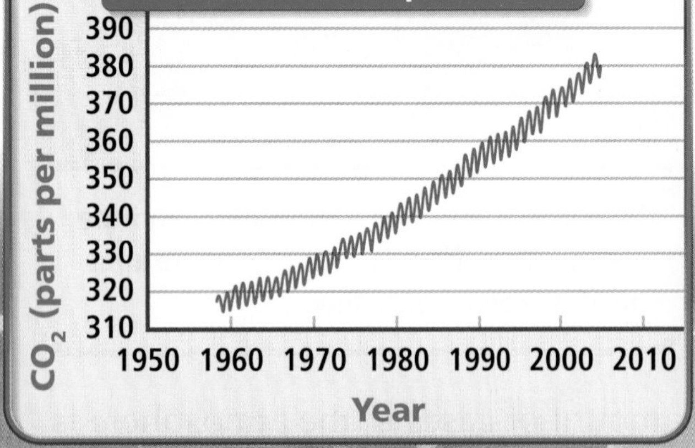

How might rising temperatures affect coastal areas on Earth? ▼

Carbon Dioxide Levels in Earth's Atmosphere

CO_2 (parts per million)

390
380
370
360
350
340
330
320
310

1950 1960 1970 1980 1990 2000 2010

Year

Visual Summary

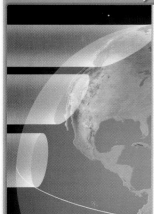

Uneven heating by the Sun causes some regions on Earth to be warmer than others.

About half of the solar energy that reaches Earth is absorbed by its surface. This energy is released by the surface as infrared radiation, warming the lower atmosphere.

Greenhouse gases in the atmosphere help moderate Earth's surface temperatures.

 STANDARDS

3.d, 4.a.

Technology

Visit **www.eduplace.com/cascp** to find out more about how Earth is heated.

Reading Review

1 MAIN IDEA What factors affect the amount of energy that Earth receives from the Sun?

2 VOCABULARY What is the *greenhouse effect*? How does it compare to an actual greenhouse?

3 READING SKILL All places on Earth are about the same distance from the Sun. Why does the Sun heat Earth unevenly?

Compare	Contrast

4 CRITICAL THINKING: Synthesize What suggestions would you make to slow down global warming?

5 INQUIRY SKILL: Compare Study today's weather map. How do temperatures compare in places across the United States? Describe trends you observe.

 TEST PRACTICE

The _____ generally receives the most direct solar radiation.

A. North Pole

B. South Pole

C. equator

D. ocean

 STANDARDS

1: 3.d., 4.b., **2:** 3.d., **3:** 4.b., **4:** 3.d., 4.a., **5:** 4.a., **Test Practice:** 4.a.

What Are Convection Currents?

Building Background

A hot air balloon rises because the hot air inside the balloon is less dense than the cooler air outside.

On a larger scale, hot air rises and cold air sinks throughout Earth's atmosphere. Warm and cold water move in similar ways. These motions distribute heat all over the planet.

PREPARE TO INVESTIGATE

Inquiry Skill

Measure When you measure, you select and use appropriate tools and units to make numerical observations.

Materials

- clear plastic container
- hot rock
- water
- ice cube
- food coloring
- thermometer

Science and Math Toolbox

For step 1, review **Using a Thermometer** on page H8.

 STANDARDS

3.c. *Students know* heat flows in solids by conduction (which involves no flow of matter) and in fluids by conduction and by convection (which involves flow of matter).
7.c. Construct appropriate graphs from data and develop qualitative statements about the relationship between variables.

Circling Around!

Procedure

1 **Collaborate** Work in a small group. In your *Science Notebook,* make a chart like the one shown.

Time	Temperature Near Ice (°C)	Temperature Near Hot Rock (°C)

2 **Experiment** Add water to the container. Carefully place the hot rock in one corner of the container. Float the ice cube in the opposite corner.

3 **Observe** When the water is still, add several drops of food coloring next to the ice cube. Observe how the food coloring moves.

4 **Measure** Use the thermometer to measure the water temperature near the rock and near the ice cube. Disturb the water as little as possible. Record each temperature. Repeat the measurements every minute for 5 minutes.

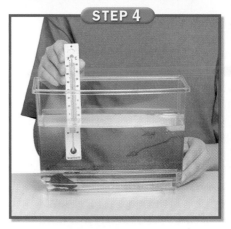

5 **Record Data** Draw and label sketches of any currents you observe in the water.

Conclusion

1. **Communicate** Uneven heating causes a liquid or gas to move in a loop called a convection current. Describe any convection currents you observed.

2. **Infer** How would the currents change if you moved the hot rock or ice cube to new positions?

3. **Analyze Data** Make a line graph to show how the water temperatures at each end change with time. How do changes in water temperature affect the convection current?

Guided Inquiry

Experiment Design an experiment that will allow you to observe convection currents in the air. With your teacher's permission, do the experiment. **Communicate** the steps and your results in a written report.

Distributing Heat

MAIN IDEA Thermal energy can be transferred by conduction, convection, or radiation.

VOCABULARY

conduction	p. 205
convection	p. 205
convection current	p. 205
density	p. 205
heat	p. 204
land breeze	p. 207
sea breeze	p. 207
temperature	p. 204
thermal energy	p. 204

READING SKILL

Main Idea and Details As you read, fill in the main ideas and details to organize the information in the lesson.

STANDARDS

3.c. *Students know* heat flows in solids by conduction (which involves no flow of matter) and in fluids by conduction and by convection (which involves flow of matter).
4.d. *Students know* convection currents distribute heat in the atmosphere and oceans.

Conduction and Convection

Have you ever heated food on a stove, warmed your hands by a fire, or watched ice melt? If so, you observed changes that involved a transfer of thermal energy. But just what is thermal energy?

All matter is made of tiny particles that are in constant, random motion. They have energy from that motion. In any sample of matter, the *total* amount of motion energy from its moving particles is called the sample's **thermal energy.** The *average* motion energy of the particles is the **temperature.** Temperature describes how hot or cold something is.

When a hot object is in contact with a cold object, thermal energy is always transferred from the hot object to the cold object. This transferred energy is called **heat.** The transfer of energy continues until both objects have the same temperature.

Thermal energy is transferred from the red-hot end of the rod to the cooler black end by conduction. ▶

◄ Currents of water or air created by the process of convection are called convection currents.

Thermal energy is transferred by one of three processes: radiation, conduction, and convection. Radiation is the transfer of thermal energy by way of electromagnetic waves. Recall that the Sun gives off energy by emitting radiation.

Conduction is the transfer of thermal energy by particle collision, such as in the example of the hot rock in cold water. The collisions transfer energy but not matter.

In the metal rod pictured on page 204, particles in the hot end have higher energy and vibrate more strongly. They collide with nearby particles, transferring some of their motion energy. As a result, energy will be transferred from the hot end across the rod toward the cooler end.

In air, water, and other fluids, thermal energy is transferred mostly by a process called convection. **Convection** is the transfer of thermal energy by mass movement of particles in a liquid or gas. Convection transports matter as well as energy.

To understand convection, look at the aquarium above. It uses a heater to warm the water that comes in contact with it. As it warms, the water expands, causing its density to decrease. **Density** is the amount of mass per unit volume of a substance. The warmer, less dense water rises.

When the rising warm water reaches the surface, it cools. Its thermal energy is transferred to surrounding water particles by collision. The water becomes denser, and sinks. Eventually, the water reaches the heater, is warmed anew, and begins another journey through the aquarium. This continuous loop of moving water is called a **convection current.**

 **MAIN IDEA AND DETAILS** How is thermal energy transferred?

Activity Card 17
Transfer Thermal Energy

Convection in Nature

Convection and convection currents play important roles in distributing heat around Earth. Just like in the aquarium example, convection currents form in the Earth's atmosphere and oceans because of uneven heating.

In Earth's oceans, water near the equator receives the most direct rays from the Sun and is therefore quite warm. Near the poles, however, sunlight strikes at an angle, so ocean water is very cold.

The temperature differences result in convection currents that form huge loops in Earth's oceans. These convection currents distribute heat throughout the oceans.

Different materials on Earth's surface absorb incoming solar radiation differently. Dark surfaces absorb a greater fraction of the incoming sunlight than do light surfaces, and become warmer.

Materials may also heat up at different rates. For example, water needs to absorb about four times as much energy as land to increase its temperature by the same amount.

Because land and ocean are heated unevenly, the air above them is heated unevenly, too. Cooler air that comes in contact with a warm surface will warm up because thermal energy is conducted from the surface to the air.

Like the warm water in the aquarium, warm air expands, becomes less dense, and rises. As the air rises, it cools, becomes denser, and sinks back down toward Earth's surface. A convection current has formed.

Ocean Surface Temperatures

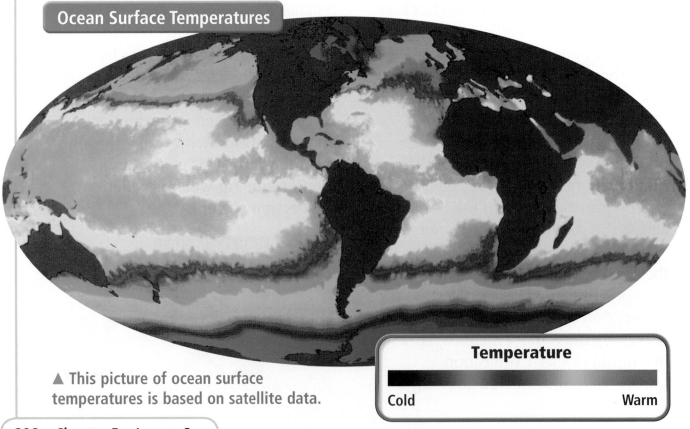

▲ This picture of ocean surface temperatures is based on satellite data.

Temperature

Cold   Warm

Warm   Cool

Cool   Warm

▲ Sea Breeze

Over land during the day, warm air rises. Cooler air from the ocean moves in to replace it, forming a sea breeze.

▲ Land Breeze

Over the ocean at night, warm air rises. Cooler air from the land replaces it, forming a land breeze.

Local Winds Have you ever spent a long day at an ocean beach? If so, you may have noticed that the local winds blow in different directions during daytime and nighttime. The same type of event happens near a large lake. What causes these changes in wind direction?

During the day, the land absorbs more of the incoming solar energy than the water does. It also heats up at a higher rate. As a result, land temperatures are higher than water temperatures. The air above land becomes warmer and less dense than the air above the water. This warm air rises and the cooler, denser air above the water moves in to replace it.

The cool air that blows along the surface from the water toward land is called a **sea breeze.** A sea breeze is really the lower half of a convection current that forms in the atmosphere over the sea and land.

At night, a convection current flows in the opposite direction. The land cools down more quickly than the water does, so the air above the water is warmer than the air above the land. Warm, less dense air rises above the water, while cool, dense air above land moves in to replace it.

The result is a cool wind blowing near the surface from land toward sea, called a **land breeze.** Sea breezes and land breezes help explain why the air is often cooler at beaches than at places farther inland.

Every moment of every day, winds are blowing across Earth. Some are mild, while others are quite strong. Yet all winds form for the same reason: the Sun heating Earth unevenly. If all points on Earth were at the same temperature, no winds would blow at all.

 **MAIN IDEA AND DETAILS** Describe some convection currents in nature.

Temperatures in California

What's the air temperature right now in California? The answer depends on where you are in the state.

In the Mojave Desert, summer temperatures may climb over 38°C (100°F). It very rarely gets that hot in the Sierra mountains, but winter temperatures may drop to −12°C (10°F) or below. By contrast, along the Pacific Ocean, air temperatures stay moderate for much of the year.

Latitude, which measures distance to the equator, explains only part of the answer. Notice that Morro Bay and the Mojave Desert are at about the same latitude. Yet their temperatures are very different throughout the year.

One important factor is the Pacific Ocean. Ocean currents, land breezes, and sea breezes all tend to moderate temperatures near the ocean.

In addition, air temperature decreases with elevation. The highest peak of Mammoth Mountain is about 3,300 meters (11,000 feet) tall. It often is covered in snow even in July!

MAIN IDEA AND DETAILS Why are temperatures different across California?

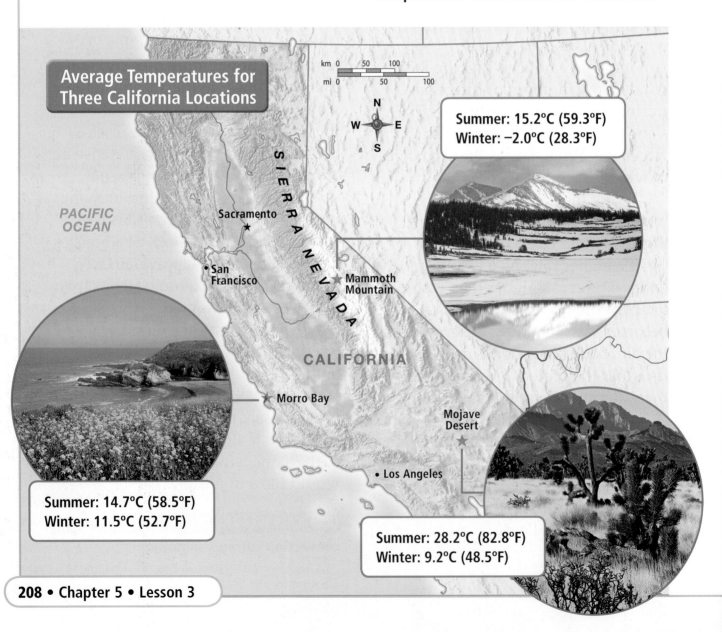

Average Temperatures for Three California Locations

km 0   50   100
mi 0   50   100

N W E S

PACIFIC OCEAN

Sacramento ★

• San Francisco

SIERRA NEVADA

Mammoth Mountain ★

CALIFORNIA

Summer: 15.2°C (59.3°F)
Winter: −2.0°C (28.3°F)

★ Morro Bay

Mojave Desert ★

• Los Angeles

Summer: 14.7°C (58.5°F)
Winter: 11.5°C (52.7°F)

Summer: 28.2°C (82.8°F)
Winter: 9.2°C (48.5°F)

Visual Summary

Thermal energy is transferred by radiation, conduction, and convection. Thermal energy transferred from a hotter object to a colder object is called heat.

Convection currents play important roles in distributing heat in Earth's atmosphere and oceans.

Land breezes and sea breezes are local winds that are caused by uneven heating of land and water.

STANDARDS

3.c., 4.d.

Technology
Visit **www.eduplace.com/cascp** to find out more about how Earth is heated.

Reading Review

1 MAIN IDEA What are the three ways in which thermal energy is transferred?

2 VOCABULARY How are *conduction* and *convection* different?

3 READING SKILL Describe how a convection current will form in an aquarium once the heater is turned on.

4 CRITICAL THINKING: Analyze
To predict air temperatures for a city, is it enough to know the city's latitude? Explain.

5 INQUIRY SKILL: Measure
A warm rock (40°C) is dropped into cool water (20°C). Predict how their temperatures will change over time.

✓ **TEST PRACTICE**

In a liquid or gas, thermal energy is transferred mostly by _____.

A. radiation

B. heat

C. conduction

D. convection

STANDARDS

1: 3.c., 3.d, **2–3:** 3.c., **4–5:** 4.d., **Test Practice:** 3.c.

209

STANDARDS 4.d. *Students know* convection currents distribute heat in the atmosphere and oceans.

Diablo Wind

The Red Wind. The Diablo Wind. Whatever you call it, when California's Santa Ana wind blows, it usually means trouble.

The Santa Ana winds are dry, hot, and fierce, whipping out of the desert from October through March. As cooling convection currents sink over the high desert in Nevada, air pressure builds. When low pressure develops offshore of California, the pressure difference causes the air to spill out of the high desert. The air rushes through mountain passes and canyons toward the ocean. As the air drops downward, it compresses and heats up.

The results can spell danger. This hot, fast wind dries out plants and makes them susceptible to fire. Once a fire is started, the Santa Ana whips it up, sometimes with hurricane force.

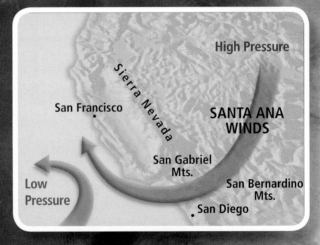

Santa Ana winds are born in high pressure that develops in the Great Basin between the Sierra Nevada and Rocky Mountain ranges.

In October of 2003 it only took two weeks for wildfires powered by the Santa Ana winds to burn almost 3000 square km of land.

Fire Areas

This satellite image shows the Santa Ana winds blowing wildfire smoke out to sea from the San Diego area.

Writing Journal

The Santa Ana is a special kind of wind called a föhn wind. Research this term and write in your journal about other famous föhn winds around the world.

211

Math in Science

You and your classmates have been recording the local air temperature twice a day for a week. All measurements have been made at 11:00 A.M. and at 7:00 P.M. The chart shows the temperatures you measured.

	Day 1	Day 2	Day 3	Day 4	Day 5	Day 6	Day 7
Temperature at 11:00 A.M.	24°C	23°C	20°C	16°C	22°C	23°C	19°C
Temperature at 7:00 P.M.	18°C	18°C	14°C	10°C	12°C	12°C	13°C

1. What is the range of temperatures in the set of data?

2. What is the mean temperature at 11:00 A.M. for the week?

3. From the data, can you conclude that 11:00 A.M. is the hottest time of day and 7:00 P.M. is the coldest? Explain.

Writing in Science
Narrative

Write a short story that includes a convection current. The current could be a local wind, a current in the ocean, or a current in an aquarium. One character should notice the current and explain it.

Architect

Buildings need stairways and elevators, systems for heating and cooling, and pipes for water. Planning all these parts is the job of an architect.

Architects are studying new ways to help buildings stay cool in summer and warm in winter. Factors that affect heat flow include the shapes of windows and doorways, and the thickness of walls. The right design keeps energy costs low.

What It Takes!

- A college degree in architecture
- Practical training and a license

Ship's Captain

What is the fastest way to travel between two places? For an ocean-going ship, the answer is not always a straight line. The captain of a ship must understand global wind patterns, ocean currents, and the way storms develop.

Captains must make good decisions. Choosing the fastest route can save thousands of dollars. Avoiding danger protects lives and property.

What It Takes!

- Knowledge of ocean ships and navigation
- Leadership and management skills

Vocabulary

Complete each sentence with a term from the list.

1. Thermal energy transferred from warmer matter to cooler matter is called ____.

2. The blanket of air surrounding Earth is called Earth's ____.

3. Radio waves, microwaves, and ultraviolet light are all part of the ____.

4. A sample's ____ describes how hot or cold the sample is.

5. The transfer of energy through the motion of a gas or liquid is called ____.

6. The amount of mass per unit volume of a substance is called ____.

7. The cool wind blowing from the ocean at night is called a(n) ____.

8. Energy from the Sun travels to Earth as ____.

9. A disturbance that transfers energy from one location to another is a(n) ____.

10. The warming of the surface and lower atmosphere of a planet is called the ____.

atmosphere p. 187
conduction p. 205
convection p. 205
convection current p. 205
density p. 205
electromagnetic radiation p. 186
electromagnetic spectrum p. 186
greenhouse effect p. 198
heat p. 204
land breeze p. 207
sea breeze p. 207
temperature p. 204
thermal energy p. 204
wave p. 184

Test Practice

Write the letter of the best answer choice.

11. Conduction, convection, and radiation are all ways that ____ can be transferred.

   A. light energy
   B. thermal energy
   C. waves
   D. land breezes

12. Thermal energy is transferred through a metal spoon by ____.

   A. conduction
   B. convection
   C. waves
   D. radiation

13. What is one reason for the uneven heating of Earth's surface?

   A. the greenhouse effect
   B. convection currents
   C. Earth's shape
   D. ocean density

14. A loop created by warm air rising and cool air sinking is called a(n) ____.

   A. greenhouse effect
   B. electromagnetic wave
   C. gamma ray
   D. convection current

Inquiry Skills

15. Communicate Write a paragraph explaining the differences between a sea breeze and a land breeze.

16. A scientist sinks a very hot rock in one corner of an aquarium. She floats several ice cubes that are kept near the opposite corner. How will the water move through the aquarium? Explain your prediction.

Map the Concept

What events are caused by the Sun's uneven heating of Earth? Show your answers in a concept map like the one shown here.

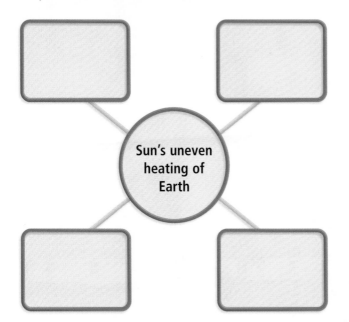

Sun's uneven heating of Earth

Critical Thinking

17. Apply Your friend forgot to put sunscreen on before going outside on a summer day. How does radiation pose a danger to her? What type of waves will cause sunburn?

18. Synthesize Explain why white clothing will keep you cooler in the summer than black clothing will.

19. Evaluate Jordan used a metal ladle to stir a pot of boiling spaghetti. He burned his hand. Explain why this happened.

20. Analyze Explain why rainbows are sometimes seen during or just after a brief rain shower.

Performance Assessment

Design a Mini Greenhouse

Your class would like to plant flowers to sell to raise money for the school science program. However, the natural light by the windows is not strong enough to grow plants effectively. Design a mini greenhouse that you and your classmates could build with everyday materials. Explain why you chose each material and describe how the greenhouse works.

Writing Journal

Review your answers to the questions on page 179 at the beginning of this chapter. Change your answers as needed, based on what you have learned.

STANDARDS

1: 3.a., **2:** 4.d., **3:** 3.a., **4:** 3.c., **5:** 4.a., **6:** 4.d., **7:** 4.a., **8:** 3.d., 4.b.,
9: 3.a., **10:** 3.d., **11:** 3.c., 3.d., **12:** 3.c., **13:** 3.d., 4.b., **14:** 3.c., 4.d.,
15–16: 4.a., 4.d., **17:** 3.d., **18:** 3.a., 3.d., **19:** 3.c., **20:** 4.b.

Chapter 6

Energy and Weather

Pigeon Point Light Station,
California State Historic Park

LESSON 1

To predict the weather, scientists study air temperature, humidity, air pressure, and other properties. What kinds of changes can take place in Earth's atmosphere?

LESSON 2

Some of Earth's waters are warm. Others are quite cold. Ocean waters are always moving. How do ocean currents affect weather across the planet?

LESSON 3

On any given day, the weather can vary widely in different parts of California. What types of climate and weather are found here?

Writing Journal

In your Writing Journal, write or draw answers to each question.

Vocabulary Preview

Vocabulary

air mass p. 226
air pressure p. 222
climate p. 236
condensation p. 225
Coriolis effect p. 234
dew point p. 225
evaporation p. 225
front p. 227
humidity p. 225
isobar p. 223
jet stream p. 235
ocean current p. 236
precipitation p. 225

Glossary

English-Spanish, p. H24

Vocabulary Skill

Find the Start

isobar

Iso comes from the Greek word *isos*, meaning "equal" or "uniform." *Bar* comes from the Greek word *baros*, meaning "weight."

air mass

a body of air that has similar temperature and water vapor content throughout

condensation

the change from a gas state to a liquid state

evaporation

the change from a liquid state to a gas state

Standard Set 4. Energy in the Earth System

4.a. *Students know* the sun is the major source of energy for phenomena on Earth's surface; it powers winds, ocean currents, and the water cycle.

4.d. *Students know* convection currents distribute heat in the atmosphere and oceans.

4.e. *Students know* differences in pressure, heat, air movement, and humidity result in changes of weather.

Standard Set 7: Investigation and Experimentation standards covered in this chapter: 7.b., 7.c., 7.d., 7.e., 7.h.

precipitation

rain, snow, hail, or other form of water that falls to Earth's surface from clouds

What Causes Weather?

Building Background

Liquid water covers about 70 percent of Earth's surface. In its gas form, water is found in the atmosphere. Every moment, water moves between the air and ground. It changes state as it passes through the stages of the water cycle.

PREPARE TO INVESTIGATE

Inquiry Skill

Use Variables The independent variable is the single factor in an experiment that is changed in order to test its effect.

Materials

- metal cup
- warm water
- thermometer
- ice water
- syringe

Science and Math Toolbox

For step 1, review **Using a Thermometer** on page H8.

STANDARDS

4.e. *Students know* differences in pressure, heat, air movement, and humidity result in changes of weather.
7.b. Select and use appropriate tools and technology (including calculators, computers, balances, spring scales, microscopes, and binoculars) to perform tests, collect data, and display data.

Discovering Dew Point

Procedure

1 **Collaborate** Work in small groups. Fill the metal cup one-third full of warm water. Lower the thermometer into the cup so that water surrounds the bulb. Record the temperature in your *Science Notebook.*

2 **Predict** When water vapor in the air meets a cold surface, it will condense into drops of liquid water. At what temperature do you predict this would happen on the metal cup? Record your prediction.

3 **Observe** Use the syringe to add ice water to the water in the metal cup. Observe the temperature change. Continue adding ice water until drops of water begin to form on the outside of the cup.

4 **Record Data** Record the temperature at which condensation begins. This is the dew point temperature in your classroom today. Compare this temperature to your earlier prediction.

Conclusion

1. **Infer** What might the dew point be if the temperature in your classroom was 20 degrees lower than it is today?

2. **Explain** Why do you think condensation formed on the outside of the metal cup?

3. **Communicate** Write a report stating your prediction, the steps you used to complete the inquiry, and whether or not your prediction agreed with your results.

STEP 1

STEP 3

STEP 4

Guided Inquiry

Ask Questions Can dew point change within a small area? Choose a location and measure the dew point there. The location you choose is the *independent variable.* **Use Variables** to test other locations and compare the results.

Weather

VOCABULARY

air mass	p. 226
air pressure	p. 222
condensation	p. 225
dew point	p. 225
evaporation	p. 225
front	p. 227
humidity	p. 225
isobar	p. 223
precipitation	p. 225

 **READING SKILL**

Main Idea and Details As you read, use headings to determine the main ideas in this lesson.

Main Idea

Detail   Detail

STANDARDS

4.a. *Students know* the sun is the major source of energy for phenomena on Earth's surface; it powers winds, ocean currents, and the water cycle.
4.e. *Students know* differences in pressure, heat, air movement, and humidity result in changes of weather.

MAIN IDEA Differences in air pressure, heat, air movement, and humidity cause changes in the weather.

Air Pressure

Nitrogen gas makes up about 78 percent of Earth's atmosphere, and oxygen makes up about 21 percent. The remaining 1 percent is mostly water vapor, argon, carbon dioxide, neon, and helium. Without the atmosphere, Earth would not have weather.

Air is matter. It has mass and takes up space. Air also has weight, because Earth's gravity pulls the molecules of air towards its surface. **Air pressure** is exerted by the weight of the air pushing on all surfaces it touches.

Air pressure decreases with altitude. Temperature also affects air pressure. Warm air is less dense and exerts less pressure than cold air.

Air pressure is all around. Air pushes on all surfaces it comes into contact with. ▶

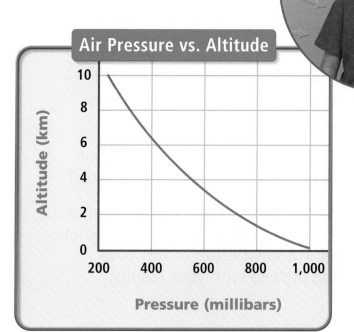

Air Pressure vs. Altitude

Altitude (km) / Pressure (millibars)

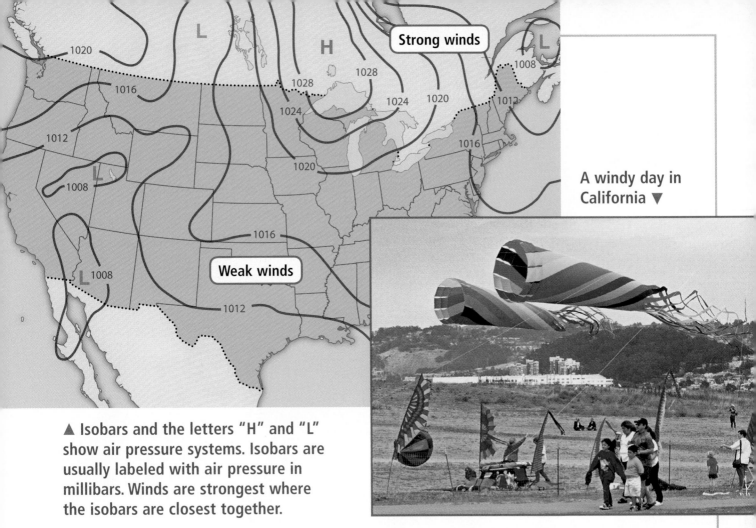

Strong winds

A windy day in California ▼

Weak winds

▲ Isobars and the letters "H" and "L" show air pressure systems. Isobars are usually labeled with air pressure in millibars. Winds are strongest where the isobars are closest together.

Winds

Winds can blow strongly or weakly, and in many different directions. In all cases, winds form from differences in air pressure. These differences are caused by uneven heating of Earth's surface by energy from the Sun.

The Sun does not heat Earth's atmosphere directly. Instead, the surface is heated, then that energy is conducted to the atmosphere.

As a result, air is warm above a warm surface and cold above a cold surface. Air pressure is different, too. Air pressure is lower above a warm surface than above a cold one.

Air tends to move from centers of higher pressure to centers of lower pressure. This movement of air is wind. The greater the pressure difference is between the two centers, the stronger the wind.

On a weather map, centers of high pressure are indicated by a blue "H," and centers of low pressure are indicated by a red "L." Lines called **isobars** are drawn on the map to connect points that have equal air pressure. Isobars also provide information about wind speed. The closer together the isobars are packed, the greater the wind speed will be.

 **MAIN IDEA AND DETAILS** What is air pressure?

Water Cycle

Water cycles among Earth's air, ground, oceans, and living things. Energy from the Sun powers the water cycle.

Rain

Snow

Hail

Precipitation

Liquid or solid water falls to the ground as rain, sleet, snow, or hail.

Condensation

When water condenses, it changes from water vapor to tiny droplets of water.

Evaporation

When water evaporates, it changes from a liquid to a gas called water vapor.

Express Lab

Activity Card 18
See Condensation

Clouds and Precipitation

Like air pressure and wind, water is an important component of weather. Water is one of the few substances that is found in nature in its three states—water vapor, liquid water, and ice.

Water is constantly circulating between Earth's surface and the atmosphere. This happens in a series of steps that make up the water cycle. Recall that much of Earth's surface—about 70 percent—is covered by water, mainly ocean water. Therefore, the oceans are the main source of water for the water cycle.

When the Sun warms the oceans or other bodies of water, the water at the surface gains enough energy to evaporate. **Evaporation** is a process that changes a liquid into a gas.

The warm, moist air rises; then, a few kilometers above Earth's surface, the air cools. In cool air, the water vapor condenses. **Condensation** is the process that changes a gas into a liquid. Clouds are formed from tiny droplets of liquid water or from ice crystals.

Eventually, the water droplets in clouds may grow and become too heavy to stay aloft. Water then falls to the ground as precipitation. **Precipitation** includes the rain, snow, sleet, and hail that falls from clouds to Earth's surface.

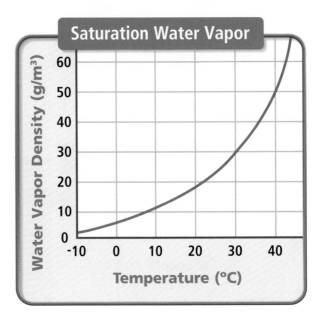

Saturation Water Vapor

Water Vapor Density (g/m³) vs. Temperature (°C)

Humidity

The amount of water vapor in the atmosphere at a given time and place is called **humidity.** Humidity can vary greatly from day to day and from place to place. Humidity also varies with air temperature.

Weather reports usually describe relative humidity. Relative humidity compares the actual amount of moisture in the air to the maximum amount the atmosphere can hold at a given temperature. Relative humidity is expressed as a percent.

At 100 percent relative humidity, the air is saturated. It is holding all the water vapor it can hold.

The temperature at which the air is saturated with water vapor is called the **dew point.** If the air temperature drops below the dew point, condensation will occur.

 **MAIN IDEA AND DETAILS** What causes clouds to form?

Air Masses

Weather can be sunny one day and stormy the next. Such major changes in weather come from the movement of air masses. An **air mass** is a large body of air that has similar temperature and moisture characteristics throughout. An air mass can cover thousands of square kilometers.

An air mass gets its characteristics from the region over which it forms. Six major source regions generate the air masses that affect North America.

Continental polar air masses form over Canada and Alaska. These air masses are cold and dry. Continental arctic air masses are even colder. These air masses form above the Arctic Circle and bring bitterly cold weather in winter and cool, dry weather in summer.

Continental tropical air masses form during summer over northern Mexico and southwestern United States. These air masses are hot and dry. If these air masses remain over a region for an extended time, they can cause droughts.

Maritime polar air masses form over oceans. These air masses are cold and moist. Those that form over the North Pacific Ocean bring rain, fog, and snow to the coast. Those that form over the North Atlantic Ocean are usually colder. They can bring strong storms to New England and eastern Canada, especially in winter.

Maritime tropical air masses are warm and moist. They form over the subtropical Pacific Ocean, the Gulf of Mexico, and the Caribbean Sea. These air masses bring hot, humid weather. They can produce heavy rains and thunderstorms.

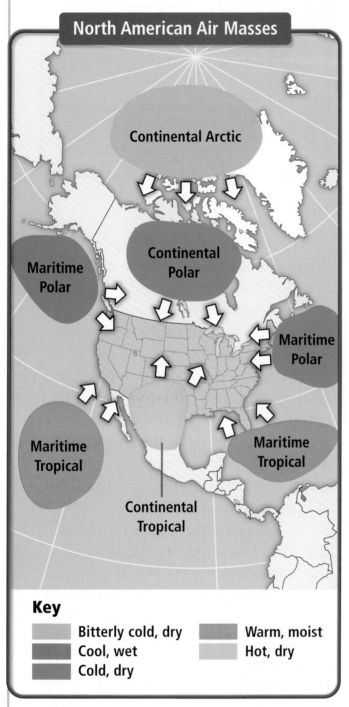

North American Air Masses

Continental Arctic

Maritime Polar

Continental Polar

Maritime Polar

Maritime Tropical

Maritime Tropical

Continental Tropical

Key

- Bitterly cold, dry
- Cool, wet
- Cold, dry
- Warm, moist
- Hot, dry

▲ Six regions produce the air masses that typically affect the weather in North America. The movements of these masses cause weather changes.

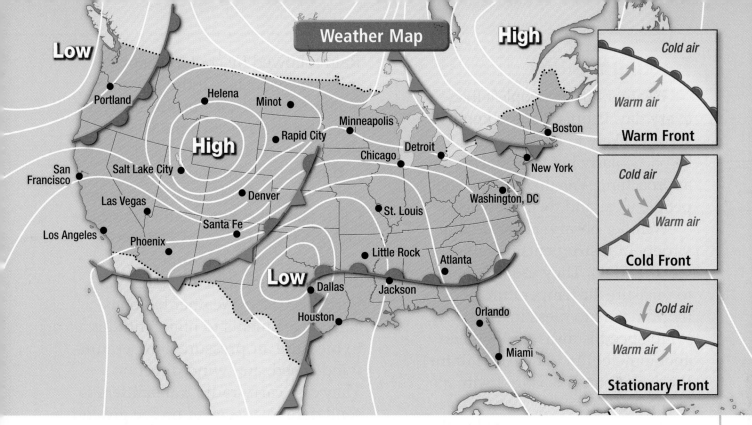

▲ The weather usually changes when a front passes over an area.

Fronts

When two air masses meet, a front forms. A **front** is the boundary between two air masses with different temperature and moisture characteristics. A front is named for the type of air mass—cold or warm—that is moving into an area. The approach of a front is usually accompanied by a change in the weather.

A cold front often brings stormy weather. At its edge, dense cold air forces warmer air ahead of the front to rise rapidly. The warm air cools as it rises. If the warm air is moist, water vapor will condense, and clouds will form. If the warm air rises quickly enough and high enough, strong thunderstorms result. Usually, a cold front moves quickly. Cooler, drier weather conditions follow it.

A warm front often brings light, steady precipitation. Along its edge, a warm air mass slides gradually up over retreating colder air. This results in light rain or snow. A warm front generally moves more slowly than a cold front. After a warm front passes, the weather is warmer.

Along a stationary front, a warm air mass meets a cold air mass, but neither is moving. The weather along the front is usually cloudy and rainy. The weather doesn't change much until the front begins moving again.

On a weather map, a cold front is shown by a blue line with triangles pointing in the direction the front is moving. A warm front is shown by a red line with half-circles facing the direction of movement. A stationary front has blue triangles on one side and red half-circles on the other.

 **MAIN IDEA AND DETAILS** What usually happens when a front approaches?

227

Tracking Weather

Weather affects people's lives every day. People want to know if snow is likely to fall, if a day will be particularly hot, or if storms are approaching. Weather affects what people wear and their activities.

Weather observers use a wide variety of instruments to gather weather data. They use thermometers to measure air temperature and hygrometers to measure humidity. Wind speed is measured with an anemometer (an uh MAHM ih tur). Precipitation is measured with a rain gauge.

Air pressure is measured with a barometer. Changes in air pressure, or barometric pressure, are important indicators of future weather. Falling barometric pressure indicates a low-pressure system is approaching.

Rain followed by cooler weather might be expected. If the pressure is falling rapidly, a storm is likely. If the pressure is steady, the weather is likely to remain the same.

Rising pressure indicates the approach of a high-pressure system. Clear skies and fair weather typically are expected.

Conditions in the upper atmosphere influence weather at Earth's surface. Weather balloons carry instruments to high altitudes to measure air pressure, temperature, wind speed, and wind direction. They also carry radio transmitters to send data to a receiver on the ground. Weather satellites send images of weather systems, including storms, to weather stations on the ground.

Weather forecasters use this information and other tools to predict the weather. They depend on radar for information about storms. Radar can show details about a storm, such as whether it contains hail or is likely to produce a tornado. Computer modeling is also a valuable tool in predicting the weather.

You can find weather information on the Internet, on the radio, in the newspaper, and on television. Learning about weather gives you a chance to make your own weather predictions.

MAIN IDEA AND DETAILS How do tools help forecast the weather?

Anemometer

Wind vane

Temperature and humidity sensor

◄ Weather forecasters use a variety of tools and instruments to collect data about the atmosphere.

Visual Summary

Uneven heating of Earth's surface by the Sun causes differences in air pressure. Winds blow from regions of high pressure to regions of low pressure.

The water cycle includes evaporation, condensation, and precipitation. The water cycle is powered by energy from the Sun.

Differences in pressure, heat, air movement, and humidity result in changes of weather.

 STANDARDS

4.a., 4.e.

Technology
Visit **www.eduplace.com/cascp** to find out more about weather.

Reading Review

1 MAIN IDEA What role does energy from the Sun play in producing Earth's weather?

2 VOCABULARY What is a *front*? What happens when a front passes over an area?

3 READING SKILL What are some important details to remember about air masses?

4 CRITICAL THINKING: Apply Is the relative humidity at a location likely to be higher in the early morning or at noon? Explain.

5 INQUIRY SKILL: Use Variables How could you observe condensation in a cup of water? What variables do you think affect the amount of condensation?

 TEST PRACTICE
A tool used to measure air pressure is a(n) _____.

A. barometer

B. anemometer

C. hygrometer

D. thermometer

STANDARDS

1: 4.a., **2–4:** 4.e., **5:** 4.d., 7.e., **Test Practice:** 7.b.

229

Predicting Hurricanes

It was 11:00 A.M. on September 2, 2004. A new hurricane, called Hurricane Frances, had formed over the Atlantic Ocean. It was heading northwest at about 21 kilometers per hour, meaning it would hit Florida in about two days. But exactly where would it hit, and when?

Tracking and predicting hurricanes is the job of the meteorologists at the National Hurricane Center. On that September day, they issued a map to show their prediction for Frances' path.

Why can't meteorologists predict a hurricane's path more precisely? Hurricanes are influenced by many factors, including changing winds and temperatures. This is why meteorologists issued warnings that day for almost all of Florida's east coast.

Several powerful hurricanes struck Florida in 2004. Yet, Floridians had evacuated areas in the hurricanes' paths. The meteorologists' predictions saved many lives.

Mexico

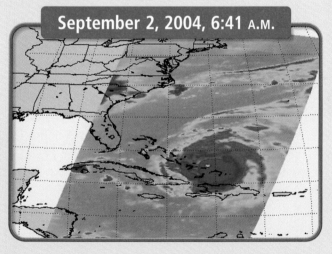

September 2, 2004, 6:41 A.M.

September 3, 2004, 8:23 P.M.

Pictures from satellites help meteorologists track the position, size, and speed of a hurricane. ▲

STANDARD
4.e. *Students know* differences in pressure, heat, air movement, and humidity result in changes of weather.

READING **LINK**

September 2, 2004

Meteorologists defined a potential track area for Hurricane Frances and predicted a specific path. How accurate did their prediction prove to be?

——— Predicted Path

——— Actual path

Potential track area

Florida

Cuba

Sharing Ideas

1. **READING CHECK** Why can't meteorologists precisely predict the path of hurricanes?

2. **WRITE ABOUT IT** Describe what you observe in the photograph on this page.

3. **TALK ABOUT IT** Why does Florida receive so many hurricanes? What should Floridians do to prepare for hurricanes?

What Are Global Weather Patterns?

Building Background

Earth is constantly rotating about its axis. You can't feel this movement because you are rotating, too.

Earth's rotation affects wind direction. Because winds usually blow from west to east across the United States, most weather systems move in this direction as well. Earth's rotation also affects ocean currents.

STANDARDS

4.e. *Students know* differences in pressure, heat, air movement, and humidity result in changes of weather.
7.d. Communicate the steps and results from an investigation in written reports and oral presentations.

PREPARE TO INVESTIGATE

Inquiry Skill

Infer When you infer, you use known facts and logical reasoning to make interpretations.

Materials

- nail
- cardboard circle, 30 cm in diameter
- pencil

Spin It!

Procedure

1 **Collaborate** Work with a partner and gather the materials.

2 **Use Models** Carefully push a nail through the center of the cardboard circle. The nail represents the North Pole. The cardboard circle represents Earth as seen from space. The circle should be able to spin easily.

3 **Use Models** Rotate the cardboard circle slowly in a counterclockwise direction. You would see Earth spinning in this direction if you were in space looking down at the North Pole. While you rotate the cardboard, have your partner use a pencil to quickly draw a straight line from the center of the circle to the edge. This line represents the direction of air movement (wind) across Earth's surface.

4 **Record Data** Draw a diagram in your *Science Notebook* showing the line's appearance.

Conclusion

1. **Analyze Data** In what direction is the line deflected, or curved?

2. **Infer** The air movement represented by the line drawn on the circle is part of a large convection cell. How might such a cell distribute energy across Earth's surface?

3. **Communicate** How does the deflection of the line relate to the way Earth's rotation affects winds and ocean currents? Write your answer in a summary report.

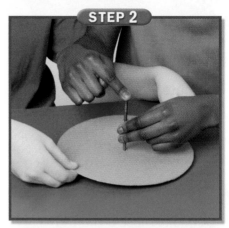

STEP 2

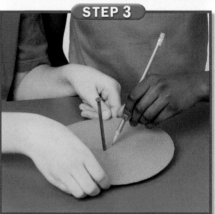

STEP 3

STEP 4

Guided Inquiry

Experiment How could you model the deflection of air in the Southern Hemisphere? Draw a diagram showing the line's deflection. Give an oral report to **communicate** your results.

Global Weather

MAIN IDEA Global weather patterns are influenced by many factors, including the distribution of air pressure and Earth's rotation.

Global Wind Patterns

As you have read, the Sun's uneven heating of Earth's surface causes differences in air pressure. Winds are part of the convection currents that form as a result. Because Earth spins on its axis, winds do not blow in straight lines. Instead, they curve. This effect is called the **Coriolis effect.** It causes winds to curve clockwise in the Northern Hemisphere and counterclockwise in the Southern Hemisphere.

Long-lasting air pressure patterns at Earth's surface are responsible for planetary wind belts. These are large regions that experience persistent winds. Wind belts in the Northern Hemisphere are generally a mirror image of those in the Southern Hemisphere. Note that these belts show general wind patterns. On any given day, the actual winds might be quite different.

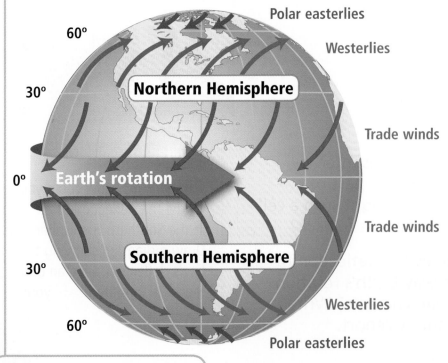

◄ The Northern Hemisphere and Southern Hemisphere each have three major wind belts. The belts form from differences in air pressure and by Earth's rotation.

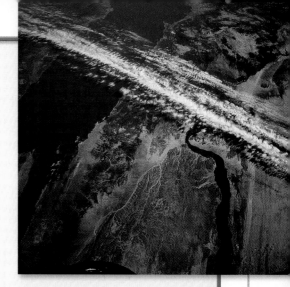

Jet streams are belts of high-speed winds high in the troposphere, the lowest layer of Earth's atmosphere. Jet streams do not follow regular paths, and their movements often affect weather.

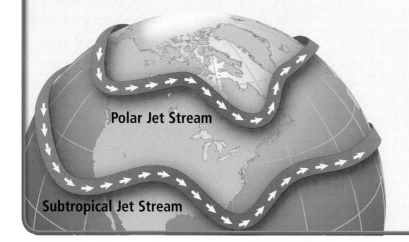

Polar Jet Stream

Subtropical Jet Stream

▲ This satellite photo shows clouds in the jet stream over the Middle East.

The wind belt around the equator is called the doldrums. The doldrums is a warm region of rising air, low air pressure, and very little wind. Rain may fall every afternoon.

Large areas of high air pressure exist at 30° north and south latitude. Here, cool air sinks toward Earth's surface. Some of this air moves across the surface toward the equator. Some moves toward the poles.

The winds that blow toward the equator are called trade winds. These steady winds powered ships on trading voyages between Europe and the Americas.

Winds between 30° and 60° latitude are called westerlies. They blow in the opposite direction to the trade winds. They blow less steadily than the trade winds.

The polar easterlies blow from high-pressure regions near each pole to about 60° latitude north or south. These winds tend to vary quite a bit in direction and speed.

Jet streams are narrow belts of high-speed winds in the upper troposphere. They generally move from west to east in both hemispheres, but can shift northward and southward, developing big loops. Jet streams often affect the movement of high- and low-pressure systems at Earth's surface. In this way, they can have a "steering" effect on weather.

Jet streams are important to commercial airlines. A pilot can fly faster and save fuel when flying with the jet stream.

SEQUENCE How does Earth's rotation affect planetary winds?

Activity Card 19
Create a Coriolis Effect

Ocean Surface Currents

Oceans cover 70 percent of Earth's surface. They affect the lands they border in many ways. Most coastal regions experience smaller daily and seasonal changes in temperature than do inland regions. One reason is because the temperature of water changes more slowly than that of land. Another reason is the effect of ocean currents.

An **ocean current** is a constant, moving stream of ocean water. All the water in a current has similar temperature and density. Ocean surface currents are produced by the prevailing winds. Like winds, currents curve to the right or left depending on which hemisphere they are in. Continents force ocean currents to change their direction.

Warm ocean currents carry warm water away from the equator. Cold ocean currents from the poles bring cooler water with them.

Climate describes the average weather conditions in an area over a long period of time. The transfer of heat by ocean currents affects climate. Many places have either warmer or colder climates because of these currents.

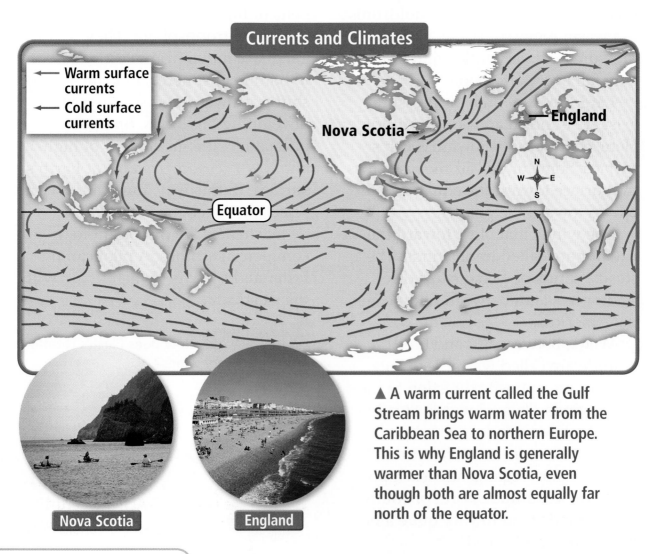

Currents and Climates

— Warm surface currents
— Cold surface currents

Nova Scotia —
— England
Equator

Nova Scotia

England

▲ A warm current called the Gulf Stream brings warm water from the Caribbean Sea to northern Europe. This is why England is generally warmer than Nova Scotia, even though both are almost equally far north of the equator.

Deep Ocean Currents

These convection currents move hot and cold water around oceans. This helps moderate temperatures of nearby land. ▶

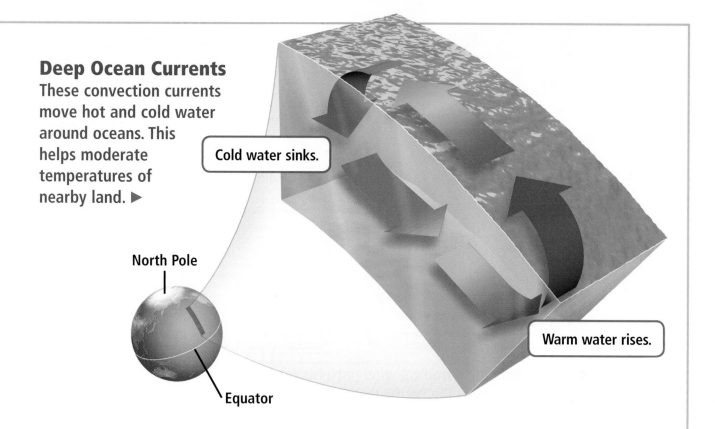

Cold water sinks.

North Pole

Equator

Warm water rises.

Deep Ocean Currents

Deep ocean currents are part of huge convection currents that circulate throughout Earth's oceans. Remember that cold water is denser than warm water. Near the poles, cold surface water sinks toward the ocean floor.

Salinity, or saltiness, also affects the density of ocean water. Saltier water is denser and sinks more rapidly than less salty water. Ice in polar regions is made up of fresh water only. When ocean water freezes, the salt is left behind. Therefore, water in polar regions tends to be both cold and salty.

A deep ocean current starts in the North Atlantic Ocean. Here, cold, salty surface water sinks, spreads out, and becomes part of a slow-moving convection current.

This deep current flows past the equator into the Southern Hemisphere. It continues past Antarctica and into the Pacific and Indian Oceans. Some of the deep waters are warmed here and rise toward the surface. The warm water returns as a surface current to the North Atlantic, where it moderates the climate.

This huge convection current is commonly described as a "conveyor belt." The water seems to move in a never-ending cycle.

Note that these currents flow very slowly. It can take as long as a thousand years for the current to make a single round trip!

SEQUENCE What happens to surface water in the northern Atlantic Ocean?

237

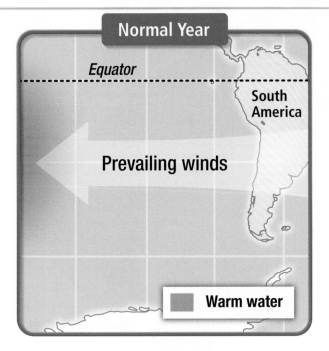

▲ In El Niño years, changes in tropical wind patterns result in a reversal of surface currents in the Pacific Ocean. Normally, surface winds near the equator drive currents east to west. During an El Niño year, reversed winds blow currents west to east.

El Niño

Can weather in the United States be affected by what happens halfway around the globe? The answer is yes!

In the tropical Pacific Ocean, the trade winds usually drive ocean currents from east to west. These currents carry warm water from the west coast of South America to the western Pacific Ocean. As surface water moves away, colder, deeper water rises along the coast of South America. This water brings nutrients to the surface. In turn, these nutrients support a large community of sea life.

In some years, however, the trade winds weaken. They are often replaced by winds that blow in the opposite direction. The surface current reverses direction, too. Unusually warm water extends across the entire Pacific Ocean. This change in wind and current patterns is called El Niño.

During an El Niño event, warm water flows along the coast of South America. The supply of nutrients to surface water is cut off. Many fish either die or leave the area, ruining the fishing industry.

Strong El Niño events affect global weather patterns, too. During El Niño years, regions that are normally dry, like southern California, might receive heavy rains. Other areas that normally have a wet climate might experience droughts. The results include floods, brush fires, and other natural disasters. Everyone is affected—from homeowners to farmers to business owners.

 **SEQUENCE**   What causes El Niño?

Lesson Wrap-Up

Visual Summary

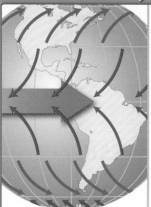

Global wind belts are part of huge convection cells in Earth's atmosphere. The Coriolis effect causes winds to curve.

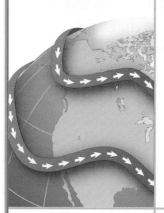

High-altitude, high-speed jet streams often affect weather systems near Earth's surface.

Ocean currents are part of huge convection cells that transport warm surface water from the equator toward the poles and cold deep ocean water from the poles toward the equator.

 STANDARDS

4.d., 4.e.

Technology
Visit **www.eduplace.com/cascp** to find out more about global weather patterns.

Reading Review

1 MAIN IDEA Name at least two factors that affect weather patterns around the world.

2 VOCABULARY What is a *jet stream*? How does it affect weather?

3 READING SKILL What events lead to the development of El Niño? What changes in the weather can El Niño cause?

1	
2	
3	
4	

4 CRITICAL THINKING: Analyze Increased melting of polar ice would make the Arctic Ocean less salty. How would this affect the North Atlantic "conveyor belt" current?

5 INQUIRY SKILL: Infer How would the planetary wind belts be affected if Earth were to stop rotating?

 TEST PRACTICE

What causes the curved shape of Earth's prevailing winds?

A. jet stream

B. Coriolis effect

C. doldrums

D. planetary wind belt

 STANDARDS

1–2: 4.e., **3–4:** 4.d., **Test Practice:** 4.e.

239

What Are California's Climates?

Building Background

Weather patterns describe the climate of a place. Some climates are hot and dry, others are cool and wet, and still others change a great deal from season to season. California is a large state that has several different climates.

PREPARE TO INVESTIGATE

Inquiry Skill

Use Numbers When you use numbers, you may do calculations to explain patterns in data.

Materials
- graph paper
- pencils
- metric ruler

STANDARDS

4.e. *Students know* differences in pressure, heat, air movement, and humidity result in changes of weather.
7.h. Identify changes in natural phenomena over time without manipulating the phenomena (e.g., a tree limb, a grove of trees, a stream, a hillslope).

Graph Your Climate!

Procedure

1 **Research** Search the National Oceanic and Atmospheric Administration (NOAA) Web site at www.noaa.gov. Find monthly average temperature and precipitation data for the past year in your town.

2 **Record Data** In your *Science Notebook,* make a table like the one shown to record your data.

3 **Use Numbers** On graph paper, draw a graph with axes like the one shown.

4 **Record Data** For each month, locate the temperature recorded in your table on the temperature scale of the graph. Use a red pencil to mark the points. Then draw a smooth line that connects the points.

5 **Use Numbers** For each month, find the amount of precipitation recorded in your table on the precipitation scale of the graph. Use a blue pencil to mark the points. Fill in a blue bar for each month up to its precipitation point.

Conclusion

1. **Analyze Data** Describe the patterns of temperature and precipitation on your graph.

2. **Infer** Study the data you gathered. What do you think determines the yearly temperature and precipitation pattern in your area?

STEP 2

Month	Total Precipitation (mm)	Average Temperature (°C)
January		
February		
March		
April		
May		
June		
July		
August		
September		
October		
November		
December		

STEP 3

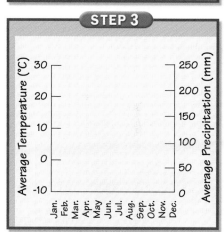

Guided Inquiry

Ask Questions Select a location in California that is very different from where you live. **Predict** how yearly weather might differ from that in your area. Make a climate graph and compare it to the one in the activity.

California Climate

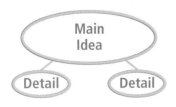
MAIN IDEA California has several different climate zones, each having different characteristics.

California Climate Zones

As you have read, the climate of a region describes the long-term average weather conditions for that area. Several factors determine climate. These include prevailing winds, persistent pressure systems, distance to large bodies of water, and nearby landforms.

Meteorologists consider two main factors when describing climate—temperature and precipitation. Using these factors, California can be divided into four climate zones, as shown on the map below.

On any given day, the weather likely is quite different among the climate zones. Mountain ranges, the Pacific Ocean, and local landforms all create very different weather across California.

For example, Los Angeles is located in a basin. It commonly has hot, dry weather. On the other hand, San Francisco is located on a bay. Its weather is often moist and cool.

LEGEND

Mediterranean (hot, dry summers with rainy mild winters)

Semi arid (dry, hot summers, cold winters)

Desert (very dry, very hot summers)

Highland (temperature varies with altitude)

OREGON
Mount Shasta ▲
Sacramento ★
San Francisco •
PACIFIC OCEAN
NEVADA
Santa Barbara •
Los Angeles •
Palm Springs •
AZ
MEXICO

N W E S

km 0 50 100
mi 0 50 100

◀ Throughout the year, weather patterns are very different across California. What does the map show about the climate of your community?

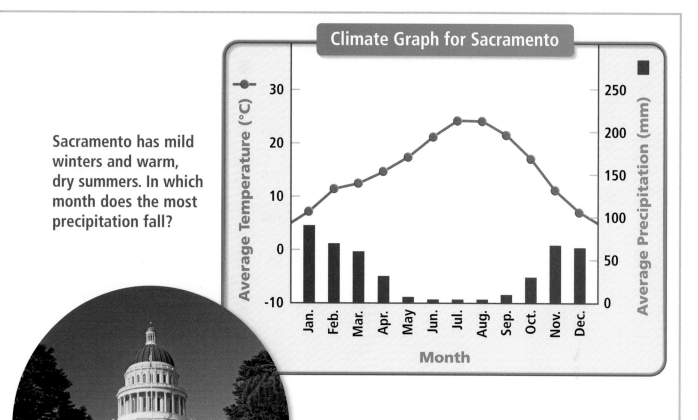

Climate Graph for Sacramento

Sacramento has mild winters and warm, dry summers. In which month does the most precipitation fall?

Sacramento

Sacramento, the capital of California, is located almost in the center of the state. Along with its role in government, Sacramento is a shipping and rail center for the region. Farm crops and other products are shipped to San Francisco by way of a channel through the Sacramento River Delta.

As shown in the graph above, Sacramento has what is known as a Mediterranean climate, with mild winters and warm, dry summers. Average yearly temperature is 16°C (61°F). Although Sacramento has distinct temperature differences during the seasons, they are not very severe. This makes Sacramento's weather quite pleasant, an important reason why it is one of the nation's faster growing cities.

Sacramento is about 65 km (40 mi) east of the foothills of the Sierra Nevadas. These mountains receive some of the heaviest snow packs in the United States. Spring melting supplies fresh water for the region.

The climate of Sacramento is ideal for growing crops. Sacramento is part of California's Central Valley, one of the most fertile regions in the world. Its farms supply almost one-fourth of the food that America eats.

 **MAIN IDEA AND DETAILS** How would you describe the climate of Sacramento?

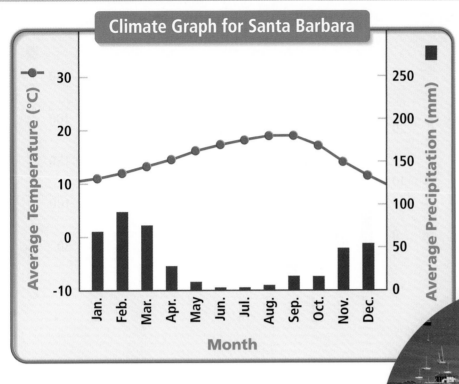

Climate Graph for Santa Barbara

Average Temperature (°C) / Average Precipitation (mm)
Month: Jan., Feb., Mar., Apr., May, Jun., Jul., Aug., Sep., Oct., Nov., Dec.

Santa Barbara has moderate, pleasant weather all year long. Compare its average temperatures to those of Sacramento.

Santa Barbara

Santa Barbara is located on the coast of California, just north of Los Angeles. Like Sacramento, Santa Barbara has mild winters and warm, dry summers. However, average temperatures tend to be slightly lower in summer and higher in winter than those of the capital.

Santa Barbara receives about 38 cm (15 in.) of rain each year. As in Sacramento, most precipitation occurs between November and March.

Two important factors influence the climate of Santa Barbara. Although most of California's coastline extends in a north-south direction, Santa Barbara is located on a section of the coast that runs east-west. This helps modify the effects of the ocean currents that cool the rest of the California coast.

The Santa Ynez Mountains also influence the climate here. These mountains come almost to the water's edge. They provide protection from the summer heat of inland areas. Yet in the spring, dry, hot winds may move down the slopes of the mountains. These winds dry out vegetation and increase the risk of wildfires.

Millions of people live along the coast between Santa Barbara and the Mexican border. Cities here include Los Angeles and San Diego, the two largest cities in California. They are popular in part because of the beautiful weather that lasts nearly all year long.

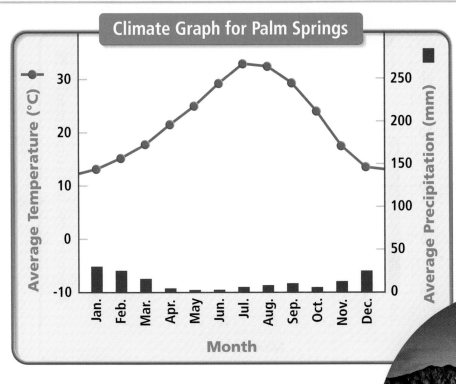

Climate Graph for Palm Springs

Average Temperature (°C) / Average Precipitation (mm) vs Month (Jan. – Dec.)

The yearly temperature and precipitation changes in Palm Springs are typical for the desert regions of the southwest United States.

Palm Springs

Find Palm Springs on the map on page 242. Notice that it is only about 100 kilometers east of Los Angeles. However, its climate is very different!

Palm Springs lies in the heart of the Sonora Desert, where the climate is very hot and very dry. Palm Springs receives less than 15 cm (6 in.) of rain each year, and that rain falls mostly in winter.

What makes southeast California so dry? The mountains just to the west are part of the answer. They cool whatever moist winds blow in from the Pacific, leaving hardly any moisture for the air farther east. In fact, desert-like conditions stretch eastward across most of the southwest United States.

Nevertheless, the lands near Palm Springs are especially fertile. Farms in this area are famous for dates, figs, and many other fruits and vegetables. Irrigation makes this possible.

Because it is so close to Los Angeles and other large cities, Palm Springs is a popular resort. It enjoys 354 days of sunshine a year!

MAIN IDEA AND DETAILS What is one reason why Santa Barbara and Palm Springs have different climates?

Express Lab

Activity Card 20
Graph Temperature

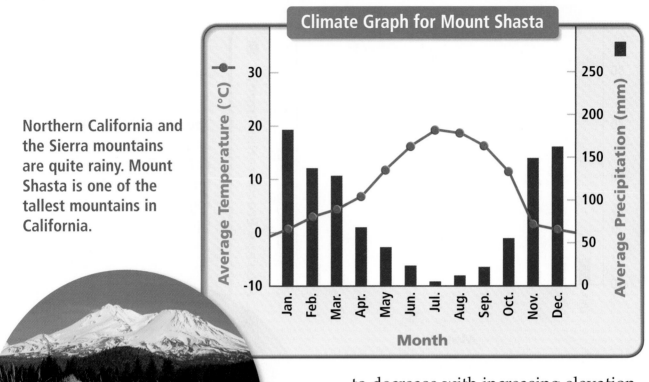

Climate Graph for Mount Shasta

Average Temperature (°C): 30, 20, 10, 0, -10

Average Precipitation (mm): 250, 200, 150, 100, 50, 0

Month: Jan., Feb., Mar., Apr., May, Jun., Jul., Aug., Sep., Oct., Nov., Dec.

Northern California and the Sierra mountains are quite rainy. Mount Shasta is one of the tallest mountains in California.

Mount Shasta

In many ways, the climate of northern California is just the opposite of the climate in the southeast part of the state. One important reason is latitude. Remember that as you move north through the United States, places receive less and less solar radiation throughout the year. In general, this means lower temperatures.

Elevation is another factor. Northern California is quite mountainous, and temperatures tend to decrease with increasing elevation. Mountains near the Pacific Ocean can be quite rainy, too.

Mount Shasta is the name of both a mountain and a nearby town. These places lie about 100 km (60 mi) south of the Oregon state line. The region experiences long, warm summers and cold, wet winters. Average yearly precipitation is almost 100 cm (39 in.), which includes a great deal of snowfall during the winter months.

All of this water, combined with warm but not scorching temperatures, makes northern California ideal for growing trees. Indeed, much of this part of the state is covered in forests. Some forest lands are protected, while many others are harvested for timber. The logging industry is important in this region.

 **MAIN IDEA AND DETAILS** **Describe the climate of northern California.**

Visual Summary

California has four distinct climate zones, based on temperature and precipitation. On any given day, the weather can be very different among these zones.

Sacramento has mild winters and warm, dry summers. The climate of Santa Barbara includes moderate temperatures throughout the year and low precipitation.

Palm Springs has a desert climate. Summers are very hot and dry. In contrast, the climate in northern California is much cooler and wetter.

STANDARD

4.e.

Technology

Visit **www.eduplace.com/cascp** to find out more about California climates.

Reading Review

1 MAIN IDEA What are the four climate zones in California?

2 VOCABULARY Write a sentence about Lesson 3 using a vocabulary term from either Lesson 1 or Lesson 2.

3 READING SKILL Describe the four different climate zones of California.

```
          Main
          Idea

   Detail        Detail
```

4 CRITICAL THINKING: Analyze How can landforms affect the climate of an area?

5 INQUIRY SKILL: Use Numbers How does the climate of Sacramento compare to that around Mount Shasta?

TEST PRACTICE

The two factors that define climate are temperature and _____.

A. elevation

B. precipitation

C. nearness to oceans

D. latitude

STANDARD

1–5: 4.e. **Test Practice:** 4.e.

EXTREME Science

SUPER WAVES!

It's the size of a five-story building. It can move at 40 km per hour. Its energy could light up a small city. What do you do with a wave that big? Surf it, of course!

Surfers on the Hawaiian island of Maui call the ocean reef where these giant waves break Peahi. Surfers around the world call the site Jaws—as in crushing, crunching danger. The extreme waves of Jaws are caused by swells formed by huge ocean storms hundreds of kilometers away.

A single wave this size produces more than 720,000 horsepower. That equals the power of 6,500 typical family cars!

Gulf of Alaska

L

USA

swells

Hawaii

Every winter, huge low-pressure systems form in the Gulf of Alaska. The energy of these extreme storms builds up massive swells. The swells travel over 965 km to the Hawaiian island, where they produce monster waves. It's the energy of an ocean that gives rise to the titans of Jaws.

Writing Journal

Calculate in your journal how long it takes a Jaws swell to travel 965 km if it travels 40 km/hr.

Math in Science

The graph shows average temperature and precipitation values based on 50 years of data. Notice the graph uses two scales: one for average temperature, another for average precipitation.

1. What is the range of average monthly temperatures for Mount Shasta?

2. What if Mount Shasta received 250 mm of precipitation next December? If the graph were revised to include next year's data, how would the bar for December change? Explain.

3. Describe the climate of Mount Shasta in your own words. Include data from the graph in your answer.

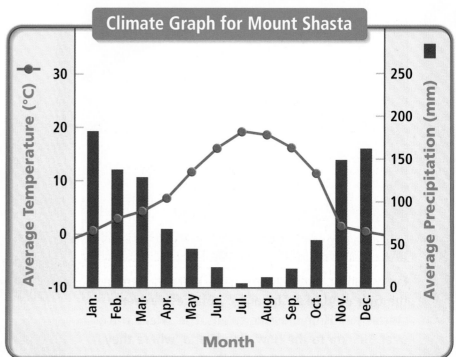

Writing in Science
Research Report

Are El Niño years more likely now than in the past? Research and report on how scientists are answering this question. Include charts, diagrams, or maps to show El Niño's causes and effects.

California

Francisco Chavez

Both anchovies and sardines are small, ocean-dwelling fish. What can be learned from studying them? Just ask Dr. Francisco Chavez, a scientist at the Monterrey Bay Aquarium Research Institute. From analyzing data on these fish, he identified a 50-year climate cycle in the Pacific Ocean.

During the cooler phase of the cycle, strong ocean currents bring nutrients to the eastern Pacific. The nutrients support anchovies in great numbers, which in turn are food for salmon, rockfish, and other fish. During the warmer phase, less nutrients are available and sardines are more common.

The sardine phase of the cycle resembles El Niño, but is milder and longer-lasting. As Dr. Chavez knows, scientists have much more to learn about climate changes and their effects on oceans.

▼ Populations of small fish, such as these anchovies, are the key to Dr. Chavez's research on climate.

Vocabulary

Complete each sentence with a term from the list.

1. The temperature at which air is saturated with water vapor is called the _____.

2. A high-speed wind in the upper troposphere is the _____.

3. The change of water from the liquid state to the gas state is _____.

4. The force exerted on a surface by the weight of the air above it is _____.

5. A large body of air that has the same temperature and moisture characteristics throughout is a(n) _____.

6. A boundary between two different air masses is a(n) _____.

7. Water, snow, or ice that falls from clouds is called _____.

8. The curving of global winds is due to the _____.

9. The long-term weather pattern for an area is its _____.

10. A line that connects points of equal air pressure on a map is a(n) _____.

air mass p. 226
air pressure p. 222
climate p. 236
condensation p. 225
Coriolis effect p. 234
dew point p. 225
evaporation p. 225
front p. 227
humidity p. 225
isobar p. 223
jet stream p. 235
ocean current p. 236
precipitation p. 225

Test Practice

Write the letter of the best answer choice.

11. The amount of water vapor in the air is called _____.

   A. fronts
   B. humidity
   C. jet stream
   D. dew point

12. The blanket of gases that surrounds a planet is known as the planet's _____.

   A. atmosphere
   B. jet stream
   C. Coriolis effect
   D. climate

13. The process of cloud formation is an example of _____.

   A. transpiration
   B. evaporation
   C. condensation
   D. precipitation

14. Continuous streams of moving ocean water that form parts of convection cells are called _____.

   A. jet streams
   B. waves
   C. ocean currents
   D. planetary winds

Inquiry Skills

15. **Infer** You hear on the morning weather report that a low-pressure system is approaching. What can you infer about the weather for later in the day?

16. Plan an investigation to determine if the climate in your area is changing over time. Describe the tools you would use, the steps you would follow, and how you would present your data.

Map the Concept

Using the Internet or local newspapers, find out what the weather forecast is in your area for the next three days. Record this information in a chart like the one below. Then monitor the weather each day and record what the weather actually was for those three days.

Forecast	Actual
Day 1:	Day 1:
Day 2:	Day 2:
Day 3:	Day 3:

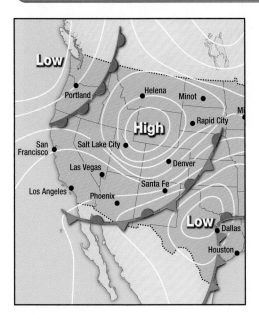

Critical Thinking

17. **Apply** Explain the movement of water in a deep ocean current in terms of convection.

18. **Synthesize** Explain how weather forecasters use information gathered from a barometer.

19. **Evaluate** Why is the south coast of Alaska much warmer, on average, than interior parts of the state? HINT: Find Alaska on the map on page 236.

20. **Analyze** Why are computers useful in forecasting the weather?

Performance Assessment

Cold Fronts

Suppose there is a cold front approaching. Draw a diagram that shows how the approaching front causes a change in the weather.

Writing Journal

Review your answers to the questions on page 217 at the beginning of this chapter. Change your answers as needed, based on what you have learned.

STANDARDS

1: 3.d., **2:** 4.a., **3:** 3.c., **4:** 2.e., **5:** 3.d., **6:** 3.b., **7:** 3.b., **8:** 3.b., **9:** 4.b., **10:** 3.b., **11–13:** 4.a., **14:** 4.d., **15:** 4.e., **16:** 7.h., **17:** 4.a., 4.d., **18:** 7.b., **19:** 4.d., **20:** 4.e., **Map the Concept:** 4.e., **Performance Assessment:** 4.e.

Write the letter of the best answer.

1. The boundary between two air masses is called a ____.
   A. front
   B. sea breeze
   C. convection current
   D. greenhouse effect

2. England and Nova Scotia are about the same distance north of the equator. Which of the following causes England to be much warmer than Nova Scotia?
   A. Coriolis effect
   B. El Niño
   C. surface area currents
   D. ozone

3. Visible light is part of the ____.
   A. convection current
   B. electromagnetic spectrum
   C. solar energy
   D. gamma rays

4. Which type of wave can travel in a vacuum?
   A. sound
   B. light
   C. water
   D. air

5. Which part of the electromagnetic spectrum causes people to need sunscreen?
   A. gamma rays
   B. ultraviolet light
   C. infrared light
   D. radio waves

6. Which region of Earth's surface is likely to receive the most direct rays of the Sun?

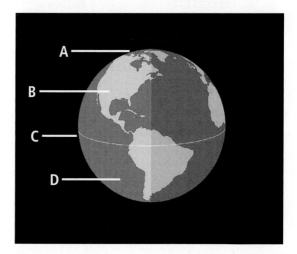

   A. A
   B. B
   C. C
   D. D

7. Which picture best shows the greenhouse effect?

A.

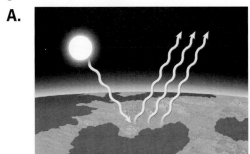

B.

C.

D.

8. Which gas is likely a cause of global warming?

- **A.** carbon dioxide
- **B.** nitrogen
- **C.** oxygen
- **D.** methane

Answer the following in complete sentences.

9. Describe the development of a convection cell in the atmosphere.

10. Why do the Mojave Desert and Mammoth Mountain have different average temperatures?

STANDARDS

1–2: 4.e., **3:** 4.b., **4:** 3.a., **5:** 4.b., **6:** 3.d., 4.a.,
7–8: 3.a., 4.b., **9:** 3.e., 4.d., **10:** 4.e.

You Can...

Discover More

A powerful fan fills a hot-air balloon with air. A gas burner heats the air, and the balloon lifts off. The balloon rises because the hot air inside it is lighter and less dense than the air around it. Whether it's in your classroom, in the atmosphere, or in a balloon, hot air always rises over cold air.

A burner changes the chemical energy in a fuel, such as propane gas, to thermal energy. The thermal energy flows to the air inside the balloon, making the air warm.

As they get warmer, air particles inside the balloon move faster and farther apart. This makes the hot air inside the balloon lighter and less dense than the cool air outside.

The hot air rises, carrying the balloon with it. Because the burner continues to heat the air inside the balloon, the balloon stays afloat.

To bring the balloon down, the pilot lets some of the hot air out through a vent near the top of the balloon. Cold air enters the balloon from the bottom. With less and less hot air to lift it, the weight of the balloon causes it to sink to the ground.

 Fly a hot-air balloon into the air. Go to **www.eduplace.com/cascp/** to see how density keeps a balloon afloat.

LIFE

UNIT D

SCIENCE

Ecology

California Connection

Visit www.eduplace.com/cascp/ to learn more about ecology and ecosystems.

Big Sur Ornithology Lab

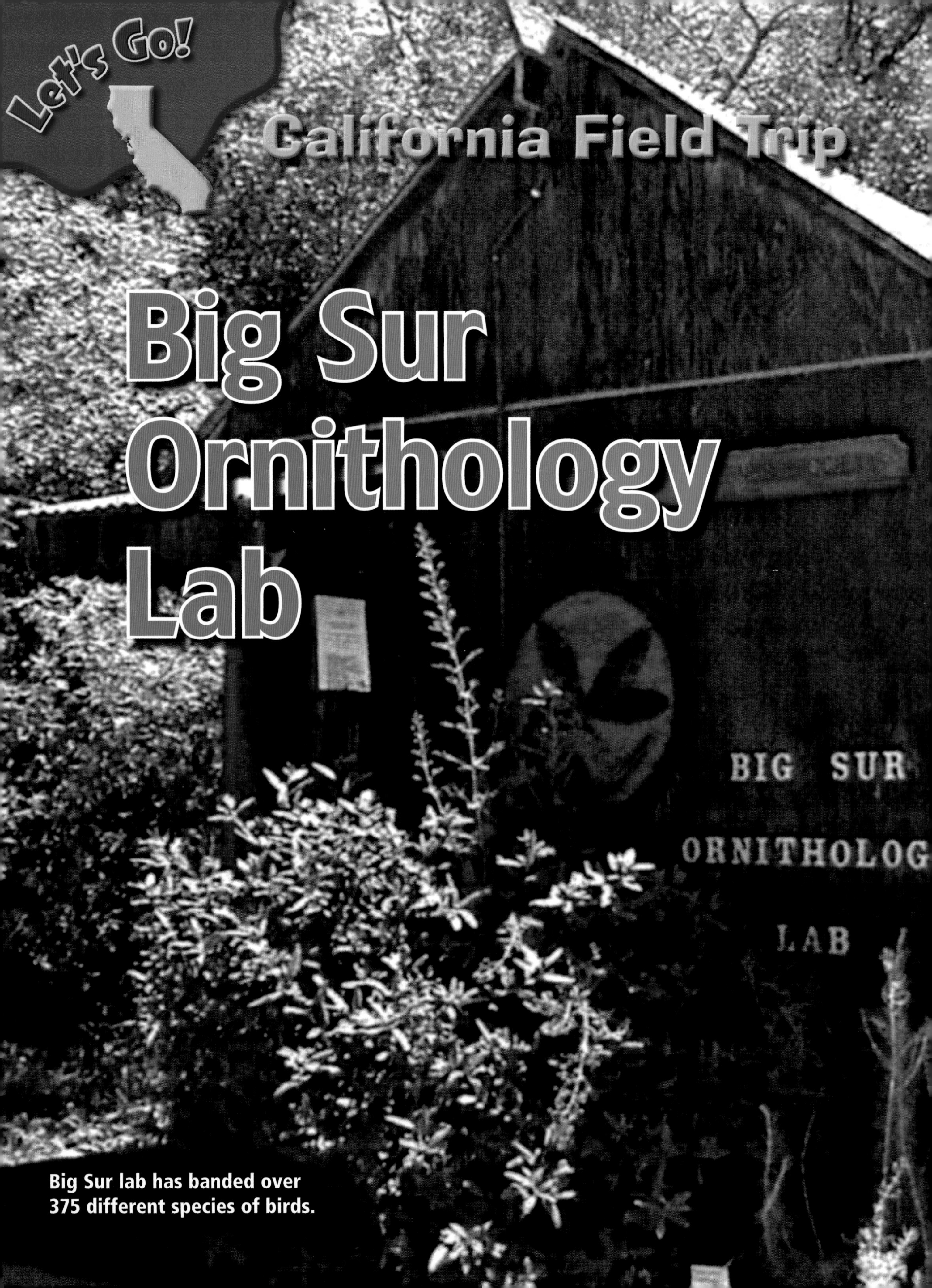

BIG SUR

ORNITHOLOG

LAB

Big Sur lab has banded over 375 different species of birds.

Banding birds can help scientists learn about the migration routes and behaviors of different species.

The California condor is making a comeback from the brink of extinction at Big Sur.

LIFE UNIT D SCIENCE

Ecology

Chapter 7
The Biosphere 258

Independent Books

- The Biosphere
- Biodiversity Hotspots
- Prairie Dogs and Black-footed Ferrets

Chapter 8
Roles of Living Things 294

Independent Books

- Roles of Living Things
- Bison and Native Americans
- Crying Wolf

Chapter 9
Populations 330

Independent Books

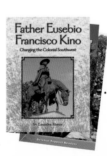

- Populations
- Father Eusebio Francisco Kino:
  Changing the Colonial Southwest
- California's Pygmy Forest

Black-tailed jackrabbit

California *Big Idea!*

Standard Set 5.
Ecology (Life Sciences)

Organisms in ecosystems exchange energy and nutrients among themselves and with the environment.

Chapter 7

The Biosphere

Brown bear and salmon in Alaska

LESSON 1

Sunlight, water, air, plants, animals, and you—how do you and other living things interact with the environment?

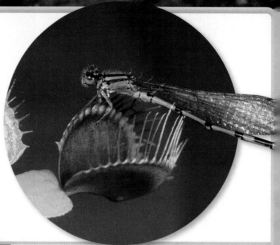

LESSON 2

Earth's biomes range from scorching deserts to steamy rain forests to the bottom of the ocean. What organisms live in these places? How do they survive?

LESSON 3

Green plants and algae use sunlight, carbon dioxide, and water to make food. How do nutrients and water cycle through the biosphere?

Writing Journal

In your Writing Journal, write or draw answers to each question.

taiga

a forest biome that has severe winters and short cool summers

Vocabulary Preview

Vocabulary

abiotic factor p. 264
adaptation p. 270
biome p. 270
biosphere p. 264
biotic factor p. 264
community p. 265
desert p. 272
ecosystem p. 264
grassland p. 272
nitrogen fixation p. 284
photosynthesis p. 280
population p. 266
respiration p. 281
taiga p. 273
temperate forest p. 271
tropical rain forest p. 271
transpiration p. 286
tundra p. 273

Glossary

English-Spanish, p. H26

Vocabulary Skill

Word Roots
biosphere

The prefix *bio-* comes from a Greek word that means life. One meaning of *sphere* is the area in which something exists. So biosphere means "area in which life exists."

desert

a very dry area, usually with sandy or rocky soil and little or no vegetation

grassland

land covered by grasses and grass-like vegetation

tundra

a cold treeless region of the far north, with mostly frozen ground

Standard Set 5. Ecology (Life Sciences)

5.a. *Students know* energy entering ecosystems as sunlight is transferred by producers into chemical energy through photosynthesis and then from organism to organism through food webs.

5.b. *Students know* matter is transferred over time from one organism to others in the food web and between organisms and the physical environment.

5.e. *Students know* the number and types of organisms an ecosystem can support depends on the resources available and on abiotic factors, such as quantities of light and water, a range of temperatures, and soil composition.

The following Set 7: Investigation and Experimentation standards covered in this chapter: 7.e., 7.h.

What Are Ecosystems?

Building Background

You live in a community made up of trees and grasses, pets and people, and all the other living things in your area. Living things interact with one another and with nonliving things. Together, they make up an ecosystem. Everything an animal or a plant needs to survive—including food, air, and a place to live—comes from living and nonliving things in its environment.

 STANDARDS

5.e. *Students know* the number and types of organisms an ecosystem can support depends on the resources available and on abiotic factors, such as quantities of light and water, a range of temperatures, and soil composition.
7.h. Identify changes in natural phenomena over time without manipulating the phenomena (e.g., a tree limb, a grove of trees, a stream, a hillslope).

PREPARE TO INVESTIGATE

Inquiry Skill

Observe When you observe, you use your senses and tools to identify properties, including changes over time.

Materials

- soil
- 500-mL beaker
- terrarium with lid
- organic matter, such as peat moss or decayed leaves
- apple peels
- earthworms
- water

Science and Math Toolbox

For step 1, review **Measuring Volume** on page H7.

A Look at Life

Procedure

Safety: Wash your hands after setting up the terrarium.

1. **Collaborate** Work in a small group. Use the beaker to measure 500 mL of soil. Pour the soil into the terrarium. Spread a thin layer of organic matter over the soil. Add earthworms and a handful of apple peels.

2. **Predict** Add water to one side of the terrarium until the soil is slightly wet. In your *Science Notebook,* predict how the earthworms will react to the water. Loosely place the lid on the terrarium. Place the terrarium out of sunlight.

3. **Classify** Draw a chart like the one shown. Classify the things in the terrarium as living or nonliving.

4. **Observe** Each day for one week, carefully observe the earthworms and their environment. Record and date your observations.

Conclusion

1. **Observe** What interactions did you observe between the earthworms and their environment? How did matter transfer to the earthworms?

2. **Infer** What do earthworms need to survive? Include evidence from this activity in your answer.

3. **Hypothesize** How would the terrarium change if the number of earthworms doubled or tripled? Explain your answer.

STEP 1

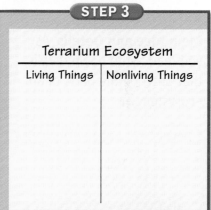

STEP 3

Terrarium Ecosystem	
Living Things	Nonliving Things

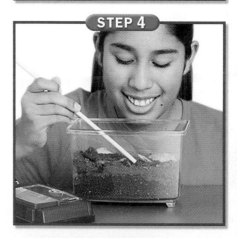

STEP 4

Guided Inquiry

Experiment Ask questions about how a small community in your schoolyard changes over time. With your teacher's permission, conduct an investigation. **Communicate** the results in a written report.

The Biosphere

MAIN IDEA An ecosystem is a community of living organisms and their environment. All of Earth's ecosystems are found in a narrow zone at or near Earth's surface, called the biosphere.

READING SKILL

Main Idea and Details As you read, write down details that describe the parts of an ecosystem.

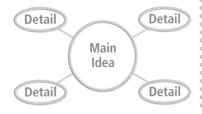

STANDARDS

5.e. *Students know* the number and types of organisms an ecosystem can support depends on the resources available and on abiotic factors, such as quantities of light and water, a range of temperatures, and soil composition.

Ecosystems and Communities

If you put your head down near the ground in a forest, what would you see? You might notice ants marching in line or worms burrowing through the soil. Fuzzy mosses might tickle your nose, and twigs and bits of leaves might stick in your hair.

A section of forest floor is one example of an ecosystem. An **ecosystem** is made up of all the living and nonliving things that interact in one place. Ecosystems can also be large—like a whole forest or a prairie. Any living part of an ecosystem is called a **biotic factor.** In a forest, biotic factors range from tiny bacteria to towering trees. Any nonliving part of an ecosystem is called an **abiotic factor.** Abiotic (ay by AHT ihk) factors include sunlight, soil, water, air, and range of temperatures.

The **biosphere** (BY uhs feer) is the narrow zone at or near Earth's surface where life is able to exist. It includes the oceans, the lower atmosphere, and the upper part of Earth's crust.

◄ Small Ecosystem
Soil, a rotting log, fungi, moss, and a lizard are all part of this small ecosystem.

Ecology is the study of interactions in ecosystems. The Mojave Desert is one of the desert ecosystems in the Joshua Tree National Park in southeastern California. The land is hot, and rainfall is scarce. Rugged mountains, exposed rock, sand, and scrubby plants make up the landscape.

The plants, animals, and other organisms of the Mojave Desert make up a community. A **community** is the group of living things found in an ecosystem. They depend upon one another for food, shelter, and other needs. They also depend upon nonliving things.

The plants and animals of the Mojave are well suited for life there. Lizards and snakes, for example, get all the water they need from their food. Scales on their bodies prevent water loss.

The habits of some animals help them survive the desert. The round-tailed squirrel curls up in a burrow and sleeps during the hottest and driest part of the summer.

Joshua trees store water in their roots, branches, and trunks. Animals get water when they eat these parts. They also provide shelter.

MAIN IDEA Give examples of the parts of an ecosystem.

Large Ecosystem
The Mohave Desert ecosystem includes a community of these and other living things.

Red-tailed hawk

◄ Joshua tree

Rattlesnake

Bighorn sheep

Populations

You can learn a lot by studying an individual plant, animal, or other organism. But to understand how an ecosystem functions, you need to study populations. A **population** consists of all the members of the same type of organism that live in an ecosystem.

The Mojave Desert ecosystem includes populations of Joshua trees, California junipers, rattlesnakes, bighorn sheep, jackrabbits, and many other species. The birth or death of one plant or animal is not likely to change the Mojave Desert very much. But what if a disease killed all the Joshua trees? Or a new animal species began to live where the jackrabbits now live? Events like these can affect the entire community.

Desert ecosystems are fragile. Suppose humans cut down large numbers of desert plants. How would the animals that depend on them survive? What if it rained even less? Desert organisms can live with limited water, but even they need some.

In every ecosystem, some species are very important for the whole community. In an ocean ecosystem, which fish would you guess are most important? Arguably, the answer is the smallest fish, including herring and mackerel. These fish are food for bigger fish, which in turn are food for sharks, killer whales, and other big animals. Without large numbers of small fish, many other animals would starve.

MAIN IDEA What are some of the populations of the Mojave Desert?

Populations in the Ocean

Express Lab

Activity Card 21
Sample Soil

Feeding Relationships
Small fish eat algae and other plant life, and they are food for larger fish. Feeding relationships like these are a part of all ecosystems.

Visual Summary

Ecosystems are made up of all the biotic and abiotic factors that interact in a given place.

A community is made up of different populations of living things in an ecosystem.

A population consists of all the members of the same type of organism that live in a community.

 STANDARD
5.e.

 **Technology**
Visit **www.eduplace.com/cascp** to find out more about ecosystems.

Reading Review

1 MAIN IDEA How do scientists classify the parts of ecosystems?

2 VOCABULARY Use the terms *community, ecosystem,* and *population* to describe the area where you live.

3 READING SKILL Why are the abiotic factors in an ecosystem important? What could happen when abiotic factors change?

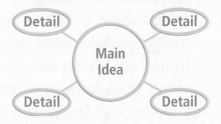

4 CRITICAL THINKING: Infer What might happen if one population in an ecosystem disappeared? Give a specific example to support your answer.

5 INQUIRY SKILL: Observe Observe a small patch of grass, a tree trunk, or an area of soil. Classify the things you observe as biotic or abiotic factors.

 TEST PRACTICE
Which of these contains the greatest number of organisms?

A. biosphere

B. population

C. community

D. ecosystem

 STANDARD
1–5: 5.e., **Test Practice:** 5.e.

267

What Are Earth's Biomes?

Building Background

Different regions on Earth support different species of plants and animals. Water, weather, soil, and other factors affect all organisms, from mountain goats to farm animals; from thick forests to tall grasses. Think about the natural environment where you live. It determines which plants and animals you see around you.

STANDARDS

5.e. *Students know* the number and types of organisms an ecosystem can support depends on the resources available and on abiotic factors, such as quantities of light and water, a range of temperatures, and soil composition.
7.e. Recognize whether evidence is consistent with a proposed explanation.

PREPARE TO INVESTIGATE

Inquiry Skill

Classify When you classify, you sort organisms, objects, or events into groups based on their characteristics.

Materials

• mixed set of picture cards

Science and Math Toolbox

For step 2, review **Making a Chart to Organize Data** on page H11.

Where Do They Live?

Procedure

1 **Collaborate** Work with a partner to classify plants and animals according to where they live. Spread out the picture cards on a table. Find the cards representing three types of natural environments: a hot and dry desert, a hot and wet rain forest, and a cold and treeless tundra.

2 **Record Data** In your *Science Notebook,* create a chart like the one shown. Use it to record your observations.

3 **Classify** Look carefully at each plant or animal card. Arrange the cards so that each organism is correctly matched with its natural environment.

4 **Record Data** Record the names of the plants and animals in the correct column in your chart.

Conclusion

1. **Analyze Data** Describe the evidence you used to match each plant and animal with its environment.

2. **Infer** Which of the three types of environments has the resources—water, sunlight, food—to support the greatest number of organisms? Explain your answer.

STEP 1

STEP 2

Desert	Rain Forest	Tundra

Guided Inquiry

Ask Questions What plants and animals live near your home and school? **Observe** them as you walk around outside. Use binoculars, if available. Make a list, then classify them into different categories.

Biomes

VOCABULARY

adaptation	p. 270
biome	p. 270
desert	p. 272
grassland	p. 272
taiga	p. 273
temperate forest	p. 271
tropical rain forest	p. 271
tundra	p. 273

MAIN IDEA Earth has six large land biomes. Each biome's climate determines what types of ecosystems may be found in the biome.

Earth's Major Biomes

A **biome** (BY ome) is a large region of similar plant life and climate. Study the map below to find the six major land biomes.

What makes biomes different from one another? The most important factor is climate, or the average weather over a long period of time. Some climates are rainy, while others are quite dry. Different climates support different biomes.

Each biome is home to organisms well adapted to live there. An **adaptation** is a trait or characteristic that helps an organism survive in its natural environment. For example, cacti have fleshy trunks and spines instead of leaves. Both adaptations allow them to conserve water.

READING SKILL

Classify Use the graphic organizer to identify the six major biomes.

STANDARDS

5.e. *Students know* the number and types of organisms an ecosystem can support depends on the resources available and on abiotic factors, such as quantities of light and water, a range of temperatures, and soil composition.

Earth is home to six major land biomes. In each biome, climate affects the native plants and animals. ▼

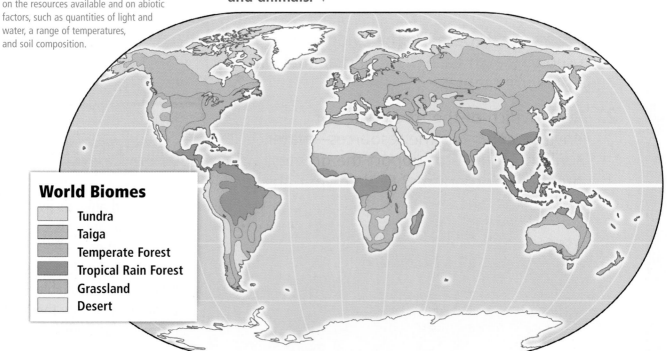

World Biomes
- Tundra
- Taiga
- Temperate Forest
- Tropical Rain Forest
- Grassland
- Desert

Tropical Rain Forests and Temperate Forests

Forests are home to tall trees and the animals that live in them. But there are different types of forest biomes. A **tropical rain forest** is very rainy and hot. Some rain forests get more than 600 cm (240 in.) of rain each year! Temperatures range from about 18°C to 35°C (64°F to 95°F), which is like a hot summer that lasts all year.

Because of the moisture and warmth, tropical rain forests are teeming with life. In fact, more kinds of plants and animals live in this biome than in any other. Its huge mass of plants produces much of Earth's oxygen. Some of these plants might supply new medicines and other useful products.

Another type of forest biome, the **temperate forest,** experiences four distinct seasons: summer, fall, winter, and spring. Temperatures range from a chilly −30°C (−22°F) to a warm 30°C (86°F). A temperate forest receives perhaps one-fifth the rainfall of a tropical forest.

These forests are home to white-tailed deer, rabbits, skunks, squirrels, and black bears. The trees include maple, oak, hickory, and beech. These trees lose their leaves in the fall and are dormant through winter. The fallen leaves add nutrients to the soil.

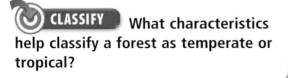

CLASSIFY What characteristics help classify a forest as temperate or tropical?

Tropical Rain Forest

Location: near the equator
Climate: warm and wet

Temperate Forest

Location: eastern North America and other places
Climate: four distinct seasons

271

Grasslands

Location: central Africa, central U.S., and other regions

Climate: distinct dry season

Desert

Location: varies

Climate: extremely dry

Grasslands and Deserts

Grasses cover the ground in the **grasslands** biome. Only a few trees grow; mainly near rivers and streams.

There are two main types of grasslands: prairies and savannas. Prairies are found in temperate regions, such as the central United States. Temperatures may dip as low as −40°C (−40°F) in winter and soar to 38°C (100°F) in summer. Prairie animals include prairie dogs, coyotes, hawks, and grouse.

Most savannas are found in warmer regions, such as central Africa. Average annual temperatures typically remain above 18°C (64°F). Elephants, giraffes, lions, and zebras call the savanna home.

A savanna receives as much as 100 cm (40 in.) of rain each year. But the savanna has a dry season, as do other grasslands. That's partly why trees are scarce. They do not thrive for long periods without water.

The **desert** is the driest biome. Most deserts receive less than 25 cm (10 in.) of rain each year. In fact, some deserts may not see a drop of rain all year long.

Cacti, sagebrush, and other plants are found in many deserts. Desert plants and animals are adapted to live with little water. Cacti, for example, have a waxy coating and spiny leaves to help reduce water loss. Yet Earth's driest deserts contain little life. These deserts are filled with sandy dunes that stretch seemingly without end.

Taiga and Tundra

The **taiga** is another forest biome. It has long, severe winters and short, cool summers. Temperatures may reach 10°C (50°F) during only one to three months each year. The taiga is fairly dry, each year receiving only about 50 cm (20 in.) of precipitation, mostly as snow.

The most common trees in the taiga forest are conifers, such as pines, firs, and spruces. The leaves of these trees are thin, waxy needles that help reduce water loss. The needles may stay attached to the tree all year long. Animals of the taiga include moose, deer, and wolves.

As harsh as the taiga can be, it is mild compared to the tundra. The **tundra** is Earth's coldest biome, having an average winter temperature of −34°C (−29°F). The ground is frozen for hundreds of meters down. The lower layers stay frozen all year long. This frozen ground is called permafrost.

In summer, temperatures hover just under 10°C (50°F). As the upper layer of ground thaws, the tundra becomes swampy and covered with mosses, lichens, and grasses and other small plants. Mosquitoes thrive in the short summer.

Other tundra animals include polar bears, wolves, caribou, and reindeer. These animals have adaptations that help them survive in this cold biome. Polar bears, for example, have a thick layer of fat to keep them warm.

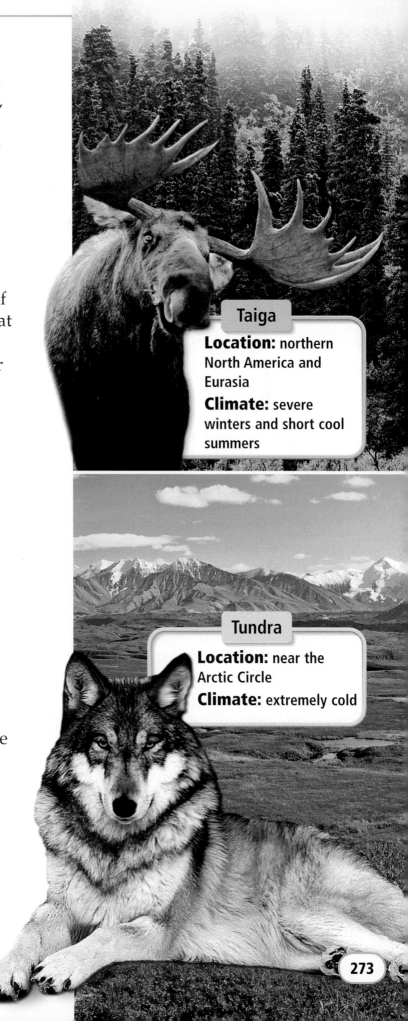

Taiga

Location: northern North America and Eurasia

Climate: severe winters and short cool summers

Tundra

Location: near the Arctic Circle

Climate: extremely cold

273

Intertidal

Neritic

Oceanic

Ocean Biome

Recall that water covers almost three-quarters of Earth's surface. There are two basic water biomes: freshwater biomes and salt water biomes. Salt water biomes include the ocean biome. As in land biomes, the ocean biome depends on plants and algae. Large green kelp is found in this biome. However, most food in the world's oceans comes from tiny algae and plankton near the surface.

Different areas, or zones of the ocean are home to organisms suited to particular conditions. The *intertidal* zone is the zone closest to land. Depending on tides and waves, this zone is either covered with water or exposed to air.

▲ The types of organisms found in each part of the ocean depend mainly on the sunlight available.

Organisms that live in the intertidal zone are adapted to crashing waves. Barnacles, for example, cling tightly to rocks.

Beyond this zone is the *neritic* zone. Here, waters are usually shallow and rich in nutrients. The zone is home to tiny algae, crabs, shrimp, mussels, sea stars, sea urchins, and many fish.

The open sea is called the *oceanic* zone. Its top layer receives the most sunlight and contains the most life. The deepest parts receive very little sunlight. These areas contain life forms that are adapted to dark, cold water and extreme pressure.

CLASSIFY What are the characteristics of the three oceanic zones?

Express Lab

Activity Card 22
Classify What You See

Visual Summary

Biomes are regions with specific climates and types of organisms.

Organisms have adaptations that make them well suited for the biome in which they live.

The ocean biome contains several different zones. Organisms in each zone are adapted to the available sunlight and other conditions.

 STANDARD

5.e.

Technology
Visit www.eduplace.com/cascp to find out more about Earth's biomes.

Reading Review

1 MAIN IDEA Describe each of the six land biomes.

2 VOCABULARY Choose a *biome*, and give an example of an *adaptation* that allows a plant or animal to live within it.

3 READING SKILL Identify the regions of the ocean biome.

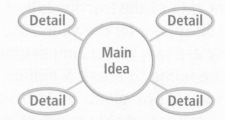

4 CRITICAL THINKING: Evaluate What might happen to the animals in a biome if Earth's temperature increased?

5 INQUIRY SKILL: Classify A certain biome has a cool summer and cold winter. There are many evergreen forests. Which biome is this?

 TEST PRACTICE

The number of organisms a biome or ecosystem can support depends on _____.

A. the number of species in it

B. biotic and abiotic factors, including water and sunlight

C. the distribution of bacteria

D. sunlight only

 **STANDARD**

1–5: 5.e., **Test Practice:** 5.e.

Rain Forests

Rain forests once covered 14 percent of Earth's surface. Yet because of human activities, today they cover only 6 percent. Some experts warn that at the current rate of destruction, all of Earth's rain forests could disappear by the year 2050.

Why are rain forests important? One reason is that they are home to about 5 million species of plants and animals. The plants yield fruits, nuts, and oils. Scientists suspect that many plants contain medicines that are waiting to be discovered.

Yet the most important product is an invisible one. More than 20 percent of the world's oxygen is produced in the Amazon rain forest alone! For this reason, rain forests affect all living things on Earth.

People are destroying rain forests to harvest trees and to make room for farms and ranches. What do you think of such actions? What do you think the world's nations should do to protect rain forests?

"Sadly, it has taken only a century of man's intervention to destroy what nature has so intricately designed to last forever."

—Leslie Taylor, medical researcher

A baby orangutan was rescued after its home was lost to deforestation. ▼

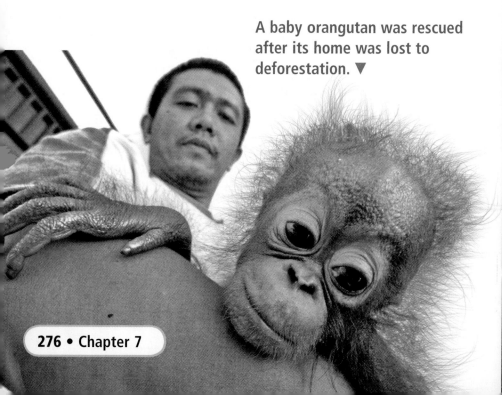

STANDARD
6.b. *Students know* different natural energy and material resources, including air, soil, rocks, minerals, petroleum, fresh water, wildlife, and forests, and know how to classify them as renewable or nonrenewable.

SOCIAL STUDIES LINK

Rain Forest Loss

Brazil

Forest Lost 37%

Original Forest
2,860,000 km²

Indonesia

Forest Lost 57%

Original Forest
1,220,000 km²

Nigeria

Forest Lost 86%

Original Forest
72,000 km²

Forest Remaining   Forest Lost

Sharing Ideas

1. **READING CHECK** Why are rain forests important, even to people who don't live near one?

2. **WRITE ABOUT IT** Where is rain forest land being destroyed?

3. **TALK ABOUT IT** What can you and your classmates do to help protect Earth's rain forests?

277

What Cycles Through the Biosphere?

Building Background

All living things need fresh water. Fortunately, rain and snow fall somewhere on Earth every day, renewing the fresh water supply. Living things also need carbon dioxide, oxygen, and nitrogen for the processes that keep them alive. Like water, these substances cycle between ground and air, passing through living things in the process.

PREPARE TO INVESTIGATE

Inquiry Skill

Infer When you infer, you use known facts and logical reasoning to make interpretations.

Materials

- leafy potted plant
- clear plastic bag
- twist tie
- water

Science and Math Toolbox

For step 1, review **Making a Chart to Organize Data** on page H11.

 STANDARDS

5.b. *Students know* matter is transferred over time from one organism to others in the food web and between organisms and the physical environment.
7.e. Recognize whether evidence is consistent with a proposed explanation.

Bag It!

Procedure

1. **Collaborate** Work in a small group. In your *Science Notebook*, make a chart like the one shown.

2. Put a plastic bag over one of the plant's leaves. Take special care not to damage the leaf. Tie the bag closed with a twist tie. The whole leaf should fit inside the bag, and the twist tie should not be too tight. Water the plant and place it near a sunny window.

3. **Predict** What do you think you will find when you check the leaves after two days? Record your prediction.

4. **Observe** After two days, observe the plant's leaves and the plastic bag. Note any changes.

5. **Record Data** Record your observations in your chart.

Conclusion

1. **Analyze Data** Look at the observations you recorded. What do they tell you about plant leaves and water?

2. **Infer** What do you think happened to the water given off by the leaves that were not covered by the plastic bag? Where do you think the water came from?

STEP 1

Plant Leaf	Prediction	Observation
Leaf in bag		
Leaf not in bag		

STEP 2

STEP 4

Guided Inquiry

Experiment Repeat the activity using two identical plants. Put one plant in a sunny window and the other in a place that stays dark. **Observe** and **compare** the leaves after two days.

VOCABULARY

nitrogen fixation   p. 284
photosynthesis   p. 280
respiration   p. 281
transpiration   p. 286

READING SKILL

Sequence Show the steps of one cycle through the biosphere.

1	
2	
3	
4	

STANDARDS

5.b. *Students know* matter is transferred over time from one organism to others in the food web and between organisms and the physical environment.
5.a. *Students know* energy entering ecosystems as sunlight is transferred by producers into chemical energy through photosynthesis and then from organism to organism through food webs.

Cycles in the Biosphere

MAIN IDEA Oxygen, carbon dioxide, nitrogen, and water cycle through the biosphere. Organisms use them again and again.

Photosynthesis and Respiration

Like the jogger below, you breathe faster and more deeply as you run because your body needs more oxygen. Did you know that algae and plants produce the oxygen in the atmosphere?

Plants provide oxygen and food through the process of photosynthesis. In **photosynthesis,** plants use energy from the Sun to change carbon dioxide and water into glucose and oxygen. The simple sugar glucose is stored in the plants' cells. It provides food and energy for plants, for animals that eat plants, and then for animals that eat other animals. The oxygen is released into the atmosphere.

◀ Trees and other plants produce oxygen during photosynthesis. People and other animals produce carbon dioxide during respiration.

Carbon Dioxide

Photosynthesis

Respiration

Oxygen

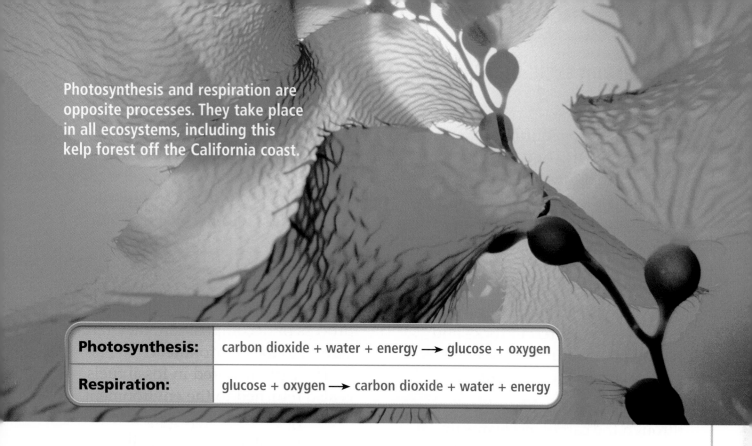

Photosynthesis and respiration are opposite processes. They take place in all ecosystems, including this kelp forest off the California coast.

Photosynthesis:	carbon dioxide + water + energy ⟶ glucose + oxygen
Respiration:	glucose + oxygen ⟶ carbon dioxide + water + energy

Plants are not the only organisms that conduct photosynthesis. Algae that live in water and some types of bacteria also carry out photosynthesis. In fact, algae in the oceans supply most of Earth's oxygen.

Most organisms are able to use the energy in food through cell respiration. **Respiration** is the process in which organisms obtain the energy stored in glucose by causing it to react with oxygen. Water and carbon dioxide are released as by-products.

Both plants and animals perform respiration, as do many other organisms. Respiration is why oxygen is so important to life on Earth, including human life. The oxygen you take in with every breath fuels respiration in your body. Your blood carries oxygen to cells throughout your body, where respiration takes place.

Do you notice anything unusual about photosynthesis and respiration? They are opposite processes. The products of photosynthesis are used in respiration. The products of respiration are used for photosynthesis. In this way, oxygen and carbon dioxide keep cycling through the biosphere.

The relationship between photosynthesis and respiration is one way that organisms depend on one another. Animals and other organisms need plants for food and oxygen. Plants rely on other organisms for the carbon dioxide they use to make food.

SEQUENCE **After an animal eats a plant, what are the steps in respiration?**

The Carbon Cycle and the Oxygen Cycle

Carbon is the fourth most abundant element on Earth and is a basic part of all living things. Carbon is part of every body cell, every sugar, and the carbon dioxide found in the air.

Carbon is also found in Earth's crust. Much of Earth's carbon is found underground in fossil fuels such as coal, oil, and natural gas. Even more is stored in rocks and sediments. Nature slowly releases this carbon to the environment.

The Carbon Cycle Carbon moves through the carbon cycle mostly as carbon dioxide gas. Recall that plants take in carbon dioxide during photosynthesis. This carbon goes into the glucose molecules formed. Later, when plant-eating organisms consume the glucose, the carbon returns to the atmosphere as carbon dioxide.

Carbon also moves through the environment in other ways. When organisms die, for example, some carbon remains in their bodies. Organisms such as bacteria and fungi break down organic matter. In the process of decomposition, they return carbon to the environment.

The carbon stored in fossil fuels is also returned to the environment. Burning fossil fuels quickly releases long-ago stored carbon into the atmosphere as carbon dioxide.

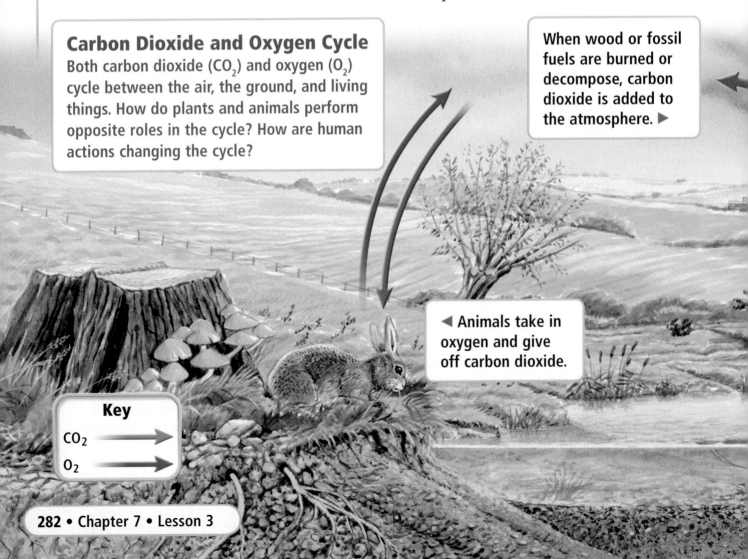

Carbon Dioxide and Oxygen Cycle
Both carbon dioxide (CO_2) and oxygen (O_2) cycle between the air, the ground, and living things. How do plants and animals perform opposite roles in the cycle? How are human actions changing the cycle?

When wood or fossil fuels are burned or decompose, carbon dioxide is added to the atmosphere. ▶

◀ Animals take in oxygen and give off carbon dioxide.

Key
CO_2 ⟶
O_2 ⟶

The Oxygen Cycle Oxygen also cycles through the environment. As you have learned, oxygen is produced during photosynthesis and consumed during respiration. Another source of oxygen is water vapor in the atmosphere, which breaks down chemically. Oxygen is also consumed during combustion, rusting, and during chemical weathering of rocks.

Because oxygen is part of carbon dioxide, the oxygen cycle is linked to the carbon cycle. Both elements cycle between living and nonliving things in the environment.

Human activity can upset these natural cycles. For example, cutting and burning forests leads to less oxygen being produced through photosynthesis. Less oxygen will enter the atmosphere and less carbon dioxide will leave.

Carbon dioxide helps Earth's atmosphere trap heat to keep Earth's surface warm. Most scientists argue that an increase in atmospheric carbon dioxide could cause an increase in global temperatures. This could lead to melting of glaciers and other land ice, causing flooding when ocean levels rise.

SEQUENCE How are the carbon cycle and oxygen cycle connected?

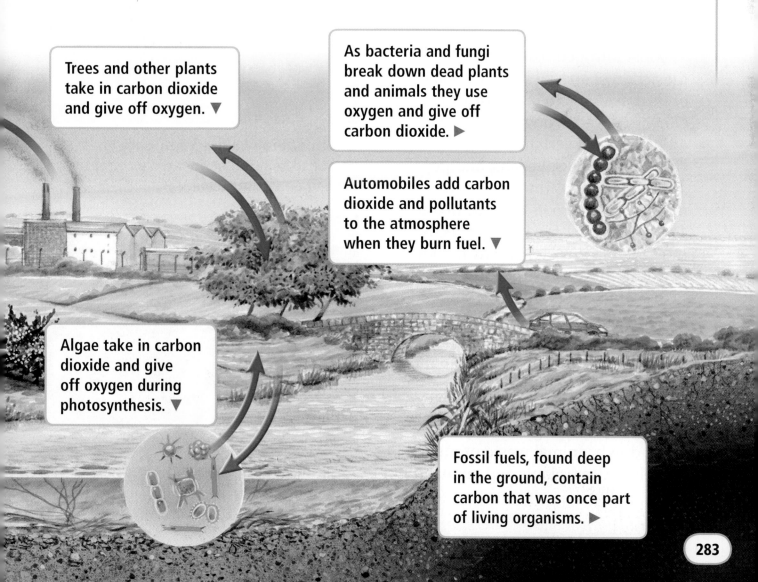

Trees and other plants take in carbon dioxide and give off oxygen. ▼

As bacteria and fungi break down dead plants and animals they use oxygen and give off carbon dioxide. ▶

Automobiles add carbon dioxide and pollutants to the atmosphere when they burn fuel. ▼

Algae take in carbon dioxide and give off oxygen during photosynthesis. ▼

Fossil fuels, found deep in the ground, contain carbon that was once part of living organisms. ▶

The Nitrogen Cycle

Nearly 80 percent of Earth's atmosphere consists of nitrogen gas. Plants and animals need nitrogen to make proteins and other important compounds. However, most living things cannot use nitrogen gas. The nitrogen must somehow be converted into the nitrogen compounds that living things can use. The process of changing nitrogen gas into usable nitrogen compounds is called **nitrogen fixation.**

Lightning is responsible for some nitrogen fixation. The energy released by lightning acts to combine nitrogen and oxygen in the air. The compounds formed dissolve in rainwater.

Most nitrogen fixation results from the action of special bacteria. Some of the bacteria live in soil or water. Other nitrogen-fixing bacteria live on the roots of certain plants, such as clover, peanuts, soybeans, and peas.

The bacteria form bumps called nodules on the roots of these plants. The bacteria get food and protection from the plant roots. In return, they perform nitrogen fixation.

If plants and animals continued to take in nitrogen compounds, eventually all the nitrogen in the environment would be stored in the bodies of living things. Of course, this does not happen. Certain kinds of bacteria and fungi decompose, or break down, animal waste products, as well as dead plants and animals.

▲ The energy that a lightning bolt releases can fix nitrogen in the air, changing nitrogen gas into nitrogen compounds.

▲ Nitrogen can be fixed artificially, then packaged as fertilizer. Today, most crops depend on fertilized soil.

▲ Nitrogen-fixing bacteria form a close relationship with many plants, including peanuts.

Nitrogen in the air

Clover uses nitrogen compounds in the soil.

Decomposers return nitrogen to the soil.

The cows get nitrogen compounds by eating clover.

Some bacteria change nitrogen back into a gas.

Nitrogen is fixed by some bacteria.

Nitrogen compounds in the soil.

As a result of the decomposition, nitrogen compounds return to the soil. Plants can then reuse the compounds. Other bacteria change nitrogen compounds in the soil into the nitrogen gas found in the air.

Human activities can alter the nitrogen cycle, sometimes adding or taking away the usable nitrogen in the soil. When crops are harvested, the nitrogen in plants is removed with the plants. Erosion and irrigation can also wash nitrogen compounds out of the soil.

To replace nitrogen, farmers add nitrogen-rich fertilizers. They also raise peanuts or other plants that support nitrogen-fixing bacteria.

SEQUENCE What must happen before nitrogen can be used by most organisms?

Express Lab

Activity Card 23
See Water in the Air

285

The Water Cycle

The water cycle is the continuous movement of water between Earth's surface and the atmosphere. Powered by the Sun, the water cycle is essential to all land ecosystems.

In the water cycle, water moves between the living and nonliving parts of the environment. The Sun heats and evaporates water from Earth's surface and oceans. Plants also release water into the atmosphere through holes in their leaves. The process through which water evaporates from plant leaves is known as **transpiration.**

Water vapor cools and condenses as it rises through the atmosphere. Clouds form. Eventually, water falls to the ground as precipitation.

Most precipitation falls on Earth's oceans. The precipitation that falls on land is absorbed into the ground, is taken up by plants, or flows to a body of water as runoff. The cycle can then begin anew.

Animals, including humans, also take part in the water cycle. They release water in their urine, perspiration, and exhaled air.

SEQUENCE How are living organisms involved in the water cycle?

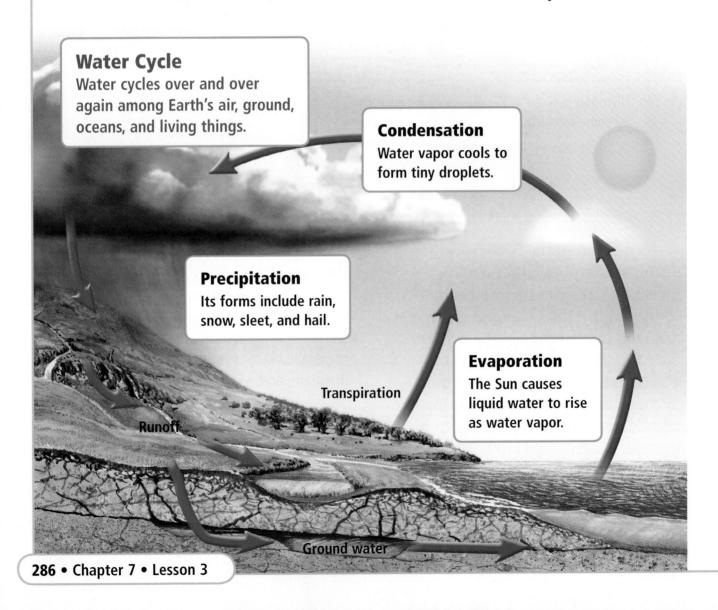

Water Cycle
Water cycles over and over again among Earth's air, ground, oceans, and living things.

Condensation
Water vapor cools to form tiny droplets.

Precipitation
Its forms include rain, snow, sleet, and hail.

Evaporation
The Sun causes liquid water to rise as water vapor.

Transpiration

Runoff

Ground water

Visual Summary

Photosynthesis and respiration are opposite processes. Plants produce oxygen that animals need and animals produce carbon dioxide that plants need.

Carbon dioxide, oxygen, and nitrogen cycle through the environment as they are used and produced by organisms.

In the water cycle, water moves between the living and nonliving parts of the environment.

STANDARDS

5.a., 5.b.

Technology
Visit **www.eduplace.com/cascp** to find out more about Earth's natural cycles.

Reading Review

1 MAIN IDEA What substances cycle through the biosphere?

2 VOCABULARY Explain the difference between *photosynthesis* and *respiration*.

3 READING SKILL Describe one path that oxygen may follow through the biosphere.

1	
2	
3	
4	

4 CRITICAL THINKING: Analyze How does driving in a car that uses gasoline connect to the carbon cycle?

5 INQUIRY SKILL: Infer Two identical plants are placed in clear plastic boxes. One plant is put on a sunny windowsill. The other is put into a closet. After a few hours, which container will hold more oxygen? Explain.

 TEST PRACTICE

Transpiration takes place in _____.

A. animals

B. plants

C. oceans

D. humans

 STANDARDS

1: 5.a., **2:** 5.b., **3–5:** 5.a., **Test Practice:** 5.b.

287

EXTREME Science

A World In Your Hands

What you see here is a world in a glass bubble. Called the EcoSphere™, this sealed globe is a miniature ecosystem that is self-contained, self-renewing, and in almost perfect biological balance. This biosphere's physical environment is simple: gravel, seawater, some trapped air, and a small branch. The inhabitants of this little world are microorganisms, algae, and tiny red shrimp.

The EcoSphere's biological cycle is a simple version of Earth's. Light and carbon dioxide in the seawater allow the algae to produce oxygen by photosynthesis. The shrimp breathe the oxygen in the water while nibbling on the algae and bacteria. The bacteria break down the animal waste into nutrients, which the algae use. The shrimp and the bacteria give off carbon dioxide, which the algae use to produce oxygen. And so the cycle repeats itself.

The first pictures of the whole Earth from outer space helped people realize that our planet is a self-contained biosphere too. Anything that disrupts the oxygen or carbon cycle threatens all life on Earth.

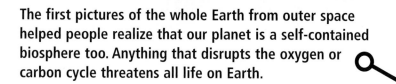

The life expectancy of these tiny shrimp is about 5 years.

Writing Journal

In your journal, write ideas on how to make a space station a self-contained, self-renewing ecosystem.

Math in Science

The circle graphs show the loss of tropical rain forest in three countries. The countries are located on different continents and are home to different animal and plant populations.

1. How many square kilometers of rain forest are left in each country?

2. Do the circle graphs tell what percent of each country's land is now covered in rain forest? Explain.

3. If people continue to cut down rain forests in these countries, how should the circle graphs be changed?

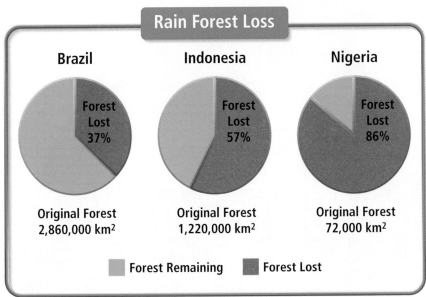

Rain Forest Loss

Brazil

Forest Lost 37%

Original Forest 2,860,000 km²

Indonesia

Forest Lost 57%

Original Forest 1,220,000 km²

Nigeria

Forest Lost 86%

Original Forest 72,000 km²

■ Forest Remaining   ■ Forest Lost

Writing in Science
Narrative

Write a story that describes the journey of a carbon atom as it moves through different parts of the carbon cycle. Try writing the story from the atom's point of view! Describe how it moves through each stage of the cycle and the things it becomes part of.

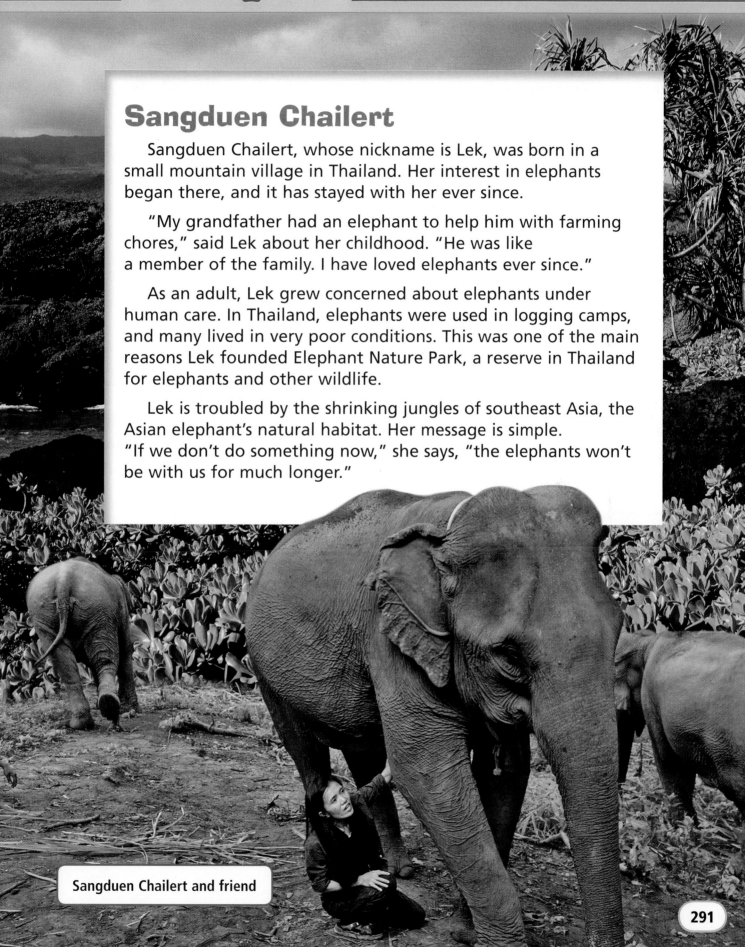

Sangduen Chailert

Sangduen Chailert, whose nickname is Lek, was born in a small mountain village in Thailand. Her interest in elephants began there, and it has stayed with her ever since.

"My grandfather had an elephant to help him with farming chores," said Lek about her childhood. "He was like a member of the family. I have loved elephants ever since."

As an adult, Lek grew concerned about elephants under human care. In Thailand, elephants were used in logging camps, and many lived in very poor conditions. This was one of the main reasons Lek founded Elephant Nature Park, a reserve in Thailand for elephants and other wildlife.

Lek is troubled by the shrinking jungles of southeast Asia, the Asian elephant's natural habitat. Her message is simple. "If we don't do something now," she says, "the elephants won't be with us for much longer."

Sangduen Chailert and friend

291

Vocabulary

Complete each sentence with a term from the list.

1. All the living and nonliving things that interact in one place are a(n) _____.

2. The driest biome is the _____.

3. A nonliving thing in an ecosystem is a(n) _____.

4. A large group of ecosystems that have similar characteristics is a(n) _____.

5. A biome covered by grasses is a(n) _____.

6. The group of living things found in an ecosystem is a(n) _____.

7. The narrow zone on Earth where life exists is the _____.

8. The _____ has long, severe winters and cool summers.

9. All the members of the same type of organism that live in an ecosystem are a(n) _____.

10. A living thing in an ecosystem is a(n) _____.

abiotic factor p. 264
adaptation p. 270
biome p. 270
biosphere p. 264
biotic factor p. 264
community p. 265
desert p. 272
ecosystem p. 264
grassland p. 272
nitrogen fixation p. 284
photosynthesis p. 280
population p. 266
respiration p. 281
taiga p. 273
temperate forest p. 271
tropical rain forest p. 271
transpiration p. 286
tundra p. 273

Test Practice

Write the letter of the best answer choice.

11. Which of these is an animal adaptation for life in the tundra?

   A. specialized eyes that see well at night
   B. tan fur to blend in with the sandy soil
   C. large ears that allow heat to escape
   D. a fatty layer that keeps the animal warm

12. Which process releases carbon dioxide into the atmosphere?

   A. respiration
   B. photosynthesis
   C. transpiration
   D. evaporation

13. What best describes the tropical rain forest?

   A. hot, humid, and rainy
   B. hot and dry
   C. cool and rainy
   D. rainy, sometimes warm, often cold

14. Which two perform nitrogen fixation?

   A. chlorophyll and special types of bacteria
   B. lightning and special types of bacteria
   C. the carbon cycle and lightning
   D. photosynthesis and respiration

Inquiry Skills

15. **Observe** Study the photo of a desert on p. 272. Describe the photo in your own words. What types of adaptations would a plant need in order to live there? Explain.

16. You are told that you live in the temperate forest biome. What evidence would you look for in order to confirm or reject this statement?

Map the Concept

Copy and use the graphic organizer to order correctly the steps in photosynthesis and respiration. Use a star (*) to indicate steps where matter is transferred between organisms and the physical environment.

Sunlight strikes plants
Carbon dioxide and water released into environment
Plants store the energy
Plants take in carbon dioxide and water from environment
Animals eat plants
Light energy is converted to chemical energy
Plant tissue is broken down by respiration to release energy

17. **Apply** Would a population that usually lives in a temperate forest thrive if it were transported to the tundra? Explain.

18. **Synthesize** Describe what would happen to an ecosystem without green plants.

19. **Analyze** Many bacteria and other single-celled organisms cause disease. They also spoil food and can ruin timber in houses and other wooden buildings. Would people be better off without these organisms? Explain.

20. **Evaluate** Are people adapted to the biome in which they live? Explain your answer.

Performance Assessment

Make a Poster

Make a poster describing the ecosystem where you live. Identify biotic and abiotic factors in the ecosystem. Include typical plants and animals. For each organism, include an adaptation it uses to survive in the ecosystem.

Writing Journal

Review your answers to the Lesson Preview questions.

STANDARDS

1–11: 5.e., **12:** 5.a., **13:** 5.e., **14:** 5.b., **15:** 5.e., **16:** 7.e., **Map the Concept:** 5.a., **17:** 5.e., **18–19:** 5.a., **20:** 5.e., **Performance Assessment:** 5.e.

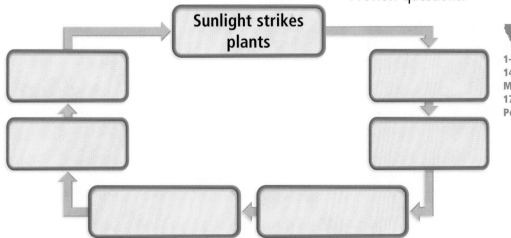

Sunlight strikes plants

Chapter 8

Roles of Living Things

Monarch butterflies in a meadow

LESSON 1

A caterpillar eats a leaf and a bird eats the caterpillar. How is energy transferred in ecosystems?

LESSON 2

What roles do different kinds of organisms play in ecosystems? How do they interact with one another?

LESSON 3

Sometimes different kinds of organisms live together very closely. What are the advantages and disadvantages of such relationships?

Writing Journal

In your Writing Journal, write or draw answers to each question.

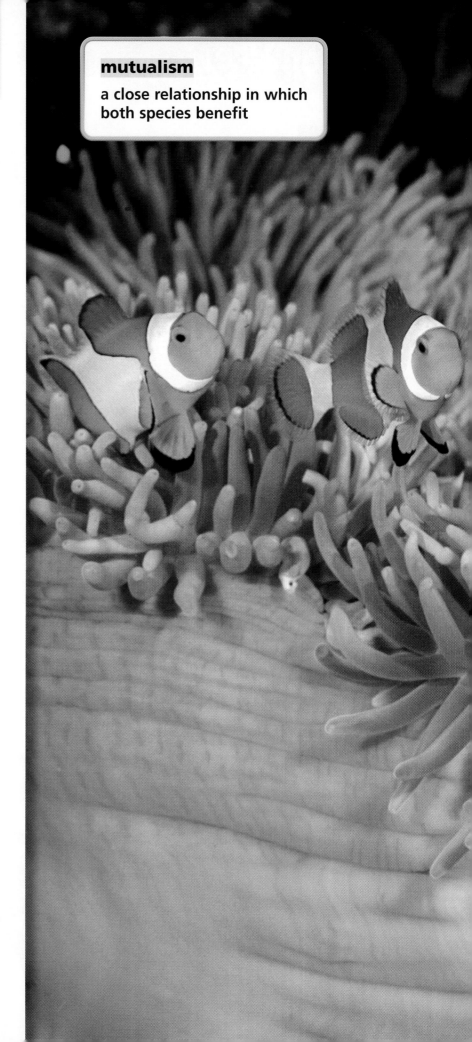

Vocabulary Preview

mutualism

a close relationship in which both species benefit

Vocabulary

carnivore p. 312

commensalism p. 319

consumer p. 300

decomposer p. 302

energy pyramid p. 303

food web p. 301

herbivore p. 312

mutualism p. 319

niche p. 310

omnivore p. 312

parasitism p. 320

predator p. 310

prey p. 310

producer p. 300

scavenger p. 302

symbiosis p. 318

trophic level p. 300

Glossary

English-Spanish, p. H26

Vocabulary Skill

Word Roots

symbiosis

Symbiosis is a close relationship between species. *Sym* comes from a Greek word meaning "together." *Bio* is from another Greek word meaning "life." So symbiosis means "living together."

carnivore

an animal that eats only meat, or the flesh of other animals

predator

an animal that hunts and eats other animals

scavenger

an animal that eats the meat of dead animals

Start with Your Standards

Standard Set 5. Ecology (Life Sciences)

5.a. *Students know* energy entering ecosystems as sunlight is transferred by producers into chemical energy through photosynthesis and then from organism to organism through food webs.

5.b. *Students know* matter is transferred over time from one organism to others in the food web and between organisms and the physical environment.

5.c. *Students know* populations of organisms can be categorized by the functions they serve in an ecosystem.

5.d. *Students know* different kinds of organisms may play similar ecological roles in similar biomes.

Set 7: Investigation and Experimentation standards covered in this chapter: 7.a., 7.d., 7.e.

What Is a Food Web?

Building Background

All living things need matter and energy to live, grow, and move. Plants make their own food. Other organisms rely on plants or animals for food.

Food chains show feeding relationships. A plant-eating animal may be eaten by a meat-eating animal, which in turn may be eaten by another meat-eater. In an ecosystem, food chains make up networks called food webs.

PREPARE TO INVESTIGATE

Inquiry Skill

Communicate You can communicate the steps and results of investigations in the form of written reports and oral presentations.

Materials

- paper
- poster board
- colored pens or pencils

Science and Math Toolbox

For step 1, review **Making a Chart to Organize Data** on page H11.

STANDARDS

5.b. *Students know* matter is transferred over time from one organism to others in the food web and between organisms and the physical environment.
7.d. Communicate the steps and results from an investigation in written and oral presentations.

Identify Your Food

Procedure

1 **Collaborate** Work in small groups to create a list of foods you might eat during one day. In your *Science Notebook*, make a chart like the one shown. Make the chart large enough to include your list of foods.

2 **Record Data** Read labels on food packages, or conduct research to identify the main ingredients in each food item. Record each ingredient in a separate row in your chart.

3 **Record Data** Identify the source of energy for each ingredient. Record it in your chart. Trace the energy source back to the Sun.

4 **Use Models** On poster board, create a food web by drawing a diagram to show how your food sources are connected. Start with yourself at the top. Draw arrows to the ingredients in the foods you eat and from them to their sources of energy. Be sure to include the Sun.

5 Circle the Sun in yellow, organisms that use the Sun as their source of energy in green, and organisms that eat them in red.

Conclusion

1. **Infer** Based on your model, what can you infer about how energy moves through an ecosystem?

2. **Communicate** Make an oral presentation to your class. Show your poster and explain the food web your group created.

STEP 1

Food	Some Ingredients	Source of Energy	Source of Energy	Source of Energy
hamburger	bun (wheat)	sun		
	meat (beef)	grain, hay, grass	sun	

STEP 4

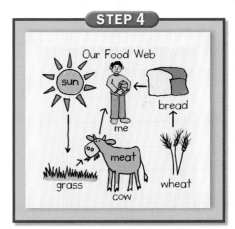

Our Food Web

sun · me · bread · grass · meat · cow · wheat

Guided Inquiry

Ask Questions What other questions do you have about food sources or food webs? Find the answers to your questions by using library or Internet resources. **Communicate** what you learn to your class.

Food Energy

MAIN IDEA Energy moves in one direction in ecosystems from producers to consumers.

Trophic Levels

Food is an organism's source of energy. As you have learned, plants and algae produce food through photosynthesis. Organisms that make food are known as autotrophs, and are also called **producers.** The producers include plants, algae, and some bacteria.

A plant breaks down some of its food for its own life processes. It stores the rest. An animal that eats a plant obtains this stored energy. In turn, the animal uses some of the energy and stores the rest. If another animal then eats the first animal, it obtains the stored energy. In this way, energy flows through an ecosystem.

Each step in the movement of energy is known as a **trophic level.** Producers make up the lowest trophic level. Organisms in the other levels cannot make their own food, and thus rely on the producers for energy. These organisms are called heterotrophs, and are also called **consumers.** Consumers gain their energy by eating, or consuming, other organisms.

An organism that feeds directly on a producer is a *primary consumer.* A mouse that eats a plant is a primary consumer. Primary consumers make up the second trophic level in an ecosystem.

An organism that eats a primary consumer is called a *secondary consumer.* A hawk that eats a mouse is a secondary consumer. Secondary consumers make up the third trophic level.

VOCABULARY

consumer	p. 300
decomposer	p. 302
energy pyramid	p. 303
food web	p. 301
producer	p. 300
scavenger	p. 302
trophic level	p. 300

READING SKILL

Sequence Use a diagram to show the sequence of organisms in trophic levels.

1	
2	
3	
4	

STANDARDS

5.a. *Students know* energy entering ecosystems as sunlight is transferred by producers into chemical energy through photosynthesis and then from organism to organism through food webs.
5.b. *Students know* matter is transferred over time from one organism to others in the food web and between organisms and the physical environment.

◄ Like other animals, this bird is a consumer. It gets the energy it needs by eating food.

Trophic Levels

	Forest	Ocean
Secondary Consumers	• Owls • Wolves • Snakes	• Sharks • Dolphins • Tuna
Primary Consumers	• Squirrels • Deer • Seed-eating birds • Insects	• Herring and other small fish • Baleen whales
Producers	• Trees • Ferns • Mosses	• Algae

A food chain describes the transfer of energy from a producer to a primary consumer, then to a secondary consumer. A plant, mouse, and hawk make up one food chain.

In nature, food chains and trophic levels may overlap. Some animals eat both producers and primary consumers. For example, bears eat fruit and fish. Some of the fish they eat may be secondary consumers that eat other fish. In addition, other animals may eat the same kind of fruit and the same kind of fish.

Overlapping food chains in an ecosystem form a **food web.** Some food webs are mainly on land. Others are in bodies of fresh water or in oceans. Some animals may belong to both a land food web and a water food web.

 **SEQUENCE** What is transferred along a food chain?

Scavengers and Decomposers

What happens to organisms when they die? In some cases, animals called scavengers eat the soft parts of the dead organisms. A **scavenger** is an animal that eats the meat of dead animals. Vultures, hyenas, and ravens are large scavengers. They eat the meat from dead animals that they find, sometimes by waiting for predators to finish their meals. Many insects are scavengers, too.

In other cases, dead organisms are left to decompose, meaning to rot or break apart. Organisms called **decomposers** live by breaking apart once-living matter into simpler parts. Bacteria are Earth's most important decomposers. Fungi and many protists are decomposers, too.

You might think of decomposers as an inconvenience or a nuisance. For example, if you leave fruits and vegetables for too long in your refrigerator or pantry, the food will rot as decomposers take hold. Farmers face similar problems with almost every crop.

In nature, however, decomposers play a very important role. By breaking down old organisms, they return minerals and nutrients to the soil so that new plants can grow.

Think what would happen without decomposers! Dead organisms and waste would pile higher and higher. The soil would gradually lose nutrients that would not be returned. Before long, plants would stop growing. The cycles of most living things would grind to a halt.

Decomposers
Bracket fungus is a decomposer. It is breaking this dead tree into simpler parts. ▼

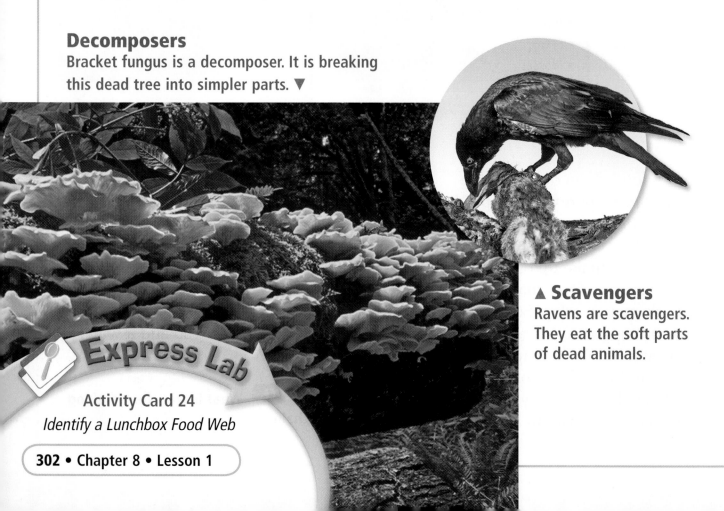

▲ **Scavengers**
Ravens are scavengers. They eat the soft parts of dead animals.

Express Lab

Activity Card 24
Identify a Lunchbox Food Web

The Energy Pyramid

Food chains and food webs show how energy is passed from one organism to another. However, they do not show the quantity of energy transferred. When an animal consumes an organism, some of the energy it gains is used for life processes. Some energy is stored and some is lost to the environment as heat. Only the energy stored in the body of an organism is passed on to another organism at the next trophic level.

An **energy pyramid** shows the availability of energy at each trophic level in an ecosystem. Note that more energy is available for use at lower levels than at higher levels. Only about 10 percent of the energy from each level is passed on to the next higher level.

Recall that water and nutrients needed to sustain life are cycled through the environment and reused. By contrast, energy that moves through an ecosystem is ultimately lost as heat and must be renewed. New food energy is continually being supplied by the producers at the base of the energy pyramid.

This loss of energy from one trophic level to the next limits the number of organisms in a food chain. For this reason, a food chain usually consists of only three or four species. Scavengers and decomposers are the final members of all food chains.

SEQUENCE **What happens to energy that is not available to the next trophic level?**

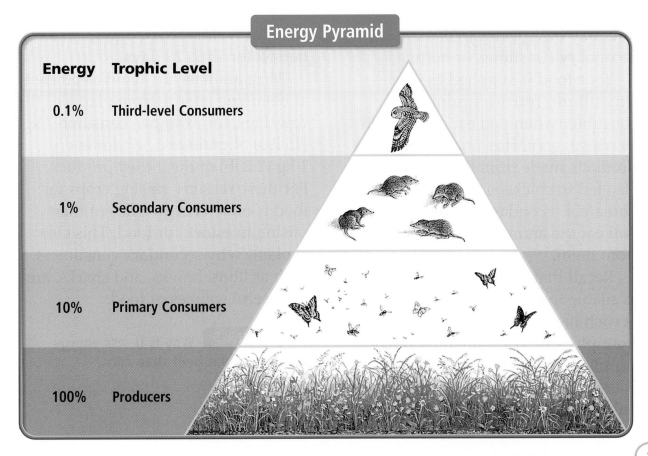

Energy Pyramid

Energy	Trophic Level
0.1%	Third-level Consumers
1%	Secondary Consumers
10%	Primary Consumers
100%	Producers

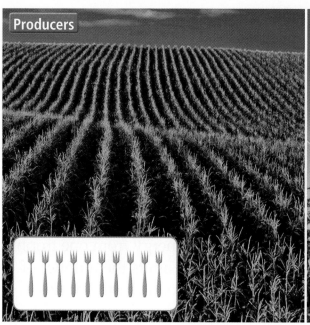

Producers

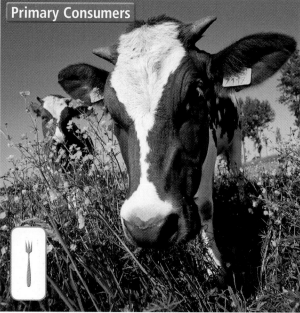

Primary Consumers

= 3,000 kilocalories

When a cow eats corn, its body takes up to 10 percent of the corn's energy. The forks represent usable energy. The ten forks of usable energy in the corn decrease to one fork of usable energy in the cow.

The Energy Pyramid and Agriculture

You are a part of many food webs. You may be a primary consumer, a secondary consumer, or both.

Your food is supplied by agriculture. You are a primary consumer when you eat plants such as wheat, corn, rice, and soybeans, or products made from them. Plants are also fed to chickens, cattle, and hogs. You are a secondary consumer when you eat the animals or products made from them.

Recall that the amount of energy available to an organism decreases at each higher trophic level. For example, suppose a quantity of corn supplies 30,000 kilocalories (kcal) of energy. If the corn is fed to a cow, only about 10% of that energy—

3,000 kcal—would be available to a consumer eating beef from the cow. While 3,000 kcal would feed a human for one or two days, the 30,000 kcal in the corn would be enough to feed a person for 15 to 20 days.

Most animals are about as efficient at obtaining energy from plants as the cow. Pigs, for example, consume 7 kg (15 lbs) of grain and soy for every 1 kg (2.2 lb) of meat they produce. For these reasons, raising crops for food is more energy efficient than raising livestock for food. This also explains why secondary consumers, such as lions, hawks, and sharks, are not useful sources of food.

SEQUENCE Why is it less energy efficient to eat beef than corn?

Visual Summary

Energy entering an ecosystem is passed from producers to primary consumers, then to secondary and third-level consumers through food webs.

Decomposers break down dead organic matter, returning nutrients to the soil.

The energy pyramid shows that the amount of energy available decreases with each higher trophic level.

Growing crops is generally a more efficient way of producing food energy for humans than raising livestock.

 STANDARDS

5.a., 5.b.

Technology
Visit **www.eduplace.com/cascp** to find out more about food energy in ecosystems.

Reading Review

1 MAIN IDEA Explain how energy is transferred when one organism eats another.

2 VOCABULARY What is the difference between a *food web* and an *energy pyramid*?

3 READING SKILL Put the following organisms in the correct order in a food chain: grasshopper, grass, bird.

1	
2	
3	
4	

4 CRITICAL THINKING: Synthesize Why do food chains stop at top-level consumers such as lions or bears?

5 INQUIRY SKILL: Communicate Create a food web that ends with a person who eats animal products such as eggs, milk, and cheese. Write a report to describe your food web.

 TEST PRACTICE
What do decomposers do?

A. Eat bacteria and fungi.

B. Produce oxygen.

C. Break down dead plant and animal matter.

D. Eat plants only.

 STANDARDS

1: 5.a., 2: 5.a., 3: 5.b., 4–5: 5.a., Test Practice: 5.b.

Food Web of the Farm

As farmers could tell you, every farm crop faces threats from other organisms. Bacteria and fungi may spoil crops before or after harvest. Weeds can crowd out or choke growing crops, while insects and other pests can eat them.

To protect their crops, most farmers treat their fields with chemicals. *Fungicides* are chemicals that kill fungi. *Herbicides* kill weeds, and *pesticides* kill pests. All are costly to purchase and to apply. They also affect the food web of the farm.

A chemical treatment may work well one year but work poorly the next. The reason is that the sturdiest weeds or pests survive the treatments. They pass along their resistance to the next generation.

In response to this problem, scientists have been using new technology to develop pest-resistant crops. In addition, a few farmers have turned to a practice called organic farming. By mixing different crops in the same field, pesticides are not needed.

Crop Dusting
Dropping pesticides from an airplane is called crop dusting. This field of lettuce will be dusted many times before harvest.

STANDARD
5.b. *Students know* matter is transferred over time from one organism to others in the food web and between organisms and the physical environment.

READING LINK

Pests ▲
The brown garden snail *(Helix aspersa)* threatens many fruits and vegetables grown in California. Other pests include certain worms and insects.

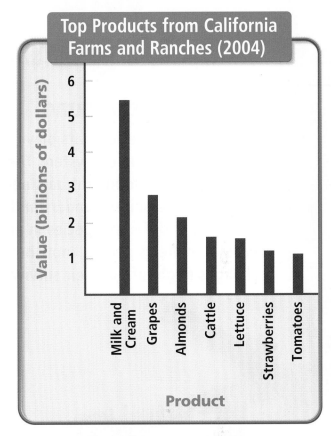

Top Products from California Farms and Ranches (2004)

Value (billions of dollars)

6
5
4
3
2
1

Milk and Cream · Grapes · Almonds · Cattle · Lettuce · Strawberries · Tomatoes

Product

California Farms and Ranches ▲
Rich soil, sunny weather, and a long growing season help California lead the nation in farming. In 2004, products from the state's farms and ranches sold for $32 billion.

Genetic Engineering ▲
Scientists have transferred certain genes from bacteria into potatoes, wheat, and other farm crops. The result has been sturdier, pest-resistant crops.

Sharing Ideas

1. **READING CHECK** List ways that organisms can threaten farm crops.

2. **WRITE ABOUT IT** Why does a pesticide become less effective every year it is used?

3. **TALK ABOUT IT** Along with fighting pests, what other challenges do farmers face?

What Roles Do Organisms Play?

Building Background

Like other species, bats play specific roles in an ecosystem. The habitat and the food that bats need to survive are unique. Understanding the roles of different species in an ecosystem helps people know how changes might affect their survival.

PREPARE TO INVESTIGATE

Inquiry Skill

Analyze Data When you analyze data, you determine whether it tends to support a hypothesis or not.

Materials

• picture cards

Science and Math Toolbox

For step 1, review **Making a Chart to Organize Data** on page H11.

STANDARDS

5.c. *Students know* populations of organisms can be categorized by the functions they serve in an ecosystem.
7.e. Recognize whether evidence is consistent with a proposed explanation.

Role Playing

Procedure

1 **Collaborate** In your *Science Notebook*, make a data table like the one shown. Include rows for 10 organisms that live in a prairie ecosystem.

2 **Observe** Study the picture cards. Record observations that help explain the organism's role in the prairie ecosystem. Note body parts that help it make food, catch food, or eat food.

3 **Classify** Classify each organism as producer, primary consumer, secondary consumer, scavenger, or decomposer. Use reference sources or the Internet, if available.

4 **Use Models** Arrange the producers and consumers into an energy pyramid. Draw the energy pyramid in your *Science Notebook*. Note the scavengers and decomposers separately.

5 **Use Models** Add arrows to the pyramid to show three food chains. Draw each arrow from food source to consumer.

Conclusion

1. **Compare** How are all food chains in the ecosystem alike? How are they different?

2. **Analyze Data** If a poison collected in the bodies of the grasshoppers, which other organisms could be affected? Explain.

3. **Infer** Identify two animals from your chart that fill very similar roles in the prairie ecosystem. Do you think their roles are exactly the same? Explain.

STEP 1

Organism	Observations	Role

◄ Great Horned Owl

▲ Richardson's Ground Squirrels

▲ Prairie Plants

Guided Inquiry

Ask Questions The American bison once grazed on the North American prairie. How does it **compare** to grazing animals of the plains of Africa? Ask questions about animals that fill similar roles in similar ecosystems. Research the answer.

Species in an Ecosystem

VOCABULARY

carnivore	p. 312
herbivore	p. 312
niche	p. 310
omnivore	p. 312
predator	p. 310
prey	p. 310

READING SKILL

Classify Use a chart to compare herbivores and carnivores.

Group	Group

STANDARDS

5.c. *Students know* populations of organisms can be categorized by the functions they serve in an ecosystem.
5.d. *Students know* different kinds of organisms may play similar ecological roles in similar biomes.

MAIN IDEA Every species in an ecosystem has a niche, which includes the species' relationships with the biotic and abiotic factors in the ecosystem.

Niche

Each organism in an ecosystem has its own niche, or role, in that ecosystem. A species' **niche** is its relationships with the biotic and abiotic factors of the ecosystem. It includes where the species lives, and how it raises its young.

Part of an animal's niche is defined by what it eats and what eats it. A **predator** is an animal, such as a lynx, that hunts and eats other animals, such as hares. The animal that is caught and eaten—the hare—is the **prey.** Both predators and prey are adapted for their niches. A lynx can run fast and can easily see and smell prey. Hares also run fast, and their fur usually blends into the background.

Some species are *generalists*, meaning they occupy a broad niche. For example, raccoons are predators that eat almost anything. They dine on nuts, berries, birds, fish, and even garbage!

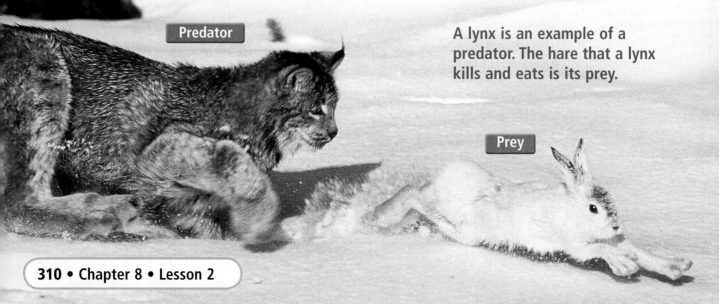

Predator

Prey

A lynx is an example of a predator. The hare that a lynx kills and eats is its prey.

Warbler Niches

Cape May Warbler

This warbler hunts in the top of the tree. It moves vertically along the edges of the branches.

Blackburnian Warbler

The Blackburnian also hunts in the top of the tree, but it moves horizontally across the entire top of the tree.

Bay Breasted Warbler

This warbler hunts in the middle section of the tree. It prefers the shaded interior.

Yellow-rumped Warbler

This warbler spends most of its time in the bottom part of the tree.

Other species are *specialists*, meaning they occupy a very specific niche. For example, evergreen forests are home to at least four species of insect-eating wood warblers. All the species hunt in the same trees in the forest. But each warbler species works in a different part of the trees.

Two species hunt in different parts of the top section of the trees. Another species hunts in parts of the middle section. One species spends most of its time hunting in the bottom section of the trees.

The warblers' niches are different in another way. They nest and raise their young at different times. Because they need more food while they are raising young, nesting at different times means that not all species need more food at the same time.

The four species of warbler can all survive in the same trees because their niches are different. When two species occupy the same niche, they compete for the same resources. Over time, the more successful species survives while the other one does not.

 **CLASSIFY** What is an example of a niche?

Herbivore

A jackrabbit is an herbivore, or a plant-eating animal.

Carnivore

A hawk is a carnivore, or a meat-eating animal.

Omnivore

A roadrunner is an omnivore, eating both plants and animals.

Food Webs

You learned that a food web shows the feeding relationships within an ecosystem. Both matter and energy are transferred through a food web.

Although each ecosystem has a different food web, all food webs have the same parts. These parts are producers, herbivores, carnivores, omnivores, and decomposers. These parts also are organized in the same way.

Producers are at the bottom of an ecosystem's food web. Producers, such as plants and algae, use the energy of the Sun to make food. This energy is passed to **herbivores,** which are plant-eating animals. Herbivores are primary consumers, the first animal in any food chain.

Animals that eat herbivores are called carnivores. **Carnivores** are also consumers, but they get their energy from eating other animals that they hunt. **Omnivores** obtain energy by eating both plants and other animals. Carnivores and omnivores are found at or near the top of a food web.

Recall that decomposers are organisms that feed on dead plants and animals, breaking them down into nutrients that enrich the soil. This transfer of nutrients from plants to animals to decomposers and back to plants occurs in every ecosystem.

Even the desert, with relatively few species, has a complex food web. Desert producers include hardy plant species such as creosote bush, sagebrush, and cactus. Rabbits, mice, and kangaroo rats are herbivores that eat these plants and their seeds.

Rattlesnakes and hawks are carnivores that hunt and eat desert herbivores. Roadrunners are omnivores. They eat whatever is available. Roadrunners eat mostly meat—insects, snakes, lizards, rodents, and even other birds. However, they eat plants in winter when desert animals are scarce. They may also scavenge on dead animals.

In healthy ecosystems, populations of each species are relatively stable.

Each population is big enough to reproduce and small enough so that it does not use up all of its food resources.

One important role in most ecosystems is the top carnivore, such as the hawk or lion. These animals indicate that an ecosystem is healthy, because they cannot survive without stable numbers of other animal and plant populations.

CLASSIFY **What are the main parts of every food web?**

Desert Food Web A food web shows all the feeding relationships in an ecosystem. Find the producers, herbivores, and carnivores shown here. Arrows between animals point from prey to predator.

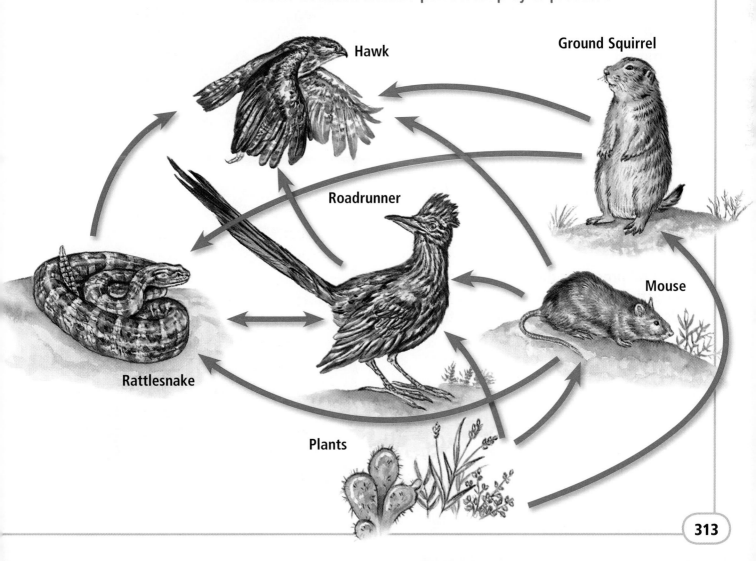

Hawk

Ground Squirrel

Roadrunner

Mouse

Rattlesnake

Plants

Biomagnification

Nutrients and energy are passed from one organism to another in a food chain. Toxins may be passed up a food chain as well.

Some toxins, or poisons, are not broken down by natural processes. Instead, the toxin stays in the body of organisms that absorb or eat them. When these organisms are eaten, the toxin is passed on up the food chain. The toxins concentrate in animals, including humans, at the top of the food chain. They receive the entire amount of toxin from all the lower levels. This effect is called *biomagnification*.

Biologist Rachel Carson (1907–1964) was one of the first scientists to observe and describe biomagnification. She observed it happening with DDT, a powerful insecticide used to kill mosquitoes. Carson showed that DDT traveled up the food chain, harming birds and other animals. She published her work in a book titled *Silent Spring*.

Thanks to Carson's work, large-scale use of DDT is banned worldwide. However, some scientists argue that DDT should be allowed limited use in certain circumstances. Mosquitoes spread malaria—a deadly disease—and DDT effectively kills mosquitoes.

CLASSIFY Which animals in a food web are most affected by biomagnification?

Natural processes do not break down the insecticide DDT, modeled here by red dots (·). Use of DDT is banned worldwide today. ▶

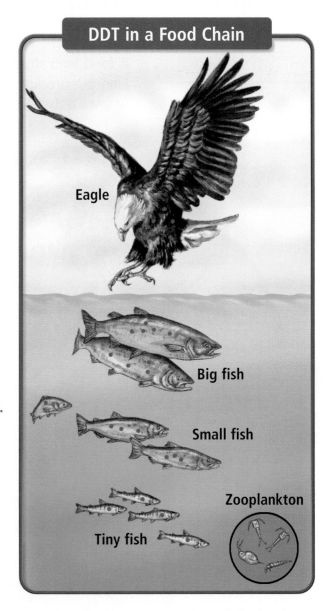

DDT in a Food Chain

Eagle

Big fish

Small fish

Tiny fish

Zooplankton

Express Lab

Activity Card 25
Make Food Connections

Visual Summary

Each species in an ecosystem has a specific role, or niche. All species depend on other species for survival. Species in different biomes may fill similar niches.

Food webs illustrate the feeding relationships among the many species of an ecosystem. A food web is made up of producers, herbivores, carnivores, and decomposers.

When toxic substances in the environment are passed up a food chain, biomagnification occurs. The top predator is harmed the most.

 STANDARDS

5.c., 5.d.

Technology
Visit **www.eduplace.com/cascp** to find out more about niches.

Reading Review

1 MAIN IDEA Describe how each species in an ecosystem depends on other species.

2 VOCABULARY Compare a *carnivore* and an *omnivore*.

3 READING SKILL Name two predators from different ecosystems. Compare the feeding relationships they form.

Group	Group

4 CRITICAL THINKING: Draw Conclusions Which species are most vulnerable to biomagnification? Explain.

5 INQUIRY SKILL: Analyze Data A scientist is studying a desert ecosystem. She observes the mouse population rising and falling greatly every year, while the snake population stays relatively constant. Should she conclude that the snakes do not prey on mice? Explain.

 TEST PRACTICE
What is a niche?

A. a type of forest biome

B. a type of tropical bird

C. a top producer

D. the specific role of a species in an ecosystem

 STANDARDS

1: 5.a., **2:** 5.c., **3–4:** 5.d., **5:** 7.a., **Test Practice:** 5.c.

315

What Is Symbiosis?

Building Background

Hummingbirds get food from flowers. As they do, they help the flowers reproduce. Both the bird and plant benefit.

All species, including humans, take part in close relationships with other species around them. Some relationships are helpful to one or both species. In others, one species is harmed.

PREPARE TO INVESTIGATE

Inquiry Skill

Hypothesize When you hypothesize, you develop an explanation of previous observations.

Materials

- 4 sheets of colored paper (red, green, blue, yellow)
- hole-puncher
- large piece of yellow cloth
- clock or stopwatch with second hand

Science and Math Toolbox

For step 1, review **Making a Chart to Organize Data** on page H11.

STANDARDS

5.c. *Students know* populations of organisms can be categorized by the functions they serve in an ecosystem.
7.a. Develop an hypothesis.

Hide and Seek!

Procedure

1 Collaborate Work in a small group. Use the hole-puncher to punch 50 dots from each sheet of colored paper. Different color dots represent different insect species. In your *Science Notebook*, create a chart like the one shown at right.

2 Predict Predict the color of insect you think would be hardest for a bird to see against a tree trunk with yellow bark. Record your prediction.

3 Use Models Lay the cloth flat. The cloth represents the yellow bark. Scatter the dots randomly on the cloth. Kneel at the edge of the cloth. When your teacher says "go," collect as many dots as possible, one at a time. Stop after 15 seconds.

4 Record Data Count the numbers of each color dots your entire group collected. Record your data in the row marked "Hunt 1." Set aside the "insects" you picked up. Then repeat step 3 two more times for Hunt 2 and Hunt 3.

Conclusion

1. **Analyze Data** Total each column. Which color insect had the fewest members collected? Explain why. Did this result match your prediction?

2. **Hypothesize** Develop a hypothesis about how a tree with yellow bark might help a yellow insect. What type of relationship would the tree and the insect have? What evidence supports your hypothesis?

STEP 1

Hunt	Blue	Yellow	Green	Red
Hunt 1				
Hunt 2				
Hunt 3				
Total				

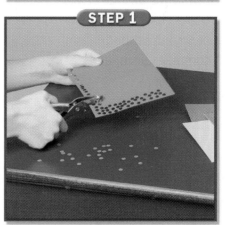

STEP 1

STEP 3

Guided Inquiry

Ask Questions What are some real organisms that help one another? What questions do you have about them? Use library and Internet resources to do **research**. Write an illustrated report to summarize your findings.

317

Symbiosis

VOCABULARY

commensalism   p. 319
mutualism   p. 319
parasitism   p. 320
symbiosis   p. 318

READING SKILL

Compare and Contrast
Use a chart to compare and contrast mutualism, commensalism, and parasitism.

Group	Group	Group

STANDARDS

5.c. *Students know* populations of organisms can be categorized by the functions they serve in an ecosystem.
5.d. *Students know* different kinds of organisms may play similar ecological roles in similar biomes.

MAIN IDEA Symbiosis is a close relationship between two different species. Symbiotic relationships include mutualism, commensalism, and parasitism.

Mutualism and Commensalism

Organisms can interact with one another in many different ways. Three major types of interactions among organisms are predation, competition, and symbiotic relationships. You have already learned about predation, in which animals eat other animals. Competition occurs when two species try to use the same limited resource, such as a food supply, a source of water, or a type of shelter. Competition is reduced when organisms occupy different niches.

In **symbiosis** (sihm bee OH sis), two species have a close living relationship. Symbiotic relationships include mutualism, commensalism, and parasitism.

Mutualism
The sea anemone's stinging tentacles keep the clownfish's predators away, and the clownfish keeps the sea anemone clean.

When two species both benefit from their relationship, the relationship is called **mutualism** (MYOO choo uh lihz uhm). One example of mutualism is the relationship between sea anemones (uh NEM uh neez) and clownfish.

Anemones feed on fish and other marine creatures. They do not move from place to place, but use stinging tentacles to capture passing creatures.

Clownfish live among the anemone tentacles, but are immune to the stings. In this way, the anemone protects the clownfish from being eaten by other fish. The clownfish in turn helps the anemone by cleaning its tentacles and chasing away fish that eat anemone tentacles.

The relationship between oxpeckers and a hippopotamus is also an example of mutualism. The birds eat ticks living on the hippo's skin.

A lichen is an alga and a fungus living in mutualism. The fungus provides a moist, nutritious home for the alga. The alga provides food by photosynthesis. ▼

▲ Commensalism
Small fish hide from predators near the poisonous tentacles of a jellyfish. The jellyfish is unaffected by the fish.

The birds benefit because they get a meal. The hippo benefits because the ticks are removed from its back.

Commensalism (kuh MEHN suh lihz uhm) is a relationship between two species, in which one species benefits while the other species is neither harmed nor helped. A robin building a nest in an oak is an example. The robin gains a safe place to lay its eggs while the oak is neither harmed nor helped.

Some barnacles attached to a whale and remoras attached to a shark are other examples. The whale and shark are not affected. The barnacles and remoras have access to more food.

Not many relationships are commensal. More often, one species is helped or harmed at least slightly.

COMPARE AND CONTRAST How are mutualism and commensalism similar, and how are they different?

Express Lab

Activity Card 26
Test Camouflage

Parasitism

Parasitism is a relationship between two species in which one species benefits while the other species is harmed. The organism causing harm is called a parasite. The harmed organism is called the host.

The tapeworm uses two different hosts in its lifecycle. ▼

The ticks that live on the skin of a hippopotamus are parasites. The hippo is the host. The ticks feed on blood that they draw from the hippo, harming the hippo.

Parasites usually weaken their hosts slowly instead of killing them quickly. By feeding on a living host, the parasite maintains a constant food supply instead of getting just a few meals.

Leeches, tapeworms, and fleas are common examples of parasites. These organisms all have specialized mouthparts allowing them to attach to the skin or other parts of their hosts. Most live off the host's blood.

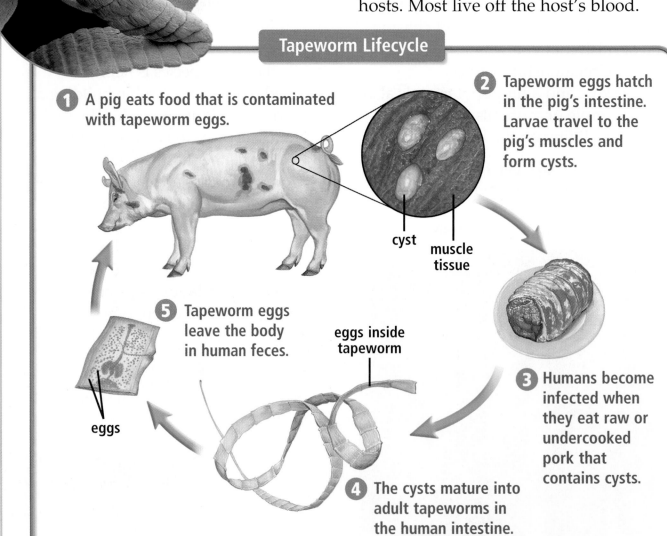

Tapeworm Lifecycle

1 A pig eats food that is contaminated with tapeworm eggs.

2 Tapeworm eggs hatch in the pig's intestine. Larvae travel to the pig's muscles and form cysts.

cyst muscle tissue

5 Tapeworm eggs leave the body in human feces.

eggs inside tapeworm

eggs

3 Humans become infected when they eat raw or undercooked pork that contains cysts.

4 The cysts mature into adult tapeworms in the human intestine.

Types of Parasites

Have you ever heard of having a puppy "wormed"? This term refers to giving the puppy a medicine that kills any tapeworms that may be living in its intestine.

Tapeworms are long, flat worms that live in the intestines of dogs, humans, and many other animals. Suckers or hooks allow the tapeworm to attach to the inner wall of the animal's intestine. There the tapeworm absorbs food. Because the host has already digested the food, the tapeworm does not need a digestive system of its own.

A tapeworm reproduces through a complex life cycle. Its fertilized eggs are released into the host's intestines and eventually leave the host's body in feces. Another animal may eat the eggs, typically with spoiled water or food.

In the second host, the eggs hatch into larvae that travel to muscle cells. There they form inactive structures called cysts. Humans and other animals become infected when they eat cyst-laden meat.

Parasites often transmit diseases that are much more harmful than the parasite itself. For example, the deer tick is a common parasite of deer, humans, and other animals. These ticks can transmit the bacteria that cause Lyme disease.

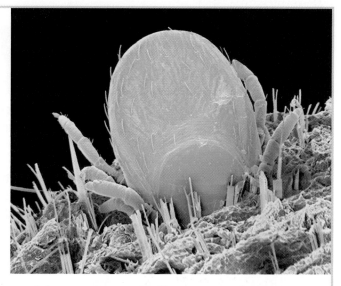

▲ Ticks can transmit diseases as they feed on a host.

Plants can have parasites, too. The dodder vine has no chlorophyll and cannot make its own food. Instead, it attaches itself to other plants and steals their food. Mistletoe grows as a parasite on oak and other trees. Its roots grow into the branches of the host tree. There, they absorb nutrients from the host, sometimes weakening or killing it.

 **COMPARE AND CONTRAST** How do parasitism and predation differ?

Mistletoe can weaken or even kill its host tree. ▶

Three Parasites of Humans		
Parasite	**Description**	**Treatment**
Plasmodium malariae (Malaria)	Infection with this protist can cause chills, fever, diarrhea, and death.	Antimalarial drugs
Sarcoptes scabei (Scabies)	Scabies are small mites that burrow under the skin of the host, forming tiny tunnels and causing an itchy rash.	Prescription medication
Pediculus humanus capitis (Lice)	Head lice live on the human scalp, and feed on human blood several times a day, causing intense itching of the scalp.	Combination of special shampoo and egg removal

Symbiosis with Humans

Although you might not realize it, other organisms are living inside and on you. In fact, many help keep you healthy!

Large numbers of bacteria live in your large intestine. These bacteria feed on food that has not been fully digested. Some of the bacteria produce vitamin K and other nutrients that humans need. This is an example of mutualism. Both species benefit.

Not all symbiotic relationships with humans are harmless. Many are parasitic. A parasitic fungus causes ringworm, a skin disease. A parasitic amoeba causes amoebic dysentery. Amoebic dysentery is a serious disease in which the parasite destroys the lining of the intestines.

Malaria is one of the world's most serious parasitic diseases. It is caused by protists. Malaria kills about 2 million people every year, and affects as many as 500 million more.

Invertebrate parasites are extremely common in the tropics. Most of these parasites are various species of worm. Humans are infected when they come into contact with water or food that has been contaminated by worms.

COMPARE AND CONTRAST What are ways that symbiotic organisms help and hurt humans?

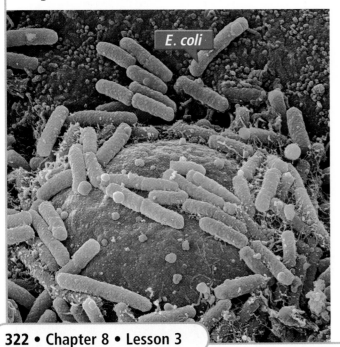
◄ *E. coli* bacteria are normally harmless inhabitants of the human digestive system.

E. coli

Visual Summary

Symbiosis means "living together." Examples of symbiosis occur in all biomes. In mutualism, two species each benefit from their relationship.

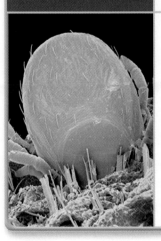

Commensalism is a relationship in which one species benefits and the other species is neither harmed nor helped.

In parasitism, one organism lives in or on another organism and harms it in some way, while benefiting itself.

STANDARDS

5.c., 5.d.

Technology

Visit **www.eduplace.com/cascp** to find out more about symbiotic relationships among organisms.

Reading Review

1 MAIN IDEA What is symbiosis?

2 VOCABULARY How is *mutualism* different from *parasitism*?

3 READING SKILL Compare and contrast mutualism and parasitism involving humans. Give one example of each.

Group	Group	Group

4 CRITICAL THINKING: Synthesize Parasites make up only a small proportion of all species. Why do you think this is so? (Hint: Think about what would happen if most species were parasitic.)

5 INQUIRY SKILL: Hypothesize Suppose you discovered a new animal species that did not have a digestive system. Develop a hypothesis about a symbiotic relationship that this species forms.

 TEST PRACTICE

A lichen is an example of _____.

A. competition

B. mutualism

C. commensalism

D. parasitism

STANDARDS

1–3: 5.d., 4–5: 5.c., **Test Practice:** 5.c.

323

STANDARDS 5.c. *Students know* populations of organisms can be categorized by the functions they serve in an ecosystem.

Dentists of the Deep

Open wide! Just like you, fish need to get their teeth cleaned every so often. You go to the dentist. Many reef fish go to the cleaner shrimp. In addition to the teeth and the mouth, cleaner shrimp work on the fish's entire body, removing food particles, dead skin, and parasites. Cleaner shrimp even perform minor surgery with their claws, clipping off dead skin and cutting out embedded parasites!

Cleaner shrimp start their workday with a vigorous tap dance that signals to fish that their cleaning station is open. Like cars at a car wash, client fish line up and patiently wait to be cleaned. Cleaners are safe in the mouths of the fiercest predators.

Cleaning fish and shrimp fill an important niche in the reef ecosystem. They help keep other fish healthy and free of diseases and parasites.

Mutualism in action!

Here you can see a scarlet cleaner shrimp cleaning the mouth of a grouper. The shrimp gets food, and the grouper gets relief from itching parasites.

Writing Journal

In your journal, discuss what would happen to a reef's fish population if all the cleaner shrimp were killed.

Math in Science

Malaria is a disease caused by a parasite. The graph shows the number of reported cases of malaria in the United States, including Guam and other territories in the southern Pacific.

1. How did malaria among U.S. citizens compare to other groups?

2. For the years shown, what was the approximate range of yearly malaria cases in the United States?

3. Propose a reason for the high number of total malaria cases in 1980. How could you evaluate your reason? What evidence would you look for?

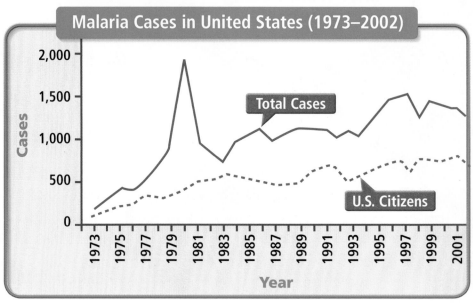

Malaria Cases in United States (1973–2002)

Total Cases

U.S. Citizens

Writing in Science
Research Report

Zebras are herbivores in the African savanna. Their niche includes eating grasses and providing food for lions and other predators. Research at least two herbivores from other grasslands around the world. Compare the different niches they fill.

California

Ann López

In 1994, Ann López read about the harsh treatment of farm workers in Mexico. Both the workers and the land were suffering. At the age of 49, López decided to do something to help. She chose to return to graduate school to become an environmental scientist.

Ann López made the most of that decision! Over the years she has visited more than 20 farms in Mexico and California. She studies how farming practices affect both the land and the people, and she proposes ways to improve life for both.

"My desire [is] to use science as a way to preserve the environment and work for social justice," says Dr. López about her career. "I learned that it is never too late to follow your passion or speak your mind."

Vocabulary

Complete each sentence with a term from the list.

1. An animal that eats both plants and animals is a(n) _____.

2. A relationship between two species in which one species benefits while the other species is neither helped nor harmed is _____.

3. A close relationship between two species is called _____.

4. Overlapping food chains in an ecosystem make up a(n) _____.

5. A relationship in which two species both benefit is called _____.

6. An organism that lives by breaking apart dead organic matter into simpler parts is a(n) _____.

7. An animal that eats other animals is a(n) _____.

8. An animal that eats only plants is a(n) _____.

9. A living relationship between two species in which one organism is harmed is called _____.

10. A species' relationship with the biotic and abiotic factors in an ecosystem is its _____.

carnivore p. 312
commensalism p. 319
consumer p. 300
decomposer p. 302
energy pyramid p. 303
food web p. 304
herbivore p. 312
mutualism p. 319
niche p. 310
omnivore p. 312
parasitism p. 320
predator p. 310
prey p. 310
producer p. 300
scavenger p. 302
symbiosis p. 318
trophic level p. 300

Test Practice

Write the letter of the best answer choice.

11. A producer is on an ecosystem's lowest _____.

   A. trophic level
   B. energy pyramid
   C. food web
   D. niche

12. What do predators hunt?

   A. parasites
   B. decomposers
   C. producers
   D. prey

13. What is at the highest level of an energy pyramid?

   A. herbivores
   B. consumers
   C. producers
   D. decomposers

14. What does a scavenger eat?

   A. only plants
   B. animals that are already dead
   C. animals that it hunts and kills
   D. only herbivores

Inquiry Skills

15. Experiment The sellers of a new insecticide claim that their product is safe for the environment. They claim the product will kill mosquitoes, but not harm other wildlife. Describe an experiment to evaluate this claim. Which animal groups would you observe?

16. Antibiotics are drugs that help the body kill bacteria. Why should you take antibiotics only under a doctor's care? Why not take antibiotics every day?

Map the Concept

Use this concept map to show the relationship between a lion and an antelope in a savanna ecosystem. Copy and fill in the concept map to identify them as predator or prey and as a primary or a secondary consumer.

Prey

Primary Consumer

Predator

Secondary Consumer

Lion	Antelope

Critical Thinking

17. Apply A disease kills all the herbivores and omnivores in an ecosystem. Can the ecosystem keep on functioning, with only producers and carnivores? Explain your answer.

18. Synthesize What would happen in an ecosystem with no decomposers?

19. Evaluate Tests performed by scientists show that eagles living near a certain river have ten times the DDT levels of the fish they catch. Do these data support the idea of biomagnification? Explain your answer.

20. Analyze What is the difference between a parasite and a predator?

Performance Assessment

Draw a Food Web

Choose an ecosystem and draw a food web that might exist within it. Include several categories of organisms: producers, primary consumers, secondary consumers, and decomposers. Then draw an energy pyramid to depict how energy is transferred between the organisms in the food web you chose.

Writing Journal

Review your answers to the Lesson Preview questions on page 295.

STANDARDS

1–2: 1.d., **3–4:** 1.b., **5:** 1.d., **6:** 1.c., 1.d., **7–8:** 1.b., **9:** 1.c., **10:** 1.b., **11:** 1.b., **12:** 1.c., **13:** 1.d., **14:** 1.b., **15:** 1.d., **16:** 1.d., 6.h., **Map the Concept:** 1.b., **17:** 1.b., 1.f., **18:** 1.d., **19:** 1.c., 1.f., **20:** 1.h., **Performance Assessment:** 1.b.

Chapter 9

Populations

Walruses on a beach

LESSON
1
Animals and other organisms constantly strive to grow and reproduce. What factors limit populations in an ecosystem?

LESSON
2

How do ecosystems respond to sudden changes, such as erupting volcanoes and raging forest fires?

LESSON
3
Humans acquire resources for their own use. How do people change ecosystems?

Writing Journal

In your Writing Journal, write or draw answers to each question.

Vocabulary Preview

secondary succession
the process in which a new community replaces an old one

Vocabulary

biodiversity p. 355

climax community p. 348

competition p. 337

disease p. 339

endangered species p. 340

extinction p. 340

invasive species p. 339

limiting factor p. 336

pioneer species p. 347

pollution p. 354

predation p. 338

primary succession p. 347

secondary succession p. 348

threatened species p. 340

Glossary

English-Spanish, p. H26

Vocabulary Skill

Word Derivations
secondary succession

Succession is the process in which communities in an ecosystem change over time. Something that is secondary happens after what has come first, or is primary. So, *secondary succession* is a process of ecosystem change that occurs after primary succession.

extinction

the complete disappearance of a species, such as the passenger pigeon

pollution

the addition of harmful substances to the environment

predation

the act of catching and eating another organism

Start with Your Standards

Standard Set 2. Shaping Earth's Surface

2.d. *Students know* earthquakes, volcanic eruptions, landslides, and floods change human and wildlife habitats.

Standard Set 5. Ecology (Life Sciences)

5.e. *Students know* the number and types of organisms an ecosystem can support depends on the resources available and on abiotic factors, such as quantities of light and water, a range of temperatures, and soil composition.

Standard Set 7: Investigation and Experimentation standards covered in this chapter: 7.a., 7.c., 7.d.

What Limits Population Growth?

Building Background

One day you see bulldozers clearing trees from a forest. Soon you see new homes and streets there—along with deer and other wild animals roaming through backyards and fields.

All animals use resources to live. Using the same resources to meet human needs pushes animals to live in new places, and it limits their population growth.

PREPARE TO INVESTIGATE

Inquiry Skill

Use Numbers When you use numbers, you may do calculations to explain patterns in data.

Materials

- paper
- pencils (2 colors)
- ruler
- calculator

Science and Math Toolbox

For step 1, review **Making a Line Graph** on page H13.

STANDARDS

5.e. *Students know* the number and types of organisms an ecosystem can support depends on the resources available and on abiotic factors, such as quantities of light and water, a range of temperatures, and soil composition.

7.c. Construct appropriate graphs from data and develop qualitative statements about the relationships between variables.

Game of Numbers

Procedure

On an island, snakes feed on mice, small birds, and other small animals. The table at right shows the populations of snakes and mice over a span of 10 years.

1 **Record Data** Create two separate line graphs to display the population data: one for the mouse population, another for the snake population. Choose useful scales for each graph. The scales on the vertical axes need not be the same.

2 **Analyze Data** Compare the graphs. Note any patterns in the mouse population that repeat in the snake population.

Conclusion

1. **Communicate** In your *Science Notebook*, describe the patterns of growth of both the mouse and snake populations. When did each increase? When did each decrease?

2. **Use Numbers** During which year did each population experience the greatest drop? Calculate the percent drop by dividing the decrease by the previous year's population.

3. **Infer** What might have caused the population drop seen in the data? Describe an event that these data would support.

4. **Ask Questions** What further information about the island would help you better analyze the data?

Island Populations

Year	Mice	Snakes
1	850	62
2	810	68
3	720	70
4	600	55
5	340	40
6	450	22
7	580	35
8	700	50
9	250	12
10	260	12

STEP 1

Guided Inquiry

Ask Questions Find out more about animal populations on islands, such as those of Hawaii, Guam, and the Galápagos Islands. Write questions to investigate. **Research** and report the answers.

Populations

VOCABULARY

competition   p. 337
disease   p. 339
endangered species   p. 340
extinction   p. 340
invasive species   p. 339
limiting factor   p. 336
predation   p. 338
threatened species   p. 340

READING SKILL

Cause and Effect List limiting factors and their effects.

Cause → Effect

STANDARD

5.e. *Students know* the number and types of organisms an ecosystem can support depends on the resources available and on abiotic factors, such as quantities of light and water, a range of temperatures, and soil composition.

MAIN IDEA Populations depend on resources, predator-prey relationships, diseases, and competition.

Limited Resources

In the photo below of the African savanna, the watering hole is drying up. How many animals can still drink from it? Perhaps 20? Only a limited number of animals can live off this water. If the population in the area exceeds that number, many animals won't get enough to drink. To survive, they must find water elsewhere.

The water available to animals at this watering hole is a limiting factor in the ecosystem. A **limiting factor** is something that restricts the growth and distribution of a population. Limiting factors include resources such as food, water, and space. They can also involve competition, predation, disease, invasive species, and human activities.

Without limiting factors, populations would increase—and keep on increasing. For example, some bacteria can double in number every 6 hours. If all offspring survived, a single bacterium could produce a colony of a quarter billion in about a week.

In any population, growth is limited by factors such as competition, predation, water, and disease.

Rain forest Rain forests receive 400 to 1,000 cm of rain each year. Plenty of water combined with warm temperatures result in abundant plant and animal populations.

Desert Water is scarce in the desert, where less than 25 cm of rain falls each year. The low availability of this resource results in small plant and animal populations.

Competition

Competition is an important limiting factor. **Competition** is the struggle among living things to use the same resources in an ecosystem.

Some competition occurs between individuals of the same species. For example, birds of the same species might compete for the best places to nest. Plants might compete for growing space in soil. Two lions might compete for the same prey.

There is also competition between different species. Owls and hawks hunt the same type of food. Their competition is limited because they hunt at different times of the day.

People compete with plants and animals for resources as well. To meet their own needs—such as for new roads and homes—people often destroy habitats for plants and animals.

Ecosystem Balance

Limiting factors determine the number of organisms an ecosystem can support. This number is called the *carrying capacity* of the ecosystem. When the carrying capacity is reached for all of its species, the ecosystem is said to be in balance.

Populations can grow above or below the carrying capacity, but only for a short time. When there are more organisms in an area than the available resources can support, only some organisms will survive. Others will have to leave the area to find resources or they will die.

When there are fewer organisms than the resources can support, the population will grow until all of the available resources are used.

 **CAUSE AND EFFECT** How does competition limit populations?

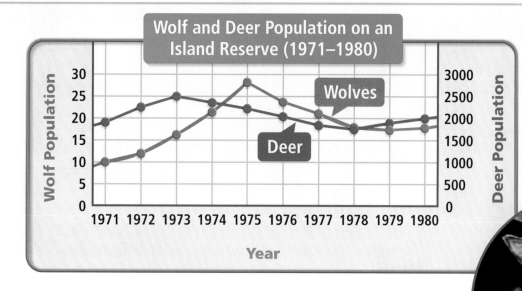

Wolf and Deer Population on an Island Reserve (1971–1980)

Wolf Population: 30, 25, 20, 15, 10, 5, 0

Deer Population: 3000, 2500, 2000, 1500, 1000, 500, 0

Year: 1971 1972 1973 1974 1975 1976 1977 1978 1979 1980

Wolves

Deer

Predators

Have you ever seen a bird snatch a worm from the ground, or a cat pounce on a mouse? Recall that this interaction is called predation. **Predation** occurs when one organism—the predator—catches and feeds on another organism—the prey.

Predation is an important limiting factor in an ecosystem. The graph above shows the populations of predators (wolves) and their prey (deer) in an ecosystem in the Midwest. The high points, or spikes, in the graph show when the populations are the largest. The low points, or dips, show when the populations are the smallest.

Notice that the spikes and dips of both populations follow a similar cycle. This cycle occurs in many predator-prey relationships and in a variety of ecosystems.

When any prey population grows, predators have plenty to eat. As a result, the predator population grows. With more wolves, many more deer are killed than are born. So the deer population drops. With its food supply reduced, the wolf population drops as well. With fewer wolves hunting them, the surviving deer enjoy a period of reduced predation. The deer population rises again. The predator-prey cycle repeats itself.

Predator and prey species can live together in this way for a long time. Their numbers cycle from high to low and back again in a natural process of population control.

Express Lab

Activity Card 27

Act Out Competition

Diseases

In 1347, a trading ship from China sailed into an Italian port. It carried not only goods but a deadly disease called bubonic plague. Rats infested with fleas that carried the disease left the ship. The disease eventually spread throughout Europe. Within five years, the Black Death, as it was known, killed 25 million people—a third of the European population.

A **disease** is a condition that prevents an organism from functioning properly. It is an important limiting factor because it can stop population growth. Diseases often appear in animal populations weakened by overcrowding or lack of food and water.

Disease can also affect plant populations. Dutch elm disease, for example, arrived in the United States with a shipment of logs around 1930. Bark beetles spread the disease. By 1970, it had killed 77 million American elms.

Fifty years ago, many city streets were lined with elm trees. Bark beetles spread Dutch elm disease, which killed most of the elms. ▼

▲ The Chinese snakehead is infesting lakes and streams in North America. It competes with native species.

Invasive Species

The natural balance of ecosystems can be destroyed when an organism arrives from elsewhere. **Invasive species** are plants or animals that are not native to an ecosystem.

One such invader is a fish called the Chinese snakehead. It was imported from Asia for aquariums and for food. But some of the snakeheads escaped. Now they have entered freshwater bodies from Florida to Maryland. Snakehead populations have exploded as they eat native fish and other animals in lakes and streams.

Invasive species harm ecosystems because they often have no natural predators. In such cases, their populations can increase quickly. They crowd out native species and consume resources. They can also destroy habitats and disrupt food chains.

CAUSE AND EFFECT What happens to prey populations when predator populations rise?

◀ Millions of passenger pigeons once lived in eastern North America. In the 1800s they were hunted for their meat, feathers, and fat. They became extinct in 1914.

Extinction

Most of the species that ever lived on Earth are now extinct. **Extinction** is the complete disappearance of a species. Extinction can occur when the conditions in an ecosystem change in a way that makes the species unable to survive.

Many species become extinct naturally. However, the actions of humans have greatly increased the rate of extinction.

In the late 1500s, for example, several European ships visited the island of Mauritius in the Indian Ocean. The ships brought pigs, rats, and cats that killed many native species, including a large flightless bird called the dodo. By the late 1600s, a combination of invasive species and other factors drove the dodo to extinction.

Perhaps the most significant way humans increase the rate of extinction is through habitat destruction. As people build homes, roads, and shopping centers, they destroy natural ecosystems. When habitats are destroyed, organisms lose the resources they need.

Rescuing Species

When a species is close to becoming extinct, it called an **endangered species**. When a species is close to becoming endangered, it is called a **threatened species**.

In the United States, the Endangered Species Act was passed in 1973. It protects plants and animals that are in danger of extinction. Other laws protect their habitats.

In some cases, captive breeding programs help rescue endangered species. The California condor once ranged across North America. By 1967, only 50 to 60 individuals remained in the wild. Many had been shot or collided with power lines.

When the wild population dropped to nine birds, wildlife experts captured them and began breeding condors in captivity. By 1992, the population had grown large enough to start releasing condors back into the wild.

CAUSE AND EFFECT What are two factors that lead to extinction of a species?

A captive breeding program is helping to save the California condor from extinction. ▶

Visual Summary

Populations grow until they reach the limits of the ecosystem's resources. Every ecosystem can support a limited number of organisms, a number called the carrying capacity.

The relationship between predators and prey is one of the many factors that help limit population growth in an ecosystem.

Extinction occurs when a species completely disappears. Human actions have caused the extinction of many species, including the passenger pigeon.

STANDARD

5.e.

Technology
Visit **www.eduplace.com/cascp** to learn more about populations.

Reading Review

1 MAIN IDEA What types of populations will be most vulnerable to disease?

2 VOCABULARY Write a short paragraph using the terms *predation* and *limiting factor.*

3 READING SKILL A species becomes extinct. Explain the possible causes for extinction.

Cause → Effect

4 CRITICAL THINKING: Evaluate A park ranger decides to open a brief hunting season for deer within a park. Why might the ranger have made this decision?

5 INQUIRY SKILL: Use Numbers Look at the graph on page 338. About how many deer were there for each wolf in 1971? In 1975? Round your answers to the nearest ten.

 TEST PRACTICE
Which of the following is NOT a limiting factor?

A. disease

B. competition

C. predation

D. population

STANDARDS

1–5: 5.e., **Test Practice:** 5.e.

341

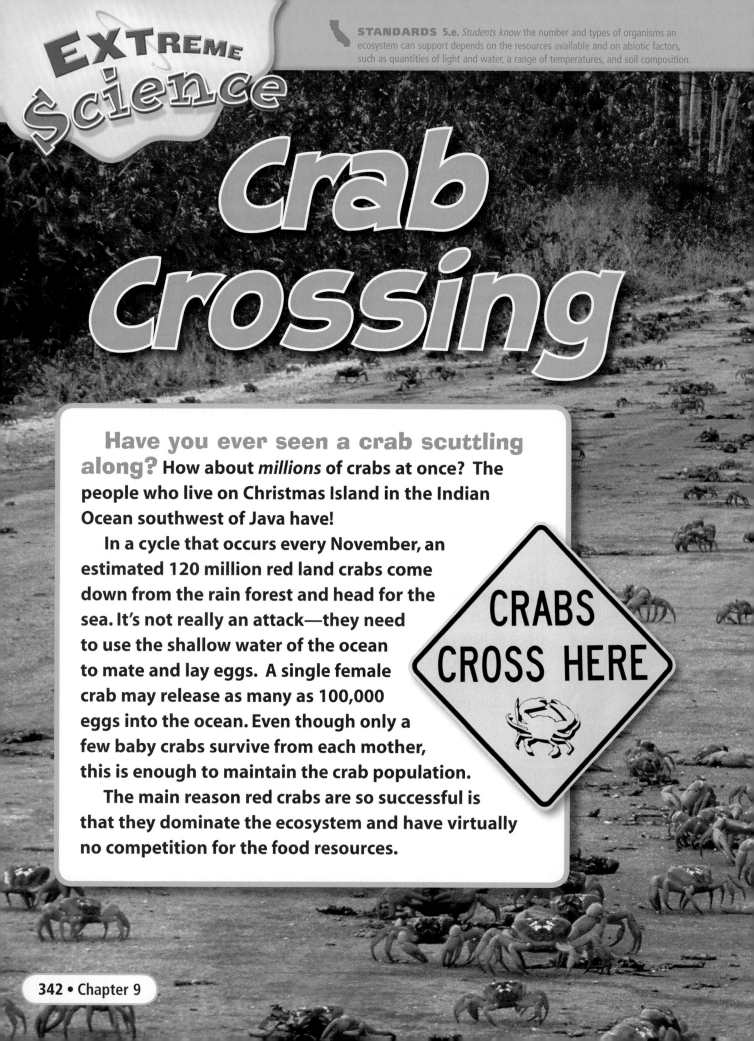

STANDARDS 5.e. *Students know* the number and types of organisms an ecosystem can support depends on the resources available and on abiotic factors, such as quantities of light and water, a range of temperatures, and soil composition.

Crab Crossing

Have you ever seen a crab scuttling along? How about *millions* of crabs at once? The people who live on Christmas Island in the Indian Ocean southwest of Java have!

In a cycle that occurs every November, an estimated 120 million red land crabs come down from the rain forest and head for the sea. It's not really an attack—they need to use the shallow water of the ocean to mate and lay eggs. A single female crab may release as many as 100,000 eggs into the ocean. Even though only a few baby crabs survive from each mother, this is enough to maintain the crab population.

The main reason red crabs are so successful is that they dominate the ecosystem and have virtually no competition for the food resources.

CRABS CROSS HERE

Dangerous Crossing
To reduce the number of crabs killed by vehicles, road closures and detours are used during peak migration periods.

Writing Journal

If half of the 120 million red land crabs were females, calculate how many eggs might be released if each female gave 100,000 eggs.

Lesson 2

What Is Ecological Succession?

Building Background

Sometimes a storm or fire will destroy the trees and plants in an area. But if you watch, you'll see wildlife slowly return. After a natural disaster, a diverse community of plants and animals will eventually thrive in even the most disturbed areas.

PREPARE TO INVESTIGATE

Inquiry Skill

Collaborate When you collaborate, you work in a team to investigate and experiment.

Materials

- paper and pencil

 **STANDARDS**

2.d. *Students know* earthquakes, volcanic eruptions, landslides, and floods change human and wildlife habitats.
7.d. Communicate the steps and results from an investigation in written reports and oral presentations.

Disaster Recovery

Procedure

A volcanic eruption blankets a community under a meter of ash. Luckily, the people left the area before the eruption. Now the returning citizens are faced with a huge cleanup job.

1. **Collaborate** How can the citizens rebuild their community? Work in a group of four students to solve this problem. Record your decisions in your *Science Notebook*.

2. **Brainstorm** the steps necessary to get the community functioning again. Consider ash cleanup, reconstruction, restarting schools and businesses, getting electricity back on, raising funds, and so on. Decide the order in which the steps need to be done.

STEP 2

3. **Classify** Determine whether each project will require government assistance and funding or private assistance and funding. Assign each project to the correct individual, group, or agency.

Conclusion

1. **Communicate** Create a flow chart to display the steps that will restore the community. Make separate branches in the chart for public and private projects. Decide who is responsible for completing each task.

2. **Communicate** Beneath your flow chart, write a brief article for the local newspaper that explains the plan to residents.

Guided Inquiry

Ask Questions Research how a community rebuilt after the 1980 eruption of Mount St. Helens in Washington. **Compare** their actions to your ideas. What questions would you ask people who live near a volcano?

345

VOCABULARY

climax community	p. 348
pioneer species	p. 347
primary succession	p. 347
secondary succession	p. 348

READING SKILL

Sequence Fill in the concept map by putting the stages of secondary succession in the correct order.

1	
2	
3	
4	

STANDARDS

2.d. *Students know* earthquakes, volcanic eruptions, landslides, and floods change human and wildlife habitats.
5.e. *Students know* the number and types of organisms an ecosystem can support depends on the resources available and on abiotic factors, such as quantities of light and water, a range of temperatures, and soil composition.

Succession

MAIN IDEA Changed ecosystems can be restored through ecological succession.

Natural Disturbances

Earthquakes, volcanic eruptions, landslides, floods, tsunamis, hurricanes, and forest fires—all can disturb or destroy stable ecosystems in a very short time. Yet a new ecosystem will eventually establish itself.

Consider Mount St. Helens, a volcano in the state of Washington. In May 1980 the volcano erupted violently. Hot lava destroyed trees over an area of 500 square kilometers. Thick deposits of ash covered the ground hundreds of kilometers away. The area surrounding the volcano became almost barren.

Yet, life slowly returned to the mountain and surrounding areas. Some plants survived the eruption. Wind blew in seeds of grasses and shrubs, which sprouted. Then larger plants moved in, followed by animals.

1980

1983

Within a few years of the Mount St. Helens eruption, flowers bloomed again on nearby slopes. ▶

1. **Volcanic activity creates a new island.**

2. **Pioneer species such as mold, bacteria, and visiting sea birds begin to form soil.**

3. **Eventually, grasses, shrubs, and other species are able to thrive.**

Primary Succession

Succession occurs in two forms: primary and secondary. These forms take place under different conditions.

In 1963, an erupting volcano broke through the ocean surface near Iceland. It formed a new island named Surtsey. The island was a barren patch of lava. Then primary succession began. **Primary succession** is the establishment of plant and animal communities on ground where organisms have never existed before.

A **pioneer species** is one of the first species to colonize new or disturbed land. These small, fast-growing organisms—such as lichens and mosses—require few nutrients. Blown in by wind, they begin to grow on rock and bare ground. They form soil by producing acids that break down rock. They trap soil particles that blow in. When the organisms die, they become part of the newly formed soil.

As soil builds up over long periods of time, grasses and other small plants can begin to grow. Then slightly larger plants and shrubs sprout, followed by trees and the arrival of larger animals.

On Surtsey, molds and bacteria were pioneer species that quickly broke down rocks to form soil. The waste of sea birds added nutrients to the soil. Soon tiny plants took hold. Today the island ecosystem includes hundreds of species.

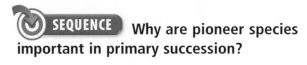 **SEQUENCE** **Why are pioneer species important in primary succession?**

Activity Card 28
Clean Up an "Oil Spill"

Secondary Succession

Fire, landslides, floods, and hurricanes can all destroy stable ecosystems in hours or even minutes. **Secondary succession** is the regular progression of new communities that form after such disturbances.

This process is quicker than primary succession because soil is already in place. Secondary succession also receives boosts from nearby plant and animal survivors.

Pioneer species are sun-loving, usually fast-growing grasses and wildflowers. Slower-growing, taller plants follow, including some small trees. Eventually, these trees create too much shade for grasses, shrubs, and even their own seedlings to survive. Other trees move in, replacing the pioneer trees. In time, stable hardwoods flourish.

The changes that occur in ecological succession occur quickly at first. Over time, the community of plants and animals reaches a fairly stable state. A mature ecosystem that remains mostly stable over time is called a **climax community.** Change is slow in the climax community—until a new disturbance hits.

Before a 1988 fire, a climax community of mature lodgepole pine trees covered most of Yellowstone National Park. The fire destroyed most of them. However, within weeks secondary succession was at work. New seedlings of lodgepole pine began to grow.

Today, a young forest grows. Someday a climax forest community will cover Yellowstone again.

SEQUENCE What may change a climax community, and what results?

Secondary Succession

1 A forest fire destroys plant life but leaves the soil behind.

2 Grasses and small plants sprout, followed by young trees.

3 Eventually, a mature forest returns.

Visual Summary

Earthquakes, volcanic eruptions, landslides, and floods change human and wildlife habitats. Ecosystems change over time through the process of succession.

Primary succession establishes plant and animal communities where none have existed before. Resources are limited at first, then develop over time.

After land is disturbed, new communities replace old ones in a process called secondary succession. Each community changes the land, providing resources for the community that follows.

 STANDARDS

2.d., 5.e.

Technology
Visit **www.eduplace.com/cascp** to find out more about ecological succession.

Reading Review

1 MAIN IDEA What is ecological succession? When will it occur?

2 VOCABULARY Explain the difference between *primary* and *secondary succession*.

3 READING SKILL Order these processes of primary succession: trees grow, lichens and mosses grow, soil is formed, small plants and shrubs grow.

4 CRITICAL THINKING: Analyze

Why do plants appear before animals during succession?

5 INQUIRY SKILL: Collaborate With a partner, research and write a news article describing a real natural disaster that devastated a population.

TEST PRACTICE

On a new island that has emerged recently from the sea, you would not find _____.

A. a pioneer species

B. barren ground

C. primary succession

D. a climax community

 STANDARDS

1–5: 2.d., 5.e., **Test Practice:** 2.d.

How Do Humans Change Ecosystems?

Building Background

Huge numbers of bison once roamed the Great Plains of North America. Yet, by 1890, humans had hunted them almost to extinction.

Over-hunting is just one example of how human activity changes ecosystems. Understanding how and why ecosystems change can help people manage their environment wisely.

 STANDARDS

5.e. *Students know* the number and types of organisms an ecosystem can support depends on the resources available and on abiotic factors, such as quantities of light and water, a range of temperatures, and soil composition.
7.a. Develop a hypothesis.

PREPARE TO INVESTIGATE

Inquiry Skill

Hypothesize When you hypothesize, you develop an explanation of previous observations.

Materials

- shallow plastic container
- modeling clay
- spray bottle
- water
- red food coloring

Tracking Water Pollution

Procedure

STEP 1

1. **Collaborate** Use clay to make a model slope inside a plastic container. The slope represents a coastal area. Place the slope at one end of the container.

2. **Use Models** Add water to the container until it covers the edge of the slope. The water represents the ocean.

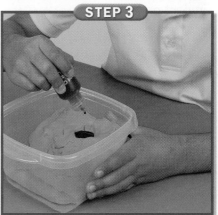
STEP 3

3. **Use Models** Using your fingers, make a smooth depression near the top of the slope. This depression represents a lawn or field. Add several drops of food coloring to the depression. The food coloring represents a fertilizer that is used to help grow plants.

4. **Predict** What do you think will happen to the "fertilizer" when it rains? Record your prediction in your *Science Notebook*.

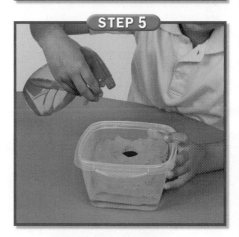
STEP 5

5. **Experiment** Carefully spray water to the land portion of the clay. This represents rain. Record what happens to the fertilizer, the lawn or field, and the ocean.

Conclusion

1. **Observe** What happened to the food coloring? How did it affect your model ocean?

2. **Hypothesize** If your model were a real coastal area, what hypothesis could you form about pollution from farms? What experiments could test your hypothesis?

Guided Inquiry

Experiment Repeat the activity, using sand in place of modeling clay. Record your observations. What can you **infer** about how pollution can contaminate groundwater and harm organisms?

351

◎ **READING SKILL**

Main Idea Fill in the concept map with ways that people can have a positive impact on ecosystems.

```
        Main
        Idea

 Detail        Detail
```

🔺 **STANDARD**

5.e. *Students know* the number and types of organisms an ecosystem can support depends on the resources available and on abiotic factors, such as quantities of light and water, a range of temperatures, and soil composition.

Tropical rain forests are being cleared for farming and logging. Many species are lost along with the forests. ▼

Human Impact on Ecosystems

MAIN IDEA Human activities can affect the number and types of organisms an ecosystem can support.

Human Activities

Rain forests are among the most valuable resources on Earth. They are home to a vast variety of plants and animals. Yet, by one account, almost 200,000 square kilometers (77,000 square miles) are lost each year! That's about 37 city blocks per minute!

Why should you care? One reason is that plants and animals may become extinct when their habitats are destroyed. Scientists believe that some rain forest plants may contain substances that could be used as medicines. In addition, rain forest plants release oxygen and take in carbon dioxide from the atmosphere.

Humans have a huge impact on ecosystems by destroying habitats. In fact, habitat loss is the main reason for rising rates of extinction. Not only are rain forests affected. Other ecosystems are affected, too.

▲ Developers cut the top off a hillside to build these houses in California.

Clear-cutting is a problem in many temperate forests in the United States. Clear-cutting means removing every tree from an area. This practice destroys ecosystems and habitats. Clear-cutting also causes extensive soil erosion.

Forests often are cut down to make way for houses, strip malls, roads, and office parks. But in the process, plant and animal habitats are destroyed.

Wetlands are sometimes drained and filled in to provide land for businesses and housing developments. Until recently, people did not understand the importance of wetlands. These ecosystems help filter harmful chemicals from groundwater.

The spongy grasses in wetlands absorb excess water during heavy rains, helping to reduce flooding. Wetlands are also important nurseries for many aquatic animal species.

Farming practices also impact ecosystems. Stable ecosystems are characterized by a great variety of species. Most farms, however, raise only a small variety of plant strains and animal breeds.

This practice can lead to entire crops being wiped out by disease. Most plant diseases affect only one type of crop. By growing a variety of crops in the same field, disease-causing organisms are less likely to spread.

MAIN IDEA How does urban sprawl affect plant and animal species?

Express Lab

Activity Card 29
Determine Habitat Loss

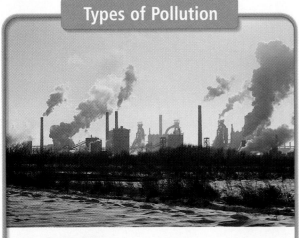

Air Pollution
Factories that burn fossil fuels can release harmful substances into the air.

Water Pollution
Oil spills can harm plants and animals that live in or near the water.

Land Pollution
Trash and garbage are often carelessly discarded, polluting the land.

Pollution

What other human activities can impact ecosystems? Burning fossil fuels is one example. Fossil fuels include oil, gas, and coal. These fuels contain stored energy that is released when they are burned. However, burning them can cause pollution. **Pollution** is the addition of harmful substances to the environment.

When fossil fuels are burned, certain gases and solid particles are released into the air. These pollutants can make the air unhealthy to breathe. Some combine with water droplets to form acids. They fall to the ground as acid rain.

Fossil fuels don't have to be burned to pose a threat to the environment. Oil, for example, is often transported on big ships called tankers. Accidental spills can damage the environment and be expensive to clean. About 300,000 birds died following a major oil spill in Alaska in 1989.

Human activities can also pollute the land. Each year, people in the United States produce hundreds of millions of tons of solid waste, including paper, plastics, and metals. Most solid waste is buried in landfills, and some is burned. However, people sometimes carelessly dump solid waste along roadsides or in bodies of water.

Some farming and lawn-care practices also cause pollution. Rain can wash fertilizers and pesticides into rivers and streams, where they damage the ecosystem.

Growth of Human Population

Hundreds of years ago, the impact of human activities was relatively small. There were no power plants or motor vehicles. And the human population was much smaller than it is today. As the graph shows, today's human population is very large, and growing larger all the time.

In 1800, only about 1 billion people lived on Earth. By 1930, that number had doubled. A mere 30 years later, the population had increased to 3 billion. Today, more than 6 billion people live on the planet.

Modern humans have been around for thousands of years. Yet population growth remained fairly steady until around 1800. Advances in medicine and technology have allowed more people to survive diseases and accidents, and to lead longer lives.

Everyone needs food, clean water, clean air, shelter, and other resources. As you have learned, however, ecosystems have limited resources. If the human population continues to grow, not enough resources will be available. In fact, in many parts of the world food and water are already scarce or poorly managed.

Human growth has also reduced **biodiversity,** the variety of species that live in an ecosystem. Wild places are home to a much greater variety of living things than a typical city, suburb, or farm.

As humans continue to grow in number, more species surely will be threatened and more habitats destroyed. Read on to find out how people are addressing these problems.

MAIN IDEA Why has the human population grown so much over the past 200 years?

Human Population Growth

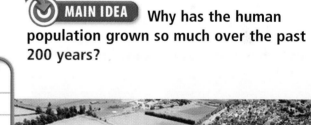

A growing human population must compete for a limited amount of resources. What is the current human population? ▶

Conservation and Preservation Efforts

As you have read, human activities often harm ecosystems. But people are also trying to repair damaged ecosystems and preserve wild places.

World governments have preserved many areas as national parks, national wildlife refuges, national monuments, and wilderness areas. The world's first national park, Yellowstone, was created in northwest Wyoming in 1872. Now there are hundreds of parks and preserves that protect ecosystems, wildlife, and unique landscapes.

When the spread of suburbs threatened to wipe out remaining stands of prairie grasses in Illinois, state agencies and private landowners cooperated to create the 5,800-acre Liberty Prairie Reserve. The reserve includes tallgrass prairie, wetland, and oak savanna. It is home to at least 21 threatened and endangered species.

Some preserves are in the ocean. The Stellwagen Bank National Marine Sanctuary is a preserve off the Massachusetts coast. These waters once were threatened by shipping traffic, sewage, mining, and oil spills. Today, the preserve is a habitat for many marine species, including the endangered northern right whale.

Zoos and other organizations run captive breeding programs to save some species and restore others. Hunting had wiped out the gray wolf in Yellowstone National Park. A program was started in the 1990s to return the wolf to the park. A similar program saved the California condor.

Muir Woods is a woodland preserve north of San Francisco. Visitors can admire California's native redwood trees. ▼

Giant Pandas are endangered in the wild. This baby receives good care in a zoo. ▼

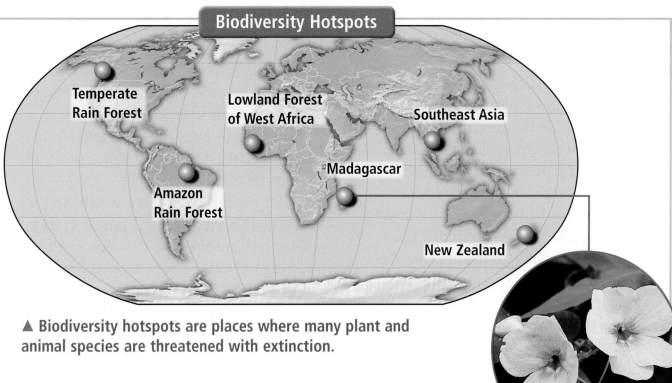

Biodiversity Hotspots

Temperate Rain Forest

Lowland Forest of West Africa

Southeast Asia

Madagascar

Amazon Rain Forest

New Zealand

▲ Biodiversity hotspots are places where many plant and animal species are threatened with extinction.

The rosy periwinkle provides a substance that fights cancer. It is native to Madagascar. ▶

Some regions of the world are particularly rich in plant and animal diversity. Threatened by human activities, these regions are called biodiversity hotspots. The Amazon rain forest is a well-known example of a biodiversity hotspot.

Rain forests may contain about half of the world's plant and animal species. Many of these species produce substances that could be useful to humans. For example, one-quarter of the medicines used today are derived from these organisms. Rain forest organisms yet to be discovered may hold the cures for many of the diseases that afflict humans.

Another biodiversity hotspot is Madagascar, a tropical island about 300 km (200 mi) off the east coast of Africa. The fourth largest island in the world, Madagascar is bigger than California! Thanks to its isolation and the late arrival of humans, a great number of plant and animal species

not found anywhere else in the world have evolved on this island.

Unfortunately, the rain forest of Madagascar is being cleared or burned for rice farming and cattle grazing. Today, less than 15 percent of the original native forest remains. Only about 2 percent of Madagascar's total area is in parks or preserves.

Scientists estimate that biodiversity hotspots contain more than 80 percent of the world's mammals. By protecting biodiversity hotspots such as the ones shown on the map, scientists hope to preserve plants and animals for the benefit of people in the future.

MAIN IDEA What have governments done to help protect ecosystems?

Saving the Salton Sea

The Salton Sea is a large, salty lake in California's Colorado Desert. The sea and its wetlands have become important desert ecosystems, with abundant fish, birds, and other wildlife. The Salton Sea is also a major stopover for hundreds of bird species that migrate along the Pacific coast.

Little rain falls in the area, so the sea is fed mostly by salty runoff from irrigated farm fields around it. Even in the hot desert, the Salton Sea has managed to exist for 100 years. But now several changes threaten its survival and its ability to support life.

In recent decades, the Salton Sea has been shrinking and getting saltier. Millions of fish have already died. If it becomes a dead lake, the birds that feed at the Salton Sea will have to find food elsewhere.

The black-necked stilt uses its long legs to wade through the water. Its health depends on the health of the Salton Sea, its home. ▶

Because 90 percent of California's wetlands have already disappeared, the Salton Sea is becoming increasingly important. To save it, government officials have suggested several ideas to reduce the amount of salt and to preserve habitats.

For example, canals could bring in freshwater. Artificial wetlands could filter polluted runoff that enters the sea. Lake water could be pumped into ponds. Then evaporation would concentrate salt in the ponds, lowering the amount of salt in the rest of the lake.

MAIN IDEA **Why is it important to maintain the health of the Salton Sea?**

Reduced runoff from nearby fields has shrunk the Salton Sea and made it saltier.

Visual Summary

Pollution is just one example of how human activities can harm ecosystems. Pollution can poison plants and animals and reduce resources available to them.

The growth of Earth's human population has put pressure on resources of natural ecosystems. Humans use land, food, and water supplies that once supported wildlife.

Individuals and governments are working to protect wildlife, and to preserve and restore ecosystems. Challenges face people in California and around the world.

 STANDARD

5.e.

 **Technology**
Visit **www.eduplace.com/cascp** to find out more about how humans affect ecosystems.

Reading Review

1 MAIN IDEA How are people harming ecosystems?

2 VOCABULARY Write a paragraph about *biodiversity*. Explain why biodiversity is important.

3 READING SKILL How are people helping to preserve ecosystems? Include specific examples.

4 CRITICAL THINKING: Evaluate Why is protection of habitats an important part of preserving a species?

5 INQUIRY SKILL: Hypothesize The salinity of the Salton Sea has been slowly increasing. What if this trend continues? Predict the future of the sea and its living things.

 TEST PRACTICE
All of these actions damage ecosystems, EXCEPT for which one?

A. captive breeding programs

B. forest clear-cutting

C. decreasing biodiversity

D. eliminating wetlands

STANDARDS
1–5: 5.e., **Test Practice:** 5.e.

359

Protecting the Environment

The timeline shows six events that helped protect the environment in California and the rest of the United States. Yet other events have harmed the environment. How do you think the environment will change in the future?

| 1890 | 1940 | | 1962 |

Yosemite National Park

California naturalist John Muir (right) and President Theodore Roosevelt (left) helped establish Yosemite as the nation's second national park. The photo shows Bridal Veil Falls, which is still falling today.

U.S. Fish and Wildlife Service

Established in 1940, today the Fish and Wildlife Service continues to promote conservation and to protect endangered species.

Silent Spring

DDT once was widely used to kill mosquitoes. In her book *Silent Spring*, Rachel Carson showed how DDT also was killing birds and other animals. Her work led to a worldwide ban of this insecticide.

STANDARD
6.b. *Students know* different natural energy and material resources, including air, soil, rocks, minerals, petroleum, fresh water, wildlife, and forests, and know how to classify them as renewable or nonrenewable.

READING **LINK**

Endangered Species Act

Enacted in 1973, this law continues to define and protect endangered species throughout the United States. One such species is the symbol of the nation: the bald eagle.

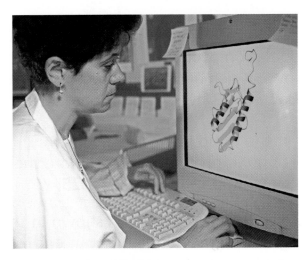

New Technology

In 2004, a computer model helped California prepare new laws to protect groundwater from pesticides.

1970   **1973**   **2004**

Earth Day

Begun in 1970, Earth Day is now celebrated on April 22nd every year. People clean parks, plant trees, and discuss issues that affect the environment.

Sharing Ideas

1. **READING CHECK** Describe three actions that people have taken to protect the environment.

2. **WRITE ABOUT IT** How have the events on the timeline affected your life?

3. **TALK ABOUT IT** How would you like to participate on the next Earth Day?

361

LINKS
for Home and School

Math in Science

Scientists are concerned about the rapid rise in human population over the past 100 years. As the human population grows, it demands more land, water, and other natural resources. Its needs often come at the expense of wildlife.

1. If the trend in world human population continues, estimate the population for the year 2025.

2. Do you think the trend shown in the graph can continue without end? Explain your reasoning.

3. Scientists have less accurate data on population long ago than for recent years. How do you think the accuracy of the data compares from year to year? Do these differences make predictions based on the graph less useful?

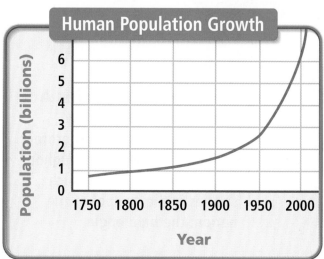

Human Population Growth

Population (billions) vs Year (1750, 1800, 1850, 1900, 1950, 2000)

Writing in Science
Persuasive

Research an environmental issue that you care about. The issue could involve endangered species, pollution, or the destruction of a natural habitat. Write an essay that shows why this issue is important. Describe and explain steps that you think should be taken.

◄ Earth's rain forests continue to be cut down for their timber and for farm land.

362 • Chapter 9

Wetlands Ecologist

Wetlands ecologists explore the unique ecosystems found in marshes, swamps, and low-lying areas near rivers. They study biodiversity, interactions among different species, and factors that contribute to environmental health.

Wetlands research is important for protecting water supplies. The fresh water from wetlands often becomes drinking water—maybe even in your community.

What It Takes!

- A degree in biology or ecology
- An interest in wild places

Zookeeper

Part rancher, part veterinarian, part museum attendant—zookeepers care for zoo animals. They maintain the animals' diet and health and display them in ways that are safe for visitors and animals alike. Zookeepers also educate the public about animals, their ecosystems, and the issues they face in the wild.

What It Takes!

- Studies in biology and zoology
- Experience caring for animals

Vocabulary

Complete each sentence with a term from the list.

1. The complete elimination of a species is called ____.

2. A mature ecosystem that remains mostly stable over time is a(n) ____.

3. The addition of harmful substances to the environment is ____.

4. One of the first species to colonize new or disturbed land is a(n) ____.

5. A species that is close to becoming extinct is a(n) ____.

6. A condition that prevents an organism from functioning properly is a(n) ____.

7. Something that restricts the growth and distribution of a population is a(n) ____.

8. A species that is close to becoming endangered is a(n) ____.

9. The regular progression of new communities that form after disturbances is ____.

10. The struggle among living things to use the same resources is ____.

biodiversity p. 355
climax community p. 348
competition p. 337
disease p. 339
endangered species p. 340
extinction p. 340
invasive species p. 339
limiting factor p. 336
pioneer species p. 347
pollution p. 354
predation p. 338
primary succession p. 347
secondary succession p. 348
threatened species p. 340

Test Practice

Write the letter of the best answer choice.

11. An invasive species is not ____.

    A. part of an ecosystem
    B. in competition with other species
    C. native to an ecosystem
    D. able to find its own food

12. In which of these areas would primary succession occur?

    A. a plowed farm field
    B. a burned forest
    C. a flooded river valley
    D. a new island covered with volcanic lava

13. What occurs when one organism hunts and feeds on another?

    A. symbiosis
    B. predation
    C. biodiversity
    D. extinction

14. The variety of species in an ecosystem is called ____.

    A. competition
    B. a climax community
    C. biodiversity
    D. commensalism

Inquiry Skills

15. **Use Numbers** A lake holds 100 trout. After fishing is banned in the lake, the number of trout doubles every year for 3 years. How many trout does the lake hold after 3 years? Do you think this pattern of growth could continue? Explain.

16. Write a paragraph about the characteristics of a diverse, healthy ecosystem. In another paragraph, explain why such ecosystems often are threatened and how people are trying to protect them.

Map the Concept

Use the graphic organizer to compare and contrast primary and secondary succession.

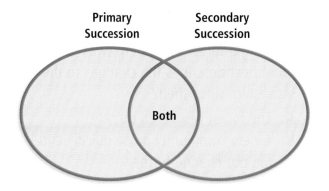

Primary Succession   Secondary Succession

Both

Critical Thinking

17. **Apply** Why are the native organisms of islands especially vulnerable to invasive species?

18. **Synthesize** How would you improve chances of keeping invasive species out of North America? Is this an important goal? Explain your answer.

19. **Evaluate** Consider this statement: "Habitat destruction is necessary for the health of the U.S. economy." Do you agree or disagree? Explain your point of view.

20. **Analyze** What is the relationship between biodiversity and ecosystem stability? Explain. Include an example in your answer.

Performance Assessment

Limits on Human Population

Human populations are rapidly growing in some countries. How are people finding the food, water, and land they need? Are these factors limiting human population growth? Research how humans meet their basic needs in your community or elsewhere in the world.

Writing Journal

Review your answers to the Lesson Preview questions on page 331.

STANDARDS

1: 5.e., **2:** 5.d., **3:** 5.c., **4–5:** 5.d., **6–7:** 5.e., **8–9:** 5.d., **10–11:** 5.e., **12:** 5.d., **13:** 5.a., **14:** 5.d., **15:** 5.e., 7.b., **16:** 5.d., 7.e., **Map the Concept:** 5.d., **17:** 5.e., **18:** 5.d., **19:** 5.e., **20:** 5.c., **Performance Assessment:** 5.e.

Write the letter of the best answer choice.

1. What is one way that energy is transferred in the ecosystem pictured above? (The arrows represent the transfer of energy.)

A. Sun ⟶ sheep ⟶ grass

B. sheep ⟶ grass ⟶ Sun

C. Sun ⟶ grass ⟶ sheep

D. Sun ⟶ both grass and sheep equally

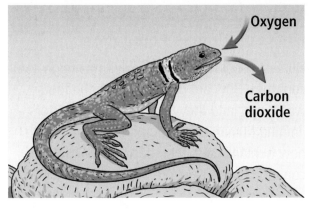

2. The diagram shows how a lizard exchanges gases with the atmosphere. Which of these organisms exchange gases in the OPPOSITE way?

A. oak tree

B. goldfish

C. alligator

D. human

3. On grasslands, hawks catch and eat mice, snakes, and other small animals. Which type of organism fills a similar role in its ecosystem?

A. redwood trees

B. bracket fungi

C. buffalo

D. sharks

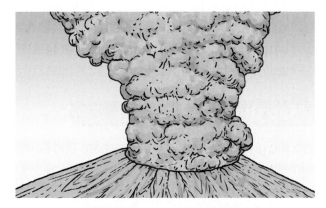

4. Mount Saint Helens erupted in 1980, covering a forest ecosystem with hot ash. What best describes the changes to the ecosystem since then?

A. The forest recovered quickly.

B. A new community arose quickly and did not change further.

C. New communities succeeded old ones, and continue to do so.

D. The mountain remains covered in ash and without life.

5. What group of organisms forms the base of the energy pyramid shown here?

A. decomposers

B. carnivores

C. primary consumers

D. producers

6. What factor most limits the growth of populations in a desert ecosystem?

A. water

B. temperature

C. predator-prey relationships

D. invasive species

7. What role do nitrogen-fixing bacteria play in the nitrogen cycle?

A. They change nitrogen into carbon or oxygen.

B. They remove nitrogen from dead plants and animals.

C. They add nitrogen gas into the soil.

D. They change nitrogen gas into a form that plants can use.

8. Where do toxins become concentrated in a process of biomagnification?

A. In the primary consumers of the food chain

B. In the animals at the top of the food chain

C. In producers and decomposers

D. In ocean waters

Answer the following in complete sentences.

9. Wolves are predators of deer. Describe the relationship between wolves and deer that this graph shows.

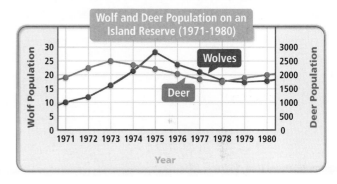

10. Describe the abiotic factors that affect the numbers and types of organisms in an ecosystem. Include a specific ecosystem as an example.

 **STANDARDS**

1: 5.a., **2:** 5.b., **3:** 5.c., **4:** 2.d., **5:** 5.a., **6:** 5.e., **7:** 5.b., **8:** 5.c., **9:** 5.e., 7.c., **10:** 5.e.

You Can...

Discover More

You wouldn't invite wood-eating termites into your home! However, they are useful in nature. By eating downed trees and old stumps, termites return nutrients to the ecosystem. They can eat wood because they form a symbiotic relationship with tiny organisms in their gut.

Termites

Wood-eating termites chew the wood into a pulp and swallow it. In the termite's gut, millions of protists and bacteria break down the wood's cellulose into glucose. The termite absorbs glucose and uses it as food. The protists and bacteria gain nutrients, too, as well as a home.

Protists in termite's gut

Symbiosis means "living together." The termite and the microorganisms inside it are an example of mutualism, a symbiotic relationship that benefits both parties. Termites are hardly the only example. Many large animals—including humans—benefit from bacteria that live in their digestive tracts.

 Learn more about symbiosis and ecosystems. Go to **www.eduplace.com/cascp/** to discover examples of different species that form symbiotic relationships.

EARTH UNIT E SCIENCE

Earth's Natural Resources

California Connection

Visit www.eduplace.com/cascp/ to learn more about natural resources.

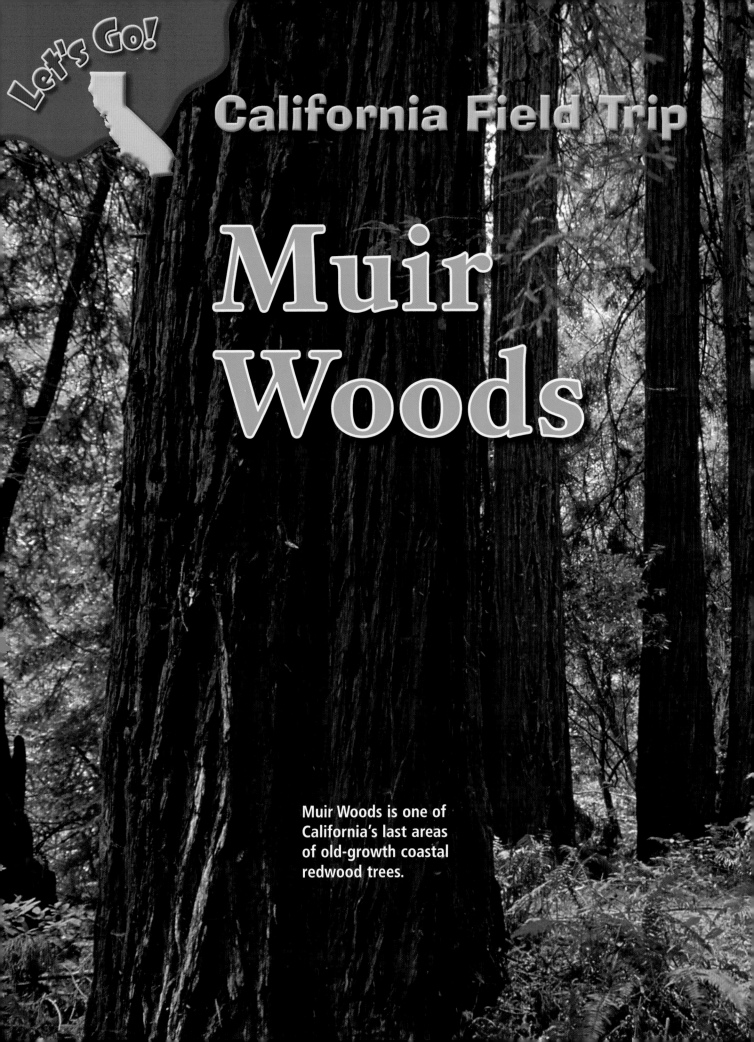

Let's Go!

California Field Trip

Muir Woods

Muir Woods is one of California's last areas of old-growth coastal redwood trees.

The Northern spotted owl can turn its head 270 degrees, which allows it to see in all directions.

Native American tribes in California baked Leopard lily bulbs and added them to soups.

Earth's Natural Resources

Chapter 10

Energy Resources 370

Independent Books

- Energy Resources
- Conserving Fossil Fuels
- How Does a Hybrid Car Work?

Chapter 11

Material Resources 412

Independent Books

- Material Resources
- Recycling Plastic
- What Are Cars Made Of?

A redwood forest in California

Standard Set 6.
Resources

Sources of energy and
materials differ in amounts,
distribution, usefulness, and
the time required for their
formation.

Chapter 10

Energy Resources

Wind turbines provide electricity in southeast California.

LESSON 1

Computers are amazing, but they won't work without a source of power. How can energy change from one form to another?

LESSON 2

What do 300-million-year-old plants have to do with the fuels people burn today?

LESSON 3

Wind, sunshine, water, and corn—how can these natural resources be used to provide energy?

Writing Journal

In your Writing Journal, write or draw answers to each question.

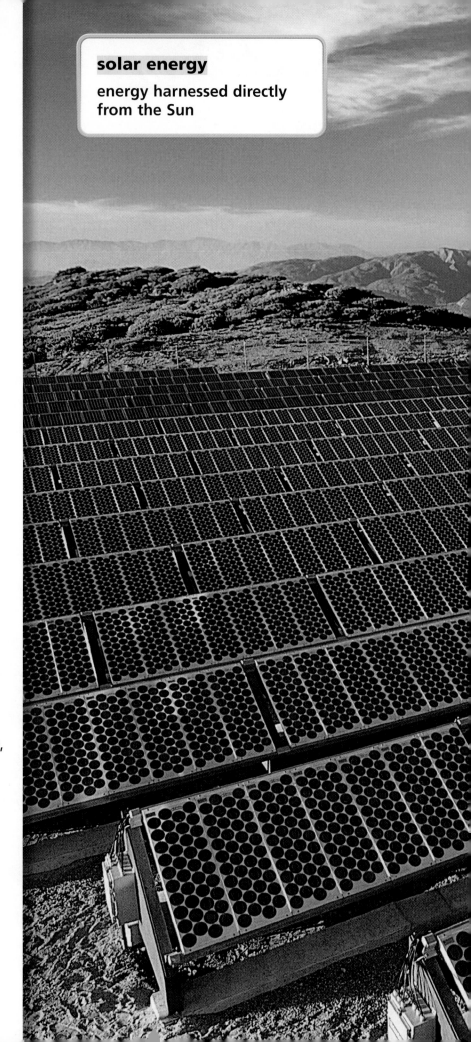

solar energy
energy harnessed directly from the Sun

Vocabulary Preview

Vocabulary

biomass p. 402
conservation p. 388
efficiency p. 379
energy p. 376
fossil fuels p. 384
geothermal energy p. 401
hydroelectric energy p. 399
natural resource p. 388
nonrenewable resource p. 386
nuclear fission p. 400
renewable resource p. 396
solar energy p. 397

Glossary
English-Spanish, p. H26

Vocabulary Skill

Antonyms and Synonyms
renewable resource
nonrenewable resource

A pair of antonyms are words that have opposite meanings. For example, the supplies of a *renewable resource* can always be restored. The opposite of *renewable* is *nonrenewable*. A nonrenewable resource could eventually be used up.

geothermal energy

energy harnessed from
Earth's hot interior

hydroelectric energy

electricity generated by
rushing water

natural resource

a material or product found
on Earth that people use

california

Start with Your Standards

**Standard Set 3. Heat (Thermal Energy)
(Physical Science)**

3.a. *Students know* energy can be carried
from one place to another by heat flow
or by waves, including water, light, and
sound waves, or by moving objects.

3.b. *Students know* that when fuel is
consumed, most of the energy released
becomes heat energy.

Standard Set 6. Resources

6.a. *Students know* the utility of energy
sources is determined by factors that
are involved in converting these sources
to useful forms and the consequences
of the conversion process.

6.b. *Students know* different natural energy
and material resources, including air,
soil, rocks, minerals, petroleum, fresh
water, wildlife, and forests, and know
how to classify them as renewable or
nonrenewable.

**Standard Set 7: Investigation and
Experimentation** standards covered in this
chapter: 7.a., 7.b., 7.c., 7.d., 7.e.

How Do People Use Energy?

Building Background

This pocket calculator can help you do math, but only when light shines on it. Its panels change light into electricity. Both light and electricity are forms of energy.

Energy can change into many different forms, but not all forms are useful for doing work. As you will discover, this explains why machines need sources of energy to keep running.

PREPARE TO INVESTIGATE

Inquiry Skill

Experiment When you experiment, you plan and conduct a test in which you identify and use variables to test a prediction.

Materials

- string
- 3 binder-style paper clips
- scissors
- book
- ruler
- meterstick

Science and Math Toolbox

For step 2, review **Using a Tape Measure or Ruler** on page H6.

 STANDARDS

3.a. *Students know* energy can be carried from one place to another by heat flow or by waves, including water, light, and sound waves, or by moving objects.
7.e. Students will recognize whether evidence is consistent with a proposed explanation.

Swing Time

Procedure

1. **Collaborate** Work with a partner. Place one ruler across the edge of your desk. Use the book to hold the ruler in place.

2. **Measure** Cut a length of string that is about three-fourths the distance from the ruler to the floor. Tie one end of the string to the ruler. Tie a binder clip to the other end. You have formed a device called a pendulum.

3. **Experiment** Raise the binder clip to the height of the desk, then let it go. Observe the pendulum until it stops. Compare the heights that it reaches with each swing. Record data and observations in your *Science Notebook.*

4. **Hypothesize** Do you think that adding binder clips to the pendulum will change the heights that it reaches? Record your hypothesis.

5. **Use Variables** Tie a second binder clip below the first, and repeat step 3. Then try a third binder clip.

Conclusion

1. **Analyze Data** Do your results support your hypothesis? Explain.

2. **Draw Conclusions** A moving pendulum carries energy. Where did this energy come from? How did it change?

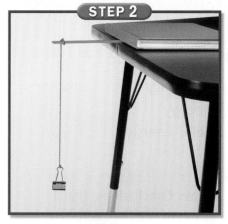
STEP 2

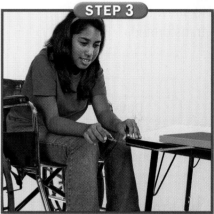
STEP 3

STEP 5

Guided Inquiry

Experiment Make two pendulums of equal length. Set one pendulum in motion so that it collides with the other one. **Infer** where the energy came from to set the second pendulum in motion.

Forms of Energy

READING SKILL

Draw Conclusions Use a diagram like the one below to show how energy is transformed.

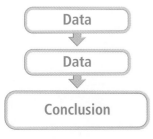

Data → Data → Conclusion

MAIN IDEA Energy takes many forms. Energy can be changed from one form to another, but it cannot be created or destroyed.

Energy Transformations

Wherever you look, you see the effects of energy. Cars driving by in the street, kids playing basketball, water boiling on the stove—all these depend on some form of energy. Energy is vital to life and to our society. The United States government even has a Department of Energy.

But what is energy? Energy is a basic component of the Universe. It is everywhere. Scientists define **energy** as the ability to do work.

Energy comes in many forms. For example, energy from the Sun is called **solar energy.**

Energy that a chemical reaction can release is called chemical energy.

Energy from position or motion is called mechanical energy. A coiled spring has mechanical energy, as does a hit baseball.

Energy Changes at a Cookout

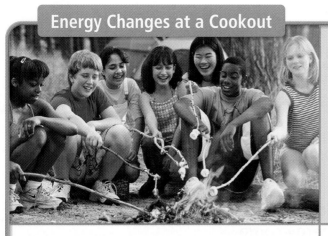

As wood burns, its chemical energy is changed into thermal energy and radiant energy. The teens will gain energy from the food they eat.

Energy Changes in a Car

This car burns gasoline in its engine. Chemical energy in the gasoline is changed into mechanical energy. Some of the energy is "lost" as thermal energy.

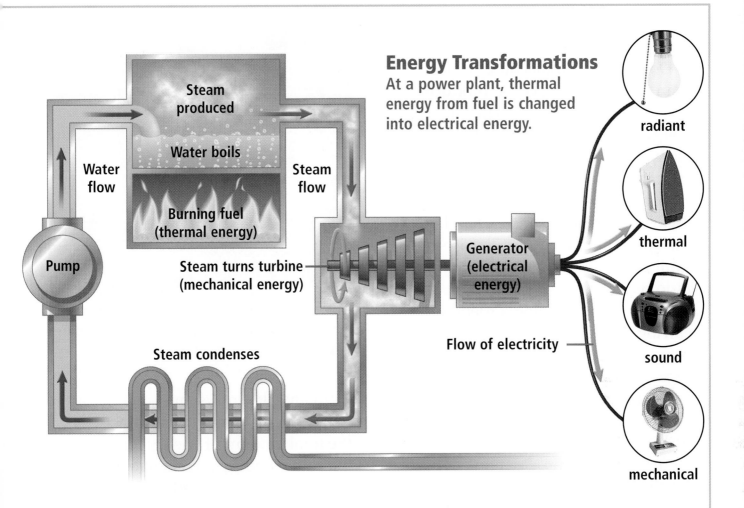

Energy Transformations
At a power plant, thermal energy from fuel is changed into electrical energy.

Steam produced

Water boils

Water flow

Steam flow

Burning fuel (thermal energy)

Pump

Steam turns turbine (mechanical energy)

Generator (electrical energy)

Flow of electricity

Steam condenses

radiant

thermal

sound

mechanical

Energy can be changed, or transformed, from one form to another. When this happens, thermal energy is released. Often, this thermal energy is not useful. In a car, for example, engine parts become hot because of friction. The thermal energy released in the engine cannot be used to do useful work.

Electricity is another form of energy. Electrical energy is changed into other forms in devices such as light bulbs, toasters, radios, and fans.

Much of modern technology relies on energy changing form, as shown in the drawing above. Examples include any device that burns fuel or that runs on electricity.

Energy transformations also play important roles in nature. Radiant energy from the Sun warms Earth and powers weather. Plants use solar energy from the Sun to grow.

Plants also convert solar energy into chemical energy, which is stored in food they produce. When the plants are eaten, this chemical energy is changed by the consumer into different forms of energy needed to carry out life processes.

DRAW CONCLUSIONS How might conditions on Earth be different if energy could not change form?

Conservation of Energy

Do you think a machine, such as an electric motor, could produce the same amount of mechanical energy as the amount of electrical energy used to make it run? No, this cannot happen. In every energy transformation, some energy is always lost as thermal energy. The total amount of energy still exists, but it is not all used by the machine to do work.

Think about pushing a friend on a swing. You push hard until your friend is swinging quite high. The force of your push has given the swing and its rider mechanical energy.

What happens when you stop pushing? The swing will slow down and eventually stop. Friction between the air and your friend's body will change the mechanical energy of the moving swing to thermal energy. So will friction between the chains of the swing and the frame.

▲ For years, people have tried to build machines that run forever without any energy input. Why is this an impossible dream?

In any closed system—one in which energy cannot enter or exit— the total amount of energy remains the same. Energy can change form, but it cannot be created or destroyed. These two concepts make up the law of conservation of energy.

All machines illustrate this law. Machines may take up energy from fossil fuels, electricity, or even the energy stored in your body. Yet that energy does not disappear. Often it is converted to thermal energy.

When the adult pushes on the swing, energy is transferred to set the swing in motion. When she stops pushing, the swing will slow to a stop. ▼

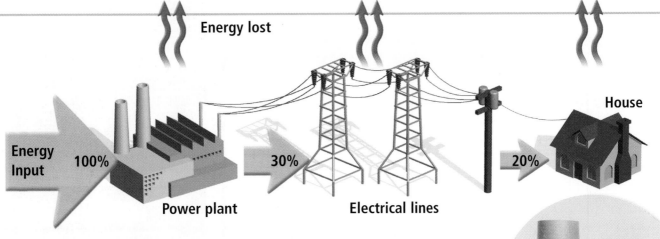

Energy lost

Energy Input   100%

Power plant

30%

Electrical lines

20%

House

▲ As energy is converted from one form to another and distributed to different places, some energy is lost as thermal energy at each step.

Energy Efficiency

As you have learned, some thermal energy is always produced when energy changes form. Because of this, most machines are not very energy efficient.

The **efficiency** of a machine compares the amount of work a machine does to the amount of energy put into the machine. Efficiency is usually expressed as a ratio of the energy output of a machine to the energy input.

No machine can be 100 percent efficient. Some simple machines, such as levers and pulleys, can come close. Because little friction is involved, the output of such machines can be almost as great as the input. However, the more moving parts a machine uses, the less efficient it is, mainly because of increased friction.

Consider an electric power system, such as the one shown in the diagram above. The output of the system is the delivery of electricity to people's homes. The input is the energy used to produce and deliver that electricity.

By the time the electric energy reaches your home, only a small fraction of the energy input is left. And when you turn on a light, only part of the electric energy is changed to light. Most of the electric energy flowing through the bulb is converted to thermal energy. The bulb gets hot!

How can energy efficiency be improved? Power plants can reduce friction in turbines and generators. They also can reduce energy losses along power lines. Customers, in turn, can use energy-saving devices, such as compact fluorescent lights.

DRAW CONCLUSIONS Why should energy efficiency be improved?

Express Lab

Activity Card 30
Observe Energy

379

San Francisco, 1860s

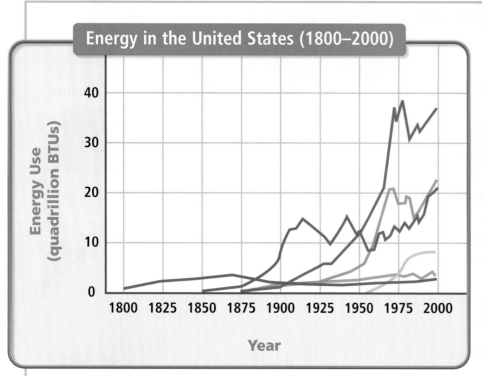

Energy in the United States (1800–2000)

Energy Use (quadrillion BTUs)

40

30

20

10

0

1800 1825 1850 1875 1900 1925 1950 1975 2000

Year

San Francisco, 2005

Key

— petroleum
— natural gas
— coal
— nuclear
— hydroelectric
— wood

Over the past 150 years, the use of energy has risen dramatically. All U.S. cities have changed much like San Francisco, shown in the photographs.

Demand for Energy Use

As the world's population has grown, the demand for energy has risen. For centuries, people relied on wood as their main source of energy. However, that changed drastically during the Industrial Revolution of the 19th century. The new machines and factories of this era ran not on wood, but on coal.

As the graph shows, the use of coal rose sharply during the late 1800s. As new technologies developed, the use of other fossil fuels rose as well.

During the 20th century, people became more aware of problems

that widespread use of fossil fuels has caused. This awareness sparked interest in alternative energy sources, such as hydroelectric energy and nuclear energy. You'll read about them later in this chapter.

Today, the United States makes up about 5 percent of the world's population. Yet the country uses about 26 percent of the world's energy. As developing countries grow and become more industrialized, their energy use likely will increase.

PROBLEM AND SOLUTION How do you think the U.S. and global demand for energy will change? Explain.

Visual Summary

Energy can change from one form to another. At a campfire, chemical energy stored in the wood is changed to thermal energy and light energy. All moving objects carry energy, as do waves.

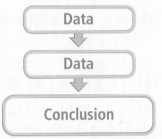

As energy is converted and distributed, some energy is always "lost" as heat. For this reason, energy efficiency is always less than 100 percent.

For centuries, people relied on wood as their main source of energy. Today, fossil fuels and other energy sources power modern technology.

STANDARDS
3.a., 3.b.

Technology
Visit **www.eduplace.com/cascp** to find out more about energy.

Reading Review

1 MAIN IDEA Describe the law of conservation of energy.

2 VOCABULARY Use the term *efficiency* in a sentence describing a machine.

3 READING SKILL How can the efficiency of a machine be improved? Describe one example.

> Data
> ↓
> Data
> ↓
> Conclusion

4 CRITICAL THINKING: Apply Why does a car's engine become hot while it is running?

5 INQUIRY SKILL: Experiment Two brands of batteries both claim that their brand provides more energy than the other brand. Write a procedure for an experiment that could test their claims.

✓ TEST PRACTICE
What does a machine need to keep running?

A. Very large parts

B. An input of energy

C. Friction between its parts

D. Very small parts

STANDARDS
1: 3.a., **2–5:** 3.b., **Test Practice:** 6.a.

381

Why Are Fossil Fuels Limited?

Building Background

People need energy to power machines in homes and factories. Where does the energy come from? In most cases, the energy source is fossil fuels. Reserves of fossil fuels are limited, and burning them can harm the environment. Using fossil fuels wisely has become more important than ever before.

STANDARDS

6.b. *Students know* different natural energy and material resources, including air, soil, rocks, minerals, petroleum, fresh water, wildlife, and forests, and know how to classify them as renewable or nonrenewable.
7.c. Construct appropriate graphs from data and develop qualitative statements about the relationships between variables.

PREPARE TO INVESTIGATE

Inquiry Skill

Use Numbers When you use numbers, you may do calculations to explain patterns in data.

Materials

- calculator (optional)

Science and Math Toolbox

For step 2, review **Using a Calculator** on page H4.

3 ... 2 ... 1...
Oil Game Over?

Procedure

1 **Collaborate** Work with a partner. Study the chart of the world's remaining oil reserves. Present the data on a bar graph. Draw a vertical scale of 0 to 300 billion barrels, with marks for every 50 billion barrels.

2 **Use Numbers** Add the amounts of oil in all of the world's proven reserves. You may use a calculator. Record the total in your *Science Notebook*.

3 **Use Numbers** In 2003, the world used an estimated 80 million barrels of oil per day. Estimate how many millions of barrels were used that year.

4 **Predict** Based on your data, estimate how long Earth's oil reserves will last at the rate people are using them.

Conclusion

1. **Use Numbers** The United States uses one-quarter of the world's oil, but has only five percent of the world's population. About how many millions of barrels of oil does the United States use each day?

2. **Analyze Data** All the countries listed in the chart are tapping their oil reserves. Predict how your bar graph would compare to one made using data from 20 years in the future.

3. **Hypothesize** How can people extend Earth's supply of oil and other fossil fuels?

STEP 1

Country	Proven Reserves (billion barrels)
Saudi Arabia	262
Iraq	112
United Arab Emirates	98
Kuwait	96
Iran	90
Venezuela	78
Russia	49
Libya	29
Mexico	28
China	24
Nigeria	24
United States	23
Qatar	15
Rest of world	106

STEP 4

Guided Inquiry

Ask Questions Find out how fossils fuels are used in your home, school, and community. **Research** ways you and your classmates can reduce the use of fossil fuels.

Fossil Fuels

MAIN IDEA Fossil fuels formed over millions of years from the remains of plants and animals. People depend on fossil fuels for most energy needs. Yet using fossil fuels can harm the environment.

VOCABULARY

conservation	p. 388
fossil fuels	p. 384
natural resource	p. 388
nonrenewable resource	p. 386

READING SKILL

Problem and Solution Fill in the chart to show a problem and solution related to use of fossil fuels.

Problem	Solution

STANDARDS

3.b. *Students know* that when fuel is consumed, most of the energy released becomes heat energy.
6.a. *Students know* the utility of energy sources is determined by factors that are involved in converting these sources to useful forms and the consequences of the conversion process.

Formation of Fossil Fuels

During the Industrial Revolution of the late 1700s, people needed energy to run factories, machines, trains, and other new devices. They turned first to coal. Later, during the 1900s, people found that oil and natural gas were useful energy sources. But where do those resources come from?

Fossil fuels are energy resources formed from the remains of plants and animals that lived more than 100 million years ago. The main fossil fuels are coal, petroleum or oil, and natural gas.

Most coal formed from the remains of plants that lived during the Carboniferous period, from 360 to 286 million years ago. During that period, Earth's climate was warm and the land was covered with swamps and shallow seas. Huge ferns and trees grew in the swamps.

Ancient swamps were thick with vegetation. After the plants died, they slowly became fossil fuels.

1 **Peat**

In thick swamps, dead organic matter builds up, forming peat. Peat can be used as a fuel.

2 **Lignite**

As peat is buried under layers of soil and sediment, the plant material is compressed and water is forced out.

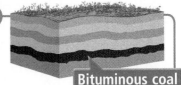

3 **Bituminous coal**

Over the years, pressure compresses the material into bituminous coal. This is the most widely used coal.

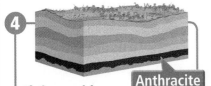

4 **Anthracite**

If the coal layer is subject to even higher temperature and pressure, it may form anthracite coal. This coal is almost pure carbon.

Coal

▲ Miners use heavy machinery to dig out underground coal deposits.

When the plants and animals died, they were buried under mud and sediments. Over time, pressure from above squeezed the remains together, forcing out the water. Left behind were substances rich in carbon and hydrogen. The remains gradually turned into coal, oil, or natural gas.

Coal was formed from dead plant matter built up in shallow swamps. Oil and natural gas formed from remains of small marine organisms that were buried on the ocean floor. The action of bacteria, heat, and pressure gradually changed the remains into oil and natural gas.

Once formed, the oil moved through cracks in rock below Earth's surface. When it reached a rock layer with no cracks, it collected into pools. If natural gas was present, it collected above the pools of oil, as shown in the diagram on the next page.

Today, deposits of fossil fuels are mined all over the world, including California. Oil fields near Bakersfield produce over half a million barrels of oil every day.

 **PROBLEM AND SOLUTION** **How quickly does coal form?**

Burning Fossil Fuels

Remember that plants get energy from sunlight and change it into food. When animals eat plants, they obtain energy that originally came from the Sun. Fossil fuels are also a part of an energy chain that begins with the Sun.

Energy from the Sun is stored in fossil fuels. Indeed, the energy is more concentrated in fossil fuels than in living plants. Burning the fuels releases most of that stored energy. Only a small fraction of that energy is locked in waste products.

How are fossil fuels used to provide this energy? Making electricity is one way, as shown on page 377.

Many power plants run on coal. Thermal energy from burning the fuel is used to boil water. The steam turns turbines, which are like large fans. Generators convert the mechanical energy of the spinning turbines to electrical energy. This can be distributed to homes, schools, and businesses.

Other fossil fuel products are burned in engines. Crude oil, or petroleum, is refined to make jet fuel for airplanes and gasoline and diesel fuel for cars, trucks, buses, and trains. The engines change the chemical energy stored in the fuel into mechanical energy.

Natural gas is used to heat more than half of all homes in the United States. Propane, a product from refined crude oil, is also used to heat homes. Propane also fuels many barbecue grills and outdoor stoves.

Are fossil fuels the best choice for meeting energy needs? Many people are asking this important question.

One problem is that fossil fuels are a **nonrenewable resource,** meaning they cannot be replaced quickly or easily. People are using fossil fuels much more quickly than natural processes are replacing them. At present rates, Earth's supply of fossil fuels will run out some day.

Burning fossil fuels also pollutes the environment. To understand how bad the problem can become, consider industrial cities such as London,

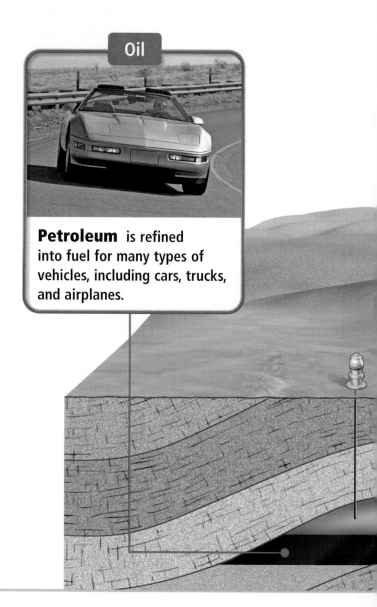

Oil

Petroleum is refined into fuel for many types of vehicles, including cars, trucks, and airplanes.

England, in the late 1800s. Smoke and soot produced by burning coal often filled the skies over London.

At times, people could barely see the Sun. Many people died from respiratory illnesses during the worst periods of pollution.

Today, strict laws and better technology help reduce pollution from fossil fuels. Even so, air pollution from factories and automobiles remains a serious problem, especially in urban areas.

Burning fossil fuels also releases carbon dioxide gas into the air. Scientists are debating the effects of this change to Earth's atmosphere. Many scientists argue that it is causing global temperatures to slowly rise, an event called global warming.

PROBLEM AND SOLUTION What are some problems caused by burning fossil fuels?

Natural Gas

Natural gas is used for heating in many homes. It is burned in fireplaces, heaters, water heaters, and stoves.

Coal

Coal has long been used as an energy source for factories and power plants.

oil derrick

coal mine

Express Lab

Activity Card 31
Model Oil Reserves

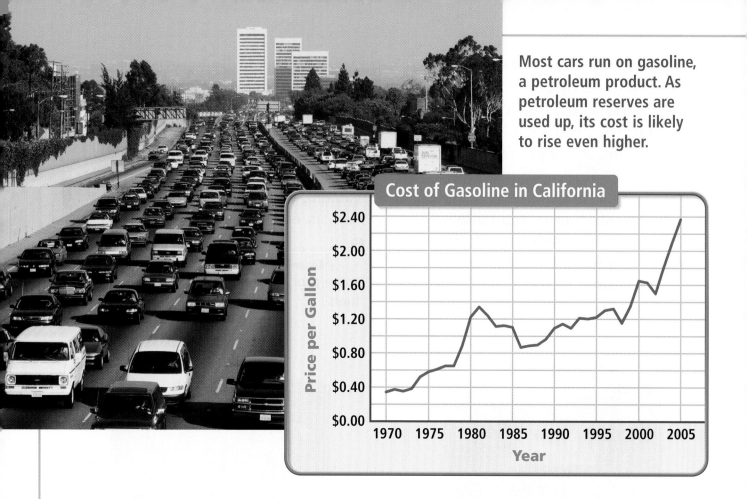

Most cars run on gasoline, a petroleum product. As petroleum reserves are used up, its cost is likely to rise even higher.

Cost of Gasoline in California

Price per Gallon

$2.40
$2.00
$1.60
$1.20
$0.80
$0.40
$0.00

1970 1975 1980 1985 1990 1995 2000 2005

Year

Conservation of Fossil Fuels

Natural resources are products and materials found in nature that people use, such as soil, air, water, and fossil fuels. The efficient use of resources is called **conservation.** Conserving nonrenewable resources is very important, because they cannot be replaced. By not wasting fossil fuels, you can save them for the future.

Another reason to conserve fossil fuels is to reduce pollution. Smoke from burning these fuels can mix with water droplets in the air to form smog, which is unhealthy to breathe.

Other waste gases from fossil fuels mix with raindrops to form acid rain, another environmental problem. Acid rain can kill trees and fish, and damage buildings and statues.

You and your family can help to conserve Earth's important resources by following some simple, common-sense practices. Use public transportation, or form carpools. Turn off electric lights and appliances when not in use.

You also can change clothes to fit the weather, instead of turning up heat or the air conditioner. Seal windows and doors. Use curtains to help keep warm or cool air inside the house. Recycle materials such as paper, plastic, and metals.

PROBLEM AND SOLUTION What problems can conservation help to solve?

Visual Summary

Fossil fuels were made from the remains of plants and animals that lived millions of years ago. When fossil fuels are burned, most of their energy is released as heat.

Fossil fuels are a convenient source of energy. Yet burning them creates air pollution and causes other problems.

Fossil fuels are a nonrenewable resource. They are being used up and cannot be replaced easily. Using public transportation helps conserve fossil fuels.

STANDARDS

3.b., 6.a., 6.b.

 Technology
Visit **www.eduplace.com/cascp** to find out more about fossil fuels.

Reading Review

1 MAIN IDEA Describe how fossil fuels were formed.

2 VOCABULARY Write a paragraph using the terms *nonrenewable resource* and *fossil fuels.* Explain why fossil fuels should be used wisely.

3 READING SKILL What are two ways to reduce the pollution that fossil fuels cause?

Problem	Solution

4 CRITICAL THINKING: Evaluate Scientists are researching new energy sources to help replace fossil fuels. Is this necessary? Why or why not?

5 INQUIRY SKILL: Use Numbers Research fluorescent and incandescent light bulbs. Find out how much energy each type uses. Create a bar graph to show your findings.

 TEST PRACTICE
Which of these fossil fuels is used to make gasoline?

A. natural gas

B. coal

C. petroleum

D. peat

STANDARDS

1: 3.b., **2:** 6.b., **3–5:** 6.a., **Test Practice:** 6.b.

389

Once There Were Fossil Fuels

How will people live without fossil fuels? Fossil fuels will run out someday. Will people be prepared? Or will they be faced with much harsher lives? Juan Arguello is about to explore these questions.

Characters

Juan Arguello
sixth grader

Guide 1 and Guide 2
guides to the future

Carl Smith
Juan's distant relative in the future

Mary Smith
Carl's daughter

STANDARD

6.b. *Students know* different natural energy and material resources, including air, soil, rocks, minerals, petroleum, fresh water, wildlife, and forests, and know how to classify them as renewable or nonrenewable.

READING LINK

Guide 1: Juan, are you tossing that plastic bottle into the trash?

Guide 2: Not the best choice, Juan.

Juan *(startled)*: Who are you?

Guide 1: We're your guides to the future.

Guide 2: Hold on! *(Each guide grabs one of Juan's hands.)* Here we go!

Scene changes to a farm. In the distance, **Mary Smith** *is leading a team of oxen as they plow a field.* **Carl Smith,** *an old farmer, is sitting on a bench.*

Juan: What…what happened? Where are we?

Guide 1: Meet your great, great, great,

Guide 2: —great, great, great, great, lots of greats—

Guide 1: —great grandson. His name is Carl.

Carl: Hello, youngster. Welcome to the future.

Juan *(confused)*: I'm…I'm pleased to meet you.

Carl: Pardon me if I don't get up. My back is aching, thanks to a lifetime of lifting, bending over, and pulling farm machinery.

Juan: Pulling farm machinery? What do you mean? Why don't you use a tractor?

Carl *(puzzled)*: A tractor? Oh, you mean one of those motorized vehicle things that ran on gasoline? Nope, we don't use tractors anymore.

Juan: Why not?

Carl: Because people in the past used up all the fossil fuels. Without gasoline, tractors became useless.

Guide 2: So did cars, trucks, and airplanes—

Guide 1: —and motorcycles, and lawn mowers, and combine harvesters!

Juan: Can't you use electricity to run motors?

Carl: We could, in theory, but electricity has become *very* expensive. People just didn't plan for life without fossil fuels. That's the problem.

Mary *(entering)*: Dad, can I quit for the day? It's going to rain soon.

Carl: All right, Mary. It's a shame we don't have one of those antique raincoats for you.

Juan: An antique raincoat? What's that?

Mary: It's something people used to wear a long time ago. It's made of a material called vinyl that we don't have anymore.

Juan: There's no more vinyl?

Mary: Of course not. Vinyl is a kind of plastic, and plastics were made from fossil fuels. Nowadays we have no

vinyl raincoats, or plastic eyeglasses, or lawn bags, or soda bottles—

Juan: Wow. I can't imagine living without those things.

Guide 1: Time's up! We're running late!

Guide 2: Hold on! *(Each guide again grabs one of Juan's hands.)* Off we go!

Scene changes to a futuristic city. Small, streamlined cars fill the streets.

Juan: Now what?

Guide 1: Welcome to a different version of the future.

Mary *(entering)*: Greetings, traveler. People from your time were very wise. They knew that fossil fuels would run out someday. To prepare, they developed alternative energy sources.

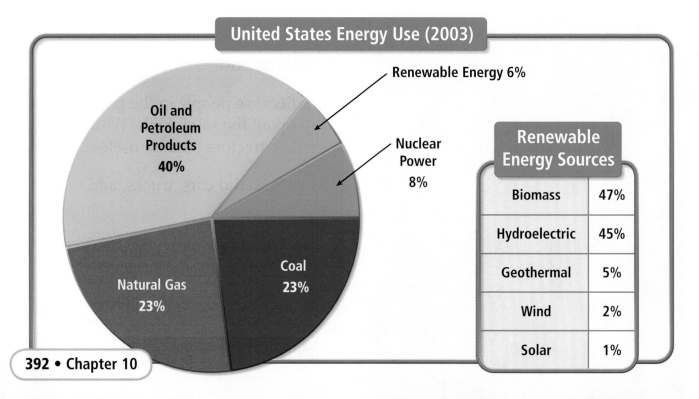

United States Energy Use (2003)

Renewable Energy 6%

Oil and Petroleum Products 40%

Nuclear Power 8%

Natural Gas 23%

Coal 23%

Renewable Energy Sources

Biomass	47%
Hydroelectric	45%
Geothermal	5%
Wind	2%
Solar	1%

Juan: You mean energy from the wind and Sun?

Mary: Yes! And geothermal energy too. People also invested in technology to capture the energy of tides.

Carl (*entering*): Don't forget the improved technology to generate hydrogen. That's used to power fuel cells.

Guide 1: And there's biomass—energy from plant matter.

Guide 2: Nuclear power and hydroelectric power are still important too.

Mary: And thanks to improved recycling, we can keep using plastic products again and again.

Juan: Wow! I think I like this future a whole lot better than the other one. But which future will come to pass?

Guide 1: Fossil fuels *will* run out someday. If people don't prepare now, future generations will face some hard choices.

Guide 2: But if people start to invest in alternative energy sources and practice recycling—

Juan: —then my children—

Carl: —and children of the future—

All: —will inherit a much better world!

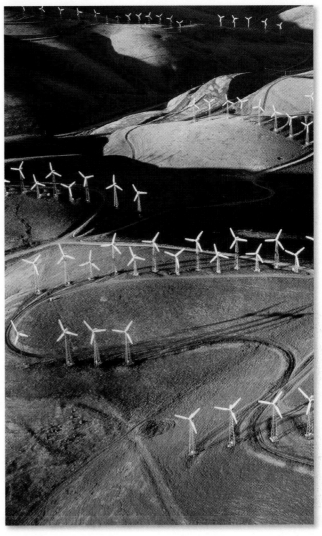

These wind turbines harness wind energy in Altamont, California. What kinds of power do you think will become more common in the future?

Sharing Ideas

1. **READING CHECK** Describe the two futures that Juan visits.

2. **WRITE ABOUT IT** What challenges will people face when fossil fuels run out?

3. **TALK ABOUT IT** What can you do to help conserve fossil fuels?

What Are Alternatives to Fossil Fuels?

Building Background

In California and elsewhere, people are searching for alternatives to using fossil fuels. The cars shown below run on electricity. Cars like these could become very common in the years ahead.

Every day, you and your family decide how to use energy resources. The more you understand about these resources, the wiser the choices you can make.

PREPARE TO INVESTIGATE

Inquiry Skill

Communicate You can communicate the steps and results of investigations in the form of written reports and oral presentations.

Materials

- Reference sources
- Internet access (optional)

STANDARDS

6.a. *Students know* the utility of energy sources is determined by factors that are involved in converting these sources to useful forms and the consequences of the conversion process.
7.b. Select and use appropriate tools and technology (including calculators, computers, balances, spring scales, microscopes, and binoculars) to perform tests, collect data, and display data.

Heating a Home

Procedure

1 **Collaborate** With a small group, discuss ways that people heat their homes. Common sources for home heating include electricity, natural gas, and oil. Other sources are propane, solar power, and geothermal power.

2 **Research** Research one type of home heating at the library or on the Internet. Find its costs, advantages and disadvantages to the homeowner, and its effect on the environment.

3 **Compare** Interview your parent, guardian, or other adult about home heating. Ask if they are satisfied with the cost and quality. Ask if they would switch heating sources if they could. Compare the information from the interview to your other research. Take notes in your *Science Notebook*.

4 **Communicate** Share your research findings with your group.

Conclusion

1. **Analyze** Which source of home heating do you think is the best choice in your community? Explain your reasoning.

2. **Infer** Do you think people in your community understand the facts about home heating? Explain why or why not.

3. **Communicate** Work with your group to present your findings in a written report. You may include pictures, charts, or graphs to illustrate your points.

NATURAL GAS

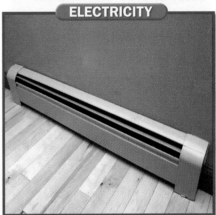
ELECTRICITY

PROPANE

Guided Inquiry

Experiment With your parents or guardian, think of five ways your family could spend less money on energy. **Predict** how effective these steps would be. Carry out your plan and observe the results.

VOCABULARY

biomass	p. 402
hydroelectric energy	p. 399
geothermal energy	p. 401
nuclear fission	p. 400
renewable resource	p. 396
solar energy	p. 397

READING SKILL

Main Idea Use the graphic organizer to record the main idea and details.

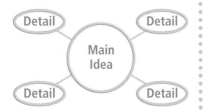

STANDARDS

6.a. *Students know* the utility of energy sources is determined by factors that are involved in converting these sources to useful forms and the consequences of the conversion process.
6.b. *Students know* different natural energy and material resources, including air, soil, rocks, minerals, petroleum, fresh water, wildlife, and forests, and know how to classify them as renewable or nonrenewable.

Renewable Energy Resources

MAIN IDEA Because fossil fuels are nonrenewable and supplies are limited, people are developing ways to use renewable energy resources. These resources include solar energy, wind, biomass, and geothermal energy.

The Importance of Renewable Energy

Imagine a world without any energy resources. Homes, schools, and businesses would have no electricity. Ships, planes, and trains could not transport goods, and people could travel no faster than horses could carry them! In many ways, people would live as they did in the early 1800s.

As you have learned, fossil fuels fill most of society's energy needs. But at the current rate of use, these nonrenewable resources will run out someday.

What will people do without fossil fuels? One solution involves preparing for the future by finding and developing renewable sources of energy. **Renewable resources,** such as the Sun, wind, and moving water, can be used day after day without running out. Renewable resources also do not pollute the atmosphere, as fossil fuels do.

However, there are disadvantages associated with any renewable energy source. Some are limited to certain areas, while others require expensive technology. Regardless, many renewable resources contribute to the energy supply today, and they hold the promise of contributing more in the future.

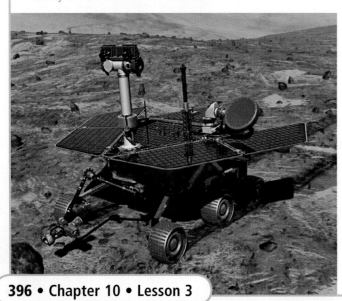

◄ Solar PV cells were used to run this Mars Rover as it explored Mars.

Solar Energy

The Sun supplies **solar energy,** an inexhaustible energy source. This means people can never use it up. It is also nonpolluting. However, harnessing solar energy can be expensive.

The diagram below shows one way to "capture" and use solar energy. In this case, solar energy is used to heat water for a house.

Simple versions of solar heaters were common in the late 1800s and early 1900s. People stopped using them when inexpensive fossil fuels became available. Now, solar heaters are becoming popular again, especially in sunny climates.

Solar energy is also used to make electricity in solar power plants. Mirrors reflect the Sun's rays onto a central collector. The heat boils water or another liquid, generating steam that turns turbines. A solar plant in the Mojave Desert provides power to 350,000 homes!

Photovoltaic cells, or PV cells, collect light and change it directly into electricity. When light hits the cells, electrons are knocked loose from atoms. The loose electrons are channeled into an electric current. Today, PV cells are used to provide electricity for calculators, home appliances, and even spacecraft.

MAIN IDEA How can energy from the Sun be collected and used?

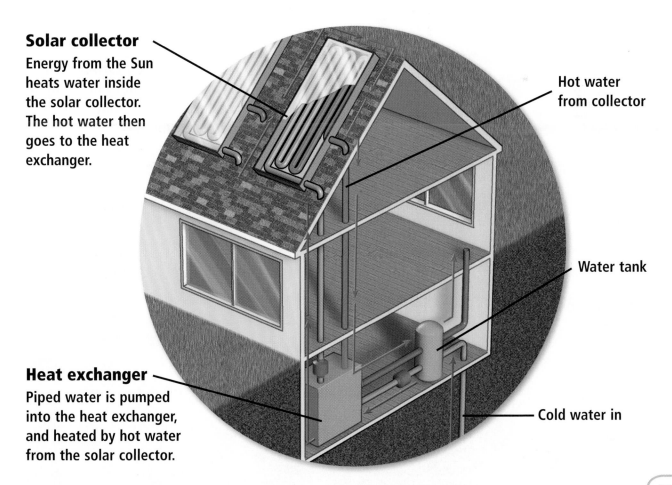

Solar collector
Energy from the Sun heats water inside the solar collector. The hot water then goes to the heat exchanger.

Hot water from collector

Water tank

Heat exchanger
Piped water is pumped into the heat exchanger, and heated by hot water from the solar collector.

Cold water in

Wind Power

People have built and used windmills for hundreds of years. The first windmills were used to grind grain or pump water. As the wind turned the blades or sails, a series of gears would turn to provide power.

Thanks to improved technology, wind power is now a promising source of electricity. In the wind turbines shown below, wind is used to spin the blades. Just as in other power plants, a generator converts the mechanical energy of the spinning turbine into electrical energy. The amount of energy depends both on the size of the turbine and the wind speed.

In some countries, wind power is very common. In Denmark, for instance, wind energy provides more than 20 percent of the country's power.

Areas with dozens of wind turbines are called wind farms. The three largest wind farms in California make enough electricity to power a city the size of San Francisco.

Wind energy does have some drawbacks, however. Wind turbines work best where steady winds blow most of the time. Wind farms also take up a lot of space, and they are noisy. Many wind farms today are in desert lands or hilly regions that otherwise would stand empty.

Winds blow because the Sun heats Earth unevenly. For this reason, the source of wind power is solar energy.

Shaft

Gear box

Generator

Blade

◄ A typical wind turbine can be as tall as a 20-story building. It has three blades that span 60 meters or longer.

Energy from Moving Water

Like wind, moving water has been used as an energy source for hundreds of years. The Romans built large water wheels on rivers, which they used to grind grain. The moving water turned the wheel. The wheel turned gears to grind the grain.

Electric energy generated from moving water is called **hydroelectric energy.** To build a hydroelectric power plant, usually the first step is to build a dam on a steep section of a river. Water is stored behind the dam in a reservoir. Near the bottom of the dam, water runs through tunnels to turbines, setting them spinning. The energy from the spinning turbines is converted into electricity.

Over the past 100 years, many large hydroelectric power plants have been built in the United States. About 15 percent of California's electricity comes from such plants.

Hydroelectric plants produce energy without polluting the air. They also rely on the water cycle—a free

▲ The Itaipú Dam on the Paraná River is one of the largest hydroelectric power plants in the world. It provides electricity to both Brazil and Paraguay.

energy source. But they can damage river ecosystems. Large dams and reservoirs change the flow of the river and can harm fish and other animals.

For example, some fish, such as salmon, migrate upstream to spawn. A series of dams can interrupt the migration. So some dams include fish ladders, which allow the fish to swim upstream at an angle.

The energy of moving water in ocean tides can also be harnessed. During high tide, water can be trapped behind a dam. Then, when the tide goes out and the water recedes into the ocean, the water passes over turbines just as in river dams. Tidal power plants work best where the difference between high tide and low tide is great.

▲ The Annapolis Tidal Generating Station uses turbines to generate electricity.

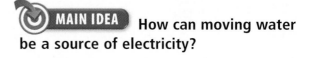 **MAIN IDEA** How can moving water be a source of electricity?

Nuclear Energy

The nucleus of a uranium atom can break apart, radiating energy in the process. For this reason, uranium and similar elements are said to be radioactive.

In a nuclear power plant, nuclei of uranium or plutonium are split in a controlled process called **nuclear fission.** This process releases vast amounts of energy. The fission of 1 kg (2.2 lb) of uranium produces more energy than burning 3 million kg (6.6 million lb) of coal!

At a nuclear power plant, bundles of rods containing uranium are placed in a thick-walled vessel called a reactor. The energy released from fission is used to boil water, producing steam. The steam turns turbines that turn generators.

Nuclear power plants offer a clean, quiet way to generate electricity. They do not add soot or carbon dioxide to the atmosphere, as burning coal or other fossil fuels do.

However, nuclear power presents risks and drawbacks. The worst risk is the accidental release of radioactive material. In the past 40 years, two terrible accidents have occurred at the world's nuclear power plants.

A more common problem comes from nuclear waste. Such wastes may stay radioactive for thousands of years. Scientists are studying ways to reuse this waste.

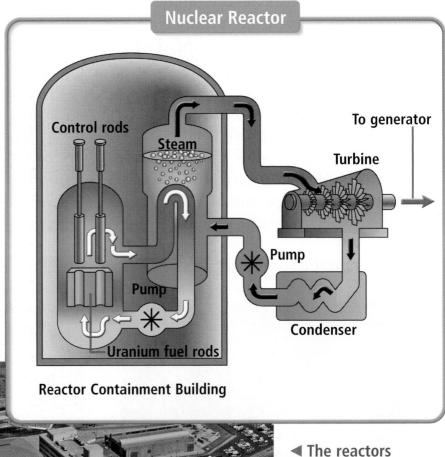

Nuclear Reactor

Control rods

Steam

To generator

Turbine

Pump

Pump

Uranium fuel rods

Condenser

Reactor Containment Building

◄ The reactors in this California nuclear power plant are located in the white-domed buildings.

At geothermal power plants, steam from hot water inside Earth is used to spin turbines, which convert mechanical energy to electrical energy. ▼

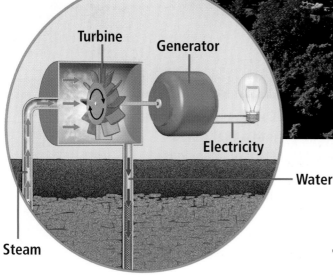

Turbine Generator

Electricity

Water

Steam

▲ Geothermal energy plant in California

Geothermal Energy

Recall that Earth is hot inside. Thermal energy from Earth's interior is called **geothermal energy.** The word stem *geo-* means "Earth," and *-thermal* refers to heat.

How does geothermal energy work? In some places, magma from Earth's interior is close to underground pools of water. If the water boils, the steam may rise through rocks to the surface. Or it may rise through a shaft that people drill. The heated water can be used to heat swimming pools and buildings.

The heated water can also be used to produce electricity. In geothermal power plants, steam or hot water is carried through underground pipes.

The steam turns turbines that turn generators. The water is sent back down through the pipes to be heated again.

Geothermal heat pumps can be used to heat individual homes. Loops of pipes are filled with water and antifreeze, then buried underground. During winter, the water carries heat from the ground into the house. During summer, heat from the house is returned to the cooler ground.

Geothermal energy is a free source of energy that will not run out. However, geothermal power plants are best suited to "hot spots"—places where molten rock from Earth's interior can heat the surface.

MAIN IDEA What is geothermal energy and how is it used?

401

Biomass

Each year, many tons of once-living matter, or **biomass,** go to waste. Biomass includes unused plant parts from farms, sawdust and bark from lumber mills, food scraps, and animal wastes. Wood is also a form of biomass.

Because biomass comes from living matter, it contains stored solar energy, just as fossil fuels do. However, the energy in biomass is much less concentrated than in fossil fuels. New technologies are needed to make biomass a cost-efficient energy source.

Biomass can be burned in a power plant to produce electricity. Another use is to allow biomass to decay on farms or in landfills. As it decays, it produces methane gas, a useful fuel.

Unwanted parts of corn plants can be used to make ethanol, a type of alcohol. Ethanol also can be burned as fuel.

When biomass burns, it causes much less air pollution than fossil fuels. Using biomass for energy also keeps it from taking space in landfills. Landfills are expensive to maintain and take up space that could be put to other uses.

Yet another use for biomass is composting. Place grass clippings, fruit rinds, potato peels, and even unwanted cotton fabric into a compost bin or pile. As these materials decay, they create a nutrient-rich material to fertilize garden plants.

Ethanol

Corn can be processed into a fuel called ethanol. Many gas stations sell gasoline mixed with ethanol.

Composting is a great way to conserve resources in your back yard! ▼

Alternative Fuels

Hydrogen fuel cells are used on spacecraft to power electric equipment. The astronauts even drink the water that the fuel cells produce!

Around the world, people have converted their diesel engines to run on used vegetable oil.

Alternative Fuels for Vehicles

Today, about two-thirds of all petroleum consumed in the United States is used for transportation. Developing and using alternative fuels for vehicles is a key to conserving petroleum.

For example, scientists are developing engines that run on ethanol only. Even vegetable oils can be used to run car engines!

Today, subways and many buses run on electricity. For an electric car, the challenge is to provide enough electricity from batteries. The batteries also need to be recharged, which may limit these cars to short trips only.

Hybrid electric cars use both a small gasoline engine and an electric motor that runs on batteries. In one model, the gasoline engine provides most of the power, but the electric motor adds power when the car accelerates. The batteries recharge when the car slows down or idles.

Hydrogen fuel cells are yet another alternative power source. In these cells, hydrogen combines with oxygen from the air. This reaction releases a lot of energy, and the only byproduct is water!

MAIN IDEA Describe alternative fuels and their uses.

Express Lab

Activity Card 32
Monitor Energy

Renewable Energy in California

Like much of the nation, California relies heavily on fossil fuels for its energy needs. About 42 percent of the state's electricity is generated by natural gas. Coal provides another 20 percent. In addition, Californians burn almost 80 million gallons of petroleum products each day.

However, alternative energy sources also play a growing role in meeting the state's energy needs. In 2004, hydroelectric energy generated nearly 15 percent of California's electricity. Nuclear power was close behind, producing 13 percent of the state's electricity. Renewable energy sources such as solar, wind, and geothermal energy generated almost 11 percent.

The California Energy Commission sets standards for energy efficiency in the state. The Commission estimates that building and appliance standards alone will save some $57 billion in energy costs by the year 2011.

California also is promoting "plug-in" hybrid vehicles. These vehicles use larger batteries than traditional hybrids, and therefore can travel longer distances on electric power, rather than gas. The goal is to produce a hybrid that is pollution-free.

MAIN IDEA **Name two ways California is conserving energy.**

This car is powered by a hydrogen fuel cell. Do you think you will drive a car like this someday? ▼

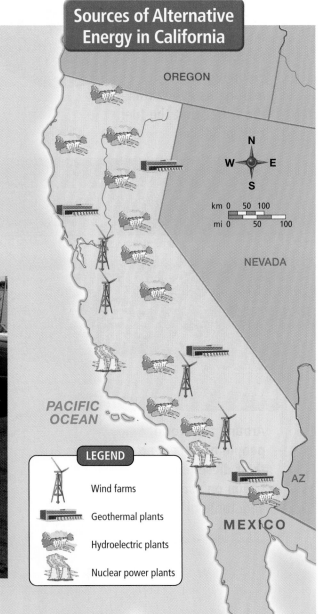

Sources of Alternative Energy in California

OREGON

NEVADA

PACIFIC OCEAN

AZ

MEXICO

LEGEND

Wind farms

Geothermal plants

Hydroelectric plants

Nuclear power plants

km 0   50   100

mi 0   50   100

Visual Summary

Many different types of renewable energy resources are being developed to replace fossil fuels.

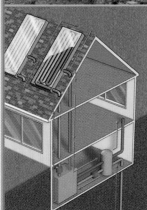

Renewable energy resources include solar, wind, hydroelectric, nuclear, biomass, and hydrogen fuel cells. Each has benefits and drawbacks.

Scientists are continuing to study and develop new energy technology. Their goals are to reduce pollution, the need for fossil fuels, and energy costs.

 STANDARDS

6.a., 6.b.

Technology
Visit **www.eduplace.com/cascp** to find out more about alternative energy sources.

Reading Review

1 MAIN IDEA Describe ways that renewable energy resources can be used to make electricity.

2 VOCABULARY Define the term *hydroelectric energy.* Describe how this kind of energy is made.

3 READING SKILL What is biomass? Why is it a renewable energy resource?

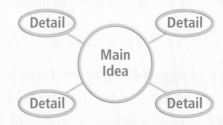

4 CRITICAL THINKING: Evaluate Should the United States build more nuclear power plants? Explain.

5 INQUIRY SKILL: Communicate Do you think people in your community are using energy resources wisely? If not, how could they improve? Write a paragraph or short essay to persuade people that your ideas are correct.

 TEST PRACTICE
What alternative energy source uses heat from Earth's interior?

A. photovoltaic (PV) cells

B. hydroelectric dams

C. geothermal plants

D. hydrogen fuel cells

 **STANDARDS**

1–3: 6.b., **4:** 6.a., **5:** 7.d., **Test Practice:** 6.a.

EXTREME Science

STANDARDS 6.a. *Students know* the utility of energy sources is determined by factors that are involved in converting these sources to useful forms and the consequences of the conversion process.

POWER Tower

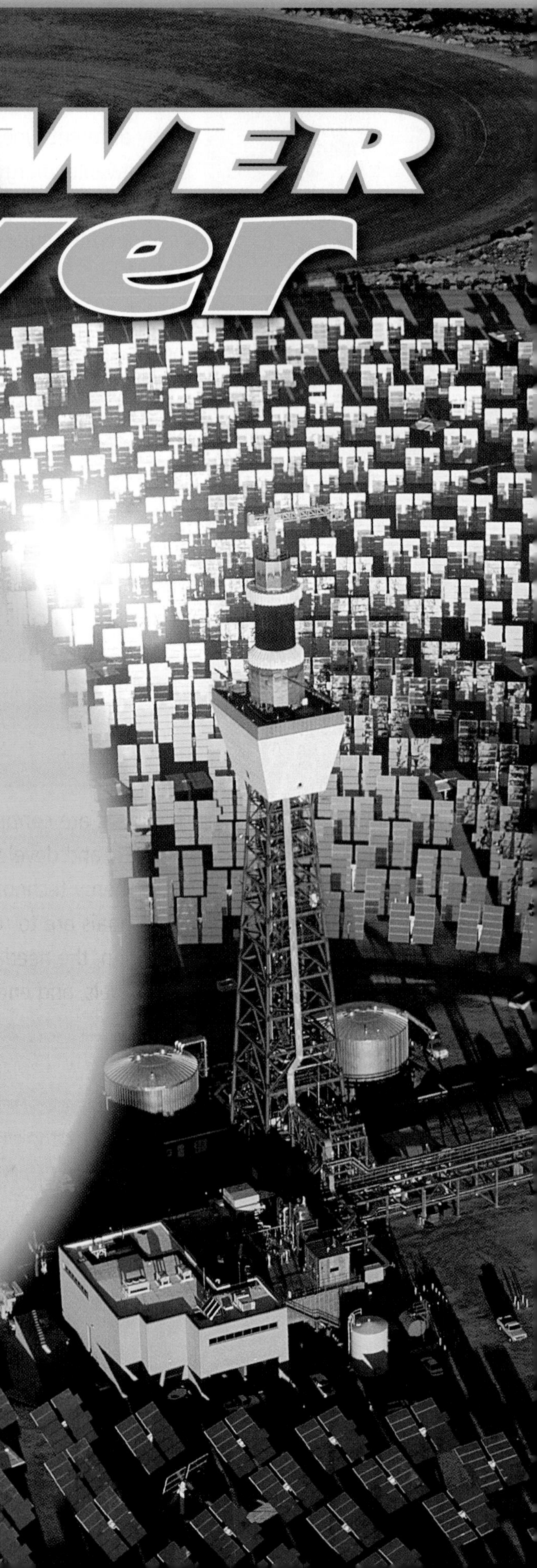

It's huge. It's powerful. It never stops giving energy. It's called the Sun. So why not tap into it?

That's just what California scientists have done at Solar Two, the experimental power plant shown here. Almost 2000 reflective mirrors focus the Sun's rays on a single collecting tower, called the Power Tower. At the focus, the temperature reaches 565° C —over 1000° F! The heat is used to create steam that runs a generator that produces usable electricity.

Why go to such lengths to catch the Sun's energy? Solar power plants use no fuel, give off no carbon emissions, and have very small impact on the environment. As the world increasingly looks for alternative energy sources, solar energy plants like Solar Two may become less extreme and more common.

In 2004, about 20% of ▶
California's total energy
needs were met by
renewable resources.

**Use of Renewable
Energy Resources in California**

Solar
1%

Hydroelectric
58%

Wind
7%

Organic Waste
10%

Geothermal
24%

Special
mirrors called
"heliostats" focus
and direct the Sun's
energy to the heat
collector at the top
of the tower.

Writing Journal

How does a plant like Solar
Two differ from a nuclear
power plant? Write down your
conclusions in your journal.

407

Math in Science

The table shows the amount of thermal energy that can be produced (measured in British thermal units, or BTU) from several different fuels.

Fuel Type	BTU Produced
Fuel oil	140,000 per gallon
Kerosene	135,000 per gallon
Propane	91,330 per gallon

1. Which fuel type is most efficient? How much energy, in BTUs, could you obtain from burning 5 gallons of that fuel?

2. Can you conclude which fuel costs the least to use? If not, what additional information do you need?

Writing in Science
Persuasive

Write a letter to the editor of your local newspaper expressing your opinion on using a specific energy source or conserving energy. In your letter, try to persuade the readers of the newspaper to support some specific action.

HVAC Technician

Is the air in your home too hot, too cold, or too stuffy? Call a heating, ventilation, and air conditioning (HVAC) technician! They install and repair cooling and heating systems.

In California and across the country, the costs of electricity, natural gas, and other energy sources have been rising every year. The need for energy-efficient cooling and heating systems is greater than ever.

What It Takes!

- Classes and training
- In many states, a professional license
- Good analytical and detective skills

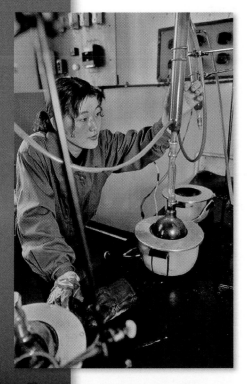

Petrochemical Engineer

All sorts of devices run on petroleum and natural gas. The job of finding and extracting these fuels belongs to the petrochemical engineer. These specialists consult with geologists to locate deposits, oversee drilling, and help process raw materials from Earth into usable fuels.

What It Takes!

- A degree in petrochemical engineering
- Willingness to work in remote regions of the world

Vocabulary

Complete each sentence with a term from the list.

1. Plant parts, sawdust, bark, and food waste are all examples of ____.

2. Because fossil fuels take millions of years to replace, they are called ____.

3. The ability to do work is called ____.

4. Hot springs and geysers are examples of ____.

5. The energy source used by photovoltaic cells is ____.

6. Electricity made from the energy of moving water is called ____.

7. The efficient use of resources is called ____.

8. Energy sources that come from the remains of long dead plants and animals are known as ____.

9. The Sun, wind, and moving water are all examples of ____.

10. The splitting of an atomic nucleus is called ____.

biomass p. 402
conservation p. 388
efficiency p. 379
energy p. 376
fossil fuels p. 384
geothermal energy p. 401
hydroelectric energy p. 399
natural resource p. 388
nonrenewable resource p. 386
nuclear fission p. 400
renewable energy p. 396
solar energy p. 397

Test Practice

Write the letter of the best answer choice.

11. Electric power plants are not very energy efficient because ____.

   A. some energy is always lost as heat
   B. some energy is always changed to mattter
   C. they use fossil fuels
   D. they use renewable resources

12. In a hydrogen fuel cell, hydrogen reacts with ____ to produce energy and water.

   A. water
   B. wind
   C. oxygen
   D. carbon dioxide

13. Nuclear power plants use ____ to produce energy.

   A. biomass
   B. coal
   C. wind
   D. uranium

14. Cars that run on ethanol are using the energy stored in ____.

   A. natural gas
   B. biomass
   C. fuel cells
   D. nuclear fuels

15. **Use Numbers** What if the world's oil reserves shrunk to 3 trillion barrels and demand was 50 billion barrels per year? At that rate of use, how much longer would the reserves last?

16. Using the illustration below as a model, explain how solar energy can be used to heat water for a house.

Place the following terms under the correct heading in the chart.

biomass
natural gas
windmill
coal
geothermal energy

gasoline
solar heating
hydroelectric energy
nuclear fission

Nonrenewable Energy Sources	Renewable Energy Sources

17. **Apply** What are some ways you can practice energy conservation in your daily life?

18. **Analyze** What is the difference between the way solar energy is used in solar collectors and in photovoltaic cells?

19. **Evaluate** How did the information in this chapter change the way you think about energy in your daily life?

20. **Synthesize** How is energy from the Sun found in both renewable and nonrenewable energy resources?

Home Designs

Imagine that you are an architect. Your client wants to build a home that relies on renewable energy sources. Based on the energy sources available in your area, design a blueprint for the home. You can use more than one renewable resource to power the home.

Review your answers to the questions on page 371 at the beginning of this chapter. Change your answers, as needed, based on what you have learned.

 STANDARDS

1–2: 6.b., **3:** 3.a., **4–6:** 6.b., **7:** 6.a., **8–10:** 6.b., **11:** 3.b., **12:** 6.a., **13–14:** 6.b., **15–16:** 6.b., **17:** 6.a., **18:** 6.b., **19:** 6.a., **20:** 3.a.

Chapter 11

Material Resources

Grapes, an important California crop

LESSON 1

Some natural resources are nonrenewable. Earth has a certain supply of them, and no more. What are some nonrenewable resources?

LESSON 2

Earth's renewable resources include soil, water, and plants and animals. Although these resources are renewable, they should still be used carefully. Why is that so?

Writing Journal

In your Writing Journal, write or draw answers to each question.

413

Vocabulary Preview

Vocabulary

humus p. 434

material resource p. 418

mineral p. 418

ore p. 419

recycling p. 422

soil p. 434

topsoil p. 434

Glossary

English-Spanish, p. H26

Vocabulary Skill

Determine Meaning

material resource

A material is a kind of matter, and a resource is something that can be used. Earth's material resources are things from Earth that are useful for making new things.

humus

a dark-colored material in soil made up of decayed plant and animal matter

Quartz

mineral

a solid crystalline chemical element or compound that occurs naturally in Earth's crust

recycling

recovering a resource from used items so they can be made into something new

ore

a rock or mineral that is mined for the valuable material it contains

Start with Your Standards

Standard Set 6. Resources

6.b. *Students know* different natural energy and material resources, including air, soil, rocks, minerals, petroleum, fresh water, wildlife, and forests, and know how to classify them as renewable or nonrenewable.

6.c. *Students know* the natural origin of the materials used to make common objects.

Standard Set 7: Investigation and Experimentation standard covered in this chapter: 7.e.

What Material Resources Are Nonrenewable?

Building Background

Why should you recycle old bottles, cans, and newspapers? One reason is to conserve Earth's resources. Recycling plastics, paper, metals, and other materials means they can be used to make new products.

PREPARE TO INVESTIGATE

Inquiry Skill

Collaborate When you collaborate, you work in a team to investigate and experiment.

Science and Math Toolbox

For step 2, review **Making a Chart to Organize Data** on page H11.

STANDARDS

6.b. *Students know* different natural energy and material resources, including air, soil, rocks, minerals, petroleum, fresh water, wildlife, and forests, and know how to classify them as renewable or nonrenewable.
7.e. Recognize whether evidence is consistent with a proposed explanation.

Recycling!

Procedure

1 **Collaborate** As a class, identify all the materials that your family, your school, and your community recycle.

2 **Record Data** In your *Science Notebook,* list the materials that the class identified. Create a chart like the one shown.

3 **Predict** Review your list and choose two types of recyclable materials that your household uses. Predict how many of these recyclable items your household uses in a week. Then predict how many of the goods will be recycled. Record your predictions.

4 **Observe** For one week, monitor your household's use of the selected recyclable goods. Record how many items are recycled and how many are thrown in the trash.

STEP 2

	Predicted data		Observed data	
	Used	Recycled	Used	Recycled
Glass bottles				
Newspaper				
Plastic				
Aluminum cans				

STEP 4

Conclusion

1. **Analyze Data** Use your data to calculate the total amount of your chosen recyclable goods used in your household that week. Then calculate the percentage of those materials that were set aside to be recycled. Did your household recycle more or less than it threw in the trash?

2. **Collaborate** Work in a small group to develop a plan that would encourage people in your community to recycle more.

Guided Inquiry

Ask Questions From your data or other observations, choose a resource that you think is wasted in your community. How could this resource be used wisely? **Communicate** your ideas in a letter, poster, or skit.

VOCABULARY

material resource	p. 418
mineral	p. 418
ore	p. 419
recycling	p. 422

READING SKILL

Problem and Solution
Use a chart to compare the pros and cons of one of the conservation solutions discussed in this lesson.

Problem	Solution

STANDARDS

6.b. *Students know* different natural energy and material resources, including air, soil, rocks, minerals, petroleum, fresh water, wildlife, and forests, and know how to classify them as renewable or nonrenewable.
6.c. *Students know* the natural origin of the materials used to make common objects.

Nonrenewable Material Resources

MAIN IDEA Many of Earth's resources cannot be easily replaced. Once they are gone, they are gone forever. People should use these resources responsibly and wisely.

Minerals and Ores

Earth provides a huge variety of **material resources,** which are things from Earth that can be used to make new products. Like energy resources, material resources are classified as either renewable or nonrenewable.

One example of a nonrenewable material resource is a mineral. A **mineral** is a solid crystalline chemical element or compound that occurs naturally in Earth's crust. Metals such as iron, copper, and gold are minerals. So are compounds such as sodium chloride, which is table salt. Minerals are considered nonrenewable because they can take thousands of years to form deep beneath Earth's surface.

Mining
Miners may dig deep into Earth or strip layers off the surface. The minerals from this mine are used to make cement. ▶

Different types of minerals combine to form rocks. An **ore** is a rock that contains enough of some mineral to make it useful. Most ores are valued for the metals they contain.

Throughout history, people have used minerals for many purposes. Minerals have been used to make tools, weapons, dyes, and jewelry. Today, many different minerals are used in a wide variety of ways, as shown in the chart.

Many metals are valuable because they are attractive and rare. Gold, silver, and platinum are called precious metals. They are often used in fine jewelry.

Most ores have to be refined to separate the desired metal from unwanted materials. Iron, for example, is found in ores such as magnetite and hematite. Copper is found in chalcopyrite (kal kuh PEYE ryt), and aluminum is found in bauxite. Refining ores is often a complex and expensive process.

Different metals have different properties that make them useful. Iron is quite strong and is used to make steel. Copper conducts heat and electricity well, and is used to make cookware and electrical wires.

Aluminum is also an excellent conductor, and it is quite lightweight. You can find aluminum in metal cans, airplane frames, and pots and pans. Long-distance power lines are also made mostly of aluminum.

 **PROBLEM AND SOLUTION** **What is the purpose of refining an ore?**

Uses of Minerals and Ores

Minerals		Ores	
	Fluorite Uses: Steel, glass, fiberglass, pottery, enamel		**Nickel ore** Uses: Stainless steel, aircraft, electrical equipment
	Gypsum Uses: Wallboard, plaster		**Iron ore** Uses: Steel for cars, railroad tracks, tools, buildings
	Quartz Uses: Glass, radios, clocks, computer chips		**Copper ore** Uses: Electrical wiring, roofing materials, coins, pipes

Where the Resources Are

In the past, people often settled in areas near important natural resources. These resources helped shape the lives and businesses of the communities in the region.

In the mid-1800s, gold was discovered in California. Settlers moved to the state by the thousands, and towns sprang up almost overnight around the gold mining industry. Similar towns were founded around silver mines. When gold and silver ran out, many of the mining towns struggled. Some eventually were abandoned.

In the 1850s, a similar situation happened on the East Coast of the United States. Oil was discovered in Pennsylvania. Towns and oil wells sprang up all over the region! Until the Texas oil boom of 1901, Pennsylvania produced half of the world's oil.

Today, resources are transported over long distances. Modern technology makes it much easier for people to use and rely on resources from all over the world. Silver ores, for example, may be mined in California, then shipped by truck or train to another state to be refined. From there, the silver may be shipped to jewelers or manufacturers in any location in the world.

As you learned earlier, the world relies on coal, oil, and other fossil fuels for most of its energy needs. Yet large deposits of these fuels are found only in a few locations. Because the world continues to use up supplies, many locations today are in remote places, including under the ocean.

Oil, or petroleum, is typically transported by large oceangoing ships called tankers. Every day, fleets of these huge tankers carry crude oil across the oceans, each carrying millions of liters. The tankers bring the oil to refineries, then the finished products are trucked to gas stations and other places where they are needed.

◀ The hunt for gold brought many people to live in California during the second half of the 1800s.

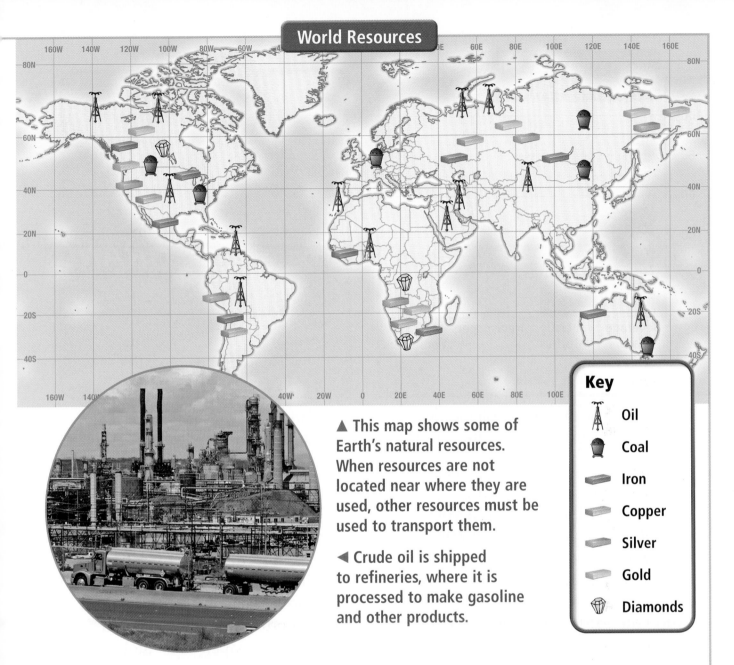

This map shows some of Earth's natural resources. When resources are not located near where they are used, other resources must be used to transport them.

◀ Crude oil is shipped to refineries, where it is processed to make gasoline and other products.

Key

🛢 Oil

⚱ Coal

▬ Iron

▬ Copper

▬ Silver

▬ Gold

◆ Diamonds

One drawback of this system is that tankers occasionally spill their cargo accidentally. Another, more typical drawback is the expense. Shipping products any distance, let alone across an ocean, costs a lot of money and energy.

Despite issues such as these, the world's system of transportation has made modern life possible. Think about the different materials you use every day. The cotton in your clothes may have been grown in India or Brazil. The aluminum in a can of tuna fish might have come from Australia. Plastics are made from petroleum, which might have been mined in Saudi Arabia.

Look again at the map shown above. What conclusions about modern life can you draw?

 **PROBLEM AND SOLUTION** How can the discovery of resources change people's lives?

Recycling Rates in the United States (2002–2003)

Percent

100%
80%
60%
40%
20%
0%

Beverage Cans | Plastic Bottles | Newspapers | Glass Containers

Recyclable Item

▲ How do you think the trash that you throw out compares to the data shown?

Recycling

354 mL   PLEASE RECYCLE   ORANG

▲ The triple-arrow symbol means that this can should be recycled.

Recycling and Conservation

Which of these items did you use today: a plastic water bottle, a cereal box, an aluminum can, a paper napkin, a tissue, and a paper towel? When you finished using them, what did you do? If you threw them away in the trash, the resources used to make these items were lost. But it doesn't have to be that way.

Recycling means recovering a resource from one item and using that resource to make another item. Recycling conserves resources and often saves energy. To conserve resources means to use them wisely.

All of the items listed above can be recycled. You can recycle both nonrenewable resources, such as plastic and aluminum, and renewable resources, such as paper.

For example, the plastic from a water bottle can be melted and molded to form another plastic container. Aluminum cans are melted down to make new aluminum cans. Paper products can be processed to make new paper. Even motor oil from a car can be recycled!

Recycling should become a priority for everyone. Look for the recycling label on the products you buy. This label will tell you whether or not the item can be recycled. The label may also tell you if the item is made from recycled products.

When you promote recycling, you are helping everyone conserve useful resources. You also are saving space in landfills, which is where communities store trash. You will learn more about landfills on pages 426 and 427.

▲ Insulation helps save energy. This fiberglass insulation helps keep a house cool in the summer and warm in the winter.

The Three R's of Conservation

Three important ways to conserve resources all begin with the letter R. They are reduce, reuse, and recycle.

Reducing simply means using less material. For example, by choosing not to use a straw in your drink, you reduce the amount of plastic you use. Every time you walk or ride a bike instead of riding in a car, you reduce the amount of fossil fuels that you use. Reducing also can save space in landfills.

Reusing is another way to conserve resources. Reusing can be as simple as using a glass cup again and again instead of throwing away a paper cup after a single use. It also means using china or plastic dinner plates instead of paper ones that are thrown away.

▲ These containers and cloth diapers can be used over and over again. What other reusable items can you name?

Reusing also means putting things to new uses. For example, gardeners often use old milk cartons as planters for starting seeds. They save money that would have been spent on plastic planters, and the milk cartons stay out of the trash for at least a few months.

By practicing the three R's of conservation, you can help save resources for the future. What examples of the three R's can you think of? Do you think they could make a difference in your community?

PROBLEM AND SOLUTION How does practicing the three R's help to conserve natural resources?

Express Lab

Activity Card 33
Identify Recyclables

New Products from Old

Scientists are constantly looking for ways to reuse and recycle the products that people use and enjoy. You may be surprised by the products that can be made from recycled materials!

For example, many companies use a material that looks like wood, but in fact comes completely from recycled plastic. Builders use this plastic product in fences, decks, docks, railroad ties, outdoor furniture, and many other items. The products can be dyed to appear painted or to look just like natural wood. They last much longer than wood, because they don't rot or become weathered.

Would you believe that broken glass is used to build roads? Most roads are paved with asphalt, which is a petroleum product. Today, some construction companies are adding recycled glass to their

▲ At a recycling center, plastic bottles are sorted by the type of plastic they contain. Eventually, the plastic is shredded into flakes or pellets, then made into new products.

asphalt mixtures.

Studies have shown that up to 30 percent of the asphalt paving on a road can be recycled glass. When the glass is ground into very small pieces, it will not damage car tires. In fact, the roughness of the glass helps to improve traction, possibly preventing some accidents.

Did you know that plastic bottles can be used to make a fleece jacket? The bottles are ground into fine pieces, then melted together, cut, and dyed.

Notice that all of these products help to both conserve resources and improve people's lives. Some people think that practicing the three R's of conservation takes too much time or costs too much money. But many examples show that the opposite often is true.

Plastic bottles can be recycled to make clothing and backpacks. ▼

PROBLEM AND SOLUTION What problems does using recycled materials help to solve?

Visual Summary

Minerals and ores are nonrenewable natural resources that should be conserved. Minerals include gold, silver, iron, and other metals.

Natural resources are found in different locations around the world. They are transported to areas that need them.

To conserve resources, practice the three R's: reduce, reuse, and recycle. Plastics are made from petroleum. They can be used in many different products.

 STANDARDS

6.b., 6.c.

Technology
Visit **www.eduplace.com/cascp** to find out more about nonrenewable resources.

Reading Review

1 **MAIN IDEA** What benefits and drawbacks come from shipping resources across the world?

2 **VOCABULARY** What is *recycling*? Give an example.

3 **READING SKILL** What problems do the three R's of conservation help to solve?

Problem	Solution

4 **CRITICAL THINKING: Analyze** Do you think you are using nonrenewable resources wisely in your daily life? How could you use them wisely and save time or money?

5 **INQUIRY SKILL: Collaborate** How do you think recycling could be improved in your school? Work with a partner to develop a poster, an announcement, or another plan to promote recycling.

 TEST PRACTICE

In the 1800s, the discovery of ____ sparked a mass movement of people to California.

A. gold

B. silver

C. diamonds

D. oil

 STANDARDS

1–2: 6.c., **3–4:** 6.b., **5:** 6.c., **Test Practice:** 6.b.

Landfills

People in the United States throw out 200 million tons of trash every year! Some gets recycled, while other trash is burned in furnaces and incinerators. However, most trash ends up in landfills.

A modern landfill is much more complex than an old-fashioned dump, which was merely a hole in the ground. Landfills are designed to store trash effectively and safely for long periods of time.

Unfortunately, all that trash fills up landfills quickly. Landfills take up a lot of room and cost money to maintain.

To make landfills last longer, you can practice the three R's of conservation—reduce, reuse, and recycle. This also conserves resources such as forests (the source of paper and wood) and petroleum (the source of plastics).

Trash is compacted and stored in individual blocks called cells. The cells are piled in layers, then covered in soil.

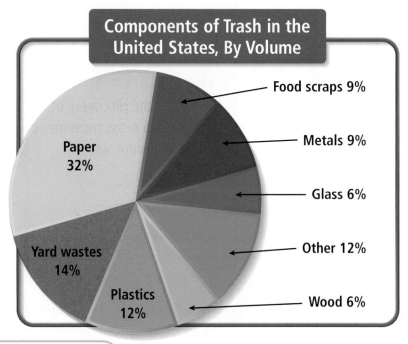

Components of Trash in the United States, By Volume

Food scraps 9%

Metals 9%

Glass 6%

Other 12%

Wood 6%

Plastics 12%

Yard wastes 14%

Paper 32%

STANDARD
6.c. *Students know* the natural origin of the materials used to make common objects.

READING **LINK**

A modern landfill is a safe, highly-organized system for processing trash. ▶

Soil

Methane is a gas that is produced as trash decomposes. Underground pipes collect the methane and vent it to the outside.

Leachate (LEE chate) is water that has seeped through the landfill. The leachate is piped into a pond, then treated.

Gravel

Clay

Sharing Ideas

1. **READING CHECK** How is a landfill different from a dump?

2. **WRITE ABOUT IT** Describe two ways that a landfill protects the environment.

3. **TALK ABOUT IT** Evaluate the amount and type of trash you produce. How could you and your classmates practice the three R's of conservation?

Soil

Bottom liners contain the landfill and protect groundwater below. Many landfills use a plastic liner sandwiched between fabric mats.

What Material Resources Are Renewable?

Building Background

Like other plants, trees can be raised as crops. Seedlings are planted, grow slowly into tall adults, then are cut down. The wood may be used for lumber, paper, and other products.

Many of Earth's resources are renewable. When managed wisely, they can be used again and again.

PREPARE TO INVESTIGATE

Inquiry Skill

Infer When you infer, you use known facts and logical reasoning to make interpretations.

Materials

- classroom objects

Science and Math Toolbox

For step 1, review **Making a Chart to Organize Data** on page H11.

STANDARDS

6.c. *Students know* the natural origin of the materials used to make common objects.
7.e. Recognize whether evidence is consistent with a proposed explanation.

What Is It Made From?

Procedure

① Collaborate Work with a partner to gather at least five different items that are available to you in the classroom. Choose at least some items that are made of more than one part, such as a pencil, a notebook, a toy, or a clock or watch.

② Record Data In your *Science Notebook*, make a chart like the one shown for each item.

③ Observe Examine each of the items. With your partner, discuss the natural resources you think were used to make that item. Research the items to confirm your ideas. Classify the natural resources as renewable (R) or nonrenewable (N).

STEP 2

Resources Used	R or N?

STEP 3

Conclusion

1. **Analyze Data** Were the items made mostly of renewable or nonrenewable materials?

2. **Infer** Aside from the resources that make up the item, what resources were used to produce the item and bring it to your classroom?

3. **Predict** When the items no longer are useful or wanted, what do you predict will happen to them?

4. **Communicate** Do you think it is important to conserve resources? Explain your answer.

Guided Inquiry

Experiment How much paper does your class throw away in one day? To **measure** the paper, select a tool such as a balance or spring scale. Discuss ways to conserve paper, then try to use less paper tomorrow.

VOCABULARY

humus	p. 434
soil	p. 434
topsoil	p. 434

READING SKILL

Main Idea Use a graphic organizer to record the important details about different types of renewable resources.

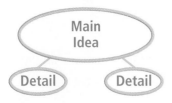

STANDARDS

6.b. Students know different natural energy and material resources, including air, soil, rocks, minerals, petroleum, fresh water, wildlife, and forests, and know how to classify them as renewable or nonrenewable.
6.c. Students know the natural origin of the materials used to make common objects.

Renewable Material Resources

MAIN IDEA Renewable resources can be used again and again. Even so, they should be conserved and used wisely.

Air

Many natural resources are renewable, meaning Earth can supply them again and again over time. The air you breathe is one very important example.

Every day, humans and other animals take in oxygen from the air and add carbon dioxide. Fortunately, green plants and algae do just the opposite. In this way, gases in the air are recycled and renewed.

However, the amount of carbon dioxide in the air has been slowly increasing over the past 100 years. Human actions are the cause. Both burning fossil fuels and cutting down rain forests have affected the carbon cycle.

Burning fuels also adds other unwanted materials to the air. When fuels burn incompletely, they can release particles of smoke or soot. These particles mix with water to form a hazy mixture called smog. Smog is not healthy to breathe, and people find it very ugly.

◀ **Cleaner Cars**
The Clean Air Act, revised in 1990, limits the pollutants from new cars. Most states, including California, require car exhaust to be tested.

Air Quality Index

	0 – 50	Good
	51 – 100	Moderate
	101 – 150	Unhealthy for sensitive groups
	151 – 200	Unhealthy
	201 – 300	Very unhealthy
	301 – 500	Hazardous

▲ Los Angeles enjoys many days with clear skies, as well as days of badly polluted air. The air quality index measures air pollution.

Many fuels also release compounds of nitrogen and sulfur when they are burned. These compounds can combine with water in the air to form acids, the cause of acid rain.

Cities and other urban areas tend to suffer the worst air pollution. The causes are factories, trucks, cars, and other devices that burn fuels.

In some cities, including Los Angeles, nearby landforms and weather patterns make air pollution worse. Typically, mountains surround such cities. As warm air moves up the mountain slopes, polluted air is "trapped" over the city. The air closer to the ground is cooler than the air above it, preventing the polluted air from rising and moving away.

Humans do not cause all air pollution. Wildfires can release huge amounts of smoke to the air. Volcanic eruptions can add tremendous amounts of soot and ash.

Air pollution can harm people's health and the health of the environment. Pollutants can become trapped in the lungs and cause many different diseases. Plants and animals can suffer, too. Acid rain can kill fish and other animals that live in lakes and rivers.

What is being done to prevent air pollution? In the United States, the government has established strict standards for cars, factories, and power plants. The Clean Air Act, revised in 1990, limits the pollutants from cars. Many states, including California, require cars to be tested regularly.

California is also encouraging new technology. Hybrid cars, which run on both gasoline and electricity, both help air quality and conserve natural resources. These cars are becoming more popular, especially as the cost of gasoline keeps rising.

 **MAIN IDEA** What is the main cause of air pollution?

431

▲ One of the largest uses of freshwater is irrigation of crops. Why is irrigation important?

Freshwater

Freshwater is another of Earth's renewable resources. Water is constantly being renewed through the water cycle.

As you know, much of Earth's surface is covered by water. However, about 97 percent of that is salt water in the ocean. Salt water cannot be used for drinking or for nourishing plants. Of the remaining 3 percent, most is locked away in glaciers.

In fact, less than 1 percent of Earth's water is freshwater that people can use. This freshwater is not spread evenly around Earth. In many places, people struggle to find a safe supply of drinking water.

People who live in dry areas often bring in water from other places. In 2000, about 34 percent of the water used in the United States was for irrigating crops.

▲ Less than 1 percent of Earth's surface water is drinkable.

◄ There are many recreational uses for Earth's freshwater.

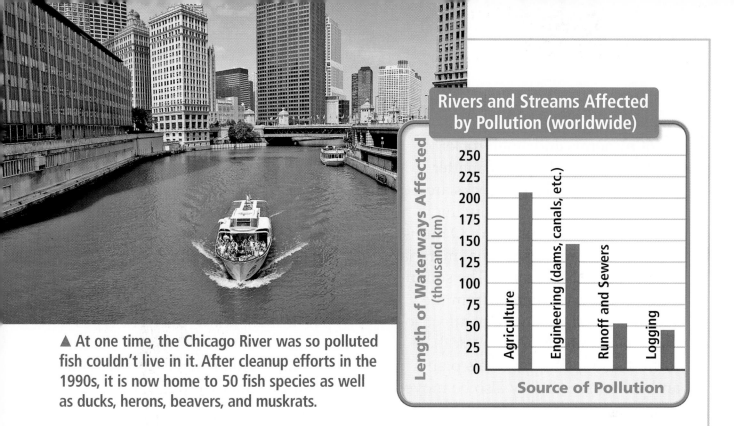

Rivers and Streams Affected by Pollution (worldwide)

Length of Waterways Affected (thousand km) vs **Source of Pollution**

- Agriculture: ~207
- Engineering (dams, canals, etc.): ~145
- Runoff and Sewers: ~53
- Logging: ~45

▲ At one time, the Chicago River was so polluted fish couldn't live in it. After cleanup efforts in the 1990s, it is now home to 50 fish species as well as ducks, herons, beavers, and muskrats.

Much of Earth's freshwater supply is found in rivers, streams, ponds, lakes, and wetlands. People use the water from these sources not only for irrigation, but also for drinking, cooking, bathing, and other everyday uses. Each person in the United States uses about 168 gallons of water every day.

Everyone must be careful to help keep Earth's freshwater clean and usable. By law, factories must not dump chemicals into bodies of water. Farmers should not let pesticides and fertilizers run off into local lakes, rivers, and streams. Landfills must be lined to keep pollutants from groundwater.

You and your family can conserve freshwater, too. Take fast showers and install showerheads that use less water. Turn off faucets while brushing teeth and rinsing dishes. Be sure to fix leaky pipes and faucets, too.

Water Sources

In a rural area, your water may come from a private well. But most communities have a system for providing water to residents. Water may be drawn from nearby lakes or rivers, pumped from groundwater, or brought in from places far away.

In the San Francisco Bay area, about 85 percent of the water comes from a watershed that includes Yosemite National Park. In the spring, snowmelt fills rivers and collects in reservoirs. This water is moved west through aqueducts.

In Southern California, the Colorado River is an important source of water. Hoover Dam on the river forms a huge reservoir behind it called Lake Mead. It supplies water for over 22 million people.

 **MAIN IDEA** Why is water conservation important?

Soil

Soil is another renewable resource. **Soil** is a natural resource made up of minerals and small rocks, water, gases, and organic matter. The minerals and small rocks are weathered bedrock. The organic matter, called **humus,** (HYOO muhs) is decayed plant and animal material.

Not all soils are alike. The soil in a desert is very different from the soil in a forest. Factors that affect soil include climate, types of rock that form the soil, and the area's plants and animals. Soil may also be moved from place to place.

Different types of soil hold water very differently. Soil made of large grains of sand has lots of air spaces. This soil is usually dry because water flows through it quickly. Clay-filled soil is denser and holds water quite well.

Soil is home to all sorts of living things. Bacteria thrive in soil. One tablespoon of soil may contain more bacteria than there are people on Earth! The bacteria help break down the organic matter in soil, recycling it for plants to use again. This also is done by fungi, algae, and protists. Earthworms and some insects aid the process.

As farmers know, different types of soil are ideal for growing different crops. California is lucky to have soils that support many crops.

Topsoil Have you ever dug a hole in the ground to plant a tree? The dark, uppermost layer of Earth's soil is called **topsoil.** Topsoil contains humus, minerals, rock fragments, bacteria and other organisms. Topsoil contains more nutrients than other layers of soil.

Three Soil Types

Sandy soil
In sandy soil, particles are medium-sized and very hard.

Clay soil
Clay soil is made up of very small, tightly-packed mineral particles.

Rocky soil
Rocky soil, or gravel, includes relatively large fragments of rock.

▲ Dust Bowl

Experts estimate that about 850 million tons of topsoil were lost in the dust storms of 1935. In part because of better soil conservation, that land is fertile again today.

Corn

Soybeans

▲ Modern Farming

These crops are different from those that were grown in the same fields a season ago. Crop rotation helps to restore nutrients to the soil.

Plants use the nutrients in topsoil in a way similar to the way your body uses vitamins and minerals. While the nutrients are not food for plants, they are necessary for healthy growth.

Topsoil is a valuable resource that needs to be protected. Poor farming practices and dry weather can change topsoil into dust. This lesson was learned in the Great Plains of the United States during the 1930s. Huge tracts of topsoil dried up and blew away in the wind, creating what was called the Dust Bowl.

As farmers learned during the Dust Bowl, topsoil must be protected from erosion by wind and water. Wind breaks help to do this. A wind break is a line of fences or trees planted along the edge of a field. They help block the wind and slow it down.

Water moving over a plowed field can also pick up soil and carry it away. In a practice called contour plowing, farmers plant crops in rows that curve with the slope of the land. This slows down the flow of water and helps prevent erosion.

What else can farmers do to manage soil successfully? One practice is to add fertilizers to the soil. Fertilizers contain nutrients that plants need. American farmers add tons of fertilizer to their crops every growing season.

Another strategy is crop rotation, the planting of different crops during different growing seasons. Each type of plant takes up different nutrients, and some plants restore certain nutrients to the soil. By rotating crops and letting fields lie unfarmed occasionally, the soil is replenished naturally.

 **MAIN IDEA** Why are nutrients important to topsoil?

Forests

Forests are very important to life on Earth, because the trees are a major source of oxygen. As you have read, plants add oxygen to the air as they perform photosynthesis.

Trees are used to make all sorts of products that you use every day. Almost every paper product you can think of came from trees. Trees also provide lumber to build homes and to make furniture. Wood from trees can be burned as a fuel.

A few hundred years ago, much of North America was covered in dense forests. Since then, much of this land has been cleared for cities, farms, and ranches. Today, only small fractions of the original forests remain.

Lumber companies often manage tree farms. Like any other crop, trees are planted, grown, and cut down when mature. Companies also harvest trees in natural forests, subject to laws and policies designed to protect the forests.

The United States has set aside land for protection from logging and other uses. In California, you can visit beautiful stands of trees in Muir Woods, Sequoia National Park, and other parks. In addition, national forests cover large areas of the northern part of the state. People often debate the amount of logging that should be allowed in such forests.

To help conserve forest land, you can use wood and paper products wisely. Learning about forests and conservation now will help you make decisions about them in the years to come.

▲ Trees are a valuable natural resource. By replacing cut-down trees, a tree farm can provide wood over and over again.

▲ At a paper mill, wood pulp is processed into long, wide sheets.

Forests and Wildlife

Tropical rain forests once covered huge areas of land in South America, Africa, and other places near the equator. Yet the forests are being cut down at an alarming rate. People are demanding the land for farms and other uses.

Why are these forests important? One reason is that they are home to more species than any place else on Earth. When the trees are cut down, the homes for these creatures are destroyed. Many species go extinct.

For an example, consider the island of Cebu in the Philippines. At one time, this island was home to 14 species of birds that lived nowhere else in the world. As the island's forests were cut down, three of those species became extinct. In each of ten other species, fewer than 100 birds are left.

The Northern Spotted Owl in California provides another example of the effects of deforestation. This owl lives in old-growth forests of redwoods and other trees in northern California and the Pacific Northwest. This owl is considered a "flagship" species, meaning its health signals the health of the whole forest. Today, only about 500 pairs of these owls remain.

Earth's forests are just one example of how humans are affecting other species. Scientists believe that up to 30 percent of the mammal, bird, and amphibian species on Earth may become extinct due to human actions.

MAIN IDEA **Why are Earth's forests important resources?**

▲ The Northern Spotted Owl is primarily found in northern California. It lives in forests with old-growth trees that have not been altered by humans.

Express Lab

Activity Card 34
Find the Renewable Resource

World Fish Catch (1950–2000)

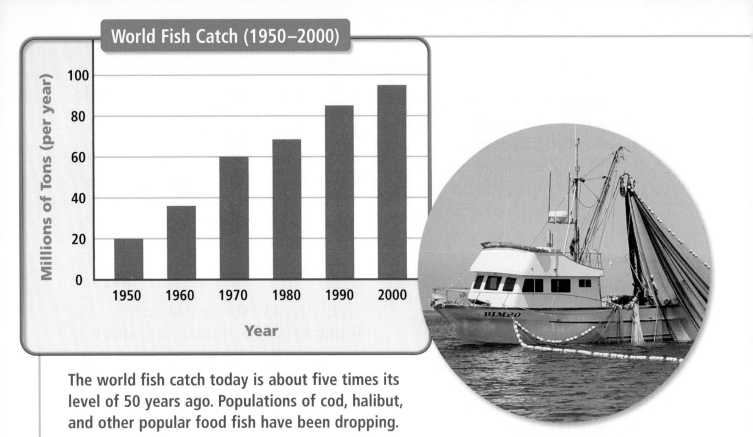

Millions of Tons (per year) vs **Year**

Year	Millions of Tons
1950	20
1960	36
1970	60
1980	68
1990	85
2000	95

The world fish catch today is about five times its level of 50 years ago. Populations of cod, halibut, and other popular food fish have been dropping.

Animals

Animals raised on farms also are renewable resources. These animals provide food, transportation, and materials such as leather and wool. Animals that live in the wild are used for food, too. Fish and other ocean animals are examples.

Sometimes, people hunt animals to the point of extinction or near extinction. In the 1820s, the Great Plains were home to more buffalo than humans. Native peoples hunted the buffalo, but not to a great extent. That changed when the Americans from the East began hunting buffalo with rifles. By 1895, only about 800 buffalo remained.

In more recent years, the humpback whale was hunted almost to extinction. These whales once thrived off the California coast, but by the 1980s were counted at a mere 88 animals. Today, these whales are protected, and their numbers are rising.

How have humans changed Earth's animals? Throughout the world, populations of native wildlife have gone down. Taking their places are cows, sheep, chickens, and a few other animals that humans breed for food and other purposes. Earth slowly is losing its great diversity of animals.

To see unusual animals today, visit a zoo or an aquarium. Years ago, a zoo's main purpose was to entertain the public. Today, zoos have a more complicated mission. They may be the last home for many animal species.

 **MAIN IDEA** How have humans changed the world's animal population?

Visual Summary

Natural resources are renewable if they can be quickly and naturally replaced. Examples of renewable resources include air, freshwater, soil, and plants and animals.

Topsoil rich in nutrients is very important for raising healthy crops. Contour plowing, crop rotation, and wind breaks help to protect topsoil from erosion.

Earth's forests, plants, and animals are important resources that should be used and managed wisely. Animals provide food, as well as products such as leather and wool.

 STANDARDS

6.b., 6.c.

Technology
Visit **www.eduplace.com/cascp** to find out more about renewable resources.

Reading Review

❶ MAIN IDEA What are three examples of renewable resources?

❷ VOCABULARY What is *humus*, and why is it important?

❸ READING SKILL: How have Americans changed the forests that once covered the continent? What have been the benefits and drawbacks of these changes?

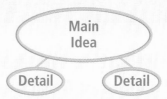

❹ CRITICAL THINKING: Analyze Choose three plants or animals that humans raise or hunt. Research and compare the different products that come from them.

❺ INQUIRY SKILL: Infer Why does having clean water often depend on keeping the land and air clean as well?

 TEST PRACTICE
Which of the following is an example of a renewable resource?

A. minerals

B. petroleum products

C. freshwater

D. air pollution

 STANDARDS

1–3: 6.b., **4:** 6.c., **5:** 6.b., **Test Practice:** 6.b.

EXTREME Science

TIRED!

What a waste! It took millions of gallons of fossil fuel and many other nonrenewable resources to make the tires in this picture. Every year, hundreds of millions of tires are thrown away. Experts estimate there are at least 1 *billion* scrap tires in the United States!

Because tires take up to 80 years to decompose, they aren't going away soon. Fortunately, recycling tires has become big business. Each year, more and more old tires are processed to produce fuel. Tires are also ground up and used to create safe, sturdy surfaces for roads, sidewalks, and playgrounds.

Tire Doctor

Dr. Jagdish Dhawan, shown here, worked with fellow chemistry professor Richard Legendre to develop a new process that recycles scrap tires into high-grade oil without any waste.

Run a rope through the billion tires in U.S. landfills today. You'll have a tire necklace long enough to circle Earth five times!

Writing Journal

Each year, about 280 million tires are discarded. If 78% of them are recycled, calculate how many are thrown in dumps.

Math in Science

The circle graph shows the uses of different sources of energy in the United States in the year 2003. The renewable sources of energy and their relative uses are listed in the table. The questions below refer to the data in the graph and table.

1. What is the ratio of oil and petroleum use to the use of renewable energy?

2. What would happen to the United States if all sources of fossil fuels ran out? Use the data to support your answer with numbers.

3. Sketch a circle graph that shows the use of renewable energy sources.

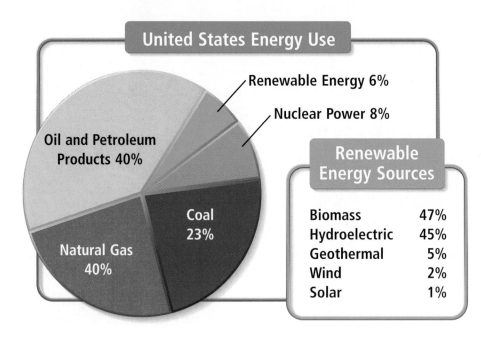

United States Energy Use

Renewable Energy 6%

Nuclear Power 8%

Oil and Petroleum Products 40%

Coal 23%

Natural Gas 40%

Renewable Energy Sources

Biomass	47%
Hydroelectric	45%
Geothermal	5%
Wind	2%
Solar	1%

Writing in Science
Persuasive

Research the debate from the 1990s over the Northern Spotted Owl. Write a report from the point of view of the loggers or the point of view of the environmentalists involved in the debate.

Michael Ableman

Over the past 100 years, much of the farmland of Southern California has been lost to growing towns and suburbs. One farm that remains is Fairview Gardens. It supplies fresh fruits and vegetables to the people of Goleta, a city that surrounds its twelve-acre plot.

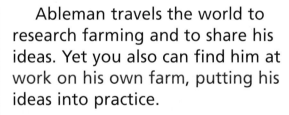

Fairview Gardens

Author and farmer Michael Ableman leads the organization that preserves and runs Fairview Gardens. He believes that small, neighborhood farms fill an important role in city life. He has shown that they can make money, too.

Ableman travels the world to research farming and to share his ideas. Yet you also can find him at work on his own farm, putting his ideas into practice.

▲ Michael Ableman and son

Vocabulary

Complete each sentence with a term from the list.

1. Something that can be used to make a product is a(n) _____.

2. A dark-colored material made from decayed plants and animals and found in soil is _____.

3. A material containing a valuable metal for which it is mined is a(n) _____.

4. A solid crystalline element or compound that occurs naturally in Earth's crust is a(n) _____.

5. The layer of soil in which plants grow is _____.

6. Making new items from used materials is _____.

7. The loose material that covers much of Earth's land is _____.

8. Gold, silver, and other metals are each an example of a(n) _____.

9. Iron _____ is a mixture of iron and other minerals.

10. Practice _____ to help conserve Earth's material resources.

humus p. 434
material resource p. 418
mineral p. 418
ore p. 419
recycling p. 422
soil p. 434
topsoil p. 434

Test Practice

Write the letter of the best answer choice.

11. About _____ of Earth's water is freshwater.

   A. 3 percent
   B. 1 percent
   C. 75 percent
   D. 97 percent

12. Using ceramic plates instead of paper plates is an example of _____.

   A. reducing paper waste
   B. reusing paper
   C. recycling paper
   D. unwise use of paper

13. Which is a common part of topsoil?

   A. fossil fuels
   B. bedrock
   C. humus
   D. oxygen

14. Wood and paper products are made from _____.

   A. fossil fuels
   B. a nonrenewable resource
   C. a renewable resource
   D. animal resources

Inquiry Skills

15. **Infer** Many oil refineries have been built along the coast of the Gulf of Mexico. Why do you think oil companies build refineries there?

16. How might people work together to reduce the amount of trash that is sent to a local landfill? Discuss positive steps that families, businesses, and communities can take.

Map the Concept

The chart shows two categories. Classify each of the natural resources listed below.

coal   oil   trees   air
water   gold   silver

Renewable Resource	Nonrenewable Resource

Critical Thinking

17. **Apply** Name three different types of natural resources that people mine from Earth. Describe uses for these resources.

18. **Synthesize** Design a plan to conserve material resources that can be used by your family. It should be practical and involve the reducing, reusing, and recycling of materials.

19. **Evaluate** How would you respond to people who say that it is not necessary to conserve natural resources, such as fossil fuels, because the supply will not run out during their lifetime?

20. **Analyze** Which natural resources are especially common in California? How do people collect them? How are they used? Research your state's resources at the library or on the Internet.

Performance Assessment

A Three-R Plan

Choose a product that you use every day. Research the different materials that are used to make the product and bring it to you. Classify these materials as renewable or nonrenewable. Discuss ways that these resources can be conserved.

Writing Journal

Review your answers to the questions at the beginning of this chapter. Change your answers as needed, based on what you have learned.

⬦ **STANDARDS**

1–13: 6.b., **14:** 6.c., **15:** 6.b., **16:** 7.d., **Map the Concept:** 6.b., **17:** 6.c., **18:** 6.b., **19:** 7.e., **20:** 6.c., **Performance Assessment:** 6.c.

Write the letter of the best answer choice.

1. Which is a renewable resource?
   A. soil
   B. coal
   C. minerals
   D. plastic

2. Which food source would benefit from contour plowing?

   A.

   B.

   C.

   D.

3. One important drawback of burning fossil fuels is _____.
   A. efficient energy
   B. air pollution
   C. solar energy
   D. filling space in landfills

4. Which is NOT a resource provided by forests?
   A. oxygen
   B. water
   C. recreational areas
   D. paper products

5. Which method of soil management is used on a sloped field?
   A. contour plowing
   B. windbreaks
   C. irrigation
   D. fertilization

6. Which energy source produces dangerous waste?

A.

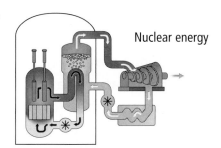

Nuclear energy

B.

Solar energy

C.

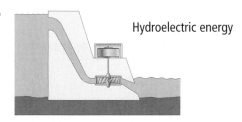

Hydroelectric energy

D.

Wind energy

7. Oxygen in the air is renewed with the help of ____.
   - **A.** people
   - **B.** plants
   - **C.** fossil fuels
   - **D.** the water cycle

8. About what percent of Earth's water is liquid freshwater?
   - **A.** 1%
   - **B.** 3%
   - **C.** 25%
   - **D.** 75%

Answer the following in complete sentences.

9. Name and describe the three Rs of conservation.

10. Describe some things people can do to increase the energy efficiency of their homes.

 STANDARDS

1–3: 6.b., **4:** 6.c., **5:** 6.b., **6:** 6.a., **7:** 5.a., **8:** 6.b., **9:** 6.b., **10:** 6.a.

You Can...

Discover More

Building a dam helps some plants and animals, but may harm others. When a dam is built, it causes flooding and creates a lake where there used to be dry land. The lake becomes a habitat for fish, birds, and other animals. It may also be a source of water that farmers can use for their crops.

The flooding caused by a dam can also have harmful effects. Water may cover land areas that were once home to a variety of plants and animals. Some plants will die, and many animals will have to find new homes.

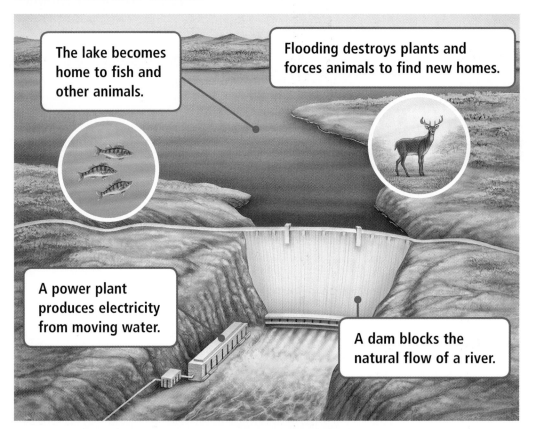

The lake becomes home to fish and other animals.

Flooding destroys plants and forces animals to find new homes.

A power plant produces electricity from moving water.

A dam blocks the natural flow of a river.

 Learn more about dams and the environment. Go to www.eduplace.com/cascp/ to run a simulation on dams.

Science and Math Toolbox

Using a Microscope H2

Making a Bar Graph H3

Using a Calculator H4

Using a Spring Scale H5

Using a Tape Measure or Ruler H6

Measuring Volume H7

Using a Thermometer H8

Using a Balance H9

Using an Equation or Formula H10

Making a Chart to Organize Data H11

Reading a Circle Graph H12

Making a Line Graph H13

Reading a Map H14

Measurements H16

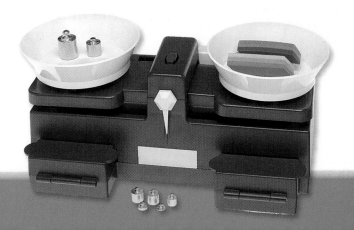

Using a Microscope

A microscope makes it possible to see very small things by magnifying them. Some microscopes have a set of lenses that magnify objects by different amounts.

Examine Some Salt Grains

Handle a microscope carefully; it can break easily. Carry it firmly with both hands and avoid touching the lenses.

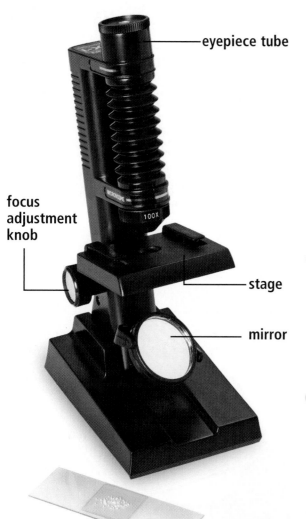

eyepiece tube

focus adjustment knob

100X

stage

mirror

microscope slide

1 Turn the mirror toward a source of light. **NEVER** use the Sun as a light source.

2 Place a few grains of salt on the slide. Put the slide on the stage of the microscope.

3 Bring the salt grains into focus. Turn the adjustment knob on the back of the microscope as you look through the eyepiece.

4 Raise the eyepiece tube to increase the magnification; lower it to decrease magnification.

Making a Bar Graph

A bar graph helps you organize and compare data. For example, you might want to make a bar graph to compare weather data for different places.

Make a Bar Graph of Annual Snowfall

For more than 20 years, the cities listed in the table have been recording their yearly snowfall. The table shows the average number of centimeters of snow that the cities receive each year. Use the data in the table to make a bar graph showing the cities' average annual snowfall.

Snowfall	
City	Snowfall (cm)
Atlanta, GA	5
Charleston, SC	1.5
Houston, TX	1
Jackson, MS	3
New Orleans, LA	0.5
Tucson, AZ	3

1. Title your graph. The title should help a reader understand what your graph describes.

2. Choose a scale and mark equal intervals. The vertical scale should include the least value and the greatest value in the set of data.

3. Label the vertical axis *Snowfall (cm)* and the horizontal axis *City*. Space the city names equally.

4. Carefully graph the data. Depending on the interval you choose, some amounts may be between two numbers.

5. Check each step of your work.

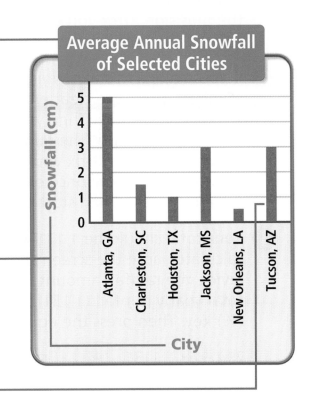

Using a Calculator

After you've made measurements, a calculator can help you analyze your data. Some calculators have a memory key that allows you to save the result of one calculation while you do another.

Add and Divide to Find Percent

The table shows the amount of rain that was collected using a rain gauge in each month of one year. You can use a calculator to help you find the total yearly rainfall. Then you can find the percent of rain that fell during January.

Rainfall	
Month	**Rain (mm)**
Jan.	214
Feb.	138
Mar.	98
Apr.	157
May	84
June	41
July	5
Aug.	23
Sept.	48
Oct.	75
Nov.	140
Dec.	108

1 Add the numbers. When you add a series of numbers, you need not press the equal sign until the last number is entered. Just press the plus sign after you enter each number (except the last).

2 If you make a mistake while you are entering numbers, press the clear entry (CE/C) key to erase your mistake. Then you can continue entering the rest of the numbers you are adding. If you can't fix your mistake, you can press the (CE/C) key once or twice until the screen shows 0. Then start over.

3 Your total should be 1,131. Now clear the calculator until the screen shows 0. Then divide the rainfall amount for January by the total yearly rainfall (1,131). Press the percent (%) key. Then press the equal sign key.

214 ÷ 1131 % =

The percent of yearly rainfall that fell in January is 18.921309, which rounds to 19%.

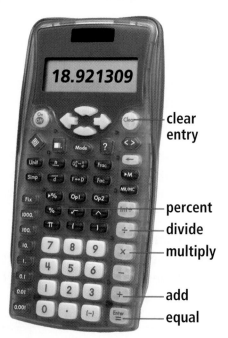

clear entry

percent
divide
multiply

add
equal

Using a Spring Scale

A spring scale is used to measure force. You can use a spring scale to find the weight of an object in newtons. You can also use the scale to measure other forces.

Measure the Weight of an Object

1 Place the object in a net bag and hang it from the hook on the bottom of the spring scale. Or, if possible, hang the object directly from the hook.

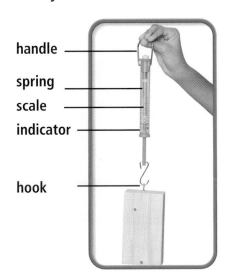

handle

spring
scale

indicator

hook

2 Slowly lift the scale by the handle at the top. Be sure the object to be weighed continues to hang from the hook.

3 Wait until the indicator inside the clear tube of the spring scale has stopped moving. Read the number next to the indicator. This number is the weight of the object in newtons.

Measure Friction

1 Hang the object from the hook at the bottom of the spring scale. Use a piece of string to connect the hook and object if needed.

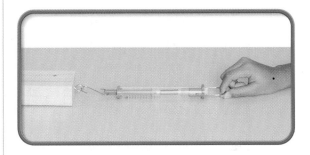

2 Gently pull the handle at the top of the scale parallel to the floor. When the object starts to move, read the number of newtons next to the indicator on the scale. This number is the force of friction between the floor and the object as you drag the object.

Using a Tape Measure or Ruler

Tape measures, metersticks, and rulers are tools for measuring length. Scientists use units such as kilometers, meters, centimeters, and millimeters when making length measurements.

Use a Meterstick

1 Work with a partner to find the height of your reach. Stand facing a chalkboard. Reach up as high as you can with one hand.

2 Have your partner use chalk to mark the chalkboard at the highest point of your reach.

3 Use a meterstick to measure your reach to the nearest centimeter. Measure from the floor to the chalk mark. Record the height.

Use a Tape Measure

1 Use a tape measure to find the circumference of, or distance around, your partner's head. Wrap the tape around your partner's head.

2 Find the line where the tape begins to wrap over itself.

3 Record the distance around your partner's head to the nearest millimeter.

Measuring Volume

A graduated cylinder, a measuring cup, and a beaker are used to measure volume. Volume is the amount of space something takes up. Most of the containers that scientists use to measure volume have a scale marked in milliliters (mL).

▲ This measuring cup has marks for every 25 mL.

▲ This beaker has marks for every 25 mL.

▲ This graduated cylinder has marks for every 1 mL.

Measure the Volume of a Liquid

1. Measure the volume of some juice. Pour the juice into a measuring container.

2. Move your head so that your eyes are level with the top of the juice. Read the scale line that is closest to the surface of the juice. If the surface of the juice is curved up on the sides, look at the lowest point of the curve.

3. Read the measurement on the scale. You can estimate the value between two lines on the scale to obtain a more accurate measurement.

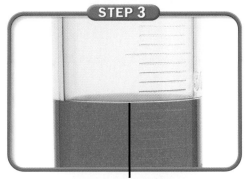

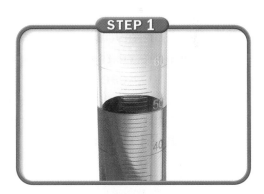

The bottom of the curve is at 50 mL.

Using a Thermometer

A thermometer is used to measure temperature. When the liquid in the tube of a thermometer gets warmer, it expands and moves farther up the tube. Different scales can be used to measure temperature, but scientists usually use the Celsius scale.

Measure the Temperature of a Liquid

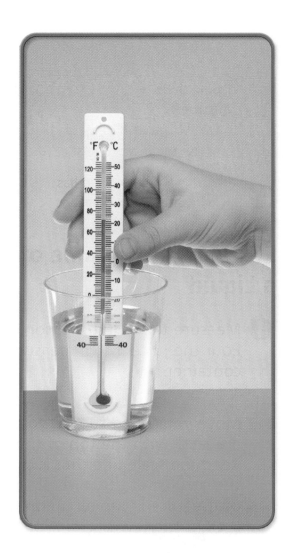

1. Half fill a cup with water or another liquid.

2. Hold the thermometer so that the bulb is in the center of the liquid. Be sure that there are no bright lights or direct sunlight shining on the bulb.

3. Wait until you see the liquid in the tube of the thermometer stop moving. Read the scale line that is closest to the top of the liquid in the tube. The thermometer shown reads 22°C (about 71°F).

Using a Balance

A balance is used to measure mass. Mass is the amount of matter in an object. To find the mass of an object, place the object in the left pan of the balance. Place standard masses in the right pan.

Measure the Mass of a Ball

1 Check that the empty pans are balanced, or level with each other. When balanced, the pointer on the base should be on the middle mark. If it needs to be adjusted, move the slider on the back of the balance a little to the left or right.

2 Place a ball in the left pan. Then add standard masses, one at a time, to the right pan. When the pointer is at the middle mark again, each pan is holding the same amount of matter, and the same mass.

3 Each standard mass is marked to show its number of grams. Add the number of grams marked on the masses in the pan. The total is the mass of the ball in grams.

Using an Equation or Formula

Equations and formulas can help you to determine measurements that are not easily made.

Use the Diameter of a Circle to Find Its Circumference

1 Find the circumference of a circle that has a diameter of 10 cm. To determine the circumference of a circle, use the formula below.

$C = \pi d$

$C = 3.14 \times 10$ cm

$C = 31.4$ cm

The circumference of this circle is 31.4 cm.

> π is the symbol for pi. Always use 3.14 as the value for π, unless another value for pi is given.

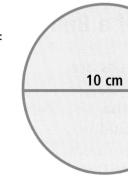

10 cm

> The circumference (C) is a measure of the distance around a circle.

> The diameter (d) of a circle is a line segment that passes through the center of the circle and connects two points on the circle.

Use Rate and Time to Determine Distance

2 Suppose an aircraft travels at 772 km/h for 2.5 hours. How many kilometers does the aircraft travel during that time? To determine distance traveled, use the distance formula below.

> d = distance
>
> r = rate, or the speed at which the aircraft is traveling.
>
> t = the length of time traveled

$d = rt$

$d = 772 \times 2.5$ km

$d = 1{,}930$ km

The aircraft travels 1,930 km in 2.5 hours.

Making a Chart to Organize Data

A chart can help you record, compare, or classify information.

Organize Properties of Elements

Suppose you collected the data shown at the right. The data presents properties of silver, gold, lead, and iron.

You could organize this information in a chart by classifying the physical properties of each element.

My Data

Silver (Ag) has a density of 10.5 g/cm^3. It melts at 961°C and boils at 2,212°C. It is used in dentistry and to make jewelry and electronic conductors.

Gold melts at 1,064°C and boils at 2,966°C. Its chemical symbol is Au. It has a density of 19.3 g/cm^3 and is used for jewelry, in coins, and in dentistry.

The melting point of lead (Pb) is 328°C. The boiling point is 1,740°C. It has a density of 11.3 g/cm^3. Some uses for lead are in storage batteries, paints, and dyes.

Iron (Fe) has a density of 7.9 g/cm^3. It will melt at 1,535°C and boil at 3,000°C. It is used for building materials, in manufacturing, and as a dietary supplement.

Create categories that describe the information you have found.

Give the chart a title that describes what is listed in it.

Make sure the information is listed accurately in each column.

Properties of Some Elements

Element	Symbol	Density g/cm^3	Melting Point (°C)	Boiling Point (°C)	Some Uses
Silver	Ag	10.5	961	2,212	jewelry, dentistry, electric conductors
Gold	Au	19.3	1,064	2,966	jewelry, dentistry, coins
Lead	Pb	11.3	328	1,740	storage batteries, paints, dyes
Iron	Fe	7.9	1,535	3,000	building materials, manufacturing, dietary supplement

Reading a Circle Graph

A circle graph shows the whole divided into parts. You can use a circle graph to compare parts to each other or to compare parts to the whole.

Read a Circle Graph of Land Area

The whole circle represents the approximate land area of all of the continents on Earth. The number on each wedge indicates the land area of each continent. From the graph you can determine that the land area of North America is 16% × 148,000,000 km², or about 24 million square kilometers.

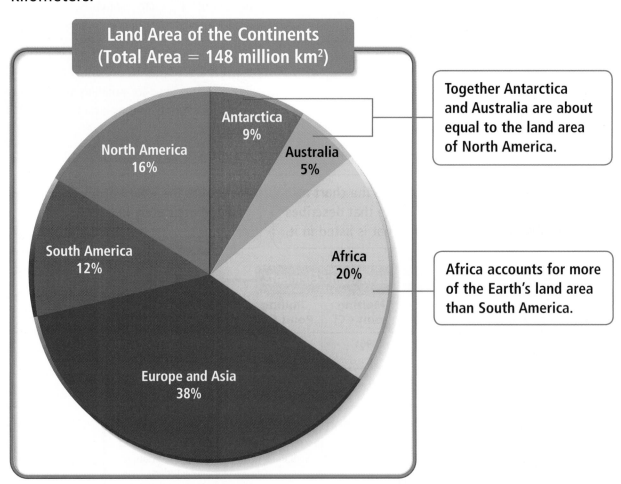

Land Area of the Continents (Total Area = 148 million km²)

Antarctica 9%

North America 16%

Australia 5%

South America 12%

Africa 20%

Europe and Asia 38%

Together Antarctica and Australia are about equal to the land area of North America.

Africa accounts for more of the Earth's land area than South America.

Making a Line Graph

A line graph is a way to show continuous change over time. You can use the information from a table to make a line graph.

Make a Line Graph of Temperatures

The table shows temperature readings over a 12-hour period at the Dallas-Fort Worth Airport in Texas. This data can also be displayed in a line graph that shows temperature change over time.

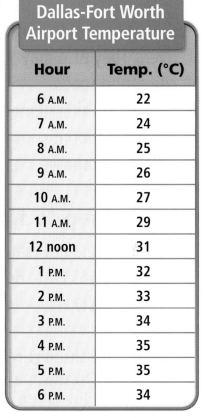

Dallas-Fort Worth Airport Temperature	
Hour	**Temp. (°C)**
6 A.M.	22
7 A.M.	24
8 A.M.	25
9 A.M.	26
10 A.M.	27
11 A.M.	29
12 noon	31
1 P.M.	32
2 P.M.	33
3 P.M.	34
4 P.M.	35
5 P.M.	35
6 P.M.	34

1. Choose a title. The title should help a reader understand what your graph describes.

2. Choose a scale and mark equal intervals. The vertical scale should include the least value and the greatest value in the set of data.

3. Label the horizontal axis *Time* and the vertical axis *Temperature* (°C).

4. Write the hours on the horizontal axis. Space the hours equally.

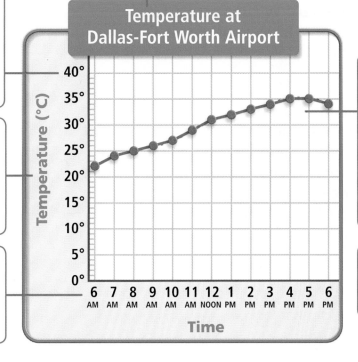

Temperature at Dallas-Fort Worth Airport

5. Carefully graph the data. Depending on the interval you choose, some temperatures will be between two numbers.

6. Check each step of your work.

Reading a Map

A map shows a section of Earth's surface. Maps may show physical features, such as coastlines, mountains, and rivers. They also may show political features, such as towns, cities, and roads.

A map's title names the place and describes the type of information it shows. Different maps are useful for different purposes.

Use a map to find location

Which body of water is farthest west: Lake Tahoe, Owens Lake, or the Salton Sea? Which is farthest east?

1. Locate these three bodies of water on the map. On this map, as on many others, the color blue is used to show water.

2. Find the closest line of longitude to each body. The line 120° W runs across Lake Tahoe. The line 118° W runs across Owens Lake. The line 116° W runs near the edge of the Salton Sea.

3. Of the three lines of longitude, the line across Lake Tahoe lies the farthest to the left of the page. As shown by the compass rose, moving left on the map means moving west. So, Lake Tahoe is the farthest west of the three bodies of water. The Salton Sea is the farthest east.

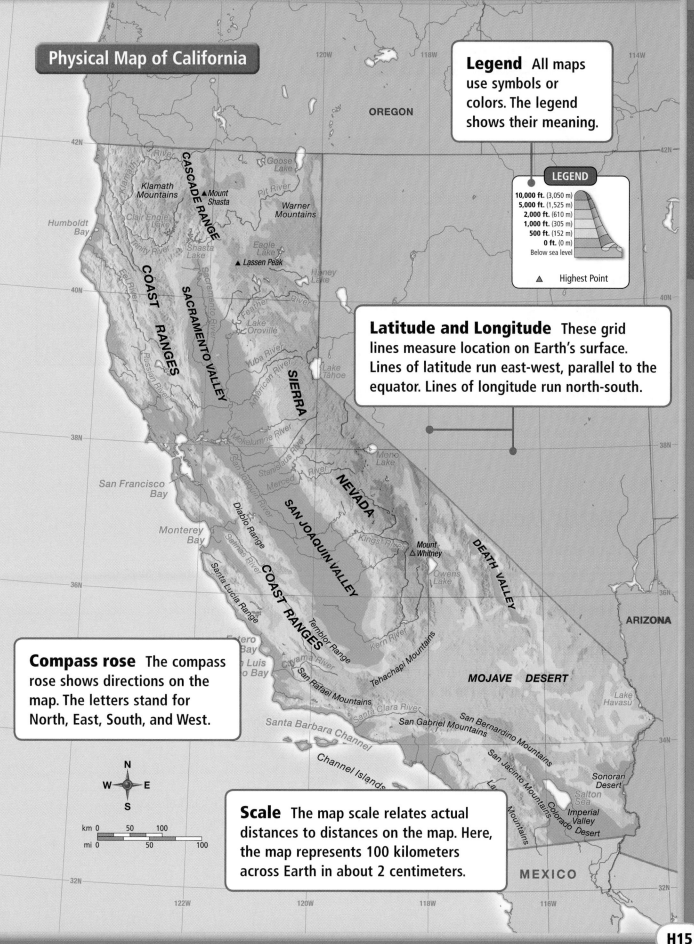

Physical Map of California

Legend All maps use symbols or colors. The legend shows their meaning.

LEGEND

10,000 ft. (3,050 m)
5,000 ft. (1,525 m)
2,000 ft. (610 m)
1,000 ft. (305 m)
500 ft. (152 m)
0 ft. (0 m)
Below sea level

△ Highest Point

Latitude and Longitude These grid lines measure location on Earth's surface. Lines of latitude run east-west, parallel to the equator. Lines of longitude run north-south.

Compass rose The compass rose shows directions on the map. The letters stand for North, East, South, and West.

Scale The map scale relates actual distances to distances on the map. Here, the map represents 100 kilometers across Earth in about 2 centimeters.

km 0   50   100
mi 0   50   100

OREGON

NEVADA

ARIZONA

MEXICO

Klamath Mountains
▲ Mount Shasta
Warner Mountains
CASCADE RANGE
Clair Engle Lake
Klamath River
Goose Lake
Pit River
Humboldt Bay
Shasta Lake
Eagle Lake
Trinity River
Honey Lake
▲ Lassen Peak
COAST RANGES
SACRAMENTO VALLEY
Eel River
Sacramento River
Lake Oroville
Feather River
Yuba River
Russian River
American River
SIERRA
Lake Tahoe
San Francisco Bay
Mokelumne River
Stanislaus River
San Joaquin River
Mono Lake
Monterey Bay
Diablo Range
Merced River
SAN JOAQUIN VALLEY
NEVADA
Kings River
Mount △ Whitney
DEATH VALLEY
Owens Lake
Salinas River
Santa Lucia Range
COAST RANGES
Temblor Range
Kern River
Estero Bay
Cuyama River
Tehachapi Mountains
MOJAVE DESERT
Lake Havasu
San Luis Obispo Bay
San Rafael Mountains
Santa Clara River
San Gabriel Mountains
San Bernardino Mountains
Santa Barbara Channel
Channel Islands
San Jacinto Mountains
Sonoran Desert
Salton Sea
Imperial Valley
Colorado Desert
Mountains

Measurements

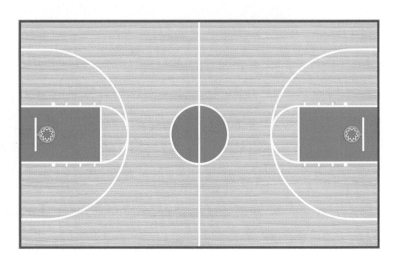

Volume

1 L of sports drink is a little more than 1 qt.

Area

A basketball court covers about 4,700 ft². It covers about 435 m².

Metric Measures

Temperature

- Ice melts at 0 degrees Celsius (°C)
- Water freezes at 0°C
- Water boils at 100°C

Length and Distance

- 1,000 meters (m) = 1 kilometer (km)
- 100 centimeters (cm) = 1 m
- 10 millimeters (mm) = 1 cm

Force

- 1 newton (N) =
  1 kilogram × 1 (meter/second) per second

Volume

- 1 cubic meter (m³) = 1 m × 1 m × 1 m
- 1 cubic centimeter (cm³) =
  1 cm × 1 cm × 1 cm
- 1 liter (L) = 1,000 milliliters (mL)
- 1 cm³ = 1 mL

Area

- 1 square kilometer (km²) = 1 km × 1 km
- 1 hectare = 10,000 m²

Mass

- 1,000 grams (g) = 1 kilogram (kg)
- 1,000 milligrams (mg) = 1 g

Temperature

The temperature at an indoor basketball game might be 27°C, which is 80°F.

Length/Distance

A basketball rim is about 10 ft high, or a little more than 3 m from the floor.

Customary Measures

Temperature

- Ice melts at 32 degrees Fahrenheit (°F)
- Water freezes at 32°F
- Water boils at 212°F

Length and Distance

- 12 inches (in.) = 1 foot (ft)
- 3 ft = 1 yard (yd)
- 5,280 ft = 1 mile (mi)

Weight

- 16 ounces (oz) = 1 pound (lb)
- 2,000 pounds = 1 ton (T)

Volume of Fluids

- 8 fluid ounces (fl oz) = 1 cup (c)
- 2 c = 1 pint (pt)
- 2 pt = 1 quart (qt)
- 4 qt = 1 gallon (gal)

Metric and Customary Rates

- km/h = kilometers per hour
- m/s = meters per second
- mph = miles per hour

Health and Fitness Handbook

As you grow, you'll be taking more responsibility for your own health. You can make choices and start habits now that will help you stay healthy for the rest of your life. In this handbook, you'll learn:

- what your respiratory and endocrine systems do and how they work;

- how to take care of others in an emergency;

- how to set goals and stay motivated to get physical activity every day;

- what Calories are and why they matter; and

- things you can do now to keep your body healthy as you grow.

You are in charge of your own health. Parents, guardians, teachers, and health care professionals can all help, but in the end the choices are up to you. Start making healthful choices today!

The Respiratory System H20
Your lungs take in oxygen and get rid of wastes.

The Endocrine System H21
Your endocrine system controls many of your body's functions.

First Aid H22
Would you know what to do if someone started to choke?

Set Fitness Goals H23
Planning physical activity can help you meet your goals.

Calories Count! H24
Knowing how much energy you need can help you choose healthful foods.

Healthy for Life H25
Starting healthful habits now can protect your health later.

The Respiratory System

The respiratory system brings oxygen into the body.
It also collects and removes carbon dioxide from the body.

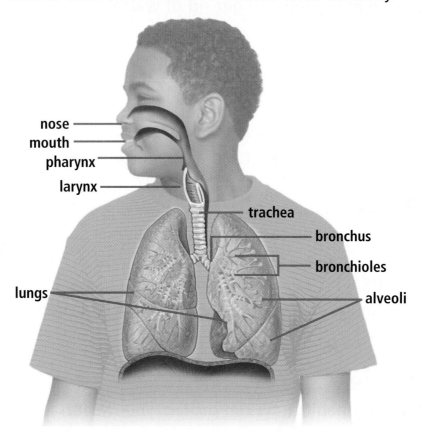

nose
mouth
pharynx
larynx
trachea
bronchus
bronchioles
lungs
alveoli

The respiratory system works automatically.
You can breathe quickly or slowly, but you can never
stop breathing on your own.

1. You breathe in air through your nose and mouth.
   The nose and mouth clean and warm the air.

2. The air moves through the pharynx, larynx,
   and trachea.

3. From the trachea, air enters the lungs through
   a tube called the bronchus. Each bronchus
   branches into smaller tubes called bronchioles.

4. The smallest bronchioles open into air sacs
   called alveoli. Oxygen passes from the alveoli
   into the blood through thin walls. Carbon
   dioxide passes into the alveoli from the blood.

5. You breathe out the carbon dioxide.

FACT

You have about
300 million alveoli!

The Endocrine System

The endocrine system is your body's messenger service. Organs called **glands** produce chemicals called **hormones**. These chemicals control body functions. Four important glands are shown below.

Thyroid Gland

The thyroid gland produces a hormone that controls how much energy your body cells produce.

Pituitary Gland

Inside your brain, your pituitary gland produces the hormones that control when and how other hormones are released. The pituitary gland also produces a hormone that controls how fast your body grows.

Pancreas

The pancreas produces insulin, a hormone that helps the body use sugar. If a person doesn't produce enough insulin, the person may develop diabetes, a disease in which a person's body cannot use sugar well.

Adrenal Glands

The adrenal glands produce a hormone called adrenalin. Adrenalin helps your body react quickly when you are surprised or threatened. It speeds up the heart rate and breathing rate.

First Aid

Do you ever baby-sit or care for a younger brother or sister? When you take care of another person, plan ahead to be sure everyone stays safe. Be sure you know:

- how to reach an adult in case of an emergency.
- where to find a flashlight and first-aid supplies.
- how to get out of the house in an emergency.
- how to perform basic first aid.

Rules for First Aid

If a person who is hurt is not breathing or has no pulse, call for help right away. In most places, you can call 9-1-1 for emergency help.

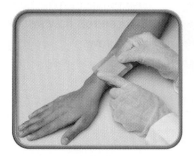

Cover a wound with a bandage.

First Aid for Bleeding If someone is bleeding, first put pressure on the wound. Wear gloves or use a cloth to protect yourself. If the bleeding is serious, raise the wound above the level of the person's heart if you can. Call for help if the bleeding will not stop.

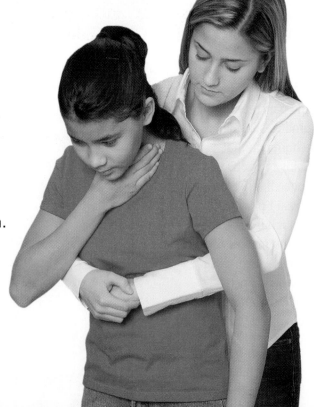

First Aid for Choking If a choking person cannot breathe, you can perform an abdominal thrust to help.

1. Wrap your arms around the person from behind.
2. Place your hands below the person's breastbone, as shown.
3. Pull quickly up and in. Repeat until the person can breathe. If the person becomes unconscious, call for help.

Set Fitness Goals

Setting physical fitness goals can help you be physically active every day and can help you maintain a healthful weight. Here are four steps that can help you set your fitness goals.

1. **Decide on fitness goals.** Think about your body. What would you like to change? Are you trying to make a school soccer team? Choose goals that make sense for you.

2. **Choose activities that you like and that are realistic.** Choose activities that are fun for you. If you like exercising in a group, try a dance class or sports team. If you like exercising alone, choose walking or biking.

   Include activities that strengthen your heart and lungs, that work your muscles, and that help your flexibility.

   Start with less strenuous activities. Move to more difficult activities as you get stronger.

3. **Plan your activity. Keep track of what you do.** Write a plan for your activity. You can use a calendar to keep track of what you do each day.

4. **Get support from others.** Sometimes it can be hard to keep going. Family and friends can help you stay motivated.

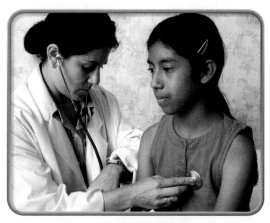

Check with your doctor before you begin any new physical activity program.

Be sure to include warm-ups and cool-downs in your activity plan.

Ask a friend to exercise with you!

Calories Count

The energy your body needs comes from food. This energy is measured in **calories.** If a person eats more calories than he or she needs, the body stores the extra energy in fat. This can lead to overweight. As a guideline, young people ages 9–13 need 2,200–2,500 calories a day. But active people and growing teens need more calories than those who are not active. Your doctor can help you decide what's right for you.

Calories in Some Common Foods

Food	Calories
Apple pie (1 slice)	405
Almonds (shelled, 1 cup)	795
Broccoli (cooked, 1 medium stalk)	50
Carrot (raw, 1 medium)	30
Cheese (cheddar, 1 slice)	70
Chicken (roasted, 1/2 breast)	140
Egg (hard-boiled, 1)	80
Fish (fried, 1 perch fillet)	185
Milk (whole, 1 cup)	150
Oatmeal (cooked, 1 cup)	145
Orange (1 medium)	60
Pork (cooked, 1 lean chop)	165
Potato (baked, 1 plain)	220

Healthy for Life

Choices you make now can help you stay healthy throughout your life. Here are some healthful habits you can start now that will help protect your health as you grow older.

- ☑ Eat a healthful diet that includes a variety of foods, and drink plenty of water. The foods give your body the nutrients it needs to work well. Water is important for just about every body function.

- ☑ Be physically active for 30 to 60 minutes every day. Physical activity reduces stress, helps you maintain a healthful weight, and keeps your muscles strong.

- ☑ Avoid using tobacco. The drugs in tobacco can harm your lungs, heart, and other body systems.

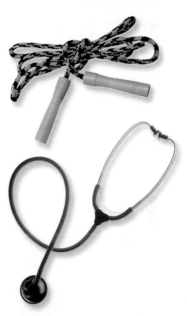

- ☑ Have regular medical and dental checkups. During checkups, doctors, nurses, and dentists check that your body is working and growing well. They can spot any problems early and suggest ways you can stay healthy.

- ☑ Always wear a seatbelt when riding in a car. Use protective gear when riding bikes, skateboards, or skates.

- ☑ Avoid risky situations.

- ☑ Find healthy ways to use your mind and express your emotions. Try new activities to keep your mind active.

- ☑ Develop strong relationships with your family and friends. These relationships can help support you when you need it.

English-Spanish Glossary

A

abiotic factor a nonliving part of an ecosystem (264)

facto abiótico parte sin vida de un ecosistema

adaptation (ad ap TAY shun) a trait or characteristic that helps an organism survive in its natural environment (270)

adaptación rasgo o característica que le sirve a un organismo para sobrevivir en su medio ambiente natural

air mass a body of air that has similar temperature and water vapor content throughout (226)

masa de aire cuerpo de aire cuya temperatura y humedad es prácticamente homogénea

air pressure the force exerted by the weight of the air pushing on all surfaces it touches (222)

presión atmosférica fuerza que ejerce el peso del aire sobre todas las superficies que toca

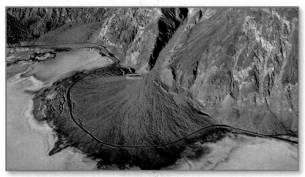

alluvial fan (ah LOO vi uhl fan) fan-shaped deposit of sediment that forms when water flows from a steep slope onto a flat plain (61)

abanico fluvial depósito de sedimento en forma de abanico que aparece cuando el agua fluye por una pendiente hacia una llanura

arch a formation caused in a narrow headland when two sea caves join (68)

arco formación que se produce en un cabo cuando dos cuevas marinas se unen

asthenosphere (as THEN uh sfir) the plastic part of the mantle beneath the lithosphere (20)

astenosfera parte flexible del manto que hay bajo la litosfera

atmosphere the blanket of air that surrounds Earth (187)

atmósfera capa de aire y otros gases que rodea la Tierra

B

barrier island a sandbar that runs parallel to the shore (69)

arrecife barrera de arena que corre paralela a la costa

beach sand or other loose sediment that has been deposited along a shoreline (69)

playa arena u otro sedimento suelto que se ha depositado a lo largo de la costa

biodiversity (BY oh dih VUR sih tee) the variety of species that live in an ecosystem (355)

biodiversidad variedad de especies que vive en un ecosistema

biomass once-living matter (402)

biomasa lo que fue antiguamente materia viva

biome (BY ome) a large group of ecosystems that have similar characteristics (270)

bioma un gran grupo de ecosistemas que tienen características similares

biosphere (BY uhs feer) the narrow zone near Earth's surface where life is able to exist (264)

biosfera zona estrecha cerca de la superficie de la Tierra y en la cual puede existir vida

biotic factor a living part of an ecosystem (264)

factor biótico parte viva de un ecosistema

C

carnivore an animal that only eats the meat of other animals (312)

carnívoro animal que se alimenta sólo de la carne de otros animales

cinder cone a volcano with slopes made mostly of rock and ash (162)

cono volcánico montaña cuyas laderas están formadas en su mayor parte por roca y ceniza volcánica

cliff steep rock feature (68)

acantilado roca muy escarpada

climate the average weather conditions in an area over a long period of time (236)

clima condiciones meteorológicas habituales en una determinada zona

climax community a mature and stable ecosystem (348)

comunidad estable ecosistema maduro que se mantiene estable

commensalism (kuh MEHN suh lihz uhm) a relationship between two species, in which one benefits while the other species is neither harmed nor helped (319)

comensalismo relación entre dos especies, en que una se beneficia y la otra no se ve beneficiada ni perjudicada

community the group of living things found in an ecosystem (265)

comunidad grupo de seres vivos que se hallan en un ecosistema

competition the struggle among living things to use the same resources in an ecosystem (337)

competencia lucha entre seres vivos por usar los mismos recursos de un ecosistema

composite volcano a volcano composed of alternating layers of lava and ash (162)

volcán compuesto volcán compuesto de capas alternas de lava y ceniza

condensation the change in a substance from a gas to a liquid state (225)

condensación cuando una sustancia cambia de gas a líquido

conduction the transfer of thermal energy by particle collision (205)

conducción transferencia de energía térmica mediante el choque de partículas

conservation the efficient use of resources (388)

conservación uso eficaz de los recursos

consumer An organism that eats, or consumes, other organisms (300)

consumidor organismo que come o consume otros organismos

contour lines lines on a topographic map that connect points with the same elevation (30)

curvas de nivel líneas sobre un mapa topográfico que conectan puntos que tienen la misma elevación

convection (kahn VEHK shuhn) the transfer of thermal energy by the mass movement of particles in a liquid or gas (110, 205)

convección transferencia de energía térmica mediante el movimiento de masa de las partículas que hay en un líquido o gas

convection current a current caused by convection that drives fluid through a circular path (110, 205)

corriente de convección corriente causada por la convección que impulsa los fluidos a través de un recorrido circular

core the innermost layer of the Earth, which extends to the center of Earth (20)

núcleo capa interna de la Tierra, que llega hasta el centro de ésta

Coriolis effect an effect that causes global winds to curve clockwise in the Northern Hemisphere, and counterclockwise in the Southern Hemisphere (234)

efecto de Coriolis efecto que hace que los vientos globales se curven en el sentido de las agujas del reloj en el hemisferio norte y en dirección contraria en el hemisferio sur

crust the outermost layer of the Earth (9)

corteza capa más externa de la Tierra

D

decomposer an organism that lives by breaking apart dead organic matter into simpler parts (302)

desintegrador organismo que vive de descomponer en partes menos complejas la materia orgánica muerta

delta a triangle-shaped plain that forms where a river enters the ocean (61)

delta llanura baja de forma triangular que se forma cuando un río llega al océano

deposition the process of dropping sediments (60)

sedimentación proceso por el cual se depositan sedimentos

density the amount of mass per unit volume of a substance (205)

densidad cantidad de masa por unidad de volumen de una sustancia

desert a very dry biome, characterized by sandy or rocky soil and little or no vegetation (272)

desierto bioma muy seco, generalmente de suelo arenoso o rocoso y sin vegetación

dew point the temperature at which the air is saturated with water vapor (225)

punto de condensación temperatura en la que el aire se satura con vapor de agua

disease a condition that prevents an organism from functioning properly (339)

enfermedad afección que impide que un organismo funcione correctamente

dome mountain a dome-shaped mound that forms when magma rises toward the surface but doesn't break through Earth's crust (136)

montaña volcánica monte con forma de cúpula que se forma cuando el magma alcanza la superficie de la Tierra pero no rompe la corteza

E

ecosystem all the living and nonliving things that interact in one place (264)

ecosistema todos los seres vivos y las cosas sin vida que interactúan en un lugar

efficiency the amount of work a machine does compared to the amount of energy put into the machine (379)

eficiencia cantidad de trabajo que hace una máquina en comparación con la cantidad de energía que necesita

electromagnetic radiation energy transferred by waves that can travel through empty space (186)

radiación electromagnética energía transferida por ondas que puede viajar a través del espacio

electromagnetic spectrum a continuous band that includes all types of electromagnetic radiation (186)

espectro electromagnético banda continua que incluye todos los tipos de radiación electromagnética

elevation height above sea level (30)

elevación altura sobre el nivel del mar

endangered species a species that is close to becoming extinct (340)

especie en peligro especie que está cerca de extinguirse

energy the ability to do work (376)

energía capacidad de trabajar

energy pyramid a pyramid that shows the availability of energy at each trophic level in an ecosystem (303)

pirámide energética pirámide que muestra la disponibilidad de energía en cada nivel trófico de un ecosistema

epicenter the point on the surface directly above the focus of an earthquake (150)

epicentro punto que en la superficie está directamente sobre el foco de un terremoto

erosion the carrying away of sediments (50)

erosión desplazamiento de sedimentos

evaporation (ih vap uh RAY shuhn) a process that changes a liquid into a gas (225)

evaporación proceso en el que un líquido cambia a gas

extinction the complete disappearance of a species (340)

extinción desaparición total de una especie

fault a crack in Earth's crust along which movement takes place (101)

falla grieta en la corteza terrestre a lo largo de la cual hay movimiento

fault-block mountain a mountain that forms from a block of crust that is pushed upward or downward along a fault (135)

montaña entre fallas montaña que se forma por un bloque de corteza que es empujado verticalmente a lo largo de una falla

focus the point underground where an earthquake begins (150)

foco punto bajo tierra donde comienza un terremoto

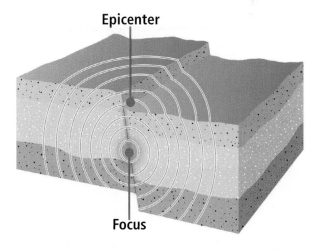

Epicenter

Focus

fold mountain a mountain that forms where continental plates collide, causing the crust to fold and crumble (134)

montaña plegada montaña que se forma donde colisionan las placas continentales, haciendo que la corteza se doble y se derrumbe

food web overlapping food chains in an ecosystem (301)

red alimenticia cadenas alimenticias que se superponen en un ecosistema

fossil the preserved remains or traces of an organism that lived in the distant past (90)

fósil restos o huellas que se conservan de un organismo que vivió en el pasado lejano

fossil fuels energy resources formed from the remains of plants and animals that lived more than 100 million years ago (384)

combustibles fósiles recursos energéticos que se forman con los restos de animales que vivieron hace más de 100 millones de años

front the boundary between two air masses with different temperature and moisture characteristics (227)

frente límite entre dos masas de aire que tienen diferentes temperaturas y niveles de humedad

geothermal energy thermal energy from Earth's interior (401)

energía geotérmica energía térmica del interior de la Tierra

grassland a boime characterized by grasses and grass-like vegetation (272)

pastizal bioma caracterizado por hierbas y pastos

greenhouse effect the trapping of heat by certain gases in Earth's atmosphere (198)

efecto invernadero acumulación de calor debida a ciertos gases en la atmósfera terrestre

headland narrow section of land that juts out into the ocean (68)

cabo parte estrecha de tierra que penetra en el océano

heat an amount of thermal energy transferred from a hotter object or regions to a colder object or region (204)

calor cantidad de energía térmica transferida de un objeto o región más caliente a un objeto o región más frío

herbivore (HUR buh vawr) an animal that eats only plants (312)

herbívoro animal que se alimenta sólo de plantas

hot spot an area of the crust above a rising plume of magma, where volcanic material can erupt through a plate, creating volcanic mountains (136)

punto caliente zona de la corteza situada sobre una columna de magma, donde es posible que el material volcánico salga a través de una placa, creando una montaña volcánica

humidity amount of water vapor in the atmosphere at a given time and place (225)

humedad cantidad de vapor de agua que hay en la atmósfera en un momento y lugar determinados

humus (HYOO muhs) decayed plant and animal material found in soil (434)

humus animales y plantas descompuestos que se hallan en el suelo

hydroelectric energy electric energy generated from moving water (399)

energía hidroeléctrica energía eléctrica generada por el agua en movimiento

intensity a measure of the amount of ground shaking an earthquake produces (151)

intensidad medida de la cantidad de temblores de tierra producidos por un terremoto

invasive species plants or animals that are not native to an ecosystem (339)

especie invasiva planta o animal que no son nativos de un ecosistema

island arc a string of volcanic islands that form where one oceanic plate sinks beneath another (161)

arco de islas conjunto de islas volcánicas que se forman cuando una placa oceánica se hunde debajo de otra

isobar (EYE suh bahr) a line drawn on a map to connect points of equal air pressure (223)

isobara línea dibujada en un mapa para conectar puntos que tienen la misma presión atmosférica

jet stream a narrow belt of high-speed winds in the upper troposphere (235)

corrientes de agua cinturón estrecho de vientos de alta velocidad que hay en la parte superior de la troposfera

land breeze a cool wind blowing near the surface from land toward sea (207)

brisa terral viento frío que sopla cerca de la superficie y va desde la tierra hacia el mar

lava magma that flows onto Earth's surface from a volcano (160)

lava magma que sale de un volcán a la superficie de la Tierra

limiting factor something that restricts the growth and distribution of a population (336)

factor limitante algo que restringe el crecimiento y la distribución de una población

lithosphere (LITH oh sfir) the rigid shell formed by the upper mantle and the crust (20)

litosfera la capa rígida formada por el manto y la corteza

magma hot melted rock below Earth's surface (102, 160)

magma roca fundida caliente que hay bajo la superficie de la Tierra

magnitude a measure of the amount of energy that an earthquake releases (151)

magnitud cantidad de energía que libera un terremoto

mantle the solid layer just below Earth's crust (20)

manto capa sólida que hay justo debajo de la corteza terrestre

material resource things from Earth that can be used to make new products (418)

recursos materiales cosas de la Tierra que pueden usarse para fabricar productos nuevos

meander (me AN duhr) a bend in a river formed when the river moves across wide, flat regions (60)

meandros curvatura de un río que se forma cuando este se mueve por superficies anchas y llanas

mineral a solid crystalline chemical element or compound that occurs naturally in Earth's crust (418)

mineral elemento o compuesto químico sólido cristalino que se da de forma natural en la naturaleza

Fluorite

Gypsum

Quartz

mutualism (MYOO choo uh lihz uhm) a close relationship in which both species benefit (319)

mutualismo relación de la que dos especies salen beneficiadas

natural resource a material found in nature that people use, such as soil, air, water, and fossil fuels (388)

recurso natural material que se encuentra en la naturaleza y que la gente usa, como el suelo, el aire, el agua y los combustibles fósiles

niche a species' relationships with the biotic and abiotic factors of its ecosystem (310)

nicho relación de una especie con los factores bióticos y abióticos de su ecosistema

nitrogen fixation the process of changing nitrogen gas into usable nitrogen compounds (284)

fijación del nitrógeno proceso que transforma el gas nitrógeno en compuestos útiles de nitrógeno

nonrenewable resource a resource that cannot be replaced quickly or easily, such as fossil fuels (386)

recurso no renovable recurso que no se puede remplazar rápida o fácilmente, como los combustibles fósiles

nuclear fission a process in which nuclei of uranium or similar elements are split apart, releasing vast amounts of energy (400)

fisión nuclear proceso en el cual los núcleos del uranio y otros elementos similares se separan y liberan grandes cantidades de energía

ocean current a continuous, moving stream of ocean water (236)

corriente oceánica corriente de agua marina que está en movimiento continuo

omnivore (AHM nuh vawr) an animal that eats both plants and other animals (312)

omnívoro animal que se alimenta de plantas y de otros animales

ore a rock that contains enough of a useful mineral to make it valuable (418)

mena roca que contiene suficiente mineral metalífero para que sea útil

parasitism a relationship between two species, in which one species benefits while the other species is harmed (320)

parasitismo relación entre dos especies, en la que una se beneficia mientras que la otra sale perjudicada

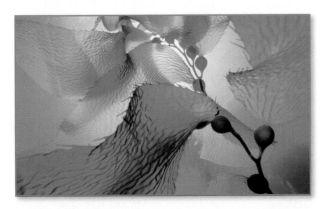

photosynthesis a process during which plants use energy from the Sun to change carbon dioxide and water into glucose and oxygen (280)

fotosíntesis proceso durante el cual las plantas usan energía del Sol para transformar el dióxido de carbono y el agua en glucosa y oxígeno

pioneer species one of the first species to colonize new or disturbed land (347)

especie pionera una de las primeras especies en colonizar tierras nuevas o conocidas

plate boundary the edge of a tectonic plate (104)

límite de la placa borde de una placa tectónica

pollution the addition of harmful substances to the environment (354)

contaminación liberación de sustancias perjudiciales en el medio ambiente

population all the members of the same type of organism that live in an ecosystem (266)

población todos los miembros del mismo tipo de organismo que viven en un ecosistema

precipitation any form of water, including the rain, snow, sleet, and hail, that falls from clouds to Earth's surface (225)

precipitación cualquier forma del agua, lluvia, nieve, granizo y aguanieve, que caen desde las nubes hasta la superficie de la Tierra

predator an animal that hunts and eats other animals (310)

depredador animal que caza y se alimenta de otros animales

predation when one organism—the predator—catches and feeds on another organism—the prey (338)

conducta predatoria cuando un organismo, el depredador, caza y se alimenta de otro organismo, la presa

prey an animal that is hunted and eaten by a predator (310)

presa animal al que un depredador caza y del cual se alimenta

primary succession the establishment of plant and animal communities in a place where organisms did not live before (347)

sucesión primaria establecimiento de comunidades animales o vegetales en lugares donde anteriormente no vivían organismos

producer an organism that makes its own food (300)

productor organismo que produce su propia comida

R

recycling recovering a resource from one item and using that resource to make another item (422)

reciclar recuperar un recurso utilizando un objeto viejo para fabricar un objeto nuevo

renewable resource a resource, such as the Sun, wind, and moving water, that can be used day after day without running out. (396)

recurso renovable un recurso como el sol, el viento y el agua en movimiento que se puede usar día tras día sin que se agote

respiration the process in which organisms obtain the energy stored in glucose by causing it to react with oxygen (281)

respiración proceso mediante el cual los organismos obtienen energía almacenada en la glucosa, haciéndola reaccionar con el oxígeno

revolution a complete orbit around an object, such the Sun (12)

revolución órbita completa alrededor de un objeto, por ejemplo, el Sol

rotation a complete turn about an axis (11)

rotación vuelta completa alrededor de un eje

S

sandbar a ridge of sand below the water's surface (69)

banco de arena cresta de arena bajo la superficie del agua

scavenger an animal that eats the meat of dead animals (302)

carroñero animal que se alimenta de la carne de animales muertos

sea breeze the cool air that blows along the surface from the water toward land (207)

brisa de mar aire frío que sopla sobre la superficie del mar y se dirige a tierra

sea cave a hole in a headland formed when weaker rock is worn away more quickly than stronger rock (68)

cueva marina agujero que se forma en un cabo cuando las rocas débiles se desgastan antes que las fuertes

sea-floor spreading a process in which magma wells up and fills the space between spreading tectonic plates (102)

relleno del lecho marino proceso mediante el cual el magma sube y rellena el espacio entre las placas tectónicas

sea stack offshore column of rock created by wave erosion (68)

islote columna de roca cerca de la costa creada por erosión producida por las olas

secondary succession the process in which a new community replaces an old one after a disturbance (348)

sucesión secundaria proceso mediante el cual una comunidad nueva remplaza a otra antigua después de una alteración

sediment small rock pieces produced by weathering (48)

sedimento trozos pequeños de roca producidos por desgaste

seismic wave (SYZ mihk wayv) a wave that carries energy released by an earthquake that travels in all directions, including up to the surface (144)

onda sísmica onda que carga energía liberada por un terremoto, y que viaja en todas direcciones, incluso hacia la superficie

seismograph a tool for recording seismic waves (146)

sismógrafo instrumento que registra las ondas sísmicas

shield volcano a volcano that has a gentle slope and is made almost entirely of layers of lava (162)

volcán con apariencia de escudo volcán que tiene una pendiente suave formada casi por entero de capas de lava

soil a natural resource made up of minerals and small rocks, water, gases, and organic matter (434)

tierra recurso natural compuesto de minerales y trozos de roca, agua, gases y materia orgánica

solar energy energy from the Sun (376)

enegía solar energía del Sol

spit sandbar that rises above the water level and has one end attached to land (69)

punta banco de arena que surge del mar y uno de sus extremos está unido a la costa

strata horizontal layers of rock (89)

estratos capas horizontales de roca

subduction a geologic process in which one tectonic plate sinks beneath another (117)

sustracción proceso geológico en el que una placa tectónica se hunde bajo otra

symbiosis (sihm bee OH sis) a close living relationship between two species (318)

simbiosis estrecha relación entre dos especies que viven juntas

taiga a forest biome characterized by long, severe winters and short, cool summers (273)

taiga bioma forestal caracterizado por inviernos largos y duros y veranos cortos y frescos

tectonic plate a giant slab of lithosphere that floats on Earth's mantle (100)

placa tectónica bloque gigantesco de litosfera que flota sobre el manto

temperate forest a forest biome that experiences four distinct seasons: summer, fall, winter, and spring (271)

bosque templado bioma forestal que tiene cuatro estaciones distintas: verano, otoño, invierno y primavera

temperature the average motion energy of particles in matter, a measure of hot or cold (204)

temperatura promedio de la energía cinética de las partículas de la materia; medida de frío o calor

thermal energy the total amount of motion energy from particles in matter (204)

energía térmica cantidad total de energía de las partículas en movimiento de la materia

threatened species a species that is close to becoming endangered (340)

especie amenazada especie que está cercana a la extinción

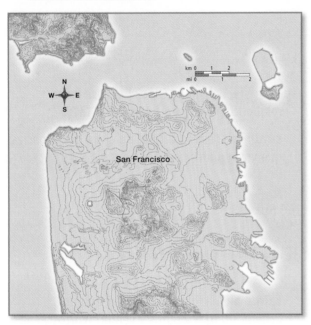

San Francisco

topographic map a map that shows the shape of surface features and their elevations (30)

mapa topográfico mapa que muestra la configuración de la superficie de un terreno y sus elevaciones

topsoil the dark uppermost layer of Earth's soil (434)

capa superficial la primera capa oscura de la Tierra

transpiration the process through which water evaporates from plant leaves (286)

transpiración proceso mediante el cual el agua se evapora de las hojas de las plantas

tributary a river or a stream feeding into a major river (58)

tributario río o corriente que desemboca en un río mayor

trophic level a step in the movement of energy through an ecosystem (300)

nivel trófico fase del movimiento de energía a través de un ecosistema

tropical rain forest a forested biome, teeming with life, characterized by rainy, hot weather (271)

selva tropical bioma forestal lleno de vida, caracterizado por un clima cálido y lluvioso

tsunami (su NOM ee) a huge sea wave produced by an earthquake, landslide, or volcanic eruption on the ocean floor (154)

maremoto gran ola marina producida por un terremoto, corrimiento de tierra o erupción volcánica en el suelo del océano

tundra Earth's coldest biome, with mostly frozen ground (273)

tundra el bioma más frío de la Tierra, cuyo suelo está en su mayoría congelado

volcano an opening in Earth's crust through which melted rock, hot gases, rock fragments, and ash reach the surface (160)

volcán abertura en la corteza terrestre a través de la cual salen a la superficie rocas fundidas, gases calientes, fragmentos de roca y cenizas

wave a disturbance that transfers energy from one location to another (184)

onda perturbación que transfiere energía de un lugar a otro

weathering the process by which rock material is broken into smaller pieces (48)

erosión el proceso por el cual el material rocoso se rompe en pedazos más pequeños

A

Abiotic factors, 264, 310
Acid rain, 388
Adaptation, 270
Adirondack Mountains, 136
African Plate, 112
Aftershocks, 146
Agriculture
    energy pyramids and, 304
    impact on ecosystems, 353
    protecting topsoil in, 435
Air, as a resource 430–431
Air masses, 218, 226
Air pollution, 354, 386–387, 402, 431
Air pressure, 222, 223
    measuring, 228
Air quality index, 431
Aleutian Islands, 118, 161
Alluvial fan, 45, 61
Alternative fuels, 403
Aluminum, 419, 421
Amazon rain forest, 357
Andes Mountains, 118, 136
Animals, 438
Annapolis Tidal Generating Station, 399
Appalachian Mountains, 29, 88
Aqueducts, 433
Arches, 68, 69
Arctic Circle, 226
Argon in atmosphere, 222
Asthenosphere, 20, 110
Atlantic Coastal Plain, 29
Atlantic Ocean, 29
Atmosphere
    of Earth, 9, 187, 188
    of Mars, 199
    of Venus, 199
Auroras, 22
Avalanches, 52
Axis of Earth, 11

B

Bacteria, 282, 284, 302, 347, 434
Balance, using, H9
Bar graphs, H3

Barometer, 228
Barometric pressure, 228
Barrier island, 69
Basalt, 20, 108
Basaltic rocks, 108, 109
Bauxite, 419
Beaches, 29, 68–72
    pollution of, 72
Bedrock, 59
Big Sur, California, 42
Biodiversity, 355
Biodiversity hotspots, 357
Biomagnification, 314
Biomass, 402
Biomes, 270–274
Biosphere, 264–266
    cycles in, 280–286
Biotic factors, 264, 310
Black Death, 339
Black Hills, 136, 137
Black sand, 70
Body waves, 144
Bridger, Jim, 18
Bryce Canyon, Utah, 50

C

Calcite, 49
Calculator, using, H4
California
    climate zones in, 242
    major earthquakes in, 151
    mountains in, 138
    renewable energy in, 404
    temperatures in, 208
    volcanoes in, 165
California Coastal Commission, 72
California condor, 340
California Energy Commission, 404
California Standards, 5, 45, 85, 131, 181, 219, 261, 297, 333, 373, 415
Calories, H24
Canyons, 29
Captive breeding programs, 340
Carbon, 282
Carbon cycle, 282

Carbon dioxide, 199, 200, 282, 283
    in atmosphere, 222, 430
Carboniferous period, 384
Careers in Science
    Architect, 213
    Building contractor, 125
    Cartographer, 39
    HVAC technician, 409
    Paleontologist, 125
    Petrochemical engineer, 409
    Ship's captain, 213
    Travel agent, 39
    Wetlands ecologist, 363
    Zookeeper, 363
Carnivores, 297, 312–313
Carrying capacity, 337
Carson, Rachel, 314
Cascade Range, 138, 161, 165
Catskill Mountains, 137
Caverns, 49
Caves, 52
    formation of, 49
Central Valley, 59, 243
Chalcopyrite, 419
Chart, making, to organize data, H11
Chemical energy, 376, 377, 386
Chemical weathering, 49, 52
Chinese snakehead, 339
Chlorofluorocarbons (CFCs), 14
Cinder cone volcanoes, 130, 162, 163
Circle graph, H12
Clay soil, 434
Clean Air Act (1990), 430, 431
Clear-cutting, 353
Cliffs, 68
Climate, 13, 236, 384
    biomes and, 270
Climax community, 348
Clouds, 225, 286
Coal, 384, 387, 404
    formation of, 385
Coastal plains, 29
Coast Ranges, 138
Cold front, 227
Colorado Desert, 358
Colorado River, 433

Commensalism, 319
Community, 265
Competition, 318, 337
Composite volcanoes, 162, 163
Composting, 402
Condensation, 218, 225, 286
Conduction, 205
Conservation, 356–357
    of energy, 378
    of fossil fuels, 388
    of nonrenewable material resources, 423
Continental Arctic air masses, 226
Continental-continental boundaries, 118
Continental crust, 108, 109
Continental drift, 91, 92
Continental polar air masses, 226
Continental tropical air masses, 226
Continents, 108
Contour lines, 4, 30
Contour plowing, 435
Convection, 110, 180, 205
    in nature, 206
Convection currents, 110, 205, 206, 207, 237
Convergent boundaries, 117, 118, 143, 161
Copper, 418, 419
Copper ore, 419
Core, 20, 21
Coriolis effect, 234, 236
Crop rotation, 435
Crust, 9, 20, 21, 48
Cysts, 321

Dams, 399, 448
Data, making chart to organize, H11
Day, 11
DDT, 314
Death Valley, California, 2, 61, 82, 135
Decision making, S22–23
Decomposers, 302, 303, 312
Deep-water currents, 237

Deer tick, 321
Deforestation, 437
Deltas, 61
Density, 205
Deposition, 60
Desert(s), 261, 272, 337
Desert ecosystems, 266, 358
Dew point, 225
Directed Inquiry
    Bag It!, 279
    Be a Time Traveler!, 87
    Circling Around!, 203
    Disaster Recovery, 345
    Discovering Dew Point, 221
    Game of Numbers, 335
    Graph Your Climate!, 241
    Heating a Home, 395
    Hide and Seek!, 317
    Identify Your Food, 299
    Light and Dark, 183
    Lighten Up!, 193
    Locating an Earthquake, 149
    A Look at Life, 263
    Make a Mountain, 133
    Make a Sundial, 7
    Make Waves!, 141
    Mantle Motion, 107
    Model a Map, 27
    A Model Earth, 17
    Model Pangaea!, 99
    Picking a Pattern, 115
    Recycling!, 417
    Rock Weathering, 47
    Role Playing, 309
    Set Up a Stream Slope, 57
    Spin It!, 233
    Swing Time, 375
    3. . . 2 . . . 1. . . Oil Game Over?, 383
    Tracking Water Pollution, 351
    Volcano Model, 159
    What Is It Made From?, 429
    Where Do They Live?, 269
    A World in a Grain of Sand, 67
Diseases, 339, 353
Divergent boundaries, 117, 118–119, 120, 136
Dodo, 340
Doldrums, 235

Dome mountains, 136
Droughts, 226
Dust Bowl, 435
Dutch elm disease, 339

Earth
    atmosphere of, 9, 187, 188
    average surface temperature on, 200
    axis of, 11
    climates on, 13
    comparison with Moon, 197
    crust of, 9
    energy balance of, 196–197
    evidence of change in, 88
    facts on, 9
    future of, 14
    gravity of, 9
    heating, 194–200
    history of, 88–92
    interior of, 19
    land features of, 29
    layers of, 20–21
    magnetic field of, 22, 103
    range of temperatures on, 8
    revolution of, 12
    rotation of, 11, 195
    as special planet, 8–9
    structure of, 18–19
    tectonic plates of, 104
    water on, 8, 28
Earthquakes, 100, 101, 104, 119, 142–146
    effects of, 152
    epicenter of, 150
    focus of, 150
    intensity of, 151
    locating, 150–154
    magnitude of, 151
    major California, 151
    measuring, 151
    preparing for, 153
Ecology, 265
Ecosystem(s), 264, 265, 300, 301, 312
    desert, 266
    human impact on, 352–358
    ocean, 266
    species in, 310–314

Ecosystem balance, 337
Electrical energy, 379
Electricity, 377, 379, 386
Electromagnetic radiation, 186
Electromagnetic spectrum, 186
Electromagnetic waves, 186, 205
Elements, radioactive, 19
Elevation, 5, 30, 246
   air pressure and, 222
El Niño, 238
Endangered species, 340, 356
Endangered Species Act (1973), 340
Endocrine system, H21
Energy, 376–380
   chemical, 376, 377, 386
   conservation of, 378
   demand for, 380
   electrical, 379
   food, 300–304
   geothermal, 373, 401
   hydroelectric, 373, 380, 399, 404
   mechanical, 376, 377, 378
   nuclear, 400
   renewable, 396–404
   solar, 184–188, 194–195, 207, 372, 376, 377, 397
   thermal, 194, 196, 204–206, 377, 378, 380, 386
   wind, 398
Energy efficiency, 379
Energy pyramid, 303
   agriculture and, 304
Energy transformations, 377, 378
Epicenter, 150
Erosion, 50, 52, 137, 285
   beach, 68–69
   preventing, 435
Erosion mountains, 137
Ethanol, 402
Eurasian Plate, 104
Evaporation, 218, 225
Extinction, 333, 340, 437, 438
Extreme Science
   Crab Crossing, 342–343
   Dentists of the Deep, 324–325

Diablo Wind, 210–211
Down in Death Valley, 36–37
It's Alive!, 122–123
Masterpiece of Erosion, 64–65
Sleeping Giant, 168–169
Super Waves, 248–249
Tired!, 440–441
A World in Your Hands, 287–288
Power Tower, 406–407

Fault-block mountains, 135, 138
Faults, 100, 101, 119, 135, 142
   types of, 143
Feeding relationships, 266
Feldspar, 70
Fertilizers, 435
First Aid, H22
Fitness goals, H23
Flood plain, 29
Floods, 62, 448
Fluorite, 419
Focus, earthquake, 131, 150
Focus On
   History of Science: Great Moments for the Electromagnetic Spectrum, 190–191
   History of Science: Protecting the Environment, 360–361
   Literature: A Journey to the Center of the Earth, 24–25
   Primary Source: Caves of the West, 54–55
   Primary Source: Rain Forests, 276–277
   Reader's Theater: Alfred Wegener and Pangaea, 94–97
   Reader's Theater: Once There Were Fossil Fuels, 390–393
   Technology: Predicting Earthquakes, 156–157

Technology: Food Web of the Farm, 306–307
Technology: Landfills, 426–427
Technology: Predicting Hurricanes, 230–231
Folding, 134
Fold mountains, 131, 134, 138
Food chain, 301, 303
Food energy, 300–304
Food webs, 301, 303, 312–313
Forests, 436–437
Fossil fuels, 380, 384–388
   burning, 14, 200, 282, 354, 386–387, 430
   conservation of, 388
   formation of, 384–385
Fossil record, 90
Fossils, 85, 90–91
   formation of, 90
   relative dating of, 91
Fresh water, 432–433
Freshwater biomes, 274
Friction, 378
Fronts, 227
Fungi, 282, 284, 302

Gabbro, 108
Gamma rays, 186
Generalists, 310
Geologic maps, 33
Geothermal energy, 373, 401
Geysers, 18, 19, 114
Glaciers, 51, 88, 432
Global Positioning System (GPS), 34, 112
Global warming, 200, 283
Global wind patterns, 234–235
Gold, 418, 419, 420
Gorda Plate, 165
Grand Teton range, 135
Granitic rocks, 109
Graphs
   bar, H3
   circle, H12
   line, H13
Grasslands, 261, 272
Gravity, 52
   of Earth, 9
Great Lakes, 51

Great Rift Valley, 100, 101, 118
Greenhouse effect, 181, 198–199
Greenhouse gases, 199, 200
Greenland, 200
Groundwater, 433
Guided Inquiry, 7, 17, 27, 47, 57, 67, 87, 99, 107, 115, 133, 141, 149, 159, 183, 193, 203, 221, 233, 241, 263, 269, 279, 299, 309, 317, 335, 345, 351, 375, 383, 395, 417, 429
Gulf Stream, 236
Gypsum, 419

Habitat loss, 352–353
Hawaiian Islands, 166
Headlands, 68
Health Handbook
    Calories Count!, H24
    Endocrine System, H21
    First Aid, H22
    Healthy for Life, H25
    Respiratory System, H20
    Set Fitness Goals, H23
    Healthy for Life, H25
Heat, 181, 204
Helium in atmosphere, 222
Herbivores, 312–313
Hetch Hetchy watershed, 433
Heterotrophs, 300–301
Hills, 29
Himalaya Mountains, 100, 101, 134
Hoover Dam, 433
Hosts, 320
Hot spots, 136, 166
    biodiversity, 357
Hot springs, 114
Human activities, 352–353
Human population, growth of, 355
Humans, parasites of, 322
Humidity, 225
Humus, 414, 434
Hurricane Katrina, 62
Hybrid cars, 403, 431
Hydroelectric energy, 373, 380, 399, 404
Hydrogen fuel cells, 403

Ice age, 88
Iceland, 118
Igneous rocks, 108
Impact craters, 88
Indian Ocean tsunami, 154
Infrared light, 187, 188
Infrared radiation, 196, 198
Inland water, 28
Inner Core, 20, 21
Inquiry model, S16
Intensity, 151
Intertidal zone, 274
Invasive species, 339, 340
Inventor, being an, S18–21
Iron, 418
Iron ore, 419
Irrigation, 245, 285, 432–433
Island arc, 161
Isobars, 223
Itaipú Dam, 399

Jet streams, 235
Joshua Tree National Park, 265
Juan de Fuca Plate, 165

Kilauea, 166
King Mountains, 138
Krakata, 164

Lake Mead, 433
Lake Pontchartrain, 62
Lakes, 28
Land breeze, 207
Land features, 29
Landfills, 402, 433
Land pollution, 354
Landslides, 52, 152
Lassen Peak, 138, 165
Latitude, 208, 246
Lava, 81, 131, 160, 162, 165

Law of the conservation of energy, 378
Leap year, 12
Levees, 62
Liberty Prairie Reserve, 356
Lice, 322
Lichens, 347
Lidar, 34
Light
    infrared, 187, 188
    speed of, 185
    ultraviolet, 187, 188
    visible, 187
Lightning, 284
Light waves, 185
Limited resources, 336, 355
Limiting factors, 336–339
Line graph, H13
Links for home and school, 38, 74, 124, 170, 212, 250, 290, 326, 408, 442
Lithosphere, 20, 100, 109
Local winds, 207
Logging industry, 246, 436
Loihi, 166
Loma Prieta earthquake, 152, 153
L-waves, 145
Lyme disease, 321

Madagascar, 357
Magma, 102, 120, 136, 160, 161, 162
Magnetic field, 22, 103
Magnetite, 70
Magnitude, 146, 151
Malaria, 322
Mammoth Mountain, 208
Mantle, 20, 21
Map scale, 32
Mariana Trench, 118
Maritime polar air masses, 226
Maritime tropical air masses, 226
Mars
    atmosphere of, 199
    average temperature on, 199

Material resources, 414, 418
nonrenewable, 418–424
renewable, 430–438
Mauna Loa, 162, 166
Meanders, 60–61
Measurements, H16–17
of volume, H7
Mechanical energy, 376, 377, 378
Mechanical weathering, 48–49
Median, finding, H14
Mediterranean climate, 243
Mercury, average temperature on, 199
Meteoroids, 9
Meteorologists, 242
Methane, 199
Microscope, using, H2
Microwaves, 186
Mid-Atlantic Ridge, 102, 118
Mid-ocean ridges, 102, 103, 118, 136, 143
Minerals, 414, 418–419
Mining, 418
Mississippi River, 61
flood of, 62
Mistletoe, 321
Modified Mercalli scale, 151, 152
Mojave Desert, 208, 265, 266, 397
Molds, 347
Moon
comparison with Earth, 197
gravitational pull of, 71
Mosses, 347
Mountains, 28, 29, 134–138
dome, 136
erosion, 137
fault-block, 135
fold, 134–135
volcanic, 136
Mountain valleys, 29
Mount Everest, 162
Mount Fuji, 162
Mount Minsi, Pennsylvania, 137
Mount Rainier, 162
Mount Saint Helens, 162, 346

Mount Shasta, 59, 138, 165, 246
Mudslides, 52
Muir Woods, 436
Mutualism, 296, 318–319

National parks, 356
Natural disturbances, 346
Natural gas, 384, 385, 386, 387, 404
Natural resources, 373
Nature of Science
Be an Inventor, S18–21
Inquiry Model, S16
Make Decisions, S22–23
Science Safety, S24
Standards, S8
What Do Scientists Do?, S10–11
WOW Manipulative, S17
You Can Think Like a Scientist, S12–15
Nazca Plate, 118
Neon in atmosphere, 222
Neritic zone, 274
Niche, 310–311
Nickle ore, 419
Night, 11
Nitrogen cycle, 284–285
Nitrogen fixation, 284
Nitrogen-fixing bacteria, 284, 285
Nitrogen in atmosphere, 9, 222, 284
Nitrous oxide, 199
Nonrenewable material resources, 386, 418–424
new products from old, 424
recycling and conservation of, 422–423
source of, 420–421
Normal faults, 143
North American Plate, 104, 111, 119, 138, 165
Northern Hemisphere, 12, 195, 234
Northern lights, 22
Northern Spotted Owl, 437
North magnetic pole, 22

North Pole, 195
Nuclear energy, 400
Nuclear fission, 400
Nuclear fusion, 10
Nuclear wastes, 400

Ocean biome, 274
Ocean crust, 109
Ocean currents, 69, 236–237
Ocean ecosystem, 266
Oceanic-continental boundaries, 118
Oceanic crust, 108
Oceanic-oceanic boundaries, 118
Oceanic zone, 274
Oceans, 28, 108
Ocean surface currents, 236
Oil, 385, 420
Oil spills, 354, 384, 421
Old Faithful Geyser, 114
Omnivores, 312–313
Ore, 415, 419
Outer core, 20, 21, 22
Oxbow lakes, 60, 61
Oxygen, 283
in atmosphere, 9, 222
Oxygen cycle, 283
Ozone, 188
Ozone layer, 14, 188

Pacific Ocean, 29, 208
Pacific Plate, 104, 111, 119, 138
Palm Springs, 245
Pangaea, 92, 111
Parasites, 320
types of, 321
Parasitism, 320
People in Science
Ableman, Michael, 443
Boehm, Alexandria, 75
Chailert, Sangduen, 291
Chavez, Francisco, 251
Lopez, Ann, 327
Malin, Peter, 171

Petroleum, 72, 384, 386, 403, 404, 420, 421
Photosynthesis, 10, 280–281, 282, 283, 300, 436
Photovoltaic cells, 397
Pioneer species, 347
Plains, 29
Planetary wind belts, 234, 235
Plasma, 10
Plastics, 421
Plateaus, 29
Plate boundaries, 104, 116–120
   types of, 117–119
Plate interactions, 116
Plate motion, 110
Plate tectonics, 81, 100
   volcanoes and, 161
Platinum, 419
Polar easterlies, 235
Pollution, 333, 354, 386–387
   air, 354, 386–387, 402, 431
   beach, 72
   land, 354
   reducing, 388
   water, 354, 433
Pompeii, 164
Populations, 266, 313, 336–340
Potassium, 19
Prairies, 272
Precipitation, 219, 225, 286
   in describing climate, 242
Predation, 318, 333, 338
Predators, 297, 310, 338, 339
Preservation, 356–357
Prevailing winds, 235
Prey, 310, 338
Primary consumer, 300, 301, 304
Primary succession, 347, 348
Producers, 300, 312
Propane, 386
P-waves, 144–145, 150

Quartz, 70, 419

Radiation, 205
   electromagnetic, 186
   infrared, 188, 196, 198
   solar, 187, 196, 197, 206
Radioactive elements, 19
Radio waves, 186
Rainbows, 187
Rain forests, 337, 352
Reading link, 25, 37, 55, 65, 123, 169, 211, 231, 249, 277, 289, 307, 325, 343, 407, 441
Recycling, 414, 422, 424
Red River, 62
Red Sea, 100, 101
Relative dating, 91
Relative humidity, 225
Renewable energy, 396–404
   in California, 404
Renewable material resources, 430–438
Reservoirs, 399, 433
Respiration, 281
Respiratory system, H20
Reusing, 423
Reverse faults, 143
Revolution
   of Earth, 4, 12
Richter, Charles, 151
Richter scale, 151
Rift valleys, 102
Ring of Fire, 120, 161
Rivers, 28, 58–59
   formation of, 58–59
River valleys, 29
Rock falls, 52
Rock record, 88, 89
Rocky Mountains, 29, 88
Rocky soil, 434
Rotation, 4
   of Earth, 11, 195
Ruler, using, H6
Runoff, 58, 72

Sacramento River, 59, 243
Sacramento River Delta, 243
Salton Sea, 358
Salt water, 432

Saltwater biomes, 274
San Andreas Fault, 100, 101, 119, 128, 143
Sandbar, 69, 70
Sand dunes, 50
Sandy soil, 434
San Francisco Bay, 59
Sanitary landfills, 354
San Jacinto Mountains, 245
San Obispo, 208
Santa Barbara, 244
Santa Cruz Mountains, 138
Santa Rosa Mountains, 245
Santz Ynez Mountains, 244
Satellites
   in making maps, 34
   weather, 228
Savanna, 272
Scabies, 322
Scavengers, 297, 302, 303
Science and Math Toolbox
   Making a Bar Graph, H3
   Making a Chart to Organize Data, H11
   Making a Line Graph, H13
   Measurements, H16–17
   Measuring Volume, H7
   Reading a Circle Graph, H12
   Reading a Map, H14–H15
   Using a Balance, H9
   Using a Calculator, H4
   Using a Microscope, H2
   Using an Equation or Formula, H10
   Using a Spring Scale, H5
   Using a Tape Measure or Ruler, H6
   Using a Thermometer, H8
Science safety, S24
Scientists
   thinking like, S12–15
   work of, S10–11
Sea breeze, 207
Sea caves, 68
Sea-floor spreading, 102, 103, 117
Sea level, changes in, 71
Seasons, 12
Sea stacks, 44, 68
Secondary consumer, 300, 301, 304

Secondary succession, 332, 347, 348
Sediment, 50, 59, 60, 61
Sediment load, 59
Seismic waves, 19, 144–145
   recording, 146
Seismogram, 146
Seismographs, 146, 150
Sequoia National Park, 436
Shield volcanoes, 162, 163, 166
Sierra Nevada mountains, 134, 138, 143, 243
Silicates, 9
Silver, 419, 420
Sinkholes, 52
Smog, 430
Sodium chloride, 418
Soil, 434–435
Solar energy, 184–188, 194–195, 207, 372, 376, 377, 397
Solar radiation, 187, 196, 197, 206
Sonar, 34
Sonora Desert, 245
Sound waves, 184–185
South American Plate, 118
Southern Hemisphere, 234
South magnetic pole, 22
South Pole, 195, 200
Specialists, 311
Spectrum
   electromagnetic, 186
   visible, 187
Spits, 45, 69
Spring scale, H15
Stationary front, 227
Stellwagen Bank National Marine Sanctuary, 356
Steno, Nicolaus, 89
Strata, 84, 89
Stratovolcanoes, 162
Strike-slip faults, 143
Subduction, 85, 117
Subduction zones, 118, 120
Succession, 346–348
   primary, 347, 348
   secondary, 347, 348

Sun, 10
   facts on, 10
   gravitational pull of, 10
   mass of, 10
Sundial, 11
   making, 7
Sun safety tips, 188
Sunset Crater, 162
Surface features, mapping, 30
Surface waves, 145
Surtsey, 347
S-waves, 144–145, 150
Symbiosis, 318–322, 322

Taiga, 260, 273
Tankers, 420–421
Tape measure, using, H6
Tapeworm lifecycle, 320, 321
Tectonic plates, 85, 100–104, 109, 134
   movement of, 110, 111, 112
Temperate forests, 271
Temperature(s), 204
   air pressure and, 222
   in California, 208
   in describing climate, 242
Tetons, 143
Thermal energy, 194, 196, 204–206, 377, 378, 380, 386
Thermometer, using, H8
Thorium, 19
Threatened species, 340, 356
Thunderstorms, 226
Tidal delta, 71
Tidal power plants, 399
Tides, 70
Topographic map, 30, 31
Top soil, 434–435
Toxins, 314
Trace fossils, 90
Trade winds, 235, 238
Transform fault boundaries, 117, 119, 143
Transpiration, 286
Trench, 161
Tributaries, 45, 58
Trophic levels, 300–301, 303
Tropical rain forests, 271, 437
Troposphere, 235

Tsunamis, 154, 164
Tundra, 261, 273

Ultraviolet light, 187, 188
Uranium, 19
U-shaped valleys, 51

Venus
   atmosphere of, 199
   average temperature on, 199
Verne, Jules, 24–25
Vesuvius, 164
Visible light, 187
Visible spectrum, 187
Vitamin D, 188
Volcanic activity, 19
Volcanic mountains, 160
Volcanoes, 52, 119, 120, 136, 160–166
   classifying, 162–163
   dormant, 164
   effects of, 164
   extinct, 164
   interior of, 160
   plate tectonics and, 161
   shield, 166
Volume, measuring, H7
V-shaped valleys, 51, 59

Warm front, 227
Water cycle, 196, 224, 225, 286, 432
Waterfalls, 58
Water pollution, 354, 433
Water sources, 433
Water vapor, 199, 286
   in atmosphere, 222
Waves, 181
   electromagnetic, 186, 205
   energy and, 184–185
   light, 185
   radio, 186
   sound, 185

Weather, 222–228
        tracking, 228
Weather balloons, 228
Weathering, 48–49
        chemical, 49, 52
        mechanical, 48–49
Weather maps, 223, 227
Weather reports, 225
Weather satellites, 228
Wegener, Alfred, 92, 100
Westerlies, 235
Wetlands, 353, 358, 433
White light, 187
White water, 58
Wildlife, 437
Wind breaks, 435

Wind energy, 398
Wind erosion, 50
Wind farms, 398
Winds, 223
        global patterns of,
        234–235
        local, 207
Wind turbines, 370, 398
WOW Manipulative, S17
Writing Journal, 3, 43, 83,
    129, 179, 217, 259, 295, 331,
    371, 413

X-rays, 186

Year, 12
Yellowstone National Park,
    18, 19, 348, 356
Yosemite National Park, 433

Zoos, 356, 438

Credits